Trade and Transitions

Trade and Transitions

A Comparative Analysis of
Adjustment Policies

Michael J. Trebilcock,
Marsha A. Chandler
and
Robert Howse

London and New York

First published 1990
by Routledge
11 New Fetter Lane, London EC4P 4EE

Simultaneously published in the USA and Canada
by Routledge
a division of Routledge, Chapman and Hall, Inc.
29 West 35th Street, New York, NY 10001

Phototypeset in 10pt Times by
Mews Photosetting, Beckenham, Kent
Printed and bound in Great Britain by
Biddles Ltd, Guildford and King's Lynn

British Library Cataloguing in Publication Data

Trebilcock, Michael J. (Michael John), *1941–*
  Trade and transitions : a comparative analysis of
  adjustment policies.
  1. Developing countries. Exports to developed countries.
  Politico-economic aspects
  I. Title II. Chandler, Marsha A., *1945–* III. Howse,
  Robert, *1958–*
  382.6091724
  ISBN 0–415–04977–6

Library of Congress Cataloging in Publication Data

Trebilcock, M.J.
    Trade and transitions : a comparative analysis of adjustment
  policies / Michael J. Trebilcock, Marsha A. Chandler, and Robert
  Howse.
      p. cm.
  Includes bibliographical references.
  ISBN 0–415–04977–6
  1. Trade adjustment assistance. I. Chandler, Marsha A., 1945–
  II. Howse, Robert, 1958– . III. Title.
HF1421.T74   1990
382'.63–dc20   90–34976
                                                         CIP

Contents

Contents

Figures and tables

Figures

Tables

Preface

This study examines how a number of industrialized countries – namely, Canada, the United States, the United Kingdom, France, West Germany, Japan, Sweden and Australia – have, over the past two decades or so, grappled with adjustment pressures induced by competitive inroads made by foreign imports in a number of sectors (steel, coal, automobiles, ship-building, textiles, clothing and footwear) that have been under stress in many of those countries. In many cases over the period, these adjustment pressures have become severe, with newly-industrialized countries (NICs) emerging as major trading powers, two oil price shocks and two world-wide recessions, increased exchange rate volatility and increasingly rapid reallocation of corporate capital as capital markets have become increasingly globalized. These pressures have increasingly strained the global trading order and threatened its future stability, as evidenced by the rise of the so-called 'New Protectionism'. Evaluation of the effectiveness of past policy responses to these adjustment pressures and proposing new domestic and international policy directions for addressing such pressures in the future is the central agenda of this study.

It is perhaps worth noting at the outset what we regard as the distinctive features of our analysis of possible policy responses to trade-induced adjustment pressures. First, the study adopts a comparative perspective in its empirical evaluation of alternative adjustment policies and reviews the experience in a number of sectors in a number of major OECD countries, thus allowing more robust inferences to be drawn as to the likely impact and implications of particular domestic adjustment policy choices. Second, the study does not confine its normative perspective to economic efficiency concerns, but recognizing that other legitimate values are at least as much at stake, evaluates the case for trade restrictions or alternative adjustment policies in import-impacted sectors against multiple normative perspectives, including efficiency, utilitarianism, distributive justice and communitarianism. Third, the book does not confine itself to a single class of policy responses to adjustment pressures, for example trade restrictions, but reviews (both positively and normatively) alternative adjustment strategies, covering not only trade restrictions, but industrial subsidies, and labour market adjustment policies.

In Chapter 1, we sketch several normative perspectives (economic efficiency, utilitarianism, social contractarianism, communitarianism) which appear to enjoy widespread support in many communities, and then evaluate the central properties of various instrumental responses to adjustment pressures (primarily trade restrictions, industrial subsidies, and labour market policies) against those frameworks. We argue that, in general, adjustment-retarding policies such as trade restrictions will rarely exhibit favourable properties and will be rarely justified according to any of these normative perspectives while labour market policies that ease the burden of adjustment for workers answer to legitimate concerns implicit in general normative perspectives.

In Chapter 2, we examine, in a comparative framework, the empirical evidence on the domestic costs and benefits of trade restrictions as a response to adjustment pressures. In almost every case, the costs to domestic consumers, per job saved, vastly outweigh the value of the jobs saved. Even in the social contractarian (distributive justice) and communitarian frameworks, the values implicated would seem capable of vindication at much lower cost through alternative policy instruments.

In Chapter 3, we consider the empirical evidence on the costs and benefits of industrial subsidies in selected countries and sectors. Although exit-oriented subsidies appear to have eased the adjustment process in some instances, subsidies for employment maintenance or modernization have not prevented employment declines in almost all of the sectors under study. Since from all three ethical perspectives the dislocation effects of change on workers are at the root of the justification for intervention, the relative incapacity of stay-oriented subsidies to prevent such dislocation suggests a rethinking of the choice for stay- rather than exit-oriented industrial subsidies as a response to industrial decline. In particular, subsidies for modernization and rationalization may be counterproductive in terms of their main ethical goals, as the evidence suggests that the productivity gains from rationalization are largely realized through labour-shedding.

In Chapter 4, we survey the major types of labour market policy instruments and profile the principal labour market strategies followed in the advanced industrialized nations. Assessing the instruments of labour adjustment according to ethical and political, as well as economic, criteria reveals that those policies which fail to maximize economic efficiency are not necessarily irrational or inappropriate. Assuming that non-economic values give rise to socially accepted claims for assistance, the problem in dealing with labour adjustment is to ensure that a morally pluralistic definition of society's interests is not used to legitimize rent-seeking and policy choices that are in fact contrary to widely shared social objectives.

In Chapter 5, we explore the strengths and limitations of public choice and institutionalist approaches to the trade and adjustment policy process. The failure of public choice theory to explain adequately or predict a wide range of policy outcomes suggests, we argue, a less deterministic view of the policy process than much of the current literature evokes. Institutions and the assumptions that have shaped them, exert influence on policy outcomes, and there are no iron laws of interest group politics which prevent us from rethinking some of these assumptions and reforming the institutions.

In Chapter 6, we examine the specific institutional dysfunctions that have led to adoption of policies which are both economically inefficient and which either serve badly, or serve at unnecessarily high cost, legitimate normative concerns such as distributive justice and community stability. Our institutional reform proposals focus upon introducing a fuller consideration of the entire range of values at issue, and instrument choices available, into a policy process which has tended – due to a traditional mercantilist bias – to exclude or marginalize anti-protection interests and values. At the international level, we adopt a neo-liberal institutionalist view of the multilateral trading order, stressing that reforms ought to aim at strengthening institutional frameworks for mutually self-interested bargaining, rather than constraining or transcending domestic self-interest. We argue that an effective multilateral system ought to contain leeway for states to renege on previous commitments, while constraining such reneging within limits so that it does not undermine confidence in the system itself. Inadequacies in the current GATT safeguards regime have led states to disguise new protection as retaliation against the supposedly 'unfair trade' of other states, thereby placing stress on the system itself, and directing attention away from the key issue: how states can respond to domestic adjustment pressures in ways that are least injurious to the welfare of their trading partners. Furthermore, we argue that inasmuch as subsidies and other non-tariff measures are injurious to the interests of foreign trading partners, the multilateral institutional framework should be adapted to facilitate their reciprocal reduction through bargaining, and to prevent these measures serving as a standing pretext for 'retaliatory protection'.

Acknowledgements

In writing this book, we have incurred a number of debts of gratitude. The Economic Council of Canada provided financial support, and Paul Gorecki of the Council has been an invaluable source of assistance to us – as a critic, as a source of information and data, and as a researcher in his own right in many of the areas embraced by this book. Comments by two anonymous Council reviewers on an earlier draft prompted extensive revisions. The International Business and Trade Law Program at the University of Toronto generously provided financial assistance that facilitated the revision process.

Throughout the writing of this book Peter Simm provided indispensable research assistance to us, and is responsible for the compilation and presentation of much of the statistical data. His advice on all facets of the study has been invaluable. Rosemin Keshvani proof read the final manuscript with admirable care. Finally, Joyce Williams, Trudy Schmidt, Margot Hall and Vera Melnyk provided expert and endlessly patient secretarial services.

Abbreviations

AAB	Adjustment Assistance Benefits (Can.)
AMS	National Labour Market Board (Swe.)
AMU	Labour Market Training Centre (Swe.)
CDS	Construction Differential Subsidy (US)
CEC	Canada Employment Centre
CEP	Community Employment Programme (Can., UK & Aus.)
CETA	Comprehensive Employment and Training Act (US)
CIASI	Inter-Ministerial Committee for the Adaption of Industrial Structure (Fr.)
CIRB	Canadian Industrial Review Board
CIRP	Canadian Industrial Review Programme
CJS	Canadian Jobs Strategy
CODIS	Inter-Ministerial Committee for the Development of Strategic Industries (Fr.)
CRAFT	Commonwealth Rebate for Apprentice Fulltime Training (Aus.)
CTST	Critical Trades Skills Training (Can.)
CVD	Countervailing duties
FTA	Free Trade Agreement (US/Can.)
GAAP	General Adjustment Assistance Programme (Can.)
GATT	General Agreement on Tariffs and Trade
GDP	Gross domestic product
GNP	Gross national product
GRT	Gross Registered Tonnage
IAC	Industries Assistance Commission (Aus.)
IAS	Industrial Adjustment Service (Can.)
ILAP	Industry and Labour Adjustment Programme (Can.)
IRBD	Industrial Renewal Board
ITC	International Trade Commission
JTPA	Jobs Training Partnership Act (US)
LAB	Labour Adjustment Benefits (Can.)

LDC	Less Developed Countries
MFA	Multifibre Arrangement
MFN	Most Favoured Nation
MFT	Multilateral free trade
MITI	Ministry of International Trade and Industry (Jap.)
MMP	Manpower Mobility Programme (Can.)
MTN	Multilateral trade negotiations
NIC	Newly industrialized country
NTB	Non-tariff barriers to trade
OECD	Organization for Economic Co-operation and Development
OMA	Orderly marketing agreements
OPEC	Organization of Petroleum Exporting Countries
PSE	Public Service Employment (US)
R&D	Research and development
STEP	Special Temporary Employment Programme (UK)
TAA	Trade Adjustment Assistance (US)
TAB	Transitional Assistance Benefits (Can.)
TES	Temporary Employment Subsidy (UK)
TOPS	Training Opportunities Scheme (UK)
TPM	Trigger price mechanism
UI	Unemployment Insurance
UIC	Unemployment Insurance Canada
VER	Voluntary export restraint

Chapter one

A conceptual framework for evaluating alternative trade-related adjustment policies

I. The dynamics of change

(a) Introduction

In all industrial societies, communities, firms and individuals are continuously confronted with myriad sources of shocks and adjustment pressures. Governments in turn confront continuous demands from affected interests to intervene to cushion these shocks and mitigate these adjustment pressures. The central concern of this study is with one class of shock: trade-induced economic and social dislocations. The question the study addresses is whether these dislocations warrant special government adjustment policies designed to cushion the impact and/or velocity of such changes.

In this chapter, we first attempt to provide a sketch of the general empirical magnitude of trade-induced dislocations relative to the many other types of dislocations that modern countries confront. We then describe three kinds of policy perspectives – economic, ethical and political – from which the case for government intevention to mitigate these dislocations can be evaluated. We go on to describe the major classes of policy instruments available to a government contemplating intervention: trade restrictions, industrial subsidies, structural policy responses, labour adjustment policies and macro-economic policies. In each case, we evaluate the central characteristics of each policy instrument against the policy perspectives described and identify convergences and divergences between these perspectives.

We seek to argue that in import-impacted sectors, government policy instruments that facilitate the exit of displaced labour by underwriting exit costs are usually most congruent with the normative economic and liberal individualist ethical perspectives, but that the positive political perspective may often lead to an inversion of the policy priorities

1

suggested by these two normative perspectives. We also consider the case for intervention from a communitarian ethical perspective, and argue that there may in some cases be a limited justification for job-preserving or creating policies to preserve community continuity and identity. We seek to argue further that the economic and ethical justifications for intervention are not limited to dislocations caused by changes in trade patterns or trade policies but have broader applications to job displacement from a variety of causes.

(b) The process of creative destruction

It is important to gain a sense of perspective on how traumatic the impacts of adjustment required by further trade liberalization are likely to be compared to the many other adjustment processes that communities, firms and individuals are already undergoing.

In Canada, for instance, each year about 136,000 firms are created and some 109,000 firms disappear. According to Statistics Canada, 503,000 firms, representing about 61 per cent of businesses in existence in Canada in 1985 had been established since 1978. During the same period, 283,000 firms, representing 47 per cent of all businesses operating in 1978, were no longer identified in 1985 (Report of Advisory Council on Adjustment 1989: 6, 7).

Green (1984) notes that of the firms and plants that accounted for almost all Canada's employment in and output from, manufacturing and mining in 1970, about one quarter had disappeared by 1976. However, an approximately equal number were born during the same period, so that the net loss was less than 3 per cent.

On an individual level, in 1981, there were 371,346 births, 171,029 deaths, 190,082 marriages and 67,671 divorces (a doubling in the divorce rate per capita from 1971). The crude birth rate (per 1,000 total population) has fallen from 28.9 in 1947 to 15.3 in 1981. In 1982, there were 30,643 consumer backruptcies reported. In 1981, 128,618 immigrants arrived in Canada from many countries of origin and in 1981-2 an estimated 41,750 emigrants left Canada. Just under 16 per cent (3.8 million) of Canadian residents were originally immigrants, as of the 1981 Census. The 1981 Census showed almost half (47.6 per cent) of Canada's population aged 5 years and over in 1981 living in a different dwelling than five years earlier; 24.9 per cent had moved within the same municipality and 22.7 per cent had moved from one municipality to another. The last group consisted of 15.1 per cent who moved within the same province, 5.1 per cent from one province to another, and 2.5 per cent from outside Canada (Statistics Canada 1985a). Between 1972 and 1984, an average of 380,000 persons a year changed residences by moving across provincial boundaries (about fifteen for every thousand

Canadians) (Macdonald Royal Commission 1985: vol. III, 124).

Today, three or four Canadian families out of a hundred are farming families. In 1885, when the first Canadian transcontinental rail line was completed, sixty families out of every hundred were farm families. In 1941, there were 733,000 farms in Canada, in 1981 the number of farms was 318,000, yet the volume of agricultural production was about 175 per cent greater in 1981 than in 1941.

Changes projected in the percentage of the labour force employed in major sectors from 1946–2000 are shown in Figure 1.1 (Advisory Council on Adjustment 1989: 27). The sharp drop in agricultural employment, the relative decline in manufacturing employment and the sharp increase in employment in the services sector imply major inter-sectoral shifts in employment over time that set in context estimates of likely inter-sectoral shifts in employment from further trade liberalization.

Between 1974 and 1982, an average of some 33 per cent of employed workers in Canadian manufacturing industries separated from their employers each year. While a large percentage of total separations consist of rehires following temporary lay-offs, and therefore do not result in a reallocation of labour, permanent lay-offs and voluntary attritions (quits and other) still amount to over 20 per cent of manufacturing employment *annually* (Economic Council of Canada 1988: 10). The labour force also shows a high degree of inter-industry mobility. Using the chemical industry as an example, between 1978 and 1983, 175,000 workers entered the industry, while 160,200 individuals left. Of those departing 127,800 individuals found work in other industries, no information was available for 23,400 and 9,000 were unemployed (Advisory Council on Adjustment 1989: 5).

With respect to education, the 376,300 full-time students in Canadian universities in 1980–1 were equivalent to 11.2 per cent of the population aged 18 to 24 – about double the proportion in 1960. In 1965, 30.4 per cent of bachelor degrees awarded were received by women; by 1982 this percentage had risen to 50.9 per cent (Statistics Canada 1985a: 131). The percentage of women participants in the Canadian labour force rose from 33.6 per cent in 1970 to 41.7 per cent in 1983, and the percentage of all women participating in the labour force rose from 38.3 per cent in 1970 to 52.6 per cent in 1983 (while the male participation rate throughout this period remained almost constant at about 77 per cent) (Statistics Canada 1985).

With respect to health, life expectancy for Canadian males at birth has increased from 60 years in 1931 to 72 years in 1981, for females from 62 to 79 years. The infant mortality rate per 1,000 live births has fallen from 102.1 in 1921 to 9.1 in 1982 (Statistics Canada 1985a: 97, 98).

Citation of this sampling of statistics is motivated by a simple

Figure 1.1 Shift in employment structure by industrial sector, 1946–2000

Per cent of employment

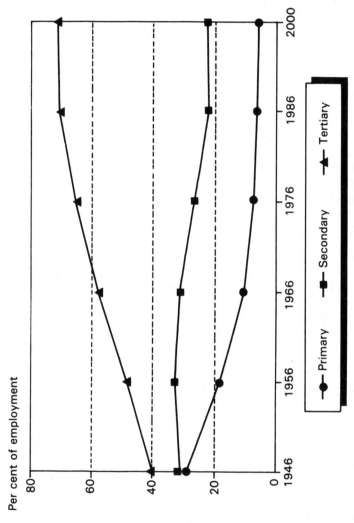

Source: Statistics Canada, *Labour Force Survey*; Employment and Immigration System, Canadian Occupational Projection System (COPS)

objective: to convey a sense of constant and often relatively dramatic transitions and adjustments that occur continuously in a modern industrialized economy. Joseph Schumpeter once wrote that a market economy involves 'a perennial gale of creative destruction' (Schumpeter 1975: 87). Even in contemporary, centrally-planned economies, with their greater rigidities, many similar processes of economic and social change are at work, as the examples of Eastern Europe and the Soviet Union dramatically exemplify. Against this background of continuous change, it is useful now to develop some perspective in the magnitude of trade-related adjustment costs.

(c) The general magnitude of trade-related adjustment costs

Harris, in his analysis of the costs and benefits for Canada of *complete multilateral free trade* (MFT) (Harris 1984) (which no one realistically envisages) estimates the gain in Canadian real income from free trade from the initial 1976 (pre-Tokyo Round) levels of protection would be of the order of 8–10 per cent of GNP. The Canadian real wage would rise on the order of 20–25 per cent, with gains in labour productivity of similar magnitudes. The pattern of adjustment to MFT primarily would be through intra-industry rationalization with improved cost efficiency in most manufacturing industries achieved through the advantages of larger scale and greater specialization. Under MFT, only the most labour-intensive sunset industries would lose. On an aggregate basis, approx-imately 6 per cent of the labour force would be required to shift inter-sectorally. Under MFT, employment would actually increase in the manufacturing sector, and the sector as a whole would move into a trade surplus position. The industrial base of the economy would expand significantly under free trade.

While Harris' estimates of future gains from MFT have been criticized as too optimistic, in part because they fail to take account of the effects of the Tokyo Round tariff reductions now in place (Whalley 1984), it would seem to be the case, for similar reasons, that they are also likely to overestimate future adjustment costs.

The size of Harris' estimated inter-sectoral shifts of labour should be compared to those experienced out of agriculture in Canada over the past fifty years and more recently the relative growth of the services sector and relative decline of the manufacturing sector in terms of employment.

Lipsey and Smith examine the process of adjustment in the twenty major Canadian manufacturing industries from 1966 to 1981 when the substantial Kennedy Round tariff reductions were phased in and the Tokyo Round tariff reductions were beginning to take effect (Lipsey and Smith 1985). Every manufacturing sector, with the single exception of knitting mills, increased the proportion of its total production that was exported. Overall, Canadian manufacturing firms exported 24 per cent of their total production in the 1966–73 period and 30 per cent in 1981. At the same time, every sector, with the single exception of petroleum and coal products, experienced an increase in the proportion of the Canadian market supplied by imports. Overall 25 per cent of the sales in Canadian manufacturing markets were served by imports in the 1966–73 period and 32 per cent in 1981 (Lipsey and Smith 1985: 106–10). Lipsey and Smith note that 'whole industries have not disappeared in either [sic] country. Instead, each industry has specialized in particular niches so that trade has increased in each direction, in each industry' (Lipsey and Smith 1985: 109). The authors also provide figures for each sector of net exports – exports minus imports – as a proportion of its total production. Comparing the 1966–73 period with 1981, half of the industries listed increased their ratio of net exports to domestic production while the other half reduced theirs. They note: 'This is just what we would expect from the operation of comparative advantage. Some industries have expanded exports relative to imports while others have contracted' (Lipsey and Smith 1985: 109). They also note that this is consistent with the experience of the European Economic Community (EEC), where the Treaty of Rome in 1958 envisaged initial tariff cuts of 10 per cent a year for five years, with provision for review, but dislocations proved so much less than had been feared that in 1960 the Community decided to increase tariff reductions to 20 per cent per year and to eliminate all quotas by the end of 1961 (Lipsey and Smith 1985: 106). Various estimates of the size of short-run adjustment costs relative to the size of long-run welfare gains from substantial trade liberalization run from ratios of 1:25 to 1:80 (Wonnacott 1987: Appendix B). It is often argued that dramatic and often unpredictable shifts in international exchange rates are likely to have more severe effects on a country's competitive position than a measured and predictable phaseout of tariffs (Wonnacott 1987: 19).

(d) *Collective responsibility for the costs of change*

The central policy issue that confronts governments, specifically in mixed market economies and liberal democracies such as Canada's, is the appropriate extent of collective responsibility for the consequences of destructive features of the processes of change, however much these may be outweighed in the aggregate and in the longer term by their creative potential. Governments in many developed economies have assumed an increasingly major role in underwriting the negative contingencies of life. Furthermore, in federal states, such as Canada, governments have also committed themselves to maintaining economic opportunity and viable communities in all regions, despite changes in comparative advantage which would, assuming perfect mobility, lead to substantial shifts of labour and capital from already disadvantaged to relatively advantaged regions.

In Canada, for example, federal equalization payments, which amounted to $5.5 billion in 1985, transfer resources from 'have' to 'have not' provinces. Federal regional development programmes, entailing expenditures of $388 million in 1985, transfer further resources to disadvantaged regions (Statistics Canada 1984: 22, 23). Federal transfer payments to the provinces to promote regional development have risen from 0.13 per cent of GDP in 1947 to 4.0 per cent in 1986.

At the level of the firm, federal government transfer payments (subsidies, capital assistance) in 1986 amounted to $7.3 billion. Provincial government transfers to business in 1986 amounted to $6 billion. Municipal transfers to business in 1986 amounted to $600 million. Foregone federal corporate tax revenues from tax expenditures were estimated in 1982 at $11.5 billion (Statistics Canada 1987: 24, 25).

At the level of the individual, with respect to social security programmes, social security expenditures by all levels of government (excluding health care expenditures and unemployment benefits) in 1985 amounted to over $37 billion (ranging over a wide variety of social security programmes including the Canada and Quebec Pension Plans, Old Age Benefits, Family Allowances, the Child Tax Credit, Workers Compensation Plans, the Canada Assistance Plan (welfare benefits) and War Veterans Allowances) (Canada Year Book 1988; Statistics Canada 1985: 6–3). This compares to expenditures in 1947 of about $3.6 billion (1985$) on all 'public welfare' programmes (including health).

With respect to unemployment benefits, the federal government paid out $10.2 billion in 1985 to approximately 3.3 million people (Canada Year Book 1988: 5–14). In 1984–5, an additional $1 billion was spent on institutional and industrial training and relocation programmes (Wonnacott 1987: 98).

Public expenditures in Canada on education have risen from $147 per capita in 1947 to $1,237 per capita in 1983–4 in real terms (1986 $), or from 1.99 per cent of GDP to 6.79 per cent (Canada Year Book 1988: 4–1; Statistics Canada 1985: 124, 129). Public expenditures on health care have risen from $54 per capita in 1947 to $1,201 per capita in 1985 in real terms (1986 $), or from 0.72 per cent of GDP to 6.18 per cent (Statistic Canada 1988: 3–36). In addition, in 1981 provincial workers' compensation programmes paid $1.6 billion in benefits to 1.2 million injured workers and their dependants or survivors (Statistics Canada 1985: 189).

Apart from these government programmes in education, health, unemployment insurance and social security, individuals, of course, often provide themselves with substantial security against various of the contingencies of life through pensions, insurance, savings, assets and access to credit.

With this mix of public and private policies, programmes and resources that provide various forms of security against some of the negative contingencies of life, the question must now be addressed as to whether trade-induced dislocations to communities, firms and individuals call for special policy responses not adequately accommodated in more broadly-cast security nets. Obviously, many existing policies – macro-economic stabilization policies, equalization and regional development policies, industrial subsidy policies, unemployment insurance, education policies and manpower training and relocation policies – are likely to be of direct relevance to sectors of the economy under import pressure. What further or alternative policy responses are required?

A concern with adjustment costs caused either by changes in trading patterns or in trade policies has long antecedents. The General Agreement on Tariffs and Trade (GATT), from its inception in 1947, provided for escape clause or safeguard relief (Article XIX) through the temporary reinstatement of previous tariff concessions if foreign imports are causing severe disruption to a domestic industry. This provision itself was borrowed from similar provisions in previous bilateral trade treaties. The Treaty of Paris, which in 1951 established the European Coal and Steel Community to promote the integration of coal and steel production in Western Europe contemplated various forms of 'orderly' adjustment in the furtherance of this goal. The Treaty of Rome, which in 1957 established the EEC, provided for a European Social Fund to provide assistance to workers to facilitate adjustment to liberalized European trade. In the US, the *Trade Expansion Act* of 1962 provided for assistance to firms and workers to ease adjustments to the Kennedy Round tariff concessions. In Canada, the Canadian-American Automotive Agreement of 1965 (the Auto Pact) provided for forms of adjustment assistance to firms and workers affected by the Agreement. The General Adjustment Assistance Programme (GAAP) adopted by Canada in 1968 provided adjustment assistance to firms under import pressure as a result of Kennedy Round tariff cuts (Banks and Tumlir 1986: chap. 2).

These and other early examples of programmes designed to address the adjustment costs of trade imports were generally not widely utilized, in part because of the high growth rates that characterized most industrialized economies throughout the 1950s and 1960s.

However, interest in adjustment assistance policies sharply intensified in the 1970s for a number of reasons: the two oil price shocks and accompanying recessions; the rise of Japan and other NICs as major international trading threats; and further trade liberalization as envisaged by the Tokyo Round tariff reductions and codes restricting the use of various non-tariff barriers to trade (NTBs). In an environment of economic stagnation and increased import competition, many governments in western industrialized countries sought strategies that would in various degrees restore international competitiveness in established industries through rationalization or modernization; achieve international competitiveness in new 'growth' industries; ease exit costs for capital and labour in industries whose comparative advantage was perceived as permanently lost; or alternatively adopt defensive policies designed to protect domestic industries from the effects of international competition. These concerns have persisted into the 1980s, intensified by the deep, world-wide recession of the early 1980s. Notwithstanding the limited economic recovery of the mid-1980s, the prospects of further regional trade liberalization under the Canada-US Free Trade Agreement, Europe 1992, the Australian-New Zealand Closer Economic Cooperation Treaty, further multilateral trade liberalization as a result of the Uruguay Round negotiations, economic liberalization in the Eastern Bloc and China, and the globalization of capital markets that has increased the speed of the capital reallocation process and exchange rate volatility, all suggest that many countries will continue to confront significant adjustment pressures and the correlative challenge of choosing appropriate adjustment policy responses to those pressures.

II. Competing perspectives on trade and adjustment policies

(a) The economic perspective

From a neo-classical economic perspective, trade restrictions are seen as having little to commend them both theoretically and empirically. By restricting the available contract opportunity set, mutual gains from exchange and specialization are foregone. Losses sustained by domestic producers from international trade are viewed as mere pecuniary externalities (private losses), which by definition are less than pecuniary gains to domestic consumers, otherwise domestic producers would cut prices to domestic consumers to neutralize the advantages to the latter of foreign trade and avoid larger losses to themselves. Recent theorizing in the international trade literature (Krugman 1986) suggests some possibilities for strategic use of trade protection policies to foster new industries and establish pre-emptive market beach-heads, but this literature is both speculative and controversial and seems of limited relevance to declining industries.

In evaluating the gains from trade liberalization, an analysis that employs comparative statistics is likely to overstate the gains: we are currently in state A, where national income is X; we could move to state

9

B, where national income will be X + Y. Richardson argues that this analysis overlooks two kinds of social costs that any dynamic analysis must take account of in evaluating the relative costs and benefits of states A and B: *dislocation costs* and *adjustment costs* incurred in moving from state A to state B (Richardson 1980: chap. 10). *Dislocation costs* entail output of goods or services sacrificed from any unemployment, temporary or otherwise, of labour and other resources caused by trade liberalization. Given common wage and input price rigidities, at least in the short-run, markets will not clear instantaneously in response to changes in the terms of trade, and resources are likely to be rendered idle. *Adjustment costs* entail resources sacrificed to retrain labour, retool machines, refurbish factories, redevelop land and relocate factors of production that trade liberalization causes to be redeployed intra-sectorally or to be shifted inter-sectorally. Richardson argues that dislocation and adjustment costs 'can be fatal to the economic welfare case for trade liberalization. They can provide an economic justification for a nation's retention of its barriers to international trade, even when free trade would be better for it in the long-run. The long-run benefits are not worth the short-run costs' (Richardson 1980: 321).

Banks and Tumlir dispute this conceptualization of the social costs of trade liberalization (Banks and Tumlir 1986: chap. 3). Defining costs in opportunity cost terms, they argue that unless some available alternative opportunity is foregone, idle resources entail no social costs. Only if cost-effective policies can be invoked (but are not) to expedite the redeployment of resources to higher valued uses, can one say that social costs have been incurred by the displacement of domestic resources by imports. It is true that such displacement will generate various kinds of private costs: with respect to firms, the write-down in the value of industry-specific assets; with respect to workers, the loss of job-specific human capital that may entail lower wages in alternative employment opportunities; loss of seniority, job security and pension rights; loss of resale value on homes in communities dependent on import-sensitive industries; psychological losses from leaving established social and cultural networks; with respect to communities, loss of tax base with industrial contraction and losses to other businesses and their employees that are dependent on the trade-impacted industry (Green 1984). Banks and Tumlir argue that these costs simply entail transfers from losers to gainers from trade liberalization, thus entailing only distributive implications but not resource costs (in an opportunity cost sense). Moreover, by assumption, the losses to the losers must be less than the gains to the gainers from trade liberalization, otherwise the losers would have been able to 'bribe' the gainers to forego the benefits of trade liberalization.

Even if this argument is correct from an economic perspective, the undeniable private dislocation and adjustment costs (henceforth for the sake of conciseness, simply adjustment costs) entailed in trade liberalization retain considerable ethical and political significance, and it remains important at this juncture to develop a general sense of these competing perspectives.

(b) Ethical perspectives

An ethical perspective on trade and adjustment policies has less straightforward implications for policy, in part because there are many ethical paradigms. Three central ethical paradigms in contemporary western political theory are utilitarianism, Kantian contractarianism and communitarianism. Utilitarianism in many ways provides the under-pinnings for modern welfare economics and would tend to suggest similar implications to the economic perspective. One difference is that utilitarianism would be unlikely to distinguish between the social and private costs of adjustment – both are sources of individual disutility and should be weighed against the gains in utility to other members of the community from trade liberalization in arriving at a determination of whether average utility (not simply income) has been increased (Trebilcock 1985a; Trebilcock and Quinn 1982). The private and psychic costs of change may be substantial (Green 1984; Olson 1985) and may significantly narrow the gap between the gains to consumers from trade liberalization and the benefits of trade protection as reflected only in incomes preserved.

A Kantian social contract perspective, at least in its modern Rawlsian version (Rawls 1971), would take the view that behind the hypothetical veil of ignorance where the social contract is constructed and where our individual lots in life and endowments are not known, we would all agree that no collective policy should be pursued that does not improve the lot of the least advantaged. In other words, we would all agree to a form of social insurance against the risk of finding ourselves in this plight.

Rawls' theory is not indifferent, however, to concerns of aggregate social welfare – he would be prepared to accept that distributive policies which benefit the least advantaged ought to be achieved at minimum necessary costs to other groups or to society in general.

A major difficulty with both the utilitarian and social contract ethical perspectives, in the international trade context, is that it is not clear why (as is often assumed) national boundaries should be assigned any special ethical significance (Brown and Shue 1981). If a global perspective is adopted, then utilitarianism would require that the disutility caused to individuals in foreign countries from domestic trade restrictions should be weighed in the utilitarian calculus. If one accepts the declining marginal utility of money and that interpersonal comparison of utilities

11

is possible (which is, admittedly controversial), one might argue that the disutility caused to low-income foreign workers from domestic trade restrictions should be assigned special weight (Singer 1979). Similarly, a global social contract perspective would require that the lot of the least well-endowed globally, should be given a special ethical pre-eminence. In both cases, a global perspective would seem to militate strongly against the maintenance of trade restrictions by industrialized countries against NICs and LDCs, or at least that foreign aid of equivalent value to the latter of trading opportunities foregone would be ethically dictated (Shue 1980). However, aid on this scale is likely to exceed the compensation required to meet all losses to domestic interests in industrialized countries from trade liberalization. Moreover, it is not clear what purpose might be specified for the aid if production of exports displacing domestic production in the importing country is foreclosed.

A third ethical perspective which has gained considerable attention in recent years is that of communitarianism. Communitarians see the autonomous individual self of Rawlsian liberal theory as reflecting an impoverished conception of human life. According to this perspective, it is 'constitutive attachments' to particular communities, groups and institutions which make human life rich and which are formative of human identities (Sandel 1982).

In a number of respects the communitarian perspective may suggest policies which diverge considerably from those driven by utilitarian or liberal individualist perspectives. First of all, while the latter *are* able to conceptualize the psychological costs of change as real costs, which may merit compensation, for the communitarian the 'exit' option – even when accompanied by such compensation – may still seem unjustified, if exit involved severing the bonds to extended family, neighbourhood, region or workplace colleagues. Loss of a significant part of one's human identity may simply not be *compensable* through redistributive policies. Policies which enhance the stay option may be preferred, where they are able to keep intact the attachments which, according to the communitarian, make life worth living. Still, even here certain 'stay' instruments would be preferred over others. For example, programmes which create long-term jobs through subsidies would be preferable to trade restrictions. Trade restrictions, unlike labour subsidies, need not prevent firms from replacing labour with capital in the production process, and hence are an uncertain hedge against the kinds of employment dislocations which communitarians seek to prevent. The rents that firms capture from trade restrictions may well be invested abroad or in other regions of the country that are not in decline or to increase capital intensity, rather than used to preserve or create employment opportunities in the affected area. Retraining policies which permit workers to find jobs in the same locality would be both attractive to communitarians and broadly consistent with the 'exit' option in the strict sense of exit from the industry that is in decline.

Of course, not all of the humanly significant attachments will be preserved (the workplace will change and with it co-workers) but as Sandel himself admits, 'each of us moves in an indefinite number of communities, some more inclusive than others, each making different claims on our allegiance' (Sandel 1982: 146). It would be hard even for a committed communitarian to argue that the government should intervene to prevent all changes in these multiple interwoven loyalties and ties.

Another variation on the communitarian perspective emphasizes the dangers to national cultural identity presented by free trade and full international mobility of labour and capital. Distinctive ways of life and cultural values are threatened by the homogenizing effects of economic and technological imperialism. This point of view, which has its roots in the critique by Rousseau and the nineteenth century political romantic movement of classical political economy, and also in the Jeffersonian alternative to the commercial republic, found its leading Canadian exponent in the philosopher George Grant (Grant 1967).

One cannot help but find somewhat unrealistic the romanticized 'closed community' conception of contemporary critics of liberalism. Traditional closed societies may have preserved distinctive customs and beliefs against external influences, but only at the cost of racial, religious and ideological intolerance, and of significant limits on individual self-development. If we were really to avoid the consequences of contemporary cosmopolitanism, trade barriers would hardly be enough – we would need strict censorship, exit visas, limits on ethnic diversity, and other measures aimed at maintaining the 'closedness' of the community. Moreover, communitarianism in its modern form lacks a coherent justification for preferring the welfare of one's own community to that of others. Domestic policies adopted to protect local communities may well, where trade restrictions are entailed, impair the vitality or viability of communities in foreign countries.

Within the mainstream of policy debate in liberal democratic societies, the economic and ethical perspectives described above have the prominence and legitimacy that come from expressing the felt needs of a susbtantial number of voting citizens. This pluralism is also reinforced by the circumstance that each perspective taken to its extreme would self-destruct or lead to a result so intolerable to a large number of citizens as, in effect, to disenfranchise their needs. A pure aggregate efficiency perspective, with no concern for the distributive consequences of adjustment, would lead to the kind of gap between rich and poor which, as the overwhelming public support for a wide range of social welfare policies suggests, has become intolerable to a majority of citizens. By

13

contrast, a society that totally neglected the social efficiency consequences of its decisions in favour of redistributive or communitarian goals would eventually find itself left with a very small pie to distribute, and with communities dying from stagnation rather than from too rapid change. Even Marxists now recognize the importance of efficiency in making social justice affordable (Markovic 1982).

Similarly, complete exclusion of community concerns would also be a disenfranchisement of important needs. Economists and liberal individualists tend to view mobility between jobs and regions as enhancing human autonomy and choice. Yet one does not need to accept the more extreme claims of communitarianism to recognize that the rapidity of change, the abrupt manner in which it dissolves long-standing relationships and routines, may outweigh possible long-term benefits, particularly for older members of the work force. Olson notes that societies characterized by high levels of geographical and employment mobility, and by rapid economic change, also typically experience certain concomitant social costs – such as high rates of suicide, mental illness, and divorce, and serious problems with alcohol and drug abuse (Olson 1985).

Banks and Tumlir (1986) argue that in the early post-war period, western societies were able to withstand massive labour dislocations, and the evidence presented earlier in the study suggests that Canadians have adjusted to various kinds of pressures for change in the last few decades, in some cases with government intervention being limited to a social security net. Yet worker dislocation may be much more traumatic in contemporary conditions, where many traditional bonds, like those of religion and family, have become weaker or more tenuous than in the past. It is interesting that the country where the exit option has been implemented most consistently, Japan, is one in which traditional norms and attachments remain comparatively strong. Moreover, change may seem more threatening and destabilizing to individuals when the general economic climate is volatile or negative. Sweden's leadership (among the countries under study) in labour shedding in the textile, clothing, footwear, shipbuilding, and coal-mining industries should be seen in the context of a particularly strong and comprehensive social safety net which may serve to reduce the general level of individuals' anxieties about the personal consequences of economic vicissitudes.

These considerations suggest a significant role for communitarian claims in the formulation of adjustment policies. For example, a policy mix to address decline in a local industry might involve relocation assistance to younger workers (often eager to move if properly compensated), retraining for other sectors in the same community or region for middle-aged employees, and an early retirement package for older workers.

To economists, of course, policies which actually retard the speed of a market-driven reallocation of labour and capital are less justifiable than those which are merely compensatory. But in a morally pluralistic society, it is not enough simply to 'pay off' the losers – the values which they hold dear must continue to have a legitimate place in the policy process. This is well-put by Calabresi:

> A decision which recognizes the values on the losing side as real and significant tends to keep us from becoming callous with respect to the moralisms and beliefs that lose out . . . . it tells the losers that, though they lost, they and their values do carry weight and are recognized in our society, even when they don't win out.
>
> (Calabresi 1985: 109)

(c) A political perspective

A political perspective on the virtues of a policy of trade liberalization may have quite different implications from both the economic and ethical perspectives. Firms and workers concentrated in declining industries will often make highly salient political demands for continuing trade protection. In contrast to the concentrated stakes of these interests, the principal cost-bearers – ultimate consumers – typically have small per capita stakes in trade liberalization and are economically, geographically and temporally a widely dispersed interest group that faces severe institutional constraints in mounting equally salient political demands for trade liberalization (Rowley and Tollison 1986; Trebilcock 1985a: chap. 1). There are, of course, other interests that also stand to gain from trade liberalization – importers of intermediate inputs, retail chains, exporters – who do not face such severe political disabilities although their capacity to make politically striking anti-protectionist demands is likely to vary widely by issue (Destler and Odell 1987). Thus, trade protection often offers concentrated, immediate and visible benefits to the recipients while sometimes rendering the costs less visible by spreading them widely over the economy and over time.

There is a complex relationship between arguments informed by the economic and ethical perspectives described above, and the political demand for protection and subsidies. Concentrated interests will usually appeal to various normative claims in order to justify to voters at large the redistributive effects being sought. Similarly, where policies are adopted in response to demands by such interests, the goals of those policies will usually be justified in terms of normative principles which are designed to make the losers (consumers) believe that these interests are not simply being sacrificed for the sake of other more concentrated interests, but rather in the name of some more general 'common good'. Voters will often not investigate whether, in practice, policies actually serve the ethical goals which are advanced to justify them (Lee 1988). This gap between rhetoric and reality is evoked by the overwhelming thrust of the empirical evidence in this study, that rarely have protection and subsidies policies come close to achieving their stated goals, or have done so only at enormous cost. Further, postponing adjustment should not be equated with phasing it in gradually. Many policies which retard exit do not soften it – the sundering of community ties comes just as suddenly and on at least as great a scale, even though it occurs at a later date. Indeed, as will be suggested in the empirical analysis which follows in subsequent chapters, retarding change may actually increase its dimensions and severity. In sum, the political explanation of trade protection and subsidies is consistent with the insight that at several levels institutions and ideas influence the formation of policies. But rent-seeking behaviour influences the interaction between legitimate values and politics, leading to ethically and economically perverse outcomes.

III. Alternative policy responses to trade-related adjustment costs

At this point, we lay out the four major classes of prospective public policy responses: (a) trade restrictions; (b) industrial subsidies; (c) structural policies and (d) labour market policies, to the costs of adjustment to trade liberalization (along with a brief comment on the relevance of macroeconomic policy), and evaluate these responses, in a general way, from economic, ethical and political perspectives. Trade restrictions, industrial subsidies and labour market policies will be explored in much greater detail in the ensuing three chapters, which will examine the empirical experience in our chosen sectors and countries with the use of these instruments. Aspects of structurally-related policy responses will be integrated into the discussion of other instruments in later chapters and will not be independently discussed.

(a) Trade restrictions

(1) Tariffs, quotas and voluntary export restraints

Within the menu of available trade protection instruments, politicians will often face strong incentives to adopt the least efficient form of trade protection (Rowley and Tollison 1986; Markusen and Melvin 1984; Blackhurst 1986). Tariffs, while distorting international comparative advantage, if applied on an MFN basis (i.e. against all foreign exporters) still leave open the possibility of the most efficient foreign firms successfully surmounting the tariff and competing effectively with domestic producers, thus maintaining competitive pressures on the latter to pursue efficient forms of adjustment or exit. Moreover, tariffs as a form of tax render the costs of protection relatively visible to the principal cost-bearers (domestic consumers). However, quotas will often be more attractive than tariffs to domestic producers and their work forces, precisely because they offer the prospect of a firmer guarantee of sustained levels of output and employment. Moreover, unlike tariffs, the costs of protection are rendered less visible to domestic consumers, manifesting themselves in scarcity rents captured by domestic producers and foreign producers in the event that they rather than importers are awarded the quotas. Not only are inefficiencies involved in guaranteeing domestic producers fixed market shares but if the quotas are applied on an historical basis they will freeze patterns of imports into pre-existing patterns, notwithstanding the possible emergence of even more efficient foreign competitors, who cannot obtain quotas. This inefficiency can be avoided and scarcity rents for foreign exporters eliminated if tradeable quotas are auctioned off by the domestic government to the highest bidders among local importers (who will buy imports from the most efficient foreign source). Domestic government also in this way avoid foregoing the tax revenues generated by tariffs (Bergsten, Elliott, Schott and Takacs 1987). The price commanded by the quotas is also a visible measure of the margin of protection.

More politically attractive again than either tariffs or quotas may be 'voluntary' export agreements or orderly marketing agreements negotiated bilaterally between an importing country and major sources of exports of a given product (Bergsten 1975). Here, like quotas and unlike tariffs, domestic producers are guaranteed market shares, foreign producers are partly mollified through the capture of scarcity rents, and the costs to domestic consumers are largely concealed. But unlike MFN tariffs or quotas imposed under the safeguard clause of the GATT (Article XIX), where compensating domestic trade concessions or retaliatory withdrawal of foreign trade concessions must be contemplated by the country seeking to impose the tariffs or quotas, nothing need be given up in return for the agreement of foreign countries to restrain exports (under the threat of unilateral action if agreement is not forthcoming). Moreover, VERs and OMAs will typically be directed primarily against the *most efficient* foreign producers, in order to minimize the impact of imports on domestic producers, even though this imposes the greatest costs on domestic consumers.

From both utilitarian and social contractarian perspectives, trade protection would seem to be the least desirable instrument to shelter workers from the negative effects of adjustment to trade. Unlike direct compensation in the form of worker adjustment assistance, trade restrictions have economic costs in that they induce a misallocation of resources within the economy. They frequently cost consumers, through increased prices, an amount greater than the full income stream for each job preserved – i.e. the costs of these restrictions are greater than would be those of a 100 per cent labour subsidy. This suggests that only a portion of the rents which accrue to producers actually benefit affected workers. In effect, after the benefits to workers have been taken into account, one is left with a substantial net transfer of wealth from consumers to producers, a transfer which has no ethical justification.

From the communitarian perspective, trade protection of declining industries would seem (in contrast to more exit-oriented policies) consistent with the concern to preserve – or at least prevent from too suddenly being dissolved – existing community and social structures. Yet such restrictions do not by any means guarantee medium or long-term preservation of employment. They may merely provide the firm with time to relocate elsewhere, after it has recovered – partly from the rents from protection – more of its sunk costs. Communitarians would at the very least insist that the rents be reinvested with a view to modernization or other measures which ensure longer-term viability of jobs in the community, although modernization, through the substitution of capital for labour, will typically itself entail prospects of job loss.

(2) 'Unfair' trade remedies

Apart from the political bias in favour of quotas, VERs and OMAs over tariffs, politicians also face strong incentives to characterize foreign competitive inroads as being the result of 'unfair' trade and to apply contingent forms of protection to them or at least to allow or encourage legal harassment of foreign producers by domestic producers through permissive access to the domestic procedures by which contingent protection determinations are reached.

Anti-dumping duties are one such form of protection for domestic producers. The legal definition of dumping – selling in the export market at prices below those at which the product is sold in the country of origin – connotes no inefficiency or distortion whatever, outside very narrow cases of predatory dumping (selling at below cost) (Trebilcock and Quinn 1979; Barcelo 1971–2: 491). But anti-dumping regimes almost never focus on these economically justifiable but exceptional cases and provide much broader-gauge protection to domestic producer interests.

Countervailing duties are another form of contingent protection. Here, the objection to foreign imports is that their competitive success in domestic markets is explained by the fact that they have been subsidized by government in the country of origin and thus their price superiority is artificially induced. While a more problematic case than 'dumping' (at least as legally defined and applied), it can be cogently argued that although global efficiency may be reduced by such subsidies, domestic interests in the importing country are actually better off in aggregate as a result of the foreign subsidies. Domestic producers are worse off to the extent that they are required to cut prices to meet the foreign subsidized price, but domestic consumers are better off by the same amount, and a further group of domestic consumers enjoy a pure welfare gain – those who could not afford the product before and now enter the market for the first time. A sober economic view of foreign subsidies of exports is that the importing country should take the foreigner's subsidies and run, noting only its regret that the subsidies are not larger and timeless. Caveats to this view relate to foreign subsidization with predatory intent, and possibly domestically destabilizing temporary or intermittent foreign subsidies (Trebilcock and Quinn 1979). To the extent that more efficient foreign exporters are being squeezed out of a market by subsidized imports, then a claim for nullification and impairment, supported by a right to compensation or retaliation against the subsidizing country, seems the appropriate response.

(3) Gradualism, reversibility, reciprocity

Short of complete rejection of trade liberalization, three other possible trade policy responses that are economically more rational than complete resistance to trade liberalization require brief noting at this juncture (Richardson 1980: 332–8). First, as was the case in the multilateral Kennedy and Tokyo Round tariff reductions, in the European Community's internal tariff reductions, and as is contemplated in the Canada-US Free Trade Agreement, trade liberalization can follow a gentle phase-in trajectory. Such a policy has two obvious and offsetting effects. It attenuates adjustment costs by providing for a temporally dispersed rather than lumpy adjustment process. However, it also attenuates the benefits from trade liberalization. Economists are generally sceptical that economic welfare is often likely to be enhanced by this policy (Kaplow 1986; Banks and Tumlir 1986), and would see Economic Darwinism as the best recipe for efficient adjustment. Utilitarians may see a phase-out of trade restrictions as an appropriate policy for reducing the private costs of rapid adjustment (and sources of disutility), and Kantians may see a less deleterious impact on the least well-endowed in society. Communitarians will emphasize the importance of ensuring that communities are not destabilized by to. rapid or too intense pressures for change. Gradual phase-in may allow for retraining or relocation to other jobs within the same community or region, or for early retirement policies which can avoid the stark choice between sundering communal bonds or forcing indefinite unemployment. Politicians may see in this policy a better temporal alignment of costs and benefits from trade liberalization. Given the short electoral time frames in which they are required to operate, policies (like trade liberalization) that may yield up-front costs and long-run benefits are antithetical to their political self-interest.

Second, provision can be made, as contemplated in Article XIX of the GATT, for temporary reinstatement of trade protection measure if trade liberalization threatens serious disruption to a domestic industry. The various implications of invoking this policy response are similar to those noted above for a phase-out strategy.

Third, trade liberalization can be made conditional on reciprocal trade concessions by trading partners. A major advantage of reciprocity is that it provides some assurance to a country seeking to liberalize its trade policies that adjustment costs caused by greater import penetration can be partially offset by increased access to export markets into which displaced resources can be redeployed (Richardson 1980: 290). Even if *on a unilateral* basis, liberalization makes sense in that the consumer welfare and allocative efficiency benefits exceed the costs of substituting adjustment policies that address worker and community dislocation, it would nonetheless usually be rational to attempt to extract some payment from other states that benefit from the liberalizing measures.

(b) Industrial subsidies

Industrial subsidies to declining sectors may take many different forms: they may be firm-specific or industry-wide; they may be designed to preserve output and employment (the stay option), or to facilitate rationalization and contraction (the exit option); they may take the form of outright grants, loans at below market interest rates, loan guarantees, or tax expenditures.

In evaluating the economic arguments for industrial subsidies to declining sectors, it is important to distinguish subsidies designed to avoid adjustment and those designed to facilitate it.

(1) Subsidies as a form of economic second-best

With respect to subsidies designed to avoid adjustments, it is arguable that if we are unwilling to live with the economic implications of unfettered international comparative advantage, subsidies are economically preferable to trade restrictions because subsidies only distort production decisions and not consumption decisions, whereas trade restrictions such as tariffs distort both (Richardson 1980). For example, a tariff on imported textiles will both encourage inefficient domestic entry into the textile industry, and inefficiently reduce demand for both imported and domestic textiles because of the tariff-induced price increases. A subsidy to domestic producers may induce the first effect, but because textiles will continue to sell at world prices, will not induce the second effect. This argument assumes that revenues needed to underwrite the subsidies can be raised by taxes that do not substantially distort consumption decisions elsewhere in the economy. This may be possible, but it is easy to imagine cases where consumption distortions will occur, for example as a result of an increase in general sales taxes. In short, from an economic perspective, the first-best policy economically is complete trade liberalization, the second-best policy industrial subsidies, and the least desirable trade restrictions.

(2) Subsidies and externalities

It has been argued that subsidies can improve the allocation of resources if they are responsive to various forms of externalities. For example, Schwartz and Harper argue that subsidies to agricultural production may be justified if there are widely held preferences in the community either that a certain portion of the population should remain engaged in agriculture and rural lifestyles or that the community should be self-sufficient in food in the event that foreign suppliers, for political or military reasons, choose not to sell food exports to us (Schwartz and Harper 1970-71). The difficulty with this argument is that while it may be true that such preferences exist and that they are unlikely to be fully registered in the prices consumers are willing to pay domestic producers for their goods, it may equally be true that such preferences do not exist. Given the absence of a market in which these preferences can reliably be revealed, industrial subsidies in all kinds of contexts could be justified by speculative conjectures as to unrevealed preferences.

(3) Industrial subsidies and capital market imperfections

The Economic Council of Canada in a recent study of programmes of government financial assistance to industry argues the possible existence of a 'credit gap' that results in firms which present objectively equal risks to investors being differentially treated by the capital market (Economic Council of Canada 1982). The Council points to disproportionately high transaction costs facing small businesses in obtaining loans, and disproportionately high costs and legal difficulties in small firms raising equity through small public offerings. These may result in a bias towards excessively highly leveraged capital structures in the classes of firms affected by such costs. This finding may then support a conclusion that government financial assistance to such firms may be warranted either on start-up or when financial difficulties are encountered.

In general, these arguments are not convincing. Other researchers have not found that small businesses encounter special difficulties in raising debt or equity capital (Trebilcock *et al.* 1985). Even if this were so, it then would have to be demonstrated that government intervention in subsidizing the availability of financing could reduce the costs that private sector financial institutions face in servicing small businesses. If real social costs are involved, what comparative advantage does government possess in reducing these costs of providing capital? Finally, even if the argument and its policy implications are cogent, only small businesses seem to fall within its scope, not larger failing firms or declining sectors generally.

(4) Industrial subsidies and modernization of obsolete capital

It is often argued (principally by industry interests) that state assistance to facilitate capital modernization may be necessary to make a distressed industry internationally competitive. However, obsolete plants are often the *result*, not the *cause* of loss of international competitiveness. Firms which are only able to cover variable costs are constrained to allow their fixed assets to run down and with them their long-term capacity. If an adequate return could be made on new fixed assets, presumably the private capital market would provide the funds required to make this investment. A government judgment that such an investment will yield long-run competitiveness and profitability will typically be at variance with this private capital market judgment and should, for this reason, be viewed with considerable circumspection.

(5) Industrial subsidies and strategic pre-emption

Richard Harris in a study for the Macdonald Royal Commission proposes three major growth strategies for Canada:

(a) multilateral or at least bilateral free trade;
(b) government support of high technology industries on a firm-specific basis;
(c) government support for accelerating automation in basic industries (Harris 1985: chap. 7).

The latter two proposals draw on some of the recent strategic trade policy literature and warrant comment.

With respect to Harris' proposal that government support the growth of high technology industries on a firm-by-firm basis and that in a small economy, 'industrial policy necessarily involves a considerable degree of targeting' (Harris 1985: 118), a series of difficulties must be noted. From a purely economic perspective, such a proposal is highly debatable. Do bureaucracies possess the kind of knowledge and expertise to evaluate technologically complex and economically highly risky projects any better than or indeed as well as private capital markets? While there may be economic advantages to a 'first mover' strategy designed to pre-empt a market position in such industries, it is possible and indeed likely, that a number of countries will pursue this 'racing' strategy simultaneously in the same sector with the risks (as Harris acknowledges) of a world glut of products in these sectors.

However, when one adds to the economic doubts of the wisdom of such a policy the practical problems of operationalizing it, it is not at all clear that the actual policy outcomes or impacts will be anything like those that Harris envisages. Harris correctly points out that across-the-board subsidies (through tax expenditures) to R&D suffer from problems of weak targeting – the pay-offs from these expenditures will vary greatly from firm-to-firm and from industry-to-industry. He notes, for example, that an aerospace firm is unlikely to be successfully promoted through what are likely to be quite inadequate across-the-board R&D subsidies.

But firm-specific targeting, whatever its theoretical economic advantages, raises a set of extremely serious policy difficulties. What firms qualify for consideration for high-tech subsidies? What is high-tech? As Roy George points out, (George 1983) if processes as well as products are included, agriculture has strong claims to be considered as an example of a highly successful high-tech industry. Most established, basic industries can make similar claims for advances in some aspects of their production technology, as Harris' premature automation proposal acknowledges. Thus, the potential catchment area of applicants for support is likely to be largely unlimited and undefined. To the extent that very substantial, discretionary subsidies to particular firms are envisaged under Harris' proposals, incentives by firms to invest resources and energy on a large scale in rent-seeking will be magnified significantly, especially if the overall level of expenditures on R&D are increased as substantially as Harris seems to advocate. In this rent-seeking environment, in which very large prizes await the winners, it seems highly unlikely that the supply function for subsidies will remain non-politicized. Harris also suggests that firms that receive support but do not grow or penetrate export markets should be 'cut off'. Unfortunately, one of the first laws of politics is that a benefit once conferred can rarely be revoked, particularly if it is claimed that failure can be turned into success with a little more assistance, thus avoiding or at least deferring the political embarrassment of acknowledging failure, especially if a significant workforce has become dependent on the firm.

While Harris argues that inter-provincial competition for favourable locational decisions by firms should be avoided (how is not made clear), he also suggests that once a decision has been made by a firm to locate in Canada, government should be prepared to 'push and pull' such firms to locate in depressed regions to mitigate the adjustment costs faced by declining sectors in those regions. This suggestion, however, explicitly introduces regional considerations into the granting of R&D subsidies on a firm-specific basis and cannot help but politicize the subsidy process further by introducing considerations that are unlikely to bear exclusively on the technical merits of proposals under review.

Many high-tech firms are not labour-intensive and it is not clear how locating such firms in regionally-depressed labour markets will help significantly in absorbing surplus labour (Bird 1984), nor is it clear how easy it is likely to be to retrain such labour (e.g. redundant textile workers) for employment in many high-tech industries. Thus, it seems inevitable that firms promising more employment opportunities, whatever a firm's high-tech or growth potential, will receive favourable consideration in such a decision-making process, thus deflecting the process further from Harris' intended objectives. Moreover, constraining the provinces from engaging in inter-jurisdictional bidding wars for high-tech industries in order to avoid gaming costs and economic distortions in the spatial alloca-tion of resources (as Harris advocates), is no easy task under the present constitutional division of powers in Canada, even if some political con-sensus were to emerge around the importance of focusing industrial assistance on high-tech firms. A further danger is that, in a federal state, even if the federal government were to focus its resources in this way, regional governments then may feel compelled to divert some of their resources to supporting economic activities from which the federal government had withdrawn its support, thus to some extent neutralizing the thrust of the federal government's industrial policies.

Other features of Harris' proposals raise similar concerns. He distinguishes between declining sectors, where orderly termination is prescribed, from basic industries (e.g. autos, rubber) facing competitive inroads from lower cost foreign competitors. As between protection, transfer of these activities to other countries, or subsidy, Harris argues for subsidies to support 'premature automation', again on a strategic pre-emption rationale. However, declining sectors will make exactly the same arguments, and policy-makers will face intractable difficulties in distinguishing between firms that fall into Harris' two categories. Again, in the absence of clear and operational criteria, the subsidy process may well degenerate into a rent-seeking process where all kinds of non-economic considerations are likely to attract weight.

(6) Industrial subsidies and job maintenance

It is often argued that evaluation of industrial subsidies designed to preserve output and jobs in a distressed sector should take account of both the direct jobs preserved and also secondary economic activities sustained or created as a result of preserving the industry.

This job maintenance argument at both the primary and secondary levels is suspect. As Usher has pointed out (Usher 1983), for industrial subsidies to be effective in preserving jobs, it is necessary to assume that a subsidy has created jobs marginal to the recipient firm (that is, jobs that the firm would not have created in the absence of the subsidy). Even if this is true, a firm-specific subsidy will not increase employ-ment in the industry of which it is part unless the jobs are marginal to the industry (that is to say, without the subsidy, other firms in the industry would not have increased their output and employment to absorb the share of the failing firm). Even if the subsidy creates jobs that are both marginal to the firm and marginal to the industry, are they marginal to the economy at large? Subsidies, by definition, have to be withdrawn from resources that would otherwise be employed elsewhere in the economy, and there is no reason to assume that the net employment effect of a subsidy will in fact be positive. The same argument holds for secondary effects. Positive multiplier effects in the sector receiving the subsidy may be offset by negative multiplier effects in the sectors from which the subsidy is raised. The effect of industrial subsidies on the overall level of economic activity must be judged against this demanding standard of incrementality, and will often be found wanting. In most cases, jobs will merely have been redistributed among sectors, with administrative costs incurred in the process and output foregone to the extent that efficient resource allocation is distorted.

(7) Industrial subsidies as a response to 'unfair' foreign competition

It is sometimes argued that industrial subsidies are an economically justifiable response to 'unfair' forms of foreign competition, in particular foreign government subsidies of these sources of competition. Where countervailing duties are unlikely to be effective in neutralizing foreign subsidies (e.g. where both domestic and foreign industries are competing for third country markets, or the product in question yields a service that cannot readily be tariffed, as in shipbuilding), domestic industrial subsidies may be looked to to neutralize the foreign subsidies. It is true that foreign subsidies may obscure or undermine considerations of comparative advantage and that countervailing domestic industrial subsidies may reinstate them. While this may improve global efficiency, as noted earlier, it is not clear that domestic interests are, on net, harmed, at least in the case of foreign subsidies of imports. In the absence of evidence of a foreign strategy of predation or evidence of destabilizing temporary or intermittent foreign subsidization, it may make economic sense for domestic consumers to enjoy the benefits of the foreign subsidies, treat them as a gift, and support the reallocation to other uses of domestic resources in the affected sectors (Trebilcock and Quinn 1979). As Krugman points out, 'in practice, an industrial policy aimed at meeting foreign [subsidized] competition would probably lead to government encouragement of investment precisely where the returns to investment are depressed by the targeting of other governments' (Krugman 1984). Subsidies designed to neutralize foreign countries' subsidies of exports into third country markets (e.g. the subsidy war in wheat) present more problematic issues. Countervailing subsidies may be temporarily required to secure some leverage in negotiating a termination of the foreign subsidies.

(8) Industrial subsidies and congestion externalities

It may be argued that in an extreme recessionary environment with very high levels of unemployment, a case can be made that in declining sectors with rigid wages and highly immobile labour, a temporary output subsidy may be cheaper than extended unemployment benefits, foregone tax revenues, additional demands on social services and other costs. In other words, as a social welfare policy (not an economic policy), it may be cheaper to provide social assistance through temporary output subsidies to firms rather than through the social welfare system (Trebilcock *et al.* 1985: chap. 3). Such an argument, however, needs to be treated with extreme caution because the action it proposes clearly retards adjustment, at least in the short run, does nothing to facilitate the redeployment of redundant labour in the long run, and to a large extent perpetuates and reinforces the conditions which may make such a policy an optimal social welfare response in the first place. Moreover, the substantial gains to free trade relative to income losses that it may cause, as reflected in data to be detailed in Chapter 2, suggest that it will be very rare indeed that these conditions are satisfied.

A similar argument that is sometimes made for temporary firm subsidies is that in generally or regionally depressed labour markets with very high levels of unemployment, mass lay-offs create congestion externalities akin to decisions to enter an already overcrowded highway or to move to an already overcrowded city (Trebilcock *et al.* 1985: chap. 3). Each worker's search efforts increase the search costs of other workers, but these costs are external to the relationships between workers and employers in firms or industries facing contractions and lay-offs. On the other hand, search efforts of workers in aggregate may create offsetting positive externalities for potential employers by reducing their recruitment costs and for workers themselves in the form of information about market conditions obtained by some workers but of use to others. In the case of mass lay-offs, however, it may well be that the negative externalities outweigh the positive. Potential policy responses might entail either taxing the source of these externalities or subsidizing the source not to produce them. The source in this context could be viewed in theory as either employer or employee in firms where mass lay-offs occur, but distributionally and operationally it might be more tenable to view the employer as the source. This would suggest taxing the employer for mass lay-offs, through such means as minimum notice periods and/or substantial severance payments or subsidizing the firm to maintain employment until the congestion in the labour market is reduced, presumably by an up-turn in the business cycle. Both policies present difficulties. Employers might view a tax on firings as constituting also an indirect tax on hirings, which might exacerbate unemployment conditions. A subsidy to maintain employment postpones the realization of the efficiency gains from reallocating the resources of the firm to more productive uses and does nothing to ensure that workers acquire skills that make them more employable in other occupations or sectors. Moreover, it is possible that the availability of subsidies to industries with potential lay-off congestion problems will encourage more firms and workers to enter such industries (a form of moral hazard problem), thus largely undermining the effects of a subsidy designed to offset the congestion.

(9) Industrial subsidies and exit costs

A further argument for industrial subsidies and related policies, while not seeking to maintain industry output and employment (as with all the above industrial subsidy rationales) but rather to facilitate downside adjustment, revolves around lumpiness in the downside adjustment process. Harris argues that firms are able to undertake an efficient adjustment to a decline in demand in competitive industries when there are no scale economies whatever (Harris 1985). Here, the decline in industrial capacity is carried out by each firm gradually lowering its own capacity and hence employment. But if there is some degree of indivisibility in plant or firm size so that efficient industry adjustment to a decline in demand requires that firms exit in some orderly temporal sequence, market forces may not produce this sequence. A case may thus arise, so it is argued, for a government role in managing adjustment to the contraction in demand, perhaps through recession cartels, active promotion of mergers, or compensation for scrapping physical capacity. This argument is difficult to evaluate. If sound, it should apply equally to expansion in imperfectly competitive industries with scale economies as well as to contraction, and it quickly then generalizes to a case for pervasive government intervention in most industrial sectors. Moreover, it assumes that government can economize on transaction costs in this context in ways not open to private firms through mergers, specialization agreements, and other means. As applied to well-functioning capital markets, this assumption seems dubious. Conversely to Harris' view, it may be plausibly argued that the contraction problem, even in imperfectly competitive markets with scale economies, entails fewer inefficiencies than the expansion problem. With expansion, there may be surplus-dissipating races to pre-empt additions to the market. With contraction, each producer drops out as its quasi-rents fall to zero. There is no racing or gaming problem, and no firm can credibly threaten to add new capacity. Exit is likely to occur in reverse order of age of facilities.

Further objections to this rationale for government intervention in the adjustment process emphasize the dangers of bureaucratic involvement in detailed industrial restructuring, in terms of relative institutional competence, and also the dangers of fostering anti-compeititive forms of collusion in the industry in seeking agreement on future industry structure (Lawrence and Litan 1986).

In sum, all the above rationales for industrial subsidies to depressed sectors are either economically unsound or appear to justify application to very narrowly circumscribed sets of circumstances. We are thus left with the principal economic vice of industrial subsidies – noted at the outset – that they distort production decisions. They also entail significant administrative costs, and rarely offer offsetting economic benefits.

From an ethical perspective, can more be said in favour of industrial subsidies to declining sectors? From a utilitarian perspective, industrial subsidies designed to preserve the stay option (i.e. preserve output and employment) mitigate both the social and private costs of adjustment. Moreover, to the extent that risk is an independent source of disutility (which, assuming that most individuals are risk averse, is a reasonable assumption), industrial subsidies mitigate the risks of change for those who stand to be prejudiced by change. However, utilitarianism would also weigh the disutilities to others from resisting change – the direct costs of the subsidies, the administrative costs of dispensing the subsidies, foregone production and consumption in other sectors from avoiding the reallocation of resources to higher valued uses. With respect to the disutility associated with risk, utilitarians may be sceptical that investors are nearly as risk-averse as employees, in that the firms in which they invest can diversify risk through product diversification and investors themselves can diversify risk through portfolio diversification. Moreover, utilitarians, like economists, would be concerned with the risk-incentive trade-offs likely to be generated by industrial subsidies (Kaplow 1986). Subsidies designed to preserve output and employment in a given sector are likely to attract additional resources into the sector – a form of moral hazard problem – that will exacerbate the original misallocation problem. And if a general and permanent policy of providing industrial subsidies to depressed sectors is announced, there will no longer be appropriate incentives to avoid over-investment in such sectors at the outset. To the extent that employees are less well able than investors to diversify away the negative risks of change, utilitarians may see a stronger case for subsidies, but would be concerned, as with investors, with the incentive effects of such subsidies (again, the risk-incentive trade-off), and would also be concerned with whether alternative policies to industrial subsidies might be devised that more finely target the risk of change for workers without also subsidizing other interests (e.g. investors), for whom private market options can yield desired risk-incentive trade-offs.

Kantian social contractarians are likely to be equally sceptical of industrial subsidies. When designed to preserve the stay option or to moderate the effects of sudden transitions, they may, on occasion, alleviate the plight of the least advantaged in our society (e.g. low-income, low-skilled, relatively immobile workers). However, in many cases the workers at risk will not fall into this class, and investors for whom risk is alleviated will almost never fall into this class. As with utilitarianism, much more finely targeted policy instruments seem indicated by this ethical perspective.

From a communitarian perspective, subsidies should ideally create jobs which have a long-term viability in the region or community whose future is threatened by industrial decline. They might therefore best be oriented towards employment creation in other sectors, or towards rationalization or modernization which reverses the process of decline. However, subsidies which merely postpone inevitable dislocations will not be justified unless this postponement genuinely makes the readjustment of community ties more gradual and natural, or permits the time needed for retraining or search for alternative work in the same community or region.

While less politically attractive than trade restrictions, because they entail on-budget expenditures, subsidies share some of the other attractive political properties of trade restrictions. To the extent that industrial subsidies are designed to preserve the stay option rather than facilitate the exit option, they avoid potentially costly acknowledgments that a sector is a loser and that government can or will do nothing to arrest its decline and avoid the consequential exit costs for interests dependent on it. Like trade restrictions, industrial subsidies can assure both investors and workers simultaneously that they will not have to bear the costs of exit, and thus the support of two major political constituencies can be engendered. The production distortions generated by industrial subsidies will have negative employment and consumption effects in other sectors over time but the impact of these costs on the bearers (future employees and consumers) will be thinly spread geographically and over time and may be barely perceived or viewed as causally related to the government's industrial subsidy policies in depressed sectors. The direct costs of underwriting industrial subsidy programmes will, of course, be borne by taxpayers. Again, like future employees and consumers, they are a widely dispersed political constituency who face major organizational and informational disabilities compared to the much more concentrated stake-holders who stand to gain from industrial subsidies. The information costs faced by taxpayers can also be exacerbated by strategic choice of the form of the industrial subsidy. By use of loans at below market interest rates, loan guarantees, credit insurance, and tax expenditures, a government may be able to move a large portion of the costs of industrial subsidies off-budget and render them less visible.

Since subsidies are expenditures from the public fisc they are unlikely – in contrast to trade restrictions – to have concentrated interests opposed to them. While importers, distributors, retailers and domestic industries stand to lose particularly heavily from trade restrictions, all taxpayers contribute, proportional to their general revenue contribution, to subsidization. An exceptional case will be firm-specific subsidies, which may be opposed by competing firms which are viable without subsidization.

It may also be argued that exit-oriented industrial subsidy policies .(e.g. compensation for scrappage of capacity) can be justified on grounds of political pragmatism. If economic efficiency would dictate the contraction of a domestic industry in the face of lower-cost or superior foreign imports, but domestic losers would seek to exert political vetoes on the withdrawal of trade restrictions, compensating the loss of domestic capital may be argued to be a necessary bribe to realize more liberal trading conditions.

There are at least two reasons for scepticism in evaluating this argument. First, exit-oriented industrial subsidies at best will buy off investor interests, not labour interests. Second, any bribe less generous than the capitalized present value of the future stream of benefits from the preservation or imposition of trade restrictions will not render investor interests indifferent between the two sets of policies. But a bribe on this scale of generosity will constitute a tax on domestic consumers and taxpayers almost equivalent to the cost to them of the trade restrictions avoided, thus largely neutralizing any gains to them. Moreover, because the bribe will entail clearly visible, determinate, up-front costs while any net gains from trade liberalization will be long-term, less determinate, and less visible, the prospect of underwriting such a bribe may have little political appeal to the cost-bearers (Quinn and Trebilcock 1982).

(c) Structural policy responses

(1) The market for corporate control

An economic perspective would generally be sceptical that an activist role on the part of government is called for in facilitating efficiency-enhancing structural adaptation in trade-impacted sectors. Economic Darwinism would be perceived as the best recipe for promoting efficient forms of rationalization, including contraction. Write-offs of the value of physical capital as a result of changes in competitive conditions are viewed as purely private losses, not social costs. Society now revalues these assets at whatever they may be worth in their next most highly valued use. There is no efficiency rationale for preventing these losses or compensating for their occurrence. For the most part, government can best facilitate the reallocation of physical capital by removing legal impediments to its mobility (Banks and Tumlir 1986). For example, unduly restrictive anti-trust policies toward firm mergers, especially in depressed sectors, restrictions on foreign take-overs or mergers, provincial securities laws that impose costly conditions on take-over bids through follow-up offer requirements, and corporate law rules that permit incumbent directors to take defensive measures in the face of a take-over bid may mute market processes that induce private rationalizations and restructurings. Tax policies that constrain the ability of acquiring companies to claim accumulated losses incurred by firms taken over may be another example. Efficiency-based modifications to these policies would all be directed to speeding up market-adjustment processes as they bear on the reallocation of physical capital, rather than retarding them (Trebilcock *et al.* 1985: chap. 10).

(2) Bankruptcy

On the other hand, it has been argued that market forces will sometimes lead to premature termination of firms in financial difficulties, resulting in inefficient reallocation of resources (Trebilcock *et al.* 1985: chap. 4; Jackson 1986: chap. 9; Quinn 1985: Bebchuk 1988). It is argued, for example, that our present bankruptcy laws may create incentives for well-secured creditors to pull the plug on firms with a potential for restructuring into new product lines, rationalizing or down-sizing productive capacity over time or modernizing production processes. Transaction cost and strategic behaviour considerations may inhibit the major stake-holders (various classes of shareholders, creditors, employees) from negotiating a post-insolvency bargain that will maximize the value of the company's assets. How serious a problem premature (economically inefficient) bankruptcy is, empirically, is difficult to judge. The costs, delays, and inefficiencies of the bankruptcy process itself create significant countervailing incentives for the major stake-holders to avoid bankruptcy in many circumstances, even perhaps in cases where, absent these costs, bankruptcy and subsequent redeployment of assets would be an efficient outcome. In this context, proposals for the adoption of bankruptcy policies modelled on Chapter XI of the *US Bankruptcy Act*, which would constrain the ability of secured creditors to enforce their security against firms undergoing court-supervised reorganizations and authorize the court to impose (cram-down) reorganizations on shareholders and creditors, may perhaps have economic merit; so, too, may suggestions for modifying voting rules with respect to voluntary proposals to reduce hold-out and strategic behaviour problems and thus facilitate voluntary reorganizations. However, in both cases the prospect of *ex post* modification of the terms of financial instruments is a risk that is likely to be reflected in the *ex ante* terms on which capital is made available to firms, so that it is difficult to be confident that constraints on the ability of creditors or shareholders to enforce the initial terms of their investments will lead to superior long-run resource allocations.

(3) Government-induced rationalization plans

More activist government strategies in promoting downside industrial restructuring would generally be viewed with scepticism by economists. For example, conditionalizing temporary trade protection or industrial subsidies on firms in a depressed industry agreeing to some government-sanctioned rationalization plan would seem to rest on the premise that market forces are unlikely to yield an efficient form of rationalization. This would seem to implicate the dubious argument concerning lumpiness in the downside adjustment process, discussed above in relation to industrial subsidies. It would also implicate the concerns noted in that context of non-expert bureaucratic involvement in detailed industry planning, and of fostering anti-competitive forms of collusion in the industry in question (Lawrence and Litan 1986; Lawrence 1987).

(4) Nationalization

The limiting case of state involvement in a depressed industry would be nationalization (state ownership). Most economists would regard this policy response as sharply antithetical to efficient adjustment. Neither the state nor its agents are likely to have nearly as strong economic incentives as private investors and their agents to utilize or redeploy the resources in question efficiently (Borcherding 1983). Moreover, once the government assumes ownership of a depressed industry, it will be perceived by affected interests as directly responsible for the future of the industry and less able to distance itself politically from the costs of transition. On the other hand, it can be argued that in particular contexts, public ownership may reduce transaction costs for government. Policy co-ordination may be most efficiently pursued by internalization of the process within a single public enterprise if the government is attempting to co-ordinate a multiplicity of policy objectives. Often these objectives cannot be precisely specified because they are, by their nature, unquantifiable or because there are novel or uncertain features in the economic, social or political environment surrounding the activities in question which call for constant redefinition of objectives or redefinition of trade-offs among objectives. In such cases, public ownership may be preferable to a less flexible, more formal, legal-orders oriented regime directed to a multiplicity of private sector economic agents. This argument derives from theories of the firm that seek to explain the integration of economic activities within firms rather than through reliance on 'contracting out' with owners of the various factors of production (Trebilcock and Prichard 1983).

In a depressed industry context, where the government is attempting to orchestrate an 'orderly' rationalization and contraction of an industry to moderate or attenuate adjustment costs, it is at least theoretically

conceivable that co-ordinating staged reductions in capacity, specialization in particular product lines, mergers, lay-offs, retraining and
relocation programmes and encouragement of new industries to locate
in the affected regions may be more efficiently achieved through a single
enterprise than through a loosely co-ordinated set of separate policies
and programmes.

From an ethical perspective, utilitarianism would seem closely to track
the economic perspective with respect to structurally-oriented policy
responses. Social contractarianism would not accept a set of structurally-
oriented policy responses as a substitute for dealing compassionately with
least advantaged workers and similarly situated individuals affected by
the adjustment process. Communitarianism also would reject structural
policies that radically disrupt deeply entrenched community ties.

Politically, laissez-faire structural policies, such as an unconstrained
market for corporate control and permissive bankruptcy policies, may
entail dislocation costs that in many contexts will prove politically difficult
to sustain. On the other hand, government-sponsored rationalization plans
will pose many of the same political difficulties as exit-oriented industrial
subsidy policies (canvassed above), as well as rendering it difficult for
government to extricate itself from a perceived role as on-going guarantor
of the welfare of the industry, thus exposing itself to the risks of
opportunism and repeated rent-seeking on a serious scale. Similarly, but
more extremely, nationalization of a declining industry dramatically
reduces a government's ability to distance itself from the subsequent fate
of the nationalized industry and makes it highly vulnerable to repeated
demands by dependent interests for further stay-oriented assistance.

(d) Labour market policies

As with the other classes of policy instruments reviewed, it is again
important to distinguish between those labour policies that respond to
adjustment pressures by attempting to preserve the stay option from those
designed to facilitate the exit option. Wage subsidies to preserve existing
jobs and to a lesser extent generous and unconditional unemployment
insurance benefits fall into the first category, while retraining
programmes, severance payments, wage subsidies and income insurance
operative on re-employment, and relocation allowances fall into the
second.

(1) Stay-oriented labour policies

From an economic perspective, the first set of labour policies is likely
to be viewed as possessing few economic virtues. Wage subsidies to
preserve existing jobs would be viewed as having least merit. Unemployment insurance may have the economic value of facilitating more

effective job search and thus promoting more efficient job matches. In addition, given that risk aversion as a source of disutility can be viewed as an economic cost that many individuals would be prepared to pay something to avoid, unemployment insurance can be viewed as reducing the costs of the risks of job displacement. However, economists would also be concerned with the risk-incentive trade-off. Generous and extended unemployment insurance benefits reduce incentives to make appropriate employment decisions at the outset as to which sector to seek employment in (if the risks of subsequent lay-offs are shifted to others) – a form of adverse selection problem – and once lay-off occurs reduces incentives to seek employment elsewhere – a form of moral hazard problem. Economists would be concerned that unemployment insurance programmes be devised so as to mitigate these adverse selection and moral hazard problems by preserving appropriate risk-incentive trade-offs.

(2) Exit-oriented labour policies

With respect to labour adjustment programmes designed to facilitate exit by easing the costs for labour associated therewith, economists would acknowledge a case for subsidizing labour adjustment costs in declining sectors in the form of subsidies for retraining and relocation. Essentially, the argument points to imperfections in the market for human capital. Particularly in the case of general (as opposed to specific) human capital that can be used in several occupations or industries, employers may under-invest in worker training because the benefits of that training can be appropriated readily by other employers without compensation. Workers themselves may be unable to finance the costs of general training by such means as wage reductions during the training period, or to meet the opportunity and direct costs of institutional training, in part because of inability to borrow against expected future income streams, which can only effectively be pledged as collateral by pledging their own future services. This arrangement might be viewed as a contingent form of indentured servitude and may not be legally enforceable. Thus a case emerges for subsidizing, at least in part, the opportunity and direct costs of general training or retraining, although the argument does not discriminate between the two and does not in itself support a case for special retraining subsidies for workers laid off in trade-impacted sectors. Rather, it supports a case for subsidizing the availability of general institutional and on-the-job training and retraining programmes for unemployed workers, whatever the source of the unemployment. In addition, even in relation to some specific forms of human capital where economies of scale or specialization in its formation make institutional training more efficient than on-the-job training by employers, efficiency objectives might be served by providing loans (although not necessarily outright grants) to trainees to finance these costs of training or retraining.

Moreover, it might be argued that in the case of highly specialized investments in human capital, the worker assumes a high degree of undiversified risk relating to the continued value of his or her investment and, if risk averse, would wish to be insured against substantial depreciation of his or her capital as a result of exogenous changes in his/her economic environment. If private insurance markets are incomplete and are unlikely to provide such insurance, a case might be made for some form of social insurance, although again problems of adverse selection and moral hazard that may explain why such insurance is not widely available in private markets may cause economists to ask whether governments are better able to contain these effects than private insurance markets (Kaplow 1986). Or, to put the issue another way, can government achieve a more efficient risk-incentive trade-off than private market arrangements?

Apart from imperfections in the market for human capital, as noted above, it is sometimes argued that in generally or regionally depressed labour markets with high levels of unemployment mass lay-offs create congestion externalities. One policy response designed to internalize these externalities and to facilitate more orderly re-integration of displaced workers into the labour force is to mandate minimum notice and severance payment requirements under plant closing laws. While it is sometimes suggested that employers may view a tax on firings as also constituting an indirect tax on hirings, presumably labour markets will re-equilibrate so that wage and benefit packages reflect the risk reallocation implicit in plant closing laws. To the extent that these laws reduce unemployment insurance costs and encourage workers to make greater investments in job-specific skills, thus enhancing their productivity, then such laws may possess efficiency-enhancing properties (Advisory Council on Adjustment 1989: chap. 9). Subsidiary advantages of plant closing laws are that in some cases they may facilitate worker buy-outs of a failing firm by providing the necessary time to organize such a strategy; in other cases advance notice requirements may signal to workers the need to consider seriously wage and other concessions if they wish to see their employer's local operations preserved.

From an ethical perspective, utilitarianism would seem closely to track the implications of the economic perspective on labour adjustment costs. It would underscore the fact that the costs of change include both social and private costs and that individuals may well be risk averse with respect to both sets of costs and desire insurance, private or social, or other forms of protection against these costs. However, utilitarians, like economists, would also be concerned with the costs, direct and indirect, of providing such insurance or protection (these costs necessarily being a source of disutility to others) and would seek to maximize average utility by maximizing benefits net of costs. It has been argued that utilitarians would be sensitive to one set of costs that may not be weighed in the economic calculus – disaffection costs. Michelman has suggested that where the source of disutility to individuals is a change in government policy (such as trade liberalization), those negatively affected may sustain 'disaffection' costs as a result of a perception that the collectivity is singling them out to bear the costs of a policy change that will benefit others but without any sharing in the gains obtained by the latter (Michelman 1967). In effect, this is a claim that the collectivity should write an *actual* Pareto superior social contract (where some gain but nobody is worse off) rather than a Kaldor–Hicks or hypothetical social contract where the gains to the gainers exceed the losses to the losers but where actual compensation to the losers need not be paid.

Kaplow has advanced a powerful critique of this view (Kaplow 1986). If the policy change in question is the result of tyrannous, malevolent of perverse behaviour on the part of its supporters, then of course it is unlikely to survive either the standard economic welfare calculus or the standard utilitarian calculus and from either of these normative standpoints should be abandoned. If, on the other hand, it can be reasonably assumed that the policy change meets these two normative standards and is, on balance, welfare or utility enhancing, Kaplow argues that no special case for compensation can be made. Kaplow gives a simple example to support his argument. Suppose a product that has been on the market for some time is now found to present serious health hazards (e.g. thalidomide, asbestos) and the government decides that social welfare would be enhanced by banning its production and sale. Is there any stronger case for compensating investors, workers and secondary dependent interests in the industry in question for losses associated with the ban than if the product in question had lost its market because of shifts in demand (e.g. buggy whips, horse-drawn carriages, obsolete computers)? Kaplow argues that the risk-incentive trade-offs are exactly the same in the two cases. In both cases, we want manufacturers, workers and related interests to face incentives in making investment or vocational decisions that take account of the probability (risk) that the product in the future may no longer increase social welfare, and to adapt their behaviour accordingly. By shifting risk to the state in either case, incentives will be created, in the case of hazardous products, to take less than optimal precautions in investigating and monitoring the safety characteristics of products offered for sale, and in the case of products that lose their market because of shifts in demand, to make less than optimal investments in R&D and marketing research to identify and develop new products that are likely to generate increases in consumer welfare.

By way of analogy, in the case of trade liberalization, we would wish firms and workers in making investments and vocational decisions to take account of possible future changes in trade policy that will enhance consumer welfare, perhaps reflecting increasing costs of trade protection as comparative advantage continues to shift. But precisely because workers face information costs and other constraints on diversification of risk that are far greater than those which face investors, compensating workers for the costs of change would seem to pose significantly less of a moral hazard problem than compensating firms (investors).

In a Kantian social contractarian ethical framework, labour adjustment policies would be endorsed to the extent that they enhance the welfare of the least advantaged in our society. Relative to the economic and utilitarian frameworks, this suggests a narrower focus on that subset of displaced workers who satisfy this criterion. Here, compensation for both social and private costs of change would seem prescribed, although the Rawlsian version of social contract theory would seem to accept that this should be done in the most efficient available way. Thus, as between stay-oriented and exit-oriented labour adjustment policies and as between 'universal' and targeted labour adjustment policies, this perspective would probably favour labour adjustment policies that ease the costs of transition for that subset of workers whose limited endowments render the costs of change to them especially burdensome.

Some communitarians may, however, be quite vehemently opposed to mobility-oriented labour adjustment policies. These policies will create incentives for the younger and better educated workers – for whom the individual self-development opportunities of change may outweigh the loss of communal ties – to leave the affected region or community. It is these workers who will be most needed for the community's economic renewal and to ensure its long-term viability.

An unresolved tension, however, in the communitarian approach is whether its focus is on the effects on *the individual* of dissolving community ties, or the intrinsic value of preserving existing communities. The latter answer is suggested by the constitutionalization, in Canada for example, of inter-regional equalization goals. The former by contrast seems to be implicit in the work of critics of liberalism such as Sandel who accept the liberal view that ethical claims must emanate from the identity and needs of the individual but argue that these needs are closely connected in most cases with community ties. On this view, exit-oriented labour policies might be targeted on those younger workers who may have more to gain psychologically by leaving than staying, with the more stay-oriented options oriented to older workers, whose community ties are likely to be more deeply entrenched.

From a political perspective, politicians will find labour adjustment policies of all kinds less attractive than either trade restrictions or industrial subsidies. First, they are responsive only to the costs of change faced by workers, and not those faced by investors or other dependent interests. Second, they entail wholly on-budget expenditures, which render the costs of the policy highly visible. Third, some labour adjustment policies may entail a potentially politically costly admission that a given sector cannot or will not be preserved on its present scale and in its present form, and that government is prepared to acquiesce in its decline. These political costs can be attenuated somewhat by adopting labour policies that favour the stay rather than the exit option. Thus, wage subsidies to preserve existing jobs and generous unemployment insurance benefits that underwrite the costs to both employees and employers of recurrent lay-offs and attenuate pressures on unionized work-forces to accept wage concessions in the face of lower wage costs on the part of foreign competitors, are likely to be given greater weight than labour adjustment policies that underwrite the costs of exit through retraining, relocation and severance subsidies.

The argument that generous assistance to displaced workers enables politicians to buy off political vetoes on welfare-enhancing changes in trade policy is likely to be viewed sceptically by politicians. First, such assistance does nothing to buy off resistance from investor and other dependent interests. Second, if the level of assistance must be such as to leave displaced workers entirely indifferent to the social and private impacts of the trade policy change in order for all resistance to be overcome, the financial implications of such a programme for taxpayers are likely to be viewed as formidable. Third, in evaluating the net political returns from such a scale of expenditures, politicians will inevitably ask themselves whether larger political returns can be garnered from a similar scale of expenditures anywhere else across the political landscape or whether other policy instruments such as trade restrictions are likely to entail lower political costs. It would seem that often the answer is likely to be affirmative (Quinn and Trebilcock 1982). Finally, it is argued that to the extent that existing rigidities in labour markets are the result of restrictive labour market practices sanctified or imposed by law, governments have no political interest in neutralizing these policies by adopting countervailing policies designed to produce opposing effects (Banks and Tumlir 1986: 30, 31). This argument is not wholly convincing. To the extent that, for example, minimum wage laws and industry-wide collective bargaining introduce wage rigidities into an industry that prevents it from responding effectively to import competition, a government may not feel politically able to attack these economy-wide 'infrastructure' policies directly, but may feel able to mute their most dysfunctional effects in particular sectors under import pressure through subsidized exit-oriented labour policies as an alternative to trade restrictions, further accelerating the substitution of capital for labour which may be the only prospect the industry has of retrieving a measure of international competitiveness.

(e) Macro-economic policies

To this point in the chapter, we have assumed that trade-related adjustment pressures are the result of genuine shifts in international comparative advantage and reflect a genuine loss of international competitiveness. This assumption cannot be taken for granted. It may be the case that trade-related adjustment pressures are at least in part a result of misconceived domestic macro-economic policies. As Krugman notes: 'Many economists believe that the US budget deficit is largely responsible for the rise in the US trade deficit, because the budget deficit drives up interest rates, [which in itself, it should be noted, raises the costs of capital for domestic firms seeking to rationalize], high interest rates attract foreign capital inflows, these inflows raise the value of the dollar, and the strength of the dollar reduces US competitiveness' (Krugman 1986: 4). In effect, a 25 per cent increase in the value of the dollar relative to the currencies of major trading partners is tantamount to a 25 per cent tax on exports and a 25 per cent reduction in the price of imports, including existing tariffs on imports. Similar arguments can be made about Canadian macro-economic policy, although it has a much less important effect on international interest rates and exchange rate movements than the much larger US economy (Wonnacott and Hill 1987). Other arguments pertain to better multilateral management of exchange rate movements to correct for serious misalignments caused by rapid international capital flows rather than goods flows (Hufbauer and Schott 1985).

Obviously, from an economic perspective, budgetary deficits should be eliminated or reduced by cutting expenditures or raising taxes or some combination of the two, if long-run economic welfare, as measured in national income statistics, is to be enhanced. Utilitarianism would probably reach similar prescriptions, although being more sensitive to the private costs of tax increases and expenditure reductions, as well as (more debatably) perhaps attaching special weight to disaffection costs. Social contractarianism would, on the other hand, resist macroeconomic policy adjustments that entailed reductions in social expenditures that accrue to least advantaged groups, presumably favouring other forms of expenditure reductions and increases in taxes on the more wealthy. From a political perspective, it seems clear that both the US and Canadian governments, struggling with chronic budget deficits, have had difficulty finding political support for either significant tax increases or expenditure reductions.

IV. Conclusions

Both the economic and utilitarian ethical perspectives are likely in most cases to favour labour adjustment policies that ease the costs of transition for labour rather than preserving the stay option, which entails sacrifices in welfare or utility for those that would stand to benefit from a more efficient allocation of resources. The social contractarian ethical perspective would focus more narrowly on the adjustment costs faced by that subset of workers who are amongst the least advantaged members of society. It may be the case that in some contexts only trade restrictions are capable of protecting their welfare because of the lack of any other viable policy, but social contractarians would accept that their welfare should be enhanced in the most efficient way (i.e. by not incurring unnecessary sacrifices in the welfare of others) and in most contexts policies other than trade restrictions, industrial subsidies, and stay-oriented labour policies would seem available that would meet this normative goal. Communitarians will prefer policies which preserve jobs within communities affected by imports, or create new jobs in other sectors in the same community or region. They will, however, prefer employment maintenance subsidies over trade restrictions, since the latter do not necessarily guarantee preservation of employment but only of output (i.e. management may still substitute capital for labour, producing the same output with fewer workers).

It seems unlikely that either the economic perspective or the three ethical perspectives would suggest any distinction between adjustment costs induced by changes in trade policy, changes in trade patterns (without changes in trade policy), or changes in resource values as a result of changes in demand, technological change or changes in productivity. Indeed, most studies have found that factors other than trade impacts tend to account for the bulk of declines in industry employment (Krueger 1980; Wonnacott 1987: 19).

The economic case for exit-oriented labour adjustment policies focuses on imperfections in human capital markets that are independent of the source of job displacement. Moreover, the administrative costs of attempting to distinguish lay-offs caused by any one of these reasons, when all are likely to be at play in any given industry are likely to be substantial. The utilitarian perspective would closely track the economic perspective, unless one accepts that special 'disaffection' costs attach to adjustment costs caused by a deliberate change in government policy. The social contractarian perspective does not require that every single transaction or policy in society meet its normative criteria provided that the 'basic structure' of society meets these criteria. If other government policies can be deployed to complement the policy change in question so as to protect or enhance the welfare of the least advantaged while not foregoing the social gains from this policy change, then such a set of policies would satisfy Rawls' 'difference' or 'maximin' principle. The communitarian perspective would seem the least consistent with the economic approach, since the stay option would seem the most obvious way of protecting existing communal or regional ties. Yet communitarians would still favour policies that allow for the long-term viability of communities and regions, not short-term job maintenance – hence communitarians as well will not be entirely insensitive to the need for positive adjustment.

From a positive or descriptive political perspective, it will have become evident from the analysis in this chapter that political incentives on the part of both demanders and suppliers of policies tend in the direction of a complete inversion of the policy prescriptions implied by both the economic and ethical normative frameworks. That is to say, in the face of trade-related adjustment pressures, politicians will face strong pressures to maintain or increase trade restrictions, whether or not the adjustment pressures are caused by prior or prospective changes in trade policy, or simply shifts in comparative advantage. As a second-best policy, industrial subsidies will be favoured. As a distinctly third-best policy, labour adjustment policies will usually be favoured, but even then with a bias towards stay-oriented labour policies rather than exit-oriented labour policies. It is not clear that the political considerations generating these biases will be significantly influenced by whether job displacement is the result of changes in trade policy, shifts in comparative advantage, productivity improvements or shifts in demand. Within a given industry where all of these factors are at play (e.g. the US steel industry), it is difficult to imagine how a government could politically defend differential treatment of workers laid off for any of these reasons (Lawrence and Litan 1986). Nor is it so obvious how a government could politically defend more generous treatment of all workers displaced for any reasons in such an industry than that provided to workers displaced in another industry unaffected by trade impacts but, for example, shifts in demand (e.g. asbestos, tobacco).

The ensuing three chapters will examine how governments in a selected number of industrialized countries have wrestled with the divergent dictates of these economic, ethical and political perspectives in formulating adjustment responses for their troubled economic sectors.

Chapter two

Trade protection instruments

I. Introduction

(a) Outline of chapter

In this chapter, we address two major classes of issues: the economic costs and benefits of trade restrictions, and the political determinants of the demand for trade protection policies. We begin our discussion of the first class of issues by sketching the basic theoretical argument underlying the case for a liberal international trading regime. We then trace the application of the liberal trade idea in the post-Second World War era. The inauguration of the General Agreement on Tariffs and Trade (GATT) in 1947 ushered in a period of substantial trade liberalization. However, beginning in the mid-1970s, in the face of oil price shocks, recessions, and the emergence of vigorous new international competitors like Japan and the NICs, we have witnessed a partial retreat from the path of increased trade liberalization and instead the rise of the so-called 'new protectionism'.

Section II of this chapter reviews the empirical evidence on the costs and benefits of trade restrictions in the countries and sectors under review, and concludes from the evidence that in all cases the costs have substantially exceeded the benefits.

(b) The basic theory of international trade

The basic economic theory of the mutual gains realizable from international trade, despite many modern refinements and elaborations (Harris 1985), is in essence simply an aspect of the more general economic theory of the mutual gains from exchange in any voluntary contractual relationship. These gains were long ago demonstrated by Adam Smith in *The Wealth of Nations*, and his famous pin-making example still today serves to illustrate the gains to be realized from specialization and exchange. Few of us find it rational to grow all our own food, produce all our own clothing, build our own shelter, administer our own medical services, etc. In its extreme form, this kind of self-sufficiency or autarky entails an existence similar to that of the hermit or caveman. In fact, most of us specialize in producing goods or services for others and for some of our own consumption needs while buying goods or services for other needs from producers who specialize in their production. But if this kind of specialization within communities is rational, Smith argued that specialization and exchange among members of different communities is equally rational. He rejected then current mercantilist notions that buying imports transferred scarce gold currency into foreign hands, diminished national wealth and reduced domestic employment. Thus, on Smith's theory of the gains from specialization, it makes no sense for Canadians to attempt to produce their own rice or pineapples if these can be purchased from foreigners more cheaply because of different endowments in climate, soil, skills, etc. On the other hand, it may make no sense for producers in these foreign countries to build their own telephone systems or hydro-electric generators if we can supply them at a higher quality or lower price.

Early in the nineteenth century, David Ricardo extended Smith's theory of absolute advantage into a theory of comparative advantage that sought to demonstrate that even countries that are less efficient than other countries in everything they produce will still find it rational to trade. Ricardo's example of Portugal and England trading wine for cloth even though England was a higher cost producer of both but enjoyed a smaller cost disadvantage in cloth, could easily have been modified to make the same point about purely domestic producers of wine and cloth with different production costs in respect of each. Indeed, Samuelson uses a similarly motivated example to show why, for example, a lawyer who also types more quickly and efficiently than her secretary will nevertheless specialize in the provision of legal services and invest in or buy secretarial services because this reflects where the lawyer's comparative advantage is greatest and where the secretary's comparative disadvantage is smallest (Samuelson and Scott 1980: 807).

Several challenges to the neo-classical theory bear mentioning, however. One of these relates to the longstanding concept of the optimal tariff'. If a country is a sole, or principal, consumer of a particular product, then it may capture a net benefit by imposing a tariff which, in driving down demand for the product, *reduces* its price. How this works is evoked by Richardson who uses the example of an American tariff on Japanese textiles: 'With a US tariff, the US demand for Japanese textiles is discouraged. Japanese textile producers are faced with reduced demand and a smaller market, and will compete harder for the limited US business. They will lower their price and improve their product and service' (Richardson 1980: 303). Where America is the only buyer of

Japanese textiles, a significant decrease in American demand could result in a large drop in world price. In order to thwart the comparative advantage of the foreign exporter, a tariff must be at least equal to the difference between world and domestic price. Hence, if world price decreases by the full amount of the tariff then American consumers are as well off as before the tariff was imposed, and Americans are *better off* collectively, since they capture the tariff revenue, which in effect is 'paid' by the foreign exporter through the lowering of its price in response to weakened demand. These conditions of monopsony are, of course, extremely rare. The literature does not contain empirical evidence about the actual use of such tariffs.

Second, it is argued that tariffs can be used strategically, either as retaliation against the trade policies of other nations or as a means of pre-empting foreign competition. The retaliatory argument is that by punishing other countries for their own protectionist policies by restrictions on their imports, it will eventually become possible to force an elimination of those protectionist policies. This is, of course, a high risk game. Important domestic political and ethical constraints fashion the available set of strategic responses. The retaliatory tariff may create, for example, its own powerful domestic constituency thus rendering its removal politically difficult or impossible, *whatever* the other state's response. Additionally, there is a high risk that the target state will retaliate in such a way as to disrupt the exports of highly politically sensitive sectors. Further counter-retaliation will do nothing in the short-run to counter the strong political demands of such sectors and it may become politically necessary, (although in purely strategic terms, unwise) to negotiate a compromise with the target state, in order to induce the removal of retaliatory restrictions against one's own highly politically sensitive sectors. This also indicates the danger of pre-emptive strategies for a particular sector (i.e. strategies premised upon levels of protection which are so high as to deter others from trying to respond through subsidies etc.): retaliation against sectors may lead to such politically devastating consequences as to induce capitulation of the would-be pre-emptor. And of course, the considerable cost to consumers of these retaliatory tariffs would have to be weighed against the highly uncertain future benefits.

An unfortunate semantic legacy of Ricardo's demonstration of the gains from international trade that has been perpetuated in the terminology of much subsequent trade literature and debate is that in international trade *countries* are trading with each other. This, of course, is rarely the case. As in purely domestic exchanges, *private economic agents* (albeit located in different countries) are trading with each other. In its most rudimentary form, all that international trade theory seeks to demonstrate is that free international trade dramatically broadens the contract opportunity set available to private economic agents and hence the mutual gains realizable from exchange as parties with different endowments of specialized skills or resources are able to reap the gains from their differential advantages and disadvantages through trade. It may be argued that in international exchanges, in contrast to domestic exchanges, part of the gains from exchange are realized by foreigners, and that a country would be advantaged by capturing all the gains from exchange for itself. However, this raises the question of whether the domestic gains foregone by foreign trade are greater or less than the additional gains from purely domestic exchange. As a matter of simple economic theory, the gains to domestic consumers from foreign trade will almost always be greater than the additional gains to domestic producers from purely domestic trade. This is so because higher domestic than foreign prices will entail a transfer of resources from domestic consumers to domestic producers (arguably creating matching decreases and increases in welfare), but *in addition* some domestic consumers will be priced out of the market by the higher domestic prices and will be forced to allocate their resources to less preferred consumption choices, entailing a dead-weight social loss. An alternative way in which to conceive of the net domestic loss from foregone foreign exchange opportunities is to ask what compensation domestic producers would need to offer domestic consumers to render them indifferent to these foregone opportunities. Presumably only domestic prices that matched foreign producers' prices would achieve this end. The inability of domestic producers to make such an offer implies that foregoing foreign trading opportunities is Pareto inferior – the gains to domestic producers and workers in the protected sectors are not sufficient fully to compensate consumers and still leave the gainers better off. As we will see in the review of the empirical evidence below, these simple theoretical propositions are amply borne out by the evidence.

International trends toward the liberalization of international trade, especially since the Second World War, reflect a recognition of the positive sum characteristics of broadened trading networks. The seven rounds of multilateral trade negotiations (MTN) since the inauguration of the General Agreement on Tariffs and Trade (GATT) in 1947 have substantially reduced tariffs in international trade. In Canada's case, tariffs on dutiable goods have fallen from about 24 per cent on average at the time of the Second World War to about 9–10 per cent on average today. These reductions were accomplished over seven multilateral negotiating rounds held within the framework of the GATT and were matched by a roughly similar or larger scale of tariff reductions by other industrialized nations. From 1947 to 1986, per capita GNP in Canada rose in real terms from $7,402 to $19,925 (1986 $) (an increase of 169.2 per cent); and civilian employment rose from 4,821,000 in 1947 to

12,295,000 in April 1988 (an increase of 155 per cent), with manufacturing employment rising 88.7 per cent over this period (Trebilcock 1988).

With respect to OECD average duties, by 1980 customs duties accounted for some 2.5 per cent of the value of imports, half the ratio ten years earlier (OECD 1985b: 26). In addition, some progress has been made, mostly in Tokyo Round negotiations, in disciplining the use of certain kinds of non-tariff barriers to trade (NTBs) through the negotiation of multilateral codes on anti-dumping, subsidies, government procurement, customs administration and technical standards.

(c) The rise of the New Protectionism

The last decade and a half – a period when the global economy experienced two oil price shocks and two world-wide recessions – has simultaneously witnessed a sharp increase in the use of quantitative restrictions: Quotas, voluntary export restraints (VERs) and orderly marketing agreements (OMAs), typically negotiated on a bilateral basis outside the safeguard provisions (Article XIX) of the GATT and in clear violation of its letter or spirit.

On one estimate, the share of restricted products in total manufactured imports increased over the period 1980 to 1983 from 6 to 13 per cent for the US, and from 11 to 15 per cent for the EEC. In 1983, the product groups subject to restriction accounted for around 30 per cent of total manufactured consumption in the OECD countries covered, up from 20 per cent in 1980. Within the protected sectors, it has been estimated that the absolute number of NTBs quadrupled between 1968 and 1983. While less than 1 per cent of OECD automobile trade was affected by discriminatory restrictions in 1973, this share had risen to nearly 50 per cent a decade later. It is also estimated that the proportion of trade under non-liberal treatment rose in recent years from 31 to 73 per cent in steel and from 53 to 81 per cent in textiles and clothing. From 1980 to 1983, the share of Japan's and the Asian NICs exports affected by discriminatory restrictions rose from 15 to over 30 per cent (OECD 1985b: 11, 12).

Non-fuel imports of industrial countries subject to selected non-tariff measures are estimated to have increased from 19 per cent of total imports in 1981 to 23 per cent in 1987. Export restraint agreements rose from 135 in September 1987 to 261 in September 1987 to May 1988, about half of which are directed at developing counties, and four-fifths of which are intended to protect the EC or US markets. The increase in non-tariff measures has significantly offset the liberalizing effect of tariff reductions in the post-war period. For example, it is estimated that the economy-wide tariff equivalent of US non-tariff barriers on textiles, steel and automobiles is about 25 per cent, bringing protection to its early post-war level (IMF 1988: 10). The distribution and recent growth of export restraint arrangements is shown in Table 2.1.

In addition to the increase in the use of quantitative restrictions, as indicated in the Tables 2.2 and 2.3 various forms of contingent protection

Table 2.1 Export-restraint arrangements, 1987–88

	September 1987	May 1988	Reported Increase Between September 1987 and May 1988
Total export restraint arrangements[1]	135	261	126[2]
By sectoral composition			
Steel	38	52	14
Agricultural and food products	20	55	35
Automobiles and transport equipment	14	17	3
Textiles and clothing[3]	28	72	44
Electronic products	11	19	8
Footwear	8	14	6
Machine tools	7	7	—
Other	9	25	16
By protected markets			
European Community	69[4]	138[5]	69
US	48	62	14
Japan	6	13	7
Other industrial countries	12	47	35
Eastern Europe	—	1	1
By restrained exporters			
Japan	25	28	3
Eastern Europe	20	45	25
Korea	24	25	1
Other industrial countries	23	59	36
Other developing countries	43	98	55

Source: International Monetary Fund, *Issues and Developments in International Trade Policy* (Washington D.C.: IMF 1988).
Notes:
[1] Includes voluntary export restraints, orderly marketing arrangements, export forecasts, basic price systems, industry-to-industry arrangements, and discriminatory import systems. Excludes restrictions under the Multifiber Arrangement.
[2] Of the reported increase, almost half were in existence prior to 1988 but were reported by GATT only in 1988.
[3] Excludes restrictions under the Multifiber Arrangement.
[4] Includes 20 arrangements involving individual EC member states.
[5] Includes 51 arrangements involving individual EC member states.

47

Table 2.2 Industrial countries: anti-dumping investigations and actions, 1981–87[1]

	1981		1982		1983		1984		1985		1986		First Half 1987[2]	
	Investi-gations	Actions	Investi-gations	Actions	Investi-gations	Actions	Investi-gations	Actions	Investi-gations	Actions	Investi-gations	Actions	Investi-gations	Actions
Australia	49	28	77	47	80	58	56	36	63	30	63	10	11	—
Industrial countries	34	14	55	25	59	44	30	26	38	15	35	7	8	—
Developing countries	15	11	20	20	21	13	21	10	19	12	20	3	3	—
Centrally planned economies	—	3	2	2	—	1	5	—	6	3	8	—	—	—
Canada	23	13	72	21	36	41	31	16	36	27	55	45	34	36
Industrial countries	12	8	54	10	27	29	20	9	18	16	21	18	21	20
Developing countries	8	1	15	7	7	10	8	5	12	8	30	17	10	12
Centrally planned economies	3	4	3	4	2	2	3	2	6	3	4	10	3	4
European Community	47	22	55	42	36	45	48	31	45	12	27	21	10	8
Industrial countries	9	8	18	9	11	12	16	9	9	9	11	9	2	3
Developing countries	3	5	15	4	9	12	5	6	16	1	8	—	4	1
Centrally planned economies	35	9	22	29	16	21	27	16	20	2	8	12	4	4
United States	14	4	61	45	47	15	71	25	65	53	70	50	47	43
Industrial countries	7	3	47	41	27	9	32	8	19	19	30	15	32	25
Developing countries	4	—	13	3	19	6	23	17	41	20	34	32	13	10
Centrally planned economies	3	1	1	1	1	—	16	—	5	14	6	3	2	8
Total	133	67	265	155	199	159	206	108	209	122	215	126	102	87
Industrial countries	62	33	174	85	124	94	98	52	84	59	97	49	63	48
Developing countries	30	17	63	34	56	41	57	38	88	41	92	52	30	23
Centrally planned economies	41	17	28	36	19	24	51	18	37	22	26	25	9	16

Source: International Monetary Fund, *Issues and Developments in International Trade Policy* (Washington D.C.: IMF 1988).
Notes: [1] The countries listed have initiated virtually all the anti-dumping investigations undertaken worldwide. Actions taken include the imposition of definitive duties and minimum price undertakings by exporting countries. Investigations include those opened in the context of reviewing an existing anti-dumping duty or after allegations of breach of an undertaking.
[2] The data are based on actions reported by signatories to the GATT Committee on Anti-dumping Practices, which exclude the actions taken against nonsignatories.

Table 2.3 Industrial countries: countervailing investigations and actions, 1981–86[1]

	1981 Investi-gations	1981 Actions	1982 Investi-gations	1982 Actions	1983 Investi-gations	1983 Actions	1984 Investi-gations	1984 Actions	1985 Investi-gations	1985 Actions	First Half 1986[2] Investi-gations	First Half 1986[2] Actions
Australia												
Industrial countries	—	—	3	—	7	9	6	—	3	—	1	2
Developing countries	—	—	3	—	7	9	5	—	3	—	—	2
Centrally planned economies	—	—	—	—	—	—	1	—	—	—	—	1
Canada												
Industrial countries	—	3	1	—	3	—	2	2	2	2	—	1
Developing countries	—	3	1	—	3	—	2	2	1	1	—	1
Centrally planned economies	—	—	—	—	—	—	—	—	—	—	—	—
European Community												
Industrial countries	—	1	3	—	2	3	1	1	—	—	—	—
Developing countries	—	1	1	—	1	1	1	1	—	—	—	—
Centrally planned economies	—	—	2	—	—	2	—	—	—	—	—	—
Japan (Industrial countries)	—	—	—	—	1	—	—	—	—	—	—	—
US												
Industrial countries	10	6	124	80	21	21	50	18	40	24	28	28
Developing countries	6	1	85	61	3	3	14	2	12	6	8	10
Centrally planned economies	4	5	39	19	16	18	34	16	27	17	20	18
Total												
Industrial countries	11	7	131	80	34	33	59	22	45	27	29	30
Developing countries	6	1	90	61	15	13	21	6	16	8	9	12
Centrally planned economies	5	6	41	19	17	20	36	16	28	18	20	18
economies	—	—	—	—	2	—	2	—	1	1	—	—

Source: International Monetary Fund. *Issues and Developments in International Trade Policy* (Washington DC.: IMF 1988).

Notes: [1] The countries listed have initiated virtually all the countervailing investigations undertaken by individual countries. Actions taken include the imposition of definitive duties and minimum price undertakings by exporting countries. Investigations include those opened in the context of reviewing an existing countervailing duty or after allegations of breach of an undertaking.

[2] The data are based on actions reported by the signatories to the GATT Committee on Subsidies and Countervailing Measures, which exclude the actions taken against nonsignatories.

Table 2.4 Recourse to Article XIX of GATT 1978–87

Country	Product	Measure	Year Introduced (Terminated)
Australia	Wool worsted yarns	Tariff quota	1978
	Round blunt chainsaw files	Quantitative restriction	1978 (1978)
	Double-edged safety razor blades	Quantitative restriction	1978 (1982)
	Sheets and plates of iron and steel	Quantitative restriction	1978 (1980)
	Certain trucks and stackers	Quantitative restriction	1980 (1982)
	Files and rasps	Quantitative restriction	1976 (1978)
	Hoops and strips of iron and steel	Tariff quota	1982 (1983)
	Certain filament lamps	Tariff increase	1983
	Nonelectrical domestic refrigerators	Tariff increase	1983 (1985)
Austria	Broken rice	Quantitative restriction	1987
Canada	Footwear other than canvas and rubber	Quantitative restriction	1977 (1981)
	Nonleather footwear	Quantitative restriction	1981[1]
	Leather footwear	Quantitative restriction	1982[1]
	Yellow onions	Specific surtax	1982 (1983)
	Fresh, chilled, and frozen beef and veal	Quantitative restriction	1985 (1985)
Chile	Sugar	Tariff surcharge	1984
	Wheat	Tariff increase	1984
	Edible vegetable oils	Tariff increase	1985
European Community	Preserved mushrooms	Quantitative restriction	1978 (1980)
	Yarn of synthetic fibers (UK only)	Quantitative restriction	1980 (1980)
	Cultivated mushrooms	Quantitative restriction	1980 (1984)
	Other cultivated mushrooms	Quantitative restriction	1980 (1980)
	Frozen cod fillets	Embargo	1981 (1981)
	Dried grapes	Compensatory tax	1982
	Certain tableware	Quantitative restriction	1983 (1983)[2]
	Certain electronic quartz watches (France)	Quantitative restriction	1984
	Morello cherries	Tariff	1985
	Preserved raspberries	Tariff	1986
	Sweet potatoes	Quantitative restriction	1986
	Certain steel products	Quantitative restriction	1987
Finland	Porous fiberboard	Tariff surcharge	1986 (1986)
Iceland	Furniture, cupboards, and cabinets: windows and doors	Import deposit	1979 (1980)
Norway	Various textile items	Quantitative restriction	1979 (1984)
Spain	Cheeses	Quantitative restriction	1980 (1980)[2]
South Africa	Certain footwear	Tariff increase	1984
	Malic acid	Tariff increase	1985
	Certain oil fatty acids, flasks, steel wire, plugs	Tariff increase	1986
Switzerland	Dessert grapes	Tariff increase	1982 (1982)

Table 2.4 (contd)

Country	Product	Measure	Year Introduced (Terminated)
US	CB radio receivers	Tariff	1978 (1981)
	High-carbon ferrochromium	Tariff	1978 (1982)
	Lag screws or bolts	Tariff	1979 (1982)
	Clothespins	Quantitative restriction	1979 (1984)
	Porcelain-on-steel cookware	Tariff	1980 (1984)
	Preserved mushrooms	Tariff	1980 (1983)
	Heavyweight motorcycles	Tariff increase	1983
	Certain specialty steels	Quantitative restriction	1983

Source: International Monetary Fund, *Issues and Developments in International Trade Policy* (Washington D.C.: IMF 1988).
Notes: [1]Partial termination in 1985.
[2]Replaced by export restraint arrangement.

– most notably anti-dumping (the US, the EC, Australia, and Canada) and countervailing duties (almost exclusively the US) – have been increasingly applied by governments, especially with respect to the trade values covered, against allegedly dumped or subsidized imports. In 1985, a full 5 per cent of US imports were challenged under at least one of the US trade remedy laws (Rugman 1986: 374). Compared to export restraint agreements and anti-dumping and countervailing duty actions, safeguard actions under Article XIX of the GATT are invoked relatively rarely, as Table 2.4 indicates.

II. The economic costs and benefits of trade restrictions

This section of the chapter reviews empirical evidence on the costs and benefits of trade restrictions in the textile and clothing, footwear, steel and automobile sectors. The shipbuilding and coalmining sectors have been omitted from this discussion as assistance to these sectors has principally taken the form of subsidies rather than trade restrictions, and they will be reviewed in this context in the following chapter.

(a) The textile and clothing industries

Historically the textile and clothing industries in most countries have been the subject of some of the most severe trade restrictions, initially in the form of high tariffs and, more recently, also in the form of quantitative restrictions. Both industries have been attractive to newly industrializing economies because of relatively low entry costs, relatively standardized technology, and heavy reliance on relatively unskilled

Table 2.5 Effective levels of protection in the textile and clothing industries

Country	Year	Item	Total Trade Barrier (%)
Australia[a]	1979–80	Textiles	61.0
		Apparel	151.0[b]
Canada	1970[c]	Cotton fabrics	32.6[d]
	1970[e]	Synthetic Fabrics	36.3
	1970[f]	Apparel	22.6
France[g]	1981	Textiles & Apparel	32.0
Sweden[h]	1981–82	Textiles & Apparel	47.0
UK	1981[i]	Textiles & Apparel	35.0
	1968[j]	Household Textiles	9.1
		Apparel	1.1
US	1983[k]	Textiles	21.0
		Apparel	39.0
		Textiles & Apparel	30.0
	1983[l]	Apparel from Hong Kong	50.0
	1983[m]	Apparel	46.0 – 76.0
	1981[n]	Textiles & Apparel	51.0
	1976[o]	Textiles & Apparel	37.4
W Germany	1970[p]	Textiles	25.6
		Apparel	25.1

Notes:
[a] Industries Assistance Commission 1980: Appendix 1.5.
[b] Amount is re apparel and footwear.
[c] Dauphin 1978: 45.
[d] This amount, and those for synthetic fabrics and apparel, (e) and (f) below, are expressed as percentages of the domestic price.
[e] Dauphin 1978.
[f] Ibid., 46.
[g] Hamilton 1984: 8.
[h] Hamilton 1984A: 105.
[i] Hamilton 1984: 8.
[j] Oulton 1976: 80.
[k] Hufbauer *et al.* 1986: 146, 149.
[l] Hamilton 1985: 21.
[m] Hickok 1985: 6. Taking quality upgrading into account, Hickok estimates that the total induced increase in the price of imported apparel is 108%.
[n] Hamilton 1984: 8.
[o] Morici and Megna 1983: 99.
[p] Hieminz 1976, 37. Amount is re imports from non-EEC countries.

labour. However, with increasingly mobile capital and technology, later entrants to the process of industrialization have been able to exploit their access to large pools of low-cost unskilled labour to secure a comparative advantage over traditional producers in these sectors. Thus, all developed industrialized economies with significant textile and clothing industries have found themselves under increasing pressure from lower-priced, foreign imports. Despite the general trend towards reduced levels of protection in international trade, at least in the first three decades since the Second World War, the textile and clothing industries have been increasingly heavily protected, beginning with the Short-Term Cotton Agreement in 1961 and expanding into what seems to have become a semi-permanent system of bilaterally negotiated quantitative restrictions under the umbrella of the Multifibre Arrangement that now applies not only to natural fibres but man-made fibres and wearing apparel. Estimates of effective levels of protection (quotas and tariffs) in these industries are shown in Table 2.5.

Despite these high levels of protection, the textile industry in most industrialized countries has undergone a substantial transformation becoming much more concentrated and capital intensive. For example, in the UK, the gain in labour productivity accounted for 70 per cent of the fall in employment in the textile and apparel sector between 1970 and 1979, although 75 per cent of the employment decline in the apparel industry in the 1970s was attributed to international competition (two-thirds of that due to LDC import penetration) (OECD 1985b: 115, 117).

The clothing industry remains structurally unconcentrated, labour intensive and employs large numbers of hard-to-redeploy marginal workers (such as the poorly educated, secondary earners, especially women, and members of ethnic minorities, often recent immigrants). In many industrialized countries, both industries tend to be regionally concentrated. The textile industry tends to be more heavily unionized than the clothing industry.

An important inference from differences in the evolution of the two industries is that if trade restrictions are removed, jobs will be lost to foreign suppliers as the domestic industry contracts, but if substantial contraction in output is to be avoided without trade restrictions, substantial job loss is also likely to be experienced through productivity gains from substituting capital for labour.

In terms of domestic producer gains from existing trade restrictions, Hufbauer *et al.* (1986) offer the following estimates (see Table 2.6). Jenkins (1980) estimated that Canadian manufacturers gained $267 million in 1979 because of quotas. Foreign producers also derive gains from quotas in the form of scarcity rents that are reflected in higher prices for imports than would prevail in the absence of such restrictions. Table 2.7 provides some estimates of the scale of these transfers.

Estimates of the employment gains and the costs per job saved from quantitative restrictions in the textile and clothing industries are set out in Table 2.8. To render these costs more concrete, Hufbauer *et al.* (1986) calculate that under MFA III, the net loss per job saved in the US textile industry was $39,000 (a $50,000 gross loss, less an $11,000 gain

Table 2.6 Annual rents to the US, textiles and apparel industries due to import barriers

	1974 (MF I)[a]	1981 (MF II)[b]	1984 (MF III)[c]
Annual Rents to US Producers	$8.7B	$18.0B[d]	$22.0B[e]
Annual Rents to US Producers Per Extra Job	$4,000	$8,700[f]	$11,100[g]
Induced Increase in US Production	2.2B lbs.	3.0B lbs.	4.0B lbs.

Notes:
[a] Hufbauer *et al.* 1986: 124–126
[b] Ibid.: 135–137.
[c] Ibid.: 147–149.
[d] Of which $5.4B is re textiles, and $12.6B is re apparel: *ibid*. 136.
[e] Of which $8.4B is re textiles, and $13,6B is re apparel: *ibid*. 148.
[f] For textiles and apparel combined. The 1981 gain from restraints to producers per job in textiles was $6,600, and in apparel was $8,700: *ibid*. 137.
[g] For textiles and apparel combined. The 1984 gain from restraints to producers per job in textiles was $11,000, and in apparel was $11,200: *ibid*: 149.

Table 2.7 Annual rents to foreign textile and apparel producers due to import quotas

Country imposing quota	Year	Item: T-Textile A-Apparel	Exporter	Annual rents ($ million)
Canada[a]	1979	T & A	All	41.4[b]
OECD[c]	1984?	T & A	All	2,000.0
US	1984[d]	T & A	All	1,800.0[e]
	1984[f]	T	Hong Kong	275.0
	1981[g]	T & A	All	350.0
	1981[h]	A	All	219.0
	1980[i]	T	Hong Kong	263.9[j]
	1974[k]	T & A	All	Negligible

Notes:
[a] Jenkins 1980: 27.
[b] Comprising 15% of total quota rents.
[c] Sundkvist 1985: 109: where, for the sake of argument, the 15% estimate from b. above was adopted.
[d] Hufbauer *et al.* 1986: 148.
[e] Of which $300M is re textiles, and $1.5B is re apparel.
[f] Tarr and Morkre 1987: 224.
[g] Hufbauer *et al.* 1986: 136.
[h] Hamilton 1984: 8,
[i] Tarr and Morkre 1984: 14.
[j] Amount is in 1983 US dollars.
[k] Hufbauer *et al.* 1986: 125.

to producers by avoiding the costs of adjustment). The resulting increase in the price of imports was calculated at 30 per cent overall (21 per cent for textiles, 39 per cent for clothing). Domestic goods increased in price by 24 per cent, representing a 17 per cent increase in the price of textiles and a 31 per cent increase in the price of clothing (Hufbauer *et al.* 1986: 149). Wolf expresses the disproportionality between the costs and benefits of trade restrictions in the textile and clothing sectors even more starkly by extrapolating as follows from findings of Jenkins on the effects of quotas in these sectors in Canada and actual post job lay-off employment experience:

> On a present value basis the economic cost of the quotas, if maintained forever, (with a 3 per cent growth of the market and a 7 per cent discount rate) would be about Canadian $360,000 per man-year of employment preserved. For tariffs the corresponding figure would be Canadian $70,000. At the same time the highest private cost of job loss would have a present value of less than Canadian $5,000 after government transfers. Thus given the government's other benefits, a social cost of Canadian $360,000 would be borne, if the bilateral restrictions were maintained indefinitely, in order to save workers who would otherwise lose their jobs from a private loss of at most Canadian $5,000 each. In other words, for every cent that a worker who would otherwise lose his job is better off, society as a whole is 72 cents worse off as a result of a permanent policy of quantitative restrictions.
>
> (Wolf 1983: 477)

In review, trade restrictions in the textile and clothing sectors have not prevented substantial job loss in these sectors. In 1953, the textile and clothing sectors accounted for over 20 per cent of OECD manufacturing employment. By 1980 their share was around 13 per cent. Over the period 1973–82, employment levels declined at an annual average rate of 4.5 per cent for textiles and 3 per cent clothing (OECD 1985b: 112). The relatively limited impact of trade restrictions on employment is explained by trade diversion caused by quantitative restrictions – Japan moving out of cotton textiles into synthetics, other less restricted NICs such as Hong Kong and Taiwan increasing their levels of exports and, additionally, in the textile industry, increasing substitution of capital for labour. Estimates suggest that no more than 8 per cent of the industry's 1976 labour force depended on tariffs for their job. In Sweden, estimates suggest that increasing the level of textile imports under voluntary restraint by 50 per cent would displace about 3 per cent of the industry's employment (OECD 1985b: 117).

While job preservation from trade restrictions in the clothing industry has been much more substantial than in the textile industry, because

Table 2.8 Domestic employment gains in textiles and apparel due to import barriers*

Country	Year	Number of extra jobs due to import barriers			Annual cost** to consumers per extra job		
		Textiles	Apparel	Combined	Textiles ($)	Apparel ($)	Combined ($)
Canada	1980[a]	—	13,474[b]	—	—	34,662[c]	—
	1978	11,091[d]	2,303[e]	13,394	63,376[f]	233,478[g]	92,624[h]
	1978[i]	—	—	—	30,400[j]	—	—
EEC[k]	1980	—	11,300	—	—	119,292	—
US	1984[l]	180,000	460,000	640,000	50,000	39,000	42,000
	1984[m]	8,900[n]	—	—	45,100[o]	—	—
	1981[p]	150,000	390,000	540,000	40,000	36,000	37,000
	1980[q]	1,840– 6,650	7,500– 25,590	9,340– 32,240	NA	NA	42,240– 57,130[r]
	1980[s]	—	8,900	—	—	156,853	—
	1978[t]	—	—	—	—	—	81,000
	1977[u]	89,280	26,910	116,190	NA	NA	13,200
	1977[v]	—	90,000	—	—	—	—
	1976[w]	(34,000)[x]	86,700[y]	52,700	NA	NA	NA
	1974[z]	120,000	300,000	420,000	—	—	22,000

Notes:

*Quotas, unless otherwise noted.
** Annually, unless otherwise noted.
[a] Jenkins 1980, 39.
[b] Of which Jenkins attributes 6,016 to quotas and 7,458 to tariffs.
[c] Jenkins 1980: 39. This amount is the weighted average: 6,016 jobs (due to quotas) at $32,959 per job, and 7,458 jobs (due to tariffs) at $36,035 per job.
[d] Hazeldine 1981: D-32. Amounts here and in f, g, and h. reflect tariffs as well as quotas. Hazeldine calculates that in 1978, the number of Canadian textiles jobs attributable to import barriers was 19,082 at high-cost firms, but that there were 7,992 fewer jobs at low-cost firms than there would be in the absence of protection: ibid: D-44.
[e] Ibid.: D-5.
[f] Ibid.: A-9, D-32. Hazeldine calculates a consumer gain of $106,9M in 1978 re the enhancement of product variety by some (high-cost) domestic suppliers. If this is taken into account, then in 1978 the annual cost to Canadian consumers per textiles job saved by protection was a mere $53.737.

g Ibid.: A-9, D-5. Hazeldine calculates a consumer gain of $3.6M in 1978 re the enhancement of product variety by some (high-cost) domestic suppliers. If this is taken into account, then in 1978 the annual cost to Canadian consumers per textiles job saved by protection was a mere $231,915.

h Weighted average of g. and h. If the 1978 consumer gain calculated by Hazeldine re enhanced product variety due to some (high-cost) domestic producers is taken into account, then the 1978 weighted average annual cost to consumers per textiles & apparel job saved by trade barriers is $84,374.

i Glenday et al. 1982: 6.

j Amount is estimated present value of cost of protecting one Sherbrooke, P.Q., textiles jobs for five years beginning 1978.

k Kalantzopoulos, per Balassa and Michopoulos 1987: 495.

l Hufbauer et al. 1986: 149.

m Tarr and Morkre 1987: 224.

n Re quotas on Hong Kong, S. Korea and Taiwan.

o Tarr and Morkre call this 'a conservative estimate', since it was calculated by dividing the annual cost to US consumers of textile quotas on Hong Kong ($401M) by the total number of US textiles jobs attributable to textiles quotas on Hong Kong, S. Korea and Taiwan.

p Hufbauer et al. 1986: 136.

q Tarr and Morkre 1984: 117. These figures are only re tariffs on apparel.

r Ibid.: 117, 119. Amount is in 1983 US dollars.

s Kalantzopoulos, per Balassa and Michapoulos 1987: 495.

t Council on Wage and Price Stability: 1978 70; per Hufbauer et al. 1986B: 136.

u Morkre and Tarr 1980: 156. Amounts are only re textile quotas.

v Morkre and Tarr, per Sundqvist 1985: 117.

w Staiger et al. 1987: 174.

x Staiger et al. calculate that if the US had removed tariffs and NTBs on textiles, domestic employment in 1976 would have risen by 15,900 and by 18,100, respectively.

y Of which Staiger et al. attribute 18,900 to tariffs and 67,800 to NTBs.

z Hufbauer et al. 1986: 125–126.

Table 2.9 Annual domestic consumer losses due to textile and apparel import barriers

Country	Year	Item: T=Textile A=Apparel	Barrier: T=Tariff Q=Quotas	Annual cost to consumers
Australia	1977–8[a]	T	T & Q	$334m[b]
		A	T & Q	$760m[c]
Canada	1978[d]	T	T & Q	S703m
		A	T & Q	$538m
	1978[e]	A	T & Q	$500m
	1979[f]	A	T & Q	$467m
Sweden	1981[g]	T & A	T & Q	SKR3,000m
		T & A	Q	SKR2,000m
US	1984[h]	T & A	T & Q	$27,000m[i]
	1984[j]	A	T & Q	$8,500m–$12,000m
	1984[k]	T	Q[l]	$401m
	1981[m]	T & A	T & Q	$20,000m[n]
	1980[o]	T & A	T	$15,000m
			Q	$3,400m[p]
	1980[q]	T	Q	$384m–$508m
	1980[r]	T	Q[s]	$308m
	1978[t]	A	T	$2,700m
	1977[u]	A	T & Q	$900m
	1977[v]	A	T	$406m
		T	T	$13m
	1974[w]	T & A	T & Q	$9,400m
	1972[x]	T[y]	Q	$2,500m
	1970[z]	T[aa]	Q	$600m

Notes:
[a] Glezer 1982: 297.
[b] Australian dollars.
[c] Australian dollars.
[d] Hazeldine 1981: A-9. Hazeldine calculates, however, that if protection on textiles had been removed, Canadian consumers would have suffered a loss in 1978 of $106.9M re reduction in product variety due to the closing of some (high-cost), domestic suppliers. If this is taken into account, then the net annual cost of textile protection to Canadian consumers was $596.0M in 1978.
[e] Glenday 1982: 1.
[f] Jenkins 1980: 33. Of this amount, $198.3M is re quotas and $269.1M is re tariffs.
[g] Hamilton 1984.
[h] Hufbauer *et al.* 1986: 148.
[i] Of which $9B was re textiles, and $18B was re apparel.
[j] Hickok 1985: 6.
[k] Tarr and Morkre 1987: 224.
[l] Re Hong Kong only.
[m] Hufbauer *et al.* 1986: 136.
[n] Of which $6B was re textiles, and $14B was re apparel.
[o] Munger 1983, per Weidenbaum and Munger 1983: 15.
[p] Weidenbaum and Munger contend that the actual amount is probably ' . . . many times larger' than that stated here: *ibid:* 17.
[q] Tarr and Morke 1984: 119.
[r] Morkre 1984: 28.

^x Re Hong Kong only.
^t Council on Wage and Price Stability: 1978: 70.
^u Guzzardi 1983: 86.
^v Morkre and Tarr 1980: 156.
^w Hufbauer *et al.* 1986: 125.
^xMintz 1973: 59.
^y Cotton, woollen, and man-made textiles.
^z Mintz 1973: 59.
^{aa}Cotton textiles.

of greater labour intensity, often internal trade diversion has occurred, for example from the north-east to the south of the US, so that trade restrictions have not protected established patterns of employment. Jobs preserved in both textile and clothing sectors have entailed costs to consumers in the form of higher prices, well in excess of gains to producers, many of which gains have accrued to foreign exporters (see Table 2.9). To the extent that trade restrictions have provided 'breathing space' for structural adjustments, German, Swiss and Italian manufacturers have concentrated on product differentiation strategies which seek to identify higher value-added, higher quality segments of the market. Japanese manufacturers have pursued similar strategies, and have also entered into joint ventures with manufacturers in low-wage developing countries. The US textile industry, with access to a large domestic market, has sought to realize economies of scale through greater concentration and capital intensity, as well as cutting costs by locating new plants in non-unionized, lower-wage regions of the country. The UK and France have promoted greater industrial concentration and integration in textiles, but economies of scale realized from mass production appear to have been insufficient to offset cost and hence price disadvantages vis-à-vis other producers. Attempting to compete primarily over price appears not to have been an optimal strategy.

(b) Footwear

Due to the nature of the product, footwear tends often to be manufactured in small, specialized plants. Barriers to entry are low, technology relatively standardized, and production relatively labour intensive. The industry's workforce is largely lower skilled, low paid and female, with low levels of unionization. In most countries the footwear industry is regionally concentrated.

All industrialized countries with footwear industries have faced increasing competition from newly industrialized countries, particularly with respect to low-cost rubber, canvas, vinyl and plastic footwear, but also more recently with respect to higher priced, higher quality footwear from countries such as Brazil.

As with textiles and clothing, a common response to foreign inroads into domestic markets in many industrialized countries has been the adoption of trade restrictions, typically a combination of tariffs and quantitative restrictions in the form of global quotas (Canada, Australia) or bilaterally negotiated OMAs or VERs (US, UK, France. Italy). Estimates of the effective levels of protection on footwear imports into various industrialized countries are shown in Table 2.10.

Table 2.10 Effective levels of protection in the footwear industry

Country	Year	Type of footwear	Total trade barrier (%)
Australia[a]	1978–9	All	151.0
Canada	1978[b]	All	29.0
	1970[c]	Rubber & Plastic	17.8
		Leather	19.2
UK[d]	1982	Non-Leather	33.0[e]
US	1983[f]	Rubber	42.0
	1981[g]	Non-rubber	18.5
W. Germany[h]	1970	All	15.1

Notes:
[a] Industries Assistance Commission 1980: Appendix 1.5. Amount is re footwear and apparel.
[b] Hazeldine 1981: A-3.
[c] Dauphin 1978: 45. Rates are expressed as percentages of the domestic prices.
[d] Greenaway 1986: 1072, 1073.
[e] Calculated as 13.0% re VERs plus 20.0% nominal tariff. Greenaway realizes [ibid: 1070] that the effective tariff exceeds the nominal tariff of 20.0% but he does not estimate the extent to which it does so.
[f] Hufbauer *et al*. 1985: 76.
[g] Ibid: 214.
[h] Hieminz and Rabeneau 1976: 37.

Table 2.11 Annual rents to domestic footwear producers due to import barriers

Country	Year	Type of footwear	Annual rents to domestic producers
Australia[a]	1977–78	All	$129.0m
Canada[b]	1978	All	$35.6m
UK[c]	1982	Non-leather	£49.9m
US	1983[d]	Rubber	$90.0m
	1981[e]	Non-rubber	$250.0m

Notes:
[a] Glezer 1982: 297. Amount is in Australian dollars.
[b] Hazeldine 1981: D-28.
[c] Greenaway 1986: 1077.
[d] Hufbauer *et al*. 1986: 76.
[e] Ibid.: 215.

Estimates of gains to domestic footwear producers as a result of import restraints are shown in Table 2.11.

Quantitative restrictions on footwear imports, as with textiles and clothing, have conferred substantial scarcity rents on foreign producers. Estimates of rents accruing to foreign footwear producers are shown in Table 2.12.

Table 2.12 Annual rents to foreign footwear producers due to import barriers

Country imposing barrier	Year	Country benefiting	Type of footwear affected	Annual rents
UK	1982[a]	Taiwan, S. Korea	Non-leather	£7.5m
	1982[b]	Unrestrained Suppliers	Non-leather	£22.4m
	1982[c]	All Other Suppliers	Non-leather	£9.7m
US	1983[d]	All	Rubber	Negligible
	1981[e]	Taiwan, S. Korea	Non-rubber	$220.0m
	1980–1981[g]	Taiwan	Non-rubber	$180.1m[f]

Notes:
[a] Greenaway 1986: 1077.
[b] Ibid.
[c] Ibid
[d] Hufbauer *et al.* 1986: 76.
[e] Ibid.: 215.
[f] Morkre and Tarr 1980.
[g] Of which $180.1m is re plastic footwear (ibid.: 129): $21.4M is re leather (ibid. 118): and $17.9M is re other (ibid.: 130).

Estimates of domestic employment gains from import restrictions and costs per job saved are shown in Table 2.13.

Estimates of domestic consumer losses due to import restrictions in the footwear industry are shown in Table 2.14.

In more concrete terms, it has been estimated that US trade restrictions on imported rubber footwear have induced a 21 per cent increase in domestic prices and a 42 per cent increase in the price of imported rubber footwear. In the case of non-rubber footwear, restrictions have induced a 5.5 per cent in domestic prices and an 18.5 per cent increase in the price of imports (Hufbauer *et al.* 1986: 76). Weidenbaum and Munger (1983: 14–18) suggest that footwear quotas and tariffs cost US consumers $77,714 per job, yielding a ratio of costs to wage compensation of 9.3:1 (average wage compensation at the time of the estimate was $8,340 p.a.).

Despite high tariffs and quantitative restrictions, the footwear industry in most industrialized countries has continued to contract. In the US, between 1968 and 1976, output fell 36 per cent, employment 34 per cent, and the number of plants 33 per cent (Trebilcock 1986: 156). In Canada,

Table 2.13 Domestic employment gains due to footwear import barriers

Country	Year	Type of footwear	Extra jobs due to trade barriers	Annual cost to consumers per extra job
Canada[a]	1978	All	1,733	$58,223
UK[b]	1982	Non-leather	7,500	£ 6,000–£13,000
US	1983[c]	Rubber	7,800	$30,000
	1981[d]	Non-rubber	12,700	$55,000
	1980–1981[f]	Non-rubber	5,536	$28,215[e]
	1980[g]	Non-rubber	3,132	$21,967
	1980[h]	All	—	$77,714
	1977–79 (Ave.)[i]	Non-rubber	15,100	—
	1977[j]	Non-rubber	10,240[k]	—
	1976[l]	All	17,000[m]	—
	1973[n]	All	7,781[o]	—

Notes:
[a] Hazeldine 1981: D-28, D-29.
[b] Greenaway 1986: 1077. Of these jobs, Greenaway attributes 3,800 to tariffs and 3,700 to VERs. Estimated adjustment costs to labour on removal of the trade barriers is 78.1m.
[c] Hufbauer *et al.* 1986: 77.
[d] Ibid: 215.
[e] Morkre and Tarr 1980: 123, 124, 125.
[f] Ibid.: 123, 124. Amounts are re OMAs with Taiwan and S. Korea.
[g] Pearson 1983: 51; per Hufbauer *et al.* 1986: 215.
[h] Weidenbaum and Munger 1983: 17.
[i] USITC 1982: 25. This amount includes induced changes in related industries – e.g. leather tanning, plastics, textiles.
[j] Morkre and Tarr 1980: 111. Amount is re OMAs with Taiwan and S. Korea.
[k] Amount is re tariffs only.
[l] Staiger *et al.* 1987: 174.
[m]Of which Staiger *et al.* attribute 1,300 to tariffs and 15,700 to NTBs.
[n] Szenberg *et al.* 1977. The present value of estimated adjustment costs to labour over 13 years (starting 1973), upon reduction of the US tariff on non-rubber footwear by 10 percentage points, discounted at 4%, is $83.5m: ibid. 87.
[o] Jobs which would have been lost in 1973, according to Szenberg *et al.*, if the US tariff on non-rubber footwear had been reduced by 10 percentage points: ibid.: 89.

the domestic market share of Canadian footwear producers dropped from 59 per cent in 1968 to 42 per cent in 1980. Employment has fallen by one-third since 1965 and the number of plants by 23 per cent (1986: 77, 92). In Australia, from 1970 to 1980, total number of establishments contracted by 30 per cent and total industry employment fell by about 36 per cent (1986: 213–15).

As with textiles and clothing, quantitative restrictions have had limited effects on industry output and employment, because of trade diversion effects with restricted suppliers moving up to higher value-

Table 2.14 Domestic consumer losses due to footwear import barriers

Country	Year	Type of footwear	Annual cost to consumers
Canada[a]	1976	All	$100.9m
UK[b]	1982	Non-leather	£117.5m
US	1983[c]	Rubber	$230.0m
	1981[d]	Non-rubber	$700.0m
	1980–1[e]	Non-rubber	$156.2m[f]
	1980[g]	Non-rubber	$1,400.0m
	1977–9	Non-rubber	$500.0m
	Ave.		

Notes:
[a] Hazeldine 1981: D-28.
[b] Greenaway 1986: 1077.
[c] Hufbauer *et al.* 1986: 76.
[d] Ibid. 215.
[e] Morkre and Tarr 1980: 125.
[f] Amount is re OMAs with Taiwan and S. Korea.
[g] Munger 1983: 9; per Hufbauer *et al.* 1986: 215. Reflects tariffs but not OMAs.
[h] Cline 1984: 42; per Hufbauer *et al.* 1986: 215. Reflects OMAs but not tariffs.

added product lines, and unrestricted suppliers increasing their exports.

In 1981, the US Administration dismantled the OMAs on footwear and in December 1985, the Canadian government, following recommendations of the Canadian Import Tribunal (Canadian Import Tribunal 1985), lifted its quota. The tribunal in its report cited research undertaken for it by the Institute for Research and Public Policy that found that quotas increased employment by only 2.1 to 4.4 per cent – about 350 to 700 jobs. Output effects were also minimal. Quotas were found to have increased production by $3.5 million in 1982 and at most $7.9 million in 1983. Quotas resulted in increased costs to consumers of $40 million in 1980 and $85 million in 1983. The bulk of the gains from the quotas were realized by importers holding quotas (41 per cent), followed by manufacturers (34 per cent) and large retailers holding quotas (26 per cent). The tribunal found that significant rationalization and restructuring had occurred within the industry but attributed this to competitive pressures from imports, and not, for the most part, to any 'breathing space' effects of the quotas.

(c) The steel industry

The steel industry in many industrialized countries has faced increased import competition from newly industrializing countries, such as Japan, and more recently from countries such as Korea, Taiwan, South Africa, Australia, Canada, Argentina, Brazil, Mexico and Venezuela. OECD countries' share of world steel exports declined from 74 per cent in 1980 to 62 per cent in 1987 (IMF 1988: 69). A global decline in the demand for steel as a result of increasing use of lighter substitutes; technologically obsolete plants; the development of specialized mini-mills; and a high wage structure reflecting in part high degrees of unionization in the sector; have all contributed to a loss of competitiveness. The structurally and regionally concentrated nature of the industry and the substantial organized work-force involved have often led to demands for trade restrictions.

In addition to tariffs, the US has employed VERs with Japan and the European Coal and Steel Community (1968–75); a trigger price mechanism (TPM) introduced in 1977, that sets price floors for imports, which if violated trigger fast-track anti-dumping proceedings, and, beginning in 1982, following further import surges, the US government negotiated VERs with the European Community, Japan, Korea, Spain, Brazil, Mexico, South Africa and Australia. By the end of 1985, a total of fifteen VERs had been negotiated covering 80 per cent of the US market (Hufbauer *et al.* 1986: 173).

European steel producers, as members of the European Coal and Steel Community, have, since 1978 adopted minimum price floors and maximum production quotas. In addition to a common effective external tariff of approximately 12 per cent and minimum import prices, beginning in 1978 VERs have also been negotiated with a number of countries, most notably Japan.

Most empirical studies that have been undertaken of the effects of trade restrictions on the steel industry relate to the US and hence principally findings from these studies are reported below.

Hufbauer *et al.* (1986: 154–86) report findings by reference to three different phases of US trade policy with respect to steel: (1) 1969–76 (VERs); (2) 1978–82 (TPM); and (3) 1982 to present (VERs).

For the first period, they report gains to US producers for 1974 of $1,330 million; gains from restraints to foreign suppliers ranging from $175 million to $330 million per year; induced increases in employment from 8,100–19,117; costs of restraints to consumers ranging from $1,254 million to $1,970 million per year; induced increases in prices of imported steel (1974) ranging from 6.3 to 13.3 per cent; induced increases in prices of domestic steel of 3.8 to 5.3 per cent; costs of restraints to US consumers per job saved ranging from $63,000 to $240,000; and gains to US producers per job (1974) of $3,400.

In the second phase, Hufbauer *et al.* report the following findings: gains from restraints to US producers ranging from $640 million (1979) to $2,770 million (1981); gains from restraints to foreign producers ranging from $519 million (1979) to $930 million (1981); induced increases in employment in the US steel industry ranging from 7,000 (1981) to 12,400 (1979); costs of restraints to US consumers ranging from

$1,135 million (1980) to $4,350 million (1981); induced increases in prices of imported steel ranging from 10.3 to 15.9 per cent; induced increases in prices of domestic steel ranging from 0.8 to 6.4 per cent; costs of restraints to US consumers per job saved ranging from $110,000 to $620,000; and gains from restraints to US producers per job of $9,700.

In the third phase, the authors report the following findings: gains from restraints to US producers ranging from $428 million to $3.4 billion p.a; gains from restraints to foreign producers ranging from $557 million to $2 billion p.a.; induced increases in employment ranging from 9,000 to 11,250; cost of restraints to US consumers ranging from $1.1 billion p.a. to $6.8 billion p.a., induced increases in prices of imported steel of 30 per cent; induced increases in prices of domestic steel of 12 per cent; costs of restraints to US consumers per job saved ranging from $113,622 to $750,000; and gains from restraints to US producers per job of $22,000.

The authors also report findings on the effects of safeguard relief for 1976–86 in the US specialty steel industry. Two figures stand out starkly: the cost of restraints to US consumers per job saved (in total 500 jobs) was $1 million (1984); the gain from restraints to US producers per job (1984) was $60,000.

Despite the extensive and (for consumers) expensive protection of the US steel industry, employment in the industry has fallen from 420,684 in 1968 to 171,000 in 1984. Imports as of 1984 held 26.7 per cent of the US steel market (up from 16.7 per cent in 1968) (Hufbauer *et al.* 1986). Together with the emergence of specialized, domestic mini-mills with highly efficient capital-intensive production technology, the large integrated US steel producers face continuing loss of competitiveness.

The experience of member countries of the EEC has been similar, with total EEC steel employment falling from 800,000 in 1974 to about 450,000 in 1984 (OECD 1985b: 53). Employment in the UK steel industry fell from 208,000 in 1977 to 100,000 in 1982; crude steel production fell from 27.9 million tons in 1970 to 11.4 million tons in 1980 (Trebilcock 1986: 180). Employment in the French steel industry fell from 157,000 in 1975 to 97,000 in 1982. Production has declined from 27 million tons in 1974 to 18.4 million tons in 1982 (Hufbauer *et al.* 1986: 257). Employment in the West German steel industry fell from 250,000 in 1974 to 180,000 in 1982, while crude steel production fell by almost 50 per cent between 1974 and 1980 (1986: 286).

There is little evidence, either from the US or European experiences, that trade restrictions are able to provide effective 'breathing spaces' for industries facing import competition to recover their competitiveness and preserve output and employment. Such attenuating effects that these restrictions have on the rate of contraction are small and come at highly disproportionate costs to consumers.

(d) Automobiles

From the beginning of the 1970s, North America and to a lesser extent European automobile industries have faced a dramatic increase in competitive inroads from Japanese auto producers.For example, in 1982, 27.3 per cent of automobile sales in the US were imports, up from 18 per cent in 1977; 22.4 per cent of all sales were accounted for by Japanese imports, up from 12.7 per cent in 1977 (OECD 1985b: 137). In 1982, imports accounted for 31.4 per cent of automobile sales in Canada; 25 per cent of all sales were Japanese imports, up 13.6 per cent from 1977 (Economic Council of Canada 1987b: Table 7-5). The emergence of Japan as a low-cost, high quality mass producer of small cars, together with the oil price shocks of the 1970s, provided a major impetus to imports. The landed cost advantage of a Japanese auto over a North American built small car was estimated in the early 1970s as between $1,500 and $2,100 – up to 40 per cent per car (Economic Council of Canada 1987b: 7-22). In addition, significant quality differences began to emerge between Japanese imports and domestically built cars (Crandall 1984). The appreciation of the US dollar against the yen reinforced underlying cost and quality differences.

In 1981, the US negotiated a three year VER with Japan. A similar agreement was negotiated between Canada and Japan. Estimates of domestic producer gains from these restrictions are shown in Table 2.15. The UK, France and Italy had previously negotiated tight, informal market share agreements with Japan, dating from the mid-1970s.

Table 2.15 Gains to domestic automobile manufacturers due to protection from imports

Country	Year	Annual gain to domestic producers
Australia	1977–8[a]	$905m
Canada	1985[b]	$200m–$1,000m[c]
	1985[d]	$570m[e]
US	1983[f]	$890m–$1,420m
	1984[g]	$120m
	1984[h]	$2,600m
	1983[i]	$115m

Notes:
[a] Glezer 1982: 297.
[b] Hazeldine and Wigington 1985.
[c] Includes gains to foreign producers.
[d] Coopers and Lybrand 1986.
[e] Includes gains to foreign producers.
[f] Crandall 1984: 14
[g] Tarr and Morkre 1987: 220. Amount is re VER with Japan.
[h] Hufbauer *et al.* 1986B: 257.
[i] Tarr and Morkre 1984: 56.

Similar understandings were subsequently reached between Japan and West Germany and Belgium (OECD 1985b: 136). In April 1985, the formal VER between the US and Japan expired and was not renewed, although Japan announced it would hold exports to 2.3 million units for 1985. Australia has for many years imposed stringent local content requirements, an extremely high tariff (57.5 per cent in 1979), and quota requirements designed to preserve 80 per cent of sales for local producers (Trebilcock 1985a: 212). For 1981, the Australian Industries Assistance Commission estimated the tariff equivalent of these policies with respect to the Australian passenger vehicle industry at 70–85 per cent (OECD 1985b: 138).

Estimates of gains from scarcity rents to Japanese producers from trade restrictions are shown in Table 2.16.

Table 2.16 Annual rents to Japanese automobile producers due to barriers to US market

Estimator	Year	Annual rents
Hufbauer *et al.*[a]	1984	$2,200m
Tarr and Morkre[b]	1984	$860m
Tarr and Morkre[c]	1983	$824m
Crandall[d]	1983	$2,000m

Notes:
[a] 1986: 258.
[b] 1987: 220.
[c] 1984: 56.
[d] 1984: 13.

Estimates of employment effects and costs to consumers from recent V ERs in the auto industry are shown in Tables 2.17 and 2.18. Estimates of induced increases in the price of imported autos as a result of the VERs in the US range from 2.4 to 15.3 per cent (or $1,000 per auto) (Hufbauer *et al.* 1986: 256). In Canada, one estimate finds that the VER with Japan increased the cost of Japanese imports by an average of $1,280 per vehicle in 1985 (Coopers and Lybrand 1986). Estimates of induced increases in the price of domestic US autos as a result of the VER with Japan range from 4 to 5 per cent (or about $400 per vehicle) (Hufbauer *et al.* 1986: 257). In Canada, one estimate finds that the price of small domestic and European cars increased on average $650 per vehicle in 1985 as a result of the VER (Coopers and Lybrand 1986).

Estimates of the annual cost of restraints to US consumers per job saved range from $105,000 to $241,235 (Hufbauer *et al.* 1986: 258). In Canada, estimates range from $179,000 (Coopers and Lybrand 1986) to $207,166 (Hazledine and Wigington 1985) per job saved in 1985.

Table 2.17 Domestic employment gains due to automobile import barriers

Country	Year	Extra jobs due to trade barriers
Canada	1985[a]	−1,577 to 879
	1982–5[b]	3,180
US	1984[c]	55,000
	1984[d]	45,000
	1984[e]	45,100
	1984[f]	4,600
	1983[g]	26,200
	1983[h]	4,600
	1980–1[i]	5,600 to 11,100

Notes:
[a] Hazeldine and Wigington 1985.
[b] Coopers and Lybrand 1986.
[c] Hufbauer *et al.* 1986B: 258.
[d] Balassa and Michalopoulus 1987: 495.
[e] USITC 1985: 41.
[f] Tarr and Morkre 1987: 220, 221.
[g] Crandall 1984: 16. Crandall calculates that the maximum possible number was 46,200: ibid.
[h] Tarr and Morkre 1984: 70.
[i] Feenstra 1984: 54; per Hufbauer *et al.* 1986B: 258. Assumes import demand elasticity of 2–3.

Gains from restraints to US producers per job (1984) have been estimated at $4,300 (Hufbauer *et al* 1986: 258).

Summarizing the effects of recent VERs on automobile production, as the OECD notes, 'the impact of trade restrictions on domestic output has been small relative to that of changes in macro-economic circumstances' (OECD 1985b: 136). Soras and Stodden estimate that US auto sales in 1982 were 4.3 million units below what past trends would have suggested they should have been, largely because of compressed incomes and rising real interest rates in the depths of the recession. The 100,000 unit increase induced by the VERs with Japan in 1982 was a very small offset to this shortfall. Feenstra estimates that induced employment increases from the US–Japan VER over the period to 1982 was no more than 22,000, while the recession was cutting required labour inputs by more than ten times this figure (OECD 1985b: 141). The appreciation of the US (and Canadian) dollar against the yen was a further adverse feature of the macro-economic environment. However, the substantial recent appreciation of the yen has significantly reduced Japan's cost advantages.

Two other factors have reduced the impact of VERs on employment in the automobile industry. First, Hunker has estimated that between 1980 and 1985 the share of small luxury cars in Japanese exports to the US would have run from 40 to 55 per cent even in the absence of the VER but in its presence rose to 63 per cent (Hunker 1984). In other

Table 2.18 Annual domestic consumer losses due to automobile import barriers

Country	Year	Annual cost to consumers
Australia	1977–8[a]	$1,170m
Canada	1985[b]	$570m
	1985[c]	$200m–1,000m
US	1984[d]	$8,520m
	1984[e]	$5,800m
	1984[f]	$5,000m
	1984[g]	$4,500m
	1984[h]	$2,007m[i]
	1984[j]	$1,157m[k]
	1983[l]	$4,680m
	1983[m]	$4,300m[n]
	1983[o]	$1,109m
	1981–84[p]	$3,920m

Notes:
[a] Glezer 1982: 297. Amount is in Australian dollars.
[b] Coopers and Lybrand 1986.
[c] Hazledine and Wiginton 1986.
[d] USTIC 1985: ix.
[e] Hufbauer *et al.* 1986: 257.
[f] Aho 1985: 249.
[g] Hickok 1985: 8
[h] Kalantzopoulos, per Balassa and Michalopoulos 1987: 495.
[i] Amount is re VERs only
[j] Tarr and Morkre 1987: 220.
[k] Or $251,600 per year per extra job: ibid: 221.
[l] USTIC 1985: ix.
[m] Crandall 1984: 16.
[n] This amount does not include additional losses in consumer welfare arising from VERs' constraint on choice of cars.
[o] Tarr and Morkre 1984: 56. This is $241.235 per year per extra job: ibid.
[p] This is an average figure. USITC 1985: ix.

words, Japanese manufacturers moved up market to higher value-added units. Second, given that the VER only related to Japan, substantial trade diversion incentives were created. In the case of Canada, Hyundai of South Korea, which exported fewer than one hundred cars to Canada in 1983, in 1985 exported 79,072 cars (almost 24 per cent of all imports) (Economic Council of Canada 1987: 7–25).

Denzau claims that the cartelization effects of VERs on Japanese automobile exports have significantly benefited Japan's major producers. The Japanese trade ministry (MITI) in establishing firm-specific quotas for exports under the VERs prevented effective price competition among Japanese auto-makers, enabling them to raise prices and increase their profits (Denzau 1988: 12). Indeed, upon announcement of the 1981 US-Japan auto VER there were substantial net-of-market increases in the stock prices of the major Japanese auto manufacturers ranging from 6.1 per cent for Mazda to 14 per cent for Nissan. Moreover, stock prices seemed to settle permanently at the new higher level (Denzau 1988: 13). This indicates that the major Japanese manufacturers actually realize a *net benefit* from the VERs, the profits from cartelization more than compensating for the restriction on the number of units exportable.

The period of VERs in the North American auto industry has witnessed significant improvements in productivity with plant rationalization, technological innovation, product quality improvements, and improved industrial relations. As well, outsourcing to multinational subsidiaries and to foreign manufacturers of component and sub-assembly production and in some cases whole units through contractual or joint venture arrangements, and the development of new local production facilities by foreign producers or through joint venture arrangements with domestic producers reflect major structural changes in the industry (often referred to, not uncritically, as 'co-operative protectionism').

(e) Summary

The recent employment of discriminatory quantitative trade restrictions (the so-called New Protectionism') by industrialized countries to protect sectors under competitive pressure from imports yields a very negative economic assessment, even if viewed solely from the perspective of the domestic economies of countries invoking such policies. Their policies have had relatively marginal effects on the preservation of employment and maintenance of output in the sectors reviewed, and such effects have been induced at wholly disproportionate costs to domestic consumers. Often, major beneficiaries have been foreign producers, who are able to capture scarcity rents from quota-induced shortages.

The weak employment effects of these policies are explained by various substitution effects that they induce, both suggested by theory (see Chapter 1) and confirmed by the empirical evidence reviewed in this chapter. These effects can be summarized as follows:

(a) VERs that restrict the number of units of imports in a given sector create incentives for foreign producers to move up-market to higher value-added, more profitable export lines. This has the perverse effect of leaving the domestic industry with a share of the product market where its comparative disadvantage is greatest and induces greater import competition in product markets where its comparative disadvantage is smallest. This trend has been evident in textiles, footwear and automobiles. It can only be countered by ever more detailed import restrictions.

(b) VERs induce entry into the market by unrestricted third country suppliers ('trade diversion'). This trend has been evident in textiles and clothing, steel, and automobiles, and can only be countered by ever broader territorial coverage of these restrictions. In some cases, such as Japanese autos, the cartelization effects of VERs (i.e. reduced/price competition) may actually place the foreign producers who participate in the VER-induced cartel in a better position than under conditions of unrestricted trade (Denzau 1988). This evokes an extremely significant transfer of wealth from domestic consumers (who must pay the higher cartel-induced prices) to foreign producers – a transfer which seems redistributively perverse from any of the ethical perspectives considered in Chapter 1.

(c) Quantitative restrictions that initially generate supra-normal profits for local producers are also likely to generate new domestic entry that may quickly compete away these profits (depending on the elasticity of supply). Thus, rationales for trade restrictions that turn on 'breathing spaces' with enhanced profitability to finance restructuring will often prove unsound. This is particularly so in industries with low entry barriers like footwear and clothing. For example, in the US one-third of the clothing and textile establishments existing at the end of 1982 had been created since 1976. In France, over one-fifth of new manufacturing firms are in the textile and clothing industries (OECD 1985b : 172). This consideration is less true of the automobile and steel industries where large specialized up-front investments discourage 'hit-and-run' entry. In the auto industry, VERs in North America may have contributed to record industry profits in the last several years (although recovery from the recession has obviously been a much more important factor), and these profits may have facilitated the restructuring and productivity improvements being realized by the industry. In the US steel industry, the established integrated steel firms have invested very few resources in productivity improvements and appear to be diversifying out of steel into unrelated sectors.

(d) Domestic price increases for a product that are induced by quantitative restrictions may induce the emergence of lower-priced substitutes, for example plastics for steel.

(e) Productivity improvements in domestic industries induced by continuing competitive pressures from domestic and foreign rivals will, even if they maintain industry output, almost certainly involve job loss as capital is substituted for labour through technological innovation and improved production techniques. This trend has been particularly evident in the textile and automobile industries and segments of the steel industry.

(f) Even where trade restrictions help preserve domestic employment, internal 'trade diversion' may occur as industries relocate to lower-wage regions of the country. This has been particularly evident in the US textile, clothing and steel industries. While new jobs are created in the low-cost regions, jobs are sacrificed in the higher-cost regions. Similar internal job substitution effects are likely to be induced by foreign producers seeking to circumvent trade restrictions by investing in new local production facilities (as in the North American auto industry).

(g) Outsourcing by domestic producers of component and sub-assembly manufacture to multinational subsidiaries or foreign producers, where this circumvents trade restrictions on fully assembled imports, again induces domestic job loss.

Two general effects of discriminatory quantitative restrictions should finally be noted. First, a ratchet effect is set in train as restrictions need to be deepened to prevent up-market substitution by restrained suppliers and broadened to prevent substitution by unrestrained third country suppliers. Also, other importing countries, concerned that restrained products will be diverted to (or 'dumped' in) their markets, will feel impelled to adopt similar restrictions (e.g. the EEC VER response to the US TPM in steel). This ratchet effect may be very difficult to reverse. Second, discriminatory quantitative restrictions promote what has been called 'co-operative protectionism' where foreign producers are partly co-opted by scarcity rents from quantitative restrictions, by various contractual and joint venture arrangements for outsourcing, and by foreign investment in local production facilities, all of which give them an increasing stake in prevailing trade restrictions. These developments seem a perversion of traditional concepts of international trade or competition and while inherently raising costs over the free trade base case, also entails significant risks over time of anti-consumer collusive or non-competitive behaviour.

To the extent that trade restrictions induce foreign producers to substitute foreign investment in local production facilities in place of exports, domestic producers are still likely to lose market share (leading them, one would predict, to demands for restrictions on foreign investments as well as trade), although local workers may be indifferent to this loss of market share if foreign producers offer terms and conditions of employment as good or better than local producers. In this event, domestic coalitions of investor and labour interests favouring trade restrictions may diverge in their attitude to foreign investment.

Apart from discriminatory quantitative restrictions, the second major aspect of the 'New Protectionism' is the escalating use of contingent protection measures, primarily anti-dumping and countervailing duties. We reserve comment on countervailing duties levied against allegedly subsidized imports until the next chapter, but a brief comment is warranted here on anti-dumping laws and the the declining importance of safeguard actions under Article XIX of the GATT.

While domestic anti-dumping laws have a long history, dating back to the turn of the century (Barcelo 1971–2), and were legitimated internationally by Article VI of the GATT in 1947, an economic rationale for their existence has, for the most part, proved elusive (Barcelo 1971–2); Trebilcock and Quinn 1979). Anti-dumping laws permit duties to be imposed in the amount of any difference between a foreign exporter's home market prices and lower prices being charged by it in importing country markets.

The only coherent economic rationale that would seem to justify such laws is predatory pricing. However, as with predation under domestic antitrust laws, the assumptions which a successful strategy of predation must meet are severe, suggesting that such cases will be rare (Dunlop, McQueen and Trebilcock 1987: chap.8). Moreover, any economic analysis of alleged predation will focus on the relationship between an alleged predator's prices and costs (which measure of cost is admittedly contentious) to determine if the predator is selling below cost with a view to recouping losses from supra-competitive prices once rivals have been driven from the market. In contrast, in anti-dumping cases the primary focus of inquiry has historically been the divergence between a foreign firm's prices in its home market and lower prices it may be charging in its export markets. Such divergence may reflect international price discrimination between the two markets, reflecting, in turn, market power that the exporter possesses in its home market that it does not possess in its export market. But this is scarcely a reason why a government in the latter market should wish, out of a perverse sense of egalitarianism, to see its own consumers monopolized in order to replicate the misery of consumers in the home market (Trebilcock and Quinn 1979). Again, the current anti-trust learning on price discrimination (Dunlop, McQueen and Trebilcock 1987: chap. 8), as with predation, needs to be brought to bear on international manifestations of the same phenomenon. Currently, US anti-dumping case-law tends increasingly to compare export market prices with the fully allocated costs of the exporter in a given year (including R & D) – a test that few domestic companies could meet and that is substantially different from cost concepts applied in domestic predation cases. Moreover, injury is determined abstracting from causation, simply by investigating whether a domestic industry has performed worse in recent time periods than in the past. Given a prior determination of 'dumping' and given that all imports, 'dumped' or not, are likely to reduce domestic producers' market share, causation is largely assumed, and duties imposed in the amount of the price differential (Cass 1989).

Very few anti-dumping cases in any jurisdiction plausibly fall within the range of a legitimate predation concern. Those few that do can be adequately dealt with under domestic anti-trust laws on predation, which further bilateral and multilateral negotiations could usefully seek to harmonize.

While efficiency arguments for anti-dumping laws are tenuous at best, it may well be the case that ethical concerns over the distributive impacts of disruptive, low-priced imports provide a firmer footing for intervention. But this concern is more properly the domain of a well conceived safeguards regime, which in its present incarnation in Article XIX of the GATT has fallen into increasing desuetude (as noted earlier in this chapter).

Article XIX permits a state to withdraw or modify previous trade concessions where these concessions have resulted in a surge of imports that are causing or threatening to cause serious injury to domestic producers of like or directly competitive products. Safeguard action may be taken for such time as may be necessary to prevent or remedy such injury. A government invoking safeguard relief normally attempts to negotiate 'compensation' with foreign governments whose exports are substantially affected by the action, typically taking the form of alternative trade concessions of equivalent value. Failing agreement on compensation, foreign governments are entitled to withdraw trade concessions of their own of equivalent value.

Efforts during and after the Tokyo Round to negotiate a new safeguards regime proved abortive. With the continuing proliferation since then of the so-called 'New Protectionism', many manifestations of which represent transparent circumventions of the letter or spirit of Article XIX, it has become a matter of even greater urgency during the current Uruguay Round to negotiate an effective agreement that imposes a higher measure of discipline on safeguard actions.

It is worth recalling what the rationales are for a safeguards regime. First, it is often argued that with an escape clause which enables a party to protect itself from the unforeseeably disruptive domestic impacts of increased imports, countries generally would be more reluctant to grant trade concessions in the first place, and thus the availability of escape clause relief, at least in extreme cases of dislocation, may actually enhance rather than retard the long-run process of trade liberalization. Second, whatever the effects of the availability of escape clause relief on the longer-term process of trade liberalization, it can plausibly be argued that non-economic norms, in particular distributive justice and communitarian values, as counterweights to efficiency or consumer welfare values, are legitimately implicated when import surges impact in serious ways on significant numbers of less well-endowed and immobile workers or on the integrity or viability of long-established communities which are substantially dependent on domestic industries that face contraction or collapse in the face of unconstrained imports.

However, with respect to these justifications for safeguard relief, it is important to ask whether alternative domestic policy instruments are available, other than trade restrictions, that are capable of cushioning adjustment shocks to domestic interests and vindicating distributive justice or communitarian values at less cost to domestic consumer welfare and to global economic efficiency than trade restrictions. In other words, to adapt a concept from Canadian constitutional law, a 'least drastic means' test seems relevant in assessing the appropriate choice of policy instrument by domestic polities in response to import surges.

Resolving the issues surrounding reform of the safeguards regime assumes a critical importance if a principled approach to the use of trade restrictions to mute the dislocating effect of unforeseeably large import surges is to be adopted. Currently, anti-dumping and countervailing duty laws have become almost complete substitutes for safeguard actions, their greater popularity being largely explained by: (i) their selective application, (ii) the absence of a requirement of compensation or a right of retaliation, and (iii) the absence of political discretion in their application. Changing the political dynamics surrounding these three regimes requires attention to these central institutional differences – a theme we pursue further in the final chapter of this study.

III. Conclusions

The evidence on the disproportionality between costs and benefits of trade protection policies is overwhelming. Arguably, from a communitarian perspective these cost/benefit disparities merely indicate how highly voters value community stability – yet despite their enormous cost to consumers and taxpayers in general, trade restrictions have, in the sectors studied, often failed to prevent major employment contraction, with the consequent disruption of communal structures. The rents captured by firms from trade restrictions are often clearly far in excess of the amount required to pay the full cost of each job maintained, suggesting that from a strong 'stay option' perspective there would be an absolute preference for even a 100 per cent labour subsidy over trade restrictions. While arguably in some cases, a 100 per cent subsidy would not be enough to induce a firm to stay in a given community, if the opportunity costs of not exiting were extremely high, in these instances an equivalent subsidy to other sectors or firms to create employment in the same community would vindicate communitarian, as well as utilitarian and liberal contractarian values, more efficiently than trade protection. For example, it makes no sense at all to 'tax' US consumers of speciality steel $1 million per year for each job preserved in the domestic speciality steel industry when the average compensation per worker was less than $60,000 or to 'tax' US consumers of automobiles $160,000 per year for each job preserved in the domestic auto industry when the average annual compensation of US autoworkers is less than one quarter of this figure (Crandall 1984: 8). Equally, in a Canadian context, it makes no sense to 'tax' consumers of footwear between $53,668 and $69,460 per year for each job saved in the industry when average earnings per worker at the time of the estimates was $7,145 p.a., or to 'tax' consumers of textile and clothing between $40,600 and $50,982 per year for each job saved when the average earnings per worker at the time of the estimates was $10,000 p.a., or to 'tax' consumers of automobiles between $179,000 and $226,394 per year for each job saved when average earnings in the industry at the time of the estimates were between $29,000 and $35,000 (Economic Council of Canada, 1988: 61, 70, 76).

Why such domestic policies are adopted by governments is a crucially important but complex question, which we pursue in Chapter 5 of this study.

Chapter three

Industrial subsidies as a response to sectoral decline

I. Outline of chapter

This chapter considers the costs, benefits and economic and political determinants of subsidies to declining industries. We consider both theoretical perspectives and empirical evidence with respect to the sectors and countries that are the focus of this study.

Our main hypothesis is that subsidization – like trade protection – does emanate from legitimate normative concerns about the dislocation costs of industrial decline. However, we see the choices of specific strategies and instruments of intervention as not in themselves driven by unalterable voter preferences, or interest group demands, but as choices that have very much to do with perceived costs and benefits of alternatives, changeable perceptions and biases of both publics and policy makers, and with actual available information about an industry's prospects, the realities of international competition, and techniques for regaining or shifting comparative advantage.

Voters are prepared to pay a significant price for the ethical concerns (distributive justice and community stability) underlying their preference for subsidization. But this does not mean that, with full information about the costs and benefits of alternatives, they will not choose the least costly means of achieving these goals. Moreover, it may be that when adequately informed about the future prospects of a given industry, or when fully aware of how high the price is of intervention, they will in some cases simply decide that intervention is not justifiable.

In our empirical analysis, we seek to highlight the extent to which – depending on their context – different strategies and instruments of intervention can entail vastly different costs and benefits, and how lack of information or incorrect assumptions or ideological and cultural biases have often been decisive in the choice of costly and ineffective strategies and instruments over less costly and more effective ones that address the same normative concerns.

We conclude that the quest for a multilateral sovereignty-limiting instrument to discipline subsidies is elusive and probably misdirected. Abolition of all subsidization is politically infeasible, if only because in ceding the right to subsidize, states would be giving away some of their most potent tools of social policy, economic control, and political survival. Yet attempts to ban some types of subsidies (i.e. regional aids or equity injections) while permitting others fall prey to the same conceptual impasses reflected in the Tokyo Round negotiations, where agreement was reached that subsidies should be subject to international discipline, only by renouncing the attempt to spell out which subsidies are permissible, and which are impermissible.

Whether a particular subsidy is an appropriate response to decline will depend on the particular country, its political culture, the structure of government-industry relations, fiscal policy, and also the problems within particular industries. For example, nationalization would be an option difficult to implement in the US, given American values and the lack of governmental structures to manage directly major industrial enterprises. In Sweden, however, it might be the most fitting response to decline, allowing state co-ordination of a strategy for adjustment accepted by government, unions, and firms. On the other hand, deregulation as an instrument of aid to industry – quite popular in the US – might be totally unacceptable in Sweden, where national values reject firms imposing social costs such as pollution on the public at large.

This illustrates that the second-best argument that some specific forms of domestic subsidization be banned is inherently problematic, since no form is inherently more destructive than any other. The costs and benefits of subsidies cannot be predicted or ranked from the form they take, but are variable depending on their context.

II. A framework for analysis of subsidy policy

(a) Decline, adjustment and subsidization

Although changing comparative advantage, changing technology, and – perhaps most importantly – changing human preferences have led to the rise and fall of many national industries over the centuries, it is only quite recently that the concept of 'industrial decline' has become a major preoccupation in debates over economic policy. In market economies where factors of production are constantly shifting between uses and even between nations, does the decline of industries or firms signify anything more than the natural, expected course of events? Indeed, one would have thought that post-war trade liberalization reflects, if anything, a heightened acceptance of the inexorable laws of comparative advantage. While specific government aid to ailing industries or firms has been practised for centuries, it is in the last decade that in North America and Western Europe 'industrial decline' has come to be seen as a crisis, requiring systematic, strategic state intervention.

This 'crisis' is a consequence of the confluence of several factors: first, during the 1970s the world economy experienced a number of 'shocks', such as the oil crises, and decline in demand for certain basic products and commodities, at a time at which most industries were investing and producing on the assumption that growth would continue; secondly, technological change was much more rapid than previously experienced; thirdly, diffusion of technology and production techniques to NICs occurred very quickly, whereas most government and industry planners in the older industrialized nations had assumed that the Third World would remain for a long time limited to primitive industrial and commodity production. In sum, there was nothing cataclysmic in what happened, but rather the sense of crisis comes largely from the contrast between new realities and the strong expectations of growth or at least stability that were built up in the 1950s and 1960s, as well as the strain on peoples and governments in adapting to and accepting change at an unprecedented rate.

Furthermore, many of the industries in decline have traditionally been identified with national strength or prestige – steel, autos and shipbuilding are prominent examples. In the US, a whole literature has developed warning of 'deindustrialization', of the supposed risk that America will become a nation of 'hamburger stands' and R & D laboratories (see, for example, Bluestein 1982). Such a scenario has been questioned as unsupportable by empirical evidence (Lawrence 1984) and some analysts consider it as offering more opportunities than losses (Reich 1983b), yet the notion of 'deindustrialization' does evoke real popular fears and anxieties about the presumed shift in the direction of a services-oriented economy (Peters 1986).

It is important then in order to analyse subsidy policies as a response to industrial decline to identify precisely the senses in which an industry may be in decline. The following are all ways in which industries may be in decline; of course, these factors often operate together to produce a 'crisis' in an industry – but separating them out is a useful, if frequently avoided, step in diagnosing the nature of the problem.

(1) Cyclical changes in demand and in factor costs

Rapid, unpredicted changes in demand, or in factor costs, can have a devastating impact on an industry's profitability. These changes may, indeed, be quite temporary, but whether a given firm or even an industry can weather the storm will depend upon its capital base, the availability of financing, and also upon hedging strategies adopted to cushion against such changes – strategies such as taking positions in futures markets, foreign exchange trading, long-term supply contracts, lay-off provisions in employment contracts and diversification. In some instances, such as the massive escalation of OPEC oil prices in the early 1970s, even firms that have taken rational measures to guard against temporary disruptions may face disaster – and in such instances public strategies for stabilization may be appropriate, and inasmuch as they counteract temporary market vicissitudes (induced in part by cartel behaviour) they may be considered as non-distortive. Of course, in their self-interested optimism, government officials, unions, and firms may seek to classify long-term or medium-term trends as mere unpredictable, temporary disruptions.

(2) Long-term decline in demand

World demand for given products changes over time, and with it the demand for inputs to make those products. The reason may be technological changes which allow cheaper substitutes to fulfil the same needs, or that needs and tastes have themselves changed. Examples of the former are slumps in the world demand for steel in the 1970s (many substitute metal alloys and plastics now perform the functions of 'ordinary' steel) (Goldberg 1986), and of the latter, a current fashion preference among consumers in industrialized countries that involves considerably lower textile consumption (OECD 1987c). In a perfectly functioning market, the effect of overall decline in world demand over the long term is that marginal firms will fail, overall output will be less and will be shared among the more efficient firms that remain. Since, given existing comparative advantage, a particular country's contribution to world output may be 'marginal', it is logical that in some cases significant decline in world demand will lead not just to exit of inefficient or marginally efficient firms but also of entire national industries from the global market.

(3) Declining competitiveness/shifting comparative advantage

The above factors focus on global trends which impact on the state of an industry in general, although clearly their effect is disproportionate, falling most heavily on the least efficient or least far-sighted firms and national industries. However, other kinds of changes can profoundly affect the share of the global market that each country has. For a very long time before political economists began discussing industrial decline, it was well known that wage costs were in general much lower outside Europe and North America. Yet in major industries, it was thought that these two continents would continue to dominate world markets: whatever disadvantage might be generated by high wage rates would be more than made up for by superior infrastructure, technology, worker productivity, and industrial organization. But in fact while the wage differential has clearly narrowed somewhat, the latter differences have, in the case of Japan and a handful of major NICs, been significantly narrowed or indeed (in the case of Japanese productivity in certain sectors and technological applications) even reversed.

Thus, it is somewhat misleading to suggest, that decline has been due to inefficiency, technological backwardness, and bureaucratic rigidity in North American industries: even if the Japanese had merely caught up to North Americans in these areas, they would still have acquired an overall comparative advantage because of the wage cost difference. However, some firms within North American industry might be able actually to do better than the Japanese or NIC producers, in these non-wage factors, and they might survive in the world market, despite a general shift of comparative advantage. This might occur if production methods were to become more capital and less labour-intensive, thereby minimizing the importance of the wage cost differential. But of course, while the result might be viable firms, it would still involve significant loss of employment, as capital replaced labour in the production process.

(b) The political economy of subsidization strategies

(1) Maintenance of output and employment

The most politically straightforward – but most economically retrograde – subsidization strategy for declining industries is to maintain output and employment in the face of declining demand and/or prices. The troubling questions of what is wrong with an industry, and how government economic and industrial policy should be changed to address what is wrong, are entirely avoided. No demands to change or adapt are made of the firms and workers involved. Where firms or industries are only in decline because of temporary changes in demand or prices, such a strategy is perhaps defensible, since once the cycle turns up, the subsidy will no longer be needed. In theory the social costs of the disruption caused by market vicissitudes (costly redeployment of assets through bankruptcy proceedings, sudden large scale lay-offs) may exceed the cost of the subsidy (Trebilcock *et al.* 1985: chap. 4).

However, as a strategy to address longer-term declines in demand or in comparative advantage, output and employment maintenance is economically disastrous. The longer adjustment is postponed, the more costly and the more difficult it becomes. The gap continues to widen between demand and subsidized output, leaving the government with the choice of either constantly increasing the rate of subsidy or abandoning its objective of output and employment maintenance (Flam, Perssom and Svenson 1983).

Of course, on an aggregate economic welfare perspective, governments may decide consciously to maintain firms or industries where the private rate of return falls below the level required to sustain them without government aid, if the social rate of return is considered to exceed that which could be captured by the firm itself. This concept of the difference between private and social return evokes the existence of non-economic goods (national security, or national prestige) not reflected in the market (positive externalities) which governments have a mandate to pursue (Denton *et al.* 1975).

Since it is often impossible to quantify these goods, it is very difficult to know whether the cost of the subsidy is lesser or greater than the positive externalities it confers. Industries such as steel and shipbuilding have traditionally been considered strategic – as essential to the industrial apparatus required for a state's self-defence or assertion of sovereignty (Hayward 1986). From the outset, for example, the US and France subsidized their shipbuilding industries to whatever extent was necessary to allow domestic production to continue, since making one's own merchant ships was considered a vital strategic asset. Although in the nuclear age this assumption no longer held, the subsidies continued, and were not even rethought until the mid-1970s. In effect, they had become a means of preserving jobs, rather than essential instruments of national strength.

It is even questionable whether production subsidies perform their primary function – to maintain employment. Since domestic subsidies cannot increase aggregate demand, the jobs they create or maintain in one firm will be lost elsewhere. Similarly, industry-wide subsidies will maintain employment in the targeted industry, but will retard the creation of jobs in other industries that would occur if factors of production were redeployed (Usher 1983). Thus, subsidies primarily affect the distribution of jobs and output within the economy.

(2) Rationalization and renewal

Instead of regarding major industries as permanent losers – as Robert Reich among others has urged (Reich 1983b) – it is more appealing to firms and politicians to consider them as salvageable through modernization and rationalization of production. Our analysis of the meaning of decline suggests that modernization in itself will often not be enough to redress shifts in comparative advantage. In some cases, however, if targeted toward the most efficient firms in the industry, it may produce a few winners which are exceptions to the general pattern of comparative disadvantage.

Where decline coincides with a period where (e.g. due to factors such as heavy public borrowing) private capital is scarce and/or very expensive, there may be an argument for government intervention in the form of loans or grants for renewal (Lawrence 1984). Yet increased debt financing may not be appropriate for firms in trouble. Their difficulties may have led to an already heavy debt load, and further loans might lead to overleveraging – a debt-to-equity ratio so skewed that the firm might collapse before it has time to renew itself (Rohatyn 1983). Why then not leave declining firms to the equity market to finance their own renewals? If investors find that a firm's prospects for renewal seem strong they will be attracted to purchase equity. Indeed, civil servants seem in general less well situated than private investors to determine whether renewal is really feasible, or which firms within a declining industry are good prospects and which are not.

Yet in a market dominated by institutional investors such as pension funds and insurance companies, firms in decline may not have the high credit ratings that such investors typically seek, or which they are required to seek by fiduciary obligations. Similar factors may also prevent a successful bond issue. Government might intervene by purchasing equity with which the firm can finance renewal, or through some form of backing that has the effect of upgrading the quality of the shares or bonds.

There are a number of important questions to be raised with respect to government-subsidized rationalization. First of all, increases in productivity or efficiency themselves are often held up as the measures of success of government subsidy programmes. Yet these are not as such public benefits or goods. If the government's purpose in subsidizing is to prevent loss of jobs, it must reckon with the prospect that the productivity and efficiency gains from rationalization may largely come from significant reductions in employment, thereby substantially mitigating the public benefit from subsidizing. Ultimately, the net jobs saved may not be worth what will often be the enormous cost of modernization, or it will be much cheaper to create new jobs in other, non-declining sectors. Second, it is difficult to estimate in advance whether even a highly successful modernization programme will involve sufficient gains to redress or counter loss of comparative advantage; even a much more efficient industry may remain marginal in terms of world markets, and if demand further declines, may become non-viable. Third, if there is an equity financing gap experienced by declining industries or firms, there may be prospects of eliminating it by means of aggressive private investment banking. It is arguable that instruments such as 'junk bonds' address themselves to just this gap. Ultimately, relaxation of legal restrictions on high-risk investment instruments may be an attractive alternative to government financing.

(3) Subsidized exit

Pioneered by the Japanese, who introduced a formal structure for subsidizing exit from declining industries with their *Structurally Depressed Industries Law* of 1978, this strategy is the most congenial to economic theory, for rather than attempting to counter or avoid changing market realities, government instead uses its resources to redistribute the costs of adapting to those realities, thereby making adjustment more palatable socially and politically (Peck *et al.* 1985; OECD 1983a). While non-Japanese industrial policy advocates such as Robert Reich (1983b) emphasize that the orderly exit strategy involves government assuming costs of exit which would normally be borne by firms and workers, it is noteworthy that the Japanese system forces the industry itself to provide a significant part of the resources that the state initially provides to buy surplus capacity and compensate workers – for example, through a special levy or tax on the industry (Peck *et al.* 1985). Also, instead of creating its own labour adjustment programme, the Japanese government relies heavily on firms themselves to retrain and redeploy workers, and subsidizes them to do so. This both reduces administrative costs to the state, and also assures workers that instead of merely a limited period of public assistance payments, they will actually obtain new permanent positions, often within the same conglomerate (Peck *et al.* 1985).

Yet, even as practised by the Japanese, exit subsidization is far from a panacea. Exit is rarely if ever as rapid as decline in demand, and the government is often left with an albeit much smaller but excessively large industry, which remains very inefficient and continues to consume subsidies. Yamazawa argues, with respect to the Japanese textile industry, that subsidized exit has 'tended to discourage voluntary, unsubsidized scrapping and to prolong survival of inefficient firms' (Yamazawa 1983: 38). This last point highlights a major difference between orderly exit (subsidized, gradual scrapping of output throughout the industry) and market-driven exit – in the latter case marginally efficient firms fail quickly, whereas the most efficient firms may well remain as survivors, while in the former, the least efficient firms have a strong incentive to prolong their existence through participation in subsidized orderly exit. A particularly controversial feature of the Japanese version of the exit strategy is the use of cartelization as a complement to subsidies. Firms are often permitted or encouraged by government to form a temporary industry cartel – allocating among themselves shares of the capacity reduction targeted for the industry. As the output of each firm is fixed by agreement, price competition is in effect eliminated. Lawrence has levelled a number of criticisms at these cartelization practices: (a) they do not lead to substantially more adjustment than would occur in a free market; (b) cartelization shifts costs onto consumers in a 'covert fashion'; (c) government-approved industry cartelization or stabilization plans entail bureaucratic involvement in industry planning which bureaucrats are rarely competent to undertake; and (d) cartelization is counterproductive if the source of an industry's declining demand is foreign competition, which is likely to increase in the face of supra-competitive domestic prices. With respect to this last point, Lawrence claims that for cartelization to have worked at all for import-impacted industries, it must have been accompanied by (hidden) protectionism (Lawrence 1987).

But comparing the Japanese exit strategy against a hypothetical free market is not particularly useful, since politically the choice is usually between different strategies of intervention. In comparison with other countries which have pursued different forms of intervention, Japan has a very good record of adjustment. In the shipbuilding industry, for example, Japan scrapped more capacity in the 1970s and 1980s than all the European Community producers combined (Todd 1985).

While it is true that consumers bear some extra cost in the form of higher prices from cartelization, it is important to remember that the firm itself in Japan is faced with paying to a significant extent for the costs of adjustment assistance. Peck *et al.* suggest that somewhat higher prices may be worth paying in order to preserve an institutional structure where firms themselves shoulder the bulk of the responsibility for the adjustment process: 'By co-ordinating capacity reduction, sometimes through cartels, public policy seeks to maintain prices at a level sufficient to permit large firms to shoulder a substantial share of the burdens of labor relocation and debt repayment' (Peck *et al.* 1985).

Finally, cartelization can be viewed as a means of shifting some of the costs of adjustment from the firm. Cartelization need not be the only means of doing this as part of an exit strategy – higher public subsidies would be an alternative. Peck *et al.* note that in Japan there is a traditional tolerance of industrial concentration, and a relatively lenient anti-trust regime. Thus, the use of cartels and direct bureaucratic involvement in planning of industry, as well, may be seen as a cultural preference, rather than a choice dictated by the economic logic of government-assisted adjustment. In any case, exit subsidization has a considerable advantage over other subsidy strategies – as the industry and its workforce decreases, the political demand for subsidization is also likely to decrease. Once an industry is marginalized it will be unlikely to mobilize enough political will to resist further adjustment, as far fewer jobs will be at stake. In the case of both employment and output maintenance, and rationalization, subsidies will often breed more demand for subsidies – in the former case, because expectations are created that, whatever happens in the market, output and employment will be sustained, and in the latter because once an industry is modernized with public funds, governments have a substantial political stake in ensuring its survival.

(c) The choice of subsidizing instrument: economic and political considerations

Given a decision to respond to political demands for intervention through one or more of the above strategies of subsidization, governments have available to them a wide variety of subsidizing instruments – ranging from tax concessions and deregulation to bailouts and nationalization. Many analysts have attempted to rank the various instruments – for example as more or less transparent, or more or less coercive and intrusive (Lowi 1970). In fact, each instrument has its own costs and benefits which must be evaluated in the context in which subsidization is to take place.

This point can be well-demonstrated by taking the four characteristics of subsidy programmes considered desirable by the OECD, as promoting positive adjustment. Subsidies should be: (a) temporary, (b) transparent; (c) linked to phasing out of surplus capacity, and (d) as little distortive as possible of international trade (OECD 1983a). No one instrument or group of instruments best embodies all these positive characteristics. For example, tax concessions are arguably much less transparent than direct grant or loan programmes; as Woodside has remarked in the Canadian context, 'tax incentives are rarely introduced either alongside detailed explanation of their goals or revenue costs, whereas direct funding forms part of the Public Estimates' (Woodside 1979: 251). On the other hand, direct subsidy programmes are more likely to create their own administrative structures and interest groups, and hence are much more likely to become permanent.

Transparency is a particularly important factor in developing efficient subsidization strategies. Enormous costs may be hidden from view, and thus public perceptions may be the consequence of a radical miscalculation of costs and benefits. Yet it is possible, by reforming domestic subsidy procedures (as noted below), to quantify and make publicly available the costs of almost any subsidy instrument. This can even include deregulation, nationalization, and bailouts (see Goldberg 1986; Wilson 1979; Trebilcock *et al.* 1985). Similarly, with conditionality (or linkage of subsidization with firm or worker support for positive adjustment policies), even an industry-wide tax credit, usually regarded as one of the most unconditional kinds of subsidies, can be made conditional on very specific kinds of investment being made by firms. On the other hand, firm-specific loans have often been granted in return for very loose promises on the part of the firms concerned. What is at stake is not only the choice of instrument itself, but ultimately the political will or determination of politicians and government managers to extract strategic concessions from firms and workers in return for aid. Exactly the same instruments were used to attempt to restructure and revitalize British Leyland in the mid-1970s and in the early 1980s. Yet the first programme was a failure, and the later one, a success. A key difference was that unlike his predecessor, the firm's new head, Sir Michael Edwardes, was able to extract key concessions from the workers in return for continued public subsidies (Dyer, Salter and Weber 1987).

III. Empirical evidence of subsidization

(a) Shipbuilding

From 1974 to 1986, world demand within the shipbuilding industry declined from 134 to 25 million gross tons (OECD 1987b). Most of the major national shipbuilding industires were already heavily subsidized, with government aid often dating back to the inception of the industry in its modern form (OECD 1976a). This massive decline in demand (especially in the tanker market, due to the OPEC-induced oil crises) was aggravated by a basic shift of comparative advantage, initially to Japan and then to NIC's such as South Korea and Yugoslavia (Mottershead 1983). The initial response of most European governments was to attempt to stem the consequences of these changes through further increases in subsidization, such that in some cases (e.g. Sweden) subsidies ended up actually exceeding value-added in the industry (Carlsson 1983). In contrast, the Japanese, almost as soon as demand began to collapse, either abolished subsidy programmes or redirected them towards reductions in capacity and assistance to unemployed workers (Boyer 1983). Between the late 1970s and the mid-1980s, however, most of the other traditional shipbuilding nations came to the realization that the increases in subsidies needed to keep the industry alive were too costly, and adopted strategics of capacity reduction and/or exit. Table 3.1 shows the trends in the extent of subsidies in OECD countries from 1952 to 1985, before this change in direction had impacted on programmes.

(1) Australia

In Australia, subsidies kept mounting to sustain the shipbuilding industry until 1976, when it required an estimated subsidy of 45 per cent of production costs to make viable construction of large merchant ships in Australian yards (Rich 1987). The government judged that to preserve the industry would require ever increasing levels of subsidy, and that decline seemed irreversible. As a consequence, subsidies were abolished altogether, with rapid collapse of the industry ensuing: within a year, one of the main yards shut, with a loss of 1800 jobs in a single, already depressed industrial community (Rich 1987). In the decade following abolition of subsidies, more shipbuilding capacity was scrapped in Australia than in all the EC countries taken together (Todd 1985).

(2) Sweden

Public aid to Sweden's nationalized shipbuilding industry continued to mount throughout the 1970s. In 1976–7 subsidies amounted to US$1,245 per employee (Hamilton 1983) and by 1978–9 actually exceeded the value added in the industry (Carlsson 1983). While subsidies mounted and

Table 3.1 Industrial subsidies as percentage of GDP[1,2]

Country	1952	1956	1960	1964	1968	1972	1976	1980	1982	1983	1984	1985
Italy	0.89	1.30	1.51	1.23	1.67	2.29	2.60	3.02	3.69	3.33	3.49	3.43
France	1.71	2.71	1.62	2.03	2.62	1.99	2.68	2.51	2.71	2.80	3.00	3.01
Canada	0.41	0.39	0.81	0.85	0.87	0.83	1.87	2.68	2.50	2.49	2.80	2.48
UK	2.68	1.76	1.93	1.56	2.06	1.82	2.72	2.50	2.15	2.13	2.44	2.22
W. Germany	0.65	0.20	0.79	0.99	1.44	1.48	1.97	2.06	1.84	1.90	2.07	2.01
Japan	0.79	0.26	0.34	0.65	1.11	1.12	1.31	1.50	1.40	1.42	1.28	1.15
US	0.11	0.20	0.25	0.44	0.50	0.59	0.33	0.40	0.49	0.66	0.61	0.58

Source: International Monetary Fund, *Issues and Developments in International Trade Policy* (Washington DC.: IMF 1988).

Notes:

[1] Countries listed in order of amount of subsidies as a percentage of GDP in 1985.

[2] The data do not include subsidies such as tax concessions. In Germany total tax concessions to enterprise averaged about 1.8 per cent of GDP a year in 1975–85 while in the US federal tax concessions to industry were about 1.5 per cent of GDP a year during 1975–87; similar data are not available for other countries.

demand declined, no national consensus developed as to whether subsidization should be linked to contraction of the industry, employment and output maintenance, or exit. Finally in the early 1980s, the non-socialist coalition government – formed in 1979 – moved to end assistance to the industry. Over a five year period, the shipbuilding activities of the nationalized firm Swedyard were phased out, workers redeployed to other industries, and the yards themselves converted to other uses (in one instance, an auto parts plant): extensive public funding was provided for capital investment in these new facilities. As a consequence, Sweden no longer has a commercial shipbuilding industry (OECD 1987b).

(3) United States

The rationale for subsidizing the US shipbuilding industry originated with the *Jones Act* of 1920, which requires that the US merchant marine operate, for national security reasons, entirely with US-made vessels. The basic subsidy was the Construction Differential Subsidy (CDS) aimed at fully compensating for the added costs of building a ship in the US rather than in a foreign location. In the mid-1970s, as the level of subsidy required to sustain the industry mounted, government policy was rethought – having merchant ships home-built no longer was of any strategic importance, and the CDS was capped at 37 per cent, with further reductions intended to eliminate it altogether. Finally, the Reagan Administration abolished the CDS in 1981, and took steps to abolish other indirect subsidies (such as government loan guarantees to domestic ship purchasers) (OECD 1987b). As a consequence, employment fell from 175,000 to 125,000 between 1980 and 1983; orders have now dried up; and one analyst has estimated that in several years exit will be completed (Todd 1985). Nevertheless, the *Jones Act* provisions prohibiting use of foreign ships for the coastal trades do remain in force, and this trade protection may mitigate tendencies to exit driven by reduced subsidization.

(4) Japan

Japan very rapidly redirected its state aid to reduction of capacity in the mid-1970s. Nineteen shipbuilding companies left the industry between 1975 and 1978, when the government and the industry agreed to a further 35 per cent reduction in capacity, to be assisted by a ¥1 billion loan from the Japan Development Bank. The loan was used to buy up excess facilities at book value, and scrap them. The loan was partly repaid by sale of these scrapped assets. However, a tax was also imposed on the price of new vessels (1.3 per cent), so that the direct burden of adjustment was borne mostly by the industry itself, not by taxpayers (Peck *et al.* 1985: 43). In addition, shipbuilders were provided with loans from a government-capitalized fund for the purpose of providing severance payments and relocation assistance to redundant workers (Boyer 1983). While in fact total reduction of capacity actually exceeded the target by 35 per cent, further reductions were clearly necessary by the mid-1980s, due to further declines in export orders (OECD 1987b). Although some additional reductions have been accepted by the industry there is clear resistance to the exit option, as evidenced by the fact that by the early 1980s a number of production oriented subsidies (such as concessional loans for domestic purchasers of Japanese ships) had been reintroduced, even as capacity was being scrapped (Kikkawa 1983: 243).

(5) France

Until the mid-1970s, French subsidy policy was directed towards both modernization of the industry and increases in output (a 30 per cent rise in capacity was realized for the 1971-5 period; OECD 1976a). Hence when the crisis of world surplus capacity peaked in 1976-7, France found itself with a growing not contracting industry. While the government did change its policy to the extent of tying subsidies to freezes in output by each shipyard (Mottershead 1983), actual reductions were not mandated. As a consequence between 1977 and 1985, virtually no capacity was scrapped (Todd 1985). As the OECD notes, even increasing subsidization will not prevent eventual collapse of the industry, since orders are drying up despite the subsidies. Costs of subsidization have been enormous, amounting in 1984 already to between FF 175,000 and 200,000 per worker, higher by 50 per cent than the average annual wage in the industrial sector (Balassa 1985: 314).

(6) United Kingdom

Long before the world crisis of surplus capacity, the British shipbuilding industry was experiencing serious difficulties. Substantial public aid was provided in the early 1970s to consolidate shipyards, modernize facilities and enhance productivity. However, unions militantly resisted any measures which would have resulted in employment reductions, particularly the closure of inefficient yards. In 1976 the industry was nationalized by the newly elected Labour government, and provided with an injection of £300 million working capital, and an additional £65 million in modernization grants (Todd 1985). The government did, eventually, proceed with substantial employment cuts, and closure of inefficient yards, buying union acquiescence through a voluntary early retirement scheme, as well as redundancy payments for those forced to retire, equivalent to £145 per year of service (Strath 1986: 153). British shipbuilders continue, however, to run substantial losses in 1986-7, these amounted to £148 million, more than £20,000 per worker (*Economist* 23 April 1988: 61). Further employment cuts (from 6,500 to 4,500 workers) are planned by the British government (*Economist* 23 April 1988: 61).

(7) Canada

In Canada, production subsidies to the shipbuilding industry began in 1961, set originally at the rate of 40 per cent to decline by 1 per cent per year until 8 per cent was reached in 1981 (OECD 1976a). In the mid-1970s, in response to industry pressure, the government expanded subsidization on a temporary basis (from 1977 to 1981). However, a Federal government policy review published in 1979 suggested that decline of the industry was inevitable, and that government aid should be redirected to scrapping of capacity. The industry strenuously opposed these recommendations (Canadian Shipbuilding and Ship Repair Association (CSSRA) 1985), and indeed demanded vastly increased subsidization to sustain employment and output. The end result was that subsidies were left in place, but not increased, leading to decreases of employment from 14,000 in 1982 to 7,022 in 1984 (CSSRA June 1985). Finally, in June 1985 the Conservative government abolished production subsidies altogether, and since that date commercial orders have declined substantially. However, government procurement policies and the renewal of the Canadian fishing fleet (with political pressure to source from Canadian yards) are likely to mitigate exit tendencies in the 1990s. De Silva notes: 'although the production subsidy was terminated, the government (has) continued to assist the shipbuilding industry in other ways such as through tariff protection, procurement, and subsidies for modernization in the form of performance improvement grants' (De Silva 1988: 81).

(b) Coal

The crisis in world demand for coal began in the mid-1950s with the rapid decline in oil prices, making oil a cheaper form of energy than coal. Subsidization responses varied from exit (Japan) to output and employment maintenance (West Germany) to capacity reduction and modernization (France, Great Britain) to regional bailouts (Canada). In the late 1970s, recovery of the industry was aided by the high oil prices consequent upon the oil crises, which made coal of considerable interest as an alternative fuel source. However, as prices have stabilized, this interest has waned, and plans to expand production and develop new coal-based energy products such as Synfuel have been shelved (e.g. in West Germany and the US).

(1) Japan

Japan initiated its strategy of subsidized exit almost immediately after oil prices began to fall in the early 1950s. In August 1955 the Coal Mining Facilities Corporation was created to provide funds to buy up the assets of uneconomic mines and for redundancy payments to displaced miners. Although funding for exit was constantly increased through the 1960s, scrapping did not occur sufficiently rapidly to prevent companies from running major losses. However, between 1960 and 1973 the number of mines was reduced from 622 (*Far East Economic Review*, 4 March 1974) and employment dropped from 231,00 in 1960 to almost one-tenth of that in the early 1980s (*Economist* 1 November 1986). Exit was never completely realized, though, and in 1986 subsidies to the remaining mines amounted to ¥40 billion. The government, in its coal plan for 1987–91, has recognized the need to close at least half of the remaining eleven mines at the rate of two a year, which will cost ¥10 billion per mine in redundancy payments (*Economist* 1 November 1986).

(2) West Germany

When demand declined in the 1950s and 1960s, the German government did not actively intervene with subsidies, since rapid growth in other sectors of the German economy meant that there were adequate jobs available for displaced miners (Lucas 1985). However, by the 1970s the government was actively subsidizing output and employment maintenance, with a DM 5 subsidy per underground worker per shift (James 1984) and subsidies to utilities to compensate them for burning coal rather than oil, this latter subsidy being funded by a 4–5 per cent tax on household and business energy consumption. Total public aid to the industry increased from 6.62 per cent of value added in 1966 to 37.3 per cent in 1978 (Black 1986: 108). While the government was prepared to invest large sums of money in R&D. to develop alternative coal-based fuel sources in the wake of the energy crisis, by the early 1980s the economic feasibility of such efforts was in doubt, and they were abandoned.

(3) France

Aid to the nationalized French coal industry, Charbonnages de France, was premised from the 1960s on rationalization and contraction of output. But despite considerable investments in modernization (e.g. FF 440 million in 1965), geological conditions kept productivity quite low – well below levels attained by West Germany and the UK (James 1984: 199). On the other hand, between 1970 and 1980, coal production was halved (Balassa 1986: 100). The socialist government decided in 1981 to reverse the policy of contraction and increase output substantially. This resulted in massive increases in subsidization in the early 1980s, amounting to FF 140,000 per worker in 1984 (Balassa 1985).

(4) United Kingdom

Until the mid-1970s the British coal industry was able to adjust through employment reduction and modernization, with little direct government aid, although the rate of return expected from the nationalized industry was below the average for the private sector (Wilson 1979). From 1956 to 1970, employment fell from 704,000 to 264,000, and the number of pits was reduced from 840 to 299 (Trebilcock *et al.* 1985). However, in the 1970s union resistance to pit closures increased, and acceptance of worker demands was reflected in government plans to actually increase output from the late 1970s through to the mid-1980s. In 1973, the government wrote off £275 million of National Coal Board debt, resulting in a savings to the industry of about £40 million per year in interest charges (Wilson 1979: 264). Almost all the losses realized by the industry in recent years have been due to inability to close inefficient pits. When the government renewed its determination to effect closures, the miners staged a year-long strike in 1983–4, with the government eventually winning agreement for closures; in 1985–6, 33,000 miners exited from the industry. The price the government paid was massive redundancy payments, amounting to £566 million in 1986 alone (*Economist* 2 August 1986: 47).

(5) Canada

In general the Canadian coal industry is not subsidized, although it has benefited from public investment in rail transportation facilities, and – in the case of British Columbia – port facilities that are crucial for reaching major markets. The port of Vancouver expanded its coal-handling capacity from 14 million tonnes in 1979 to 30 million in the mid-1980s, and as of 1984 construction of a coal terminal at Prince Rupert was underway. Additional rail links between coalfields in northern British Columbia and Prince Rupert are under development, with costs in the $250–315 range; a significant portion of these expenditures will be borne by the Federal government (James 1984: 174). These investments have clearly been premised on steady or increasing demand for British Columbia coal – an assumption cast in doubt by heightened competition with Australia to retain the Japanese market share, and by intense pressure for price cuts by Japanese buyers (Anderson 1986).

The major instance of subsidization, however, is to be found in the Cape Breton Development Corporation, probably Canada's most important experiment with public enterprise as a response to a declining regional industry (the history of Devco, and the costs and benefits of Federal support for the company, are detailed in Trebilcock *et al.* 1985). In 1984, in response to continuing and increasing losses, a major review and restructuring of Devco's operations was undertaken. Problem areas identified were: poor financial control, absenteeism, a high accident rate, and failure to develop new markets (Cape Breton Development Corporation 1985). A team of consultants was brought in, and the structure of management was overhauled to emphasize rigorous accountability for expenditure at every level of the enterprise. New health and safety procedures reduced accidents by 17 per cent and absenteeism in general by 25 per cent in less than a year. Renewed efforts were made to develop dormant European and South American markets (Cape Breton Development Corporation 1985: *Globe and Mail* 4 May 1985; *Globe and Mail* 14 May 1985).

The results of these changes were substantial: Devco's coal operations went from a loss of $49 million in 1983–84 to a break-even position in 1984–5 (Cape Breton Development Corporation 1985). Devco proceeded with capital expenditures of about $90 million in 1985, aimed at developing new mines at Phalen and Donkin, to be in operation by the end of the 1980s. The new facilities will incorporate recent technologies to greatly increase worker productivity (*Globe and Mail ROB* 14 May 1985). It is estimated that the Donkin project will create 900 new jobs (*Globe and Mail ROB* 14 May 1985).

In 1985–6 Devco was back in a loss position (about $16 million). This was due in part to the closure of one of the three mines, which was gutted by fire in April 1984. The Corporation not only lost the output from the burnt-out mine, but also had to bear the cost of providing alternative employment or redundancy settlements for the miners who had worked there (Cape Breton Development Corporation 1986). Undoubtedly, if not shouldered by Devco, this labour adjustment burden would have fallen on other Federal government programs, whether unemployment insurance or regional assistance. Also, a further 10 per cent reduction in absenteeism and 8 per cent decline in accidents were realized in 1985–6 (Cape Breton Development Corporation 1986). In March 1987, Devco announced that it had signed major delivery contracts with companies in Brazil, Italy, West Germany and Sweden. The Brazilian and Swedish deals together could lead to purchases of about half a million tonnes of coal, almost 25 per cent of current output (*Globe and Mail* 14 March 1987: B3).

While some efficiency gains and modest market expansion have occurred at Devco, the decision to expand mining operations, and add an entirely new mining facility represents a reversal of the government's previous commitment to reduce the Cape Breton community's dependence on coal mining. While investment plans were premised upon increases in the price of coal in the early 1980s, it is unlikely that demand and price will be sustained in the future at such levels as to make Devco's coal operations profitable. Increased dependence on coal in Cape Breton is likely to only perpetuate dependence upon government subsidies.

(c) *Textiles, clothing and footwear*

Trade restrictions have been the major form of government response to decline in the textile, clothing and footwear industries (see previous chapter). Subsidization has been directed ostensibly at funding modernization necessary for firms to regain competitiveness, with a view eventually to eliminating what were supposed to be temporary trade restrictions (the MFA). However, in the UK, France, Sweden and Canada, subsidies have also performed an employment maintenance role, at odds with modernization objectives which require replacement of labour by capital-intensive technology. Japan has used subsidies to induce partial exit from the industry, but for modernization goals as well. As the OECD notes, none of the industrialized countries has adopted a strategy of outright exit, nor accepted as inevitable 'the shift of large segments of low capital-intensive and highly unskilled labour-intensive industries to the NICs and LCDs' (OECD 1987c: 7).

As there is a paucity of discrete data concerning subsidy programmes and sectoral strategy for the footwear industry alone, we have focused below on textiles and clothing. Where programmes apply to all three industries (as is the case with the Canadian IBRD subsidies) we have attempted to indicate this in the text.

(1) United Kingdom

In the UK, the goal of subsidization policy has long oscillated between employment maintenance and modernization and concentration of the industry. Throughout the 1960s and 1970s, government aid focused on financing conversion of the industries to high technology, and diversion of production away from specialization in fashion/clothing towards mass production of raw textiles (Hartmann 1985). From the mid-1970s to the early 1980s, the principal form of assistance became wage subsidies, aimed solely at maintaining jobs (Shepherd 1983: 45). In 1985, the government established a new four-year £20 million scheme to fund investment by small and medium sized firms in textile, clothing and footwear sectors in high technology equipment – which may result in some firms surviving, but will unquestionably lead to major job losses (Hartmann 1985).

(2) France

French policy was oriented to wage subsidies in the 1950s and 1960s, which managed to preserve a large number of small family-owned firms into the 1970s, but which, as Mytelka argues, created a major disincentive to invest in labour-saving modernization. However, in the 1970s the policy emphasized grants to finance mergers of smaller firms, with a view to capitalizing on mass-production techniques and eliminating excess capacity (Mytelka 1983). While several major enterprises emerged as relatively competitive, output and employment fell considerably in the late 1970s (OECD 1983c). In clear contradiction with the strategy of modernization and contraction of the industry, the 1981 French Plan for textiles included a direct production/employment subsidy in the form of a reduction of the employer's social security contribution in return for a commitment to maintain jobs (OECD 1987c: 67).

(3) Canada

From 1955 to 1982, employment in the textile industries declined by about 14 per cent. The number of firms in the industry actually increased slightly in the same period, from 977 to 989 (Trebilcock 1986: 76–7). Ahmad notes that:

the major part of employment declines, . . . , is due less to falling domestic production and more to up-grading of skill requirements due to change in capital intensity, and the fact that new jobs do not go to workers displaced as a result of the change in production methods.

(Ahmad 1988: 100)

Indeed, labour productivity grew between 1971 and 1982 at an average of 2.4 per cent per year (Ahmad 1988: 57). Increased imports, by contrast, have contributed in the 1978–1987 period only by a factor of 8 per cent to employment declines (1988: 52). The age and skill levels of workers in the industry have resulted in relatively lengthy periods of unemployment following redundancies in the industry (Glenday and Jenkins 1981).

While some aids were provided previously (mainly regional assistance), a strategy of subsidization for the Canadian textile industry only emerged in 1970 with the establishment of a Canadian 'textile policy'. The core of the policy was to continue to protect the industry by trade restrictions, while providing labour adjustment asistance (to help displaced workers find jobs in other sectors) and investment grants for modernization, so that eventually protection could be reduced or eliminated (Ahmad 1988). In 1981 administration of these programmes was consolidated in the Canadian Industrial Renewal Board (CIRB). The costs of the CIRB are summarized in Table 3.2.

This complex of programmes (aimed at creating jobs in other sectors in communities hard hit by declining textile employment) was expected to create about 5,200 manufacturing jobs between 1982 to 1988 – the subsidy cost per job to average around $18,000. Significantly, however, an independent review of the effectiveness of the programme found that a subsidy of 25 per cent less would have been sufficient to create the same number of jobs (Price Waterhouse 1986). Modernization assistance has been little more than a means of sustaining firms and creating

Table 3.2 Federal government assistance to the Canadian textile, clothing and footwear industries

Programme	Objective	Government Assistance Programmes (million dollars) Type of assistance	Total expenditure textile clothing, footwear
CIRB Canadian Industrial Renewal Board 1981–1986	Promote the revitalization and international competitiveness of the TCF sectors	Loans, loan insurance, contributions to consulting costs and capital expenses	274.7 (SFP and LAP)
— SFP Sector Firms Programme	Promote restructuring and modernization	223.10	
— LAP Labour Adjustment Programme	Provide assistance to workers affected by foreign competition in the TCF sectors	Wage subsidies, mobility assistance enhanced training allowance incentives	51.60

Source: Ahmad 1988.

temporary employment; even the recipients admitted that the modernization projects did little to improve the international competitiveness of their firms (Price Waterhouse 1986: 63). Moreover, it appears that two-thirds of the projects would have been undertaken eventually even without subsidy.

Furthermore, although one of the distinctive features of the CIRB's programme was to aid the stronger and larger firms in the industries – i.e. to create 'winners' rather than perpetuate the existence of 'losers' – there is no conclusive evidence that in fact the programme has had that effect (Price Waterhouse 1986; Ahmad 1988). One reason may be that the low cost of entry for new small firms militates against the strategy of concentration – the would-be 'winners' are constantly faced with competition from new entrants in the market, and so even preferential government subsidy policies cannot ensure for them a stable or growing market share.

(4) Sweden

Until the 1970s, Swedish policy was not to intervene in the textile industry, which was undertaking its own process of modernization and employment reduction. More recently, the Swedish government has provided massive wage subsidies in the face of rapidly declining demand. Between 1971 and 1982 subsidies in total amounted to about S Kr140,000 per worker. While costly, these measures did little to halt the rapid decline in employment – from 132,000 in 1964 to 18,200 in 1982 (OECD 1984a). They have also managed to neutralize completely any positive effect of Sweden's modest modernization programme (worth S Kr20 million). With output falling faster than employment, labour intensity has actually been increasing in the industry in the 1970s and 1980s (Herin and Haltunen 1983: 7).

(5) West Germany

While the German textile industry's survival was in question at the beginning of the 1970s, two decades of rationalization, technological innovation and specialization in capital intensive segments of the market have produced a remarkable recovery. While capacity declined between 1970 and 1983 by about 1.2 per cent per year, sales per worker increased from DM 71,000 in 1970 to DM 122,000 in 1983. The percentage of product exported almost tripled in the same period while employment was halved from 500,000 to 236,000. In recent years, there have not been further declines in employment, despite the absence of subsidy, suggesting that Germany has ended up with a viable, modernized industry at lower but relatively stable levels of employment. This, of course, has been the purported but unachieved goal of much subsidization in other countries.

West Germany's extraordinary success is due to several factors: (a) earlier rationalization than in most of the other countries; (b) a lack of production or wage subsidies to retard adjustment; and (c) a very high level of specialization in capital intensive products (Hartmann 1985).

(6) Japan

Japanese strategy has focused on: (a) technological innovation; (b) concentration of firms; and (c) scrapping of capacity. The Textile Industry Rationalization Agency has been providing loans and grants to the industry for new technology since the 1960s. By the late 1970s, however, it became evident that these policies had not been very successful in facilitating positive adjustment, and the Agency's focus has now shifted to R&D. Initial expenditures were small (US$5 million in 1982) but quickly increased, and there is now in progress a US$40 million project to build by 1995 a prototype of an almost completely automated textile plant, with on-line linkage to distribution systems (Dore 1986).

Linked to technological innovation has been subsidization of industrial concentration, since it is considered that new technologies will not be affordable for small firms. Loans have been made available for mergers at preferential interest rates. Up to the present, few mergers have been created by these incentives, although it will be still several years before the major technologies they are intended to make affordable will be available (Dore 1986). Finally, scrapping of capacity both in the synthetic fibre and cotton and wool textile industries has been accomplished under the 1978 Structurally Depressed Industries Law. Loans have been made available to industry trade associations to buy up surplus capacity and sell it for conversion to other uses; total costs of the programme are not available, but it is known that loans for the wool industry amounted to US$42 million between 1978–83 (Peck *et al.* 1986).

In contrast to other sectors, such as shipbuilding, Japan's industry-contraction policies in textiles and clothing have so far not proven particularly effective in inducing positive adjustment (Dore 1986). It is too early to tell whether the longer-term strategy of total automation will restore some margin of comparative advantage. In any case this strategy – premised entirely on increased capital intensivity of production – will invariably lead to substantial employment reductions if it does succeed.

(d) Automobiles

As detailed in the previous chapter, trade protection has been a major instrument of policy response to the rise of Japanese competition in European and North American markets. However, subsidization has also occurred, primarily in the form of bailouts or (in the case of national-ized industries) capital injections aimed at facilitating restructuring of ailing firms. The other two main forms of subsidization have been regional grants and loans to influence location of new plants and to ensure that plant modernization occurs rather than closure, and R&D funding. The incidence of these subsidies in recent years is summarized in Table 3.3.

The three major bailout/recapitalization exercises of the 1980s – British Leyland, Chrysler (US and Canada), and Renault – have all achieved their objective of putting the firms back on the path to profitability, although rationalization has involved in most instances major employment reductions, and in some instances, wage cuts for workers.

(1) United Kingdom

In the case of British Leyland (nationalized in 1975), capital injections of over £1 billion in the late 1970s as well as an ambitious restructuring programme failed to revive the firm – partly due to the militant unions' success in forestalling plans for employment reductions and work force restructuring. In 1977, Sir Michael Edwardes was appointed chairman of BL, and proceeded immediately to close down outmoded plants,

Table 3.3 Government assistance to the automobile industries in selected OECD countries 1975–85: selected firm-specific subsidies

France			
Eve research project	1981/85 PSA/Renault	FF560m	$62m
FIM modernization	1984/85 PSA	FF2,700m	$300m
loans	1984/85 Renault	FF2,750m	$306m
Capital Injections	1975/80 Renault	FF1,520m	$169m
	1982/85 Renault	FF7,200m	$800m
	1986/87 Renault (projected)	FF15,000m	$1,670m
W. Germany			
Auto 2,000 research project	1980/84 VK/DBenz/ Berlin V.	DM148m	$50m
UK			
Capital injection	1978/83 BL	£2,009m	$2,612m
Regional & other	1976/83 Ford	£158m	$205m
grants	1979/82 PSA	£59m	$77m
	1979/83 GM Vauxhall	£25m	$33m
	1988/91 Nissan (projection)	£112m	$146m
USA			
Loan Guarantees	1981 Chrysler	$1,500m	$1,500m
Canada			
Grants	1985/86 AMC	$120m	$164m

Source: K. Bhaskar, *State aid to the European motor industry*, East Anglia University, 1984, and press cuttings.
Note: $ amounts calculated at 1985 exchange rates.
Warning: This Table is included for illustrative purposes only and is in no way a comprehensive summary of state aid to the motor industry.

limit wage increases, and rationalize employment structures, which had been held hostage to an anachronistic division of the workplace among different unions. Between 1978 and 1983 employment was reduced by 25,000, product lines were streamlined, and in some plants worker productivity nearly tripled (Dyer, Salter and Webber 1987). As a consequence, in 1983 BL showed its first profit in a decade. Since then the Jaguar division has been privatized, and the remaining Rover enterprise continues to achieve productivity gains.

(2) United States

The bailout of Chrysler involved Federal government loan guarantees of $1.5 billion, in return, however, for concessions from all the major actors (workers, state and local governments, creditors) who stood to lose if Chrysler went bankrupt. Reich estimates the concessions totalled $2.6 billion. Their distribution is shown in Table 3.4.

Table 3.4 Concessions made by other parties as conditions for US government backing of the Chrysler bailout

Concessions Agreed by July: *$2.6 Billion*
Employees (35%)   Lenders (24%)   Sales of Assets (24%)   Other governments (14%)   Suppliers and dealers (3%)

Source: From Reich 1985.

Within two years, Chrysler was again profitable, and in 1983 paid back in full the federally guaranteed loan. Rationalization of the firm, however, involved not only new product lines and joint ventures with foreign producers but also major employment cuts – employment fell from 121,800 in 1979 to 83,900 in 1985 (Reich 1985). These cuts were cushioned by disbursements of Trade Adjustment Assistance (TAA) to workers by the Federal government. Claims by redundant auto workers are considered largely to account for the increase in TAA claimants from 131, 722 to 388,265 over one year, of which former Chrysler workers constituted a significant proportion (Aho and Bayard 1984: 179–80). Workers did not fully recoup the wage cuts and fringe benefit deferments that were conceded as part of the restructuring, although the firm's profits soared to US$2.5 billion in 1984. Similarly, Chrysler's creditors have never been fully compensated for the concessions they made to facilitate the bailout.

(3) Canada

As noted by Trebilcock *et al.* the Chrysler bailout in Canada had a somewhat different character – rather than being contingent on concessions by creditors or restructuring of Chrysler's Canadian operations, the government loan guarantees were instead linked to promises to maintain employment levels (Trebilcock *et al.* 1985: 285–6). Although the $170 million in Canadian loan guarantees were never used, they were an essential condition of Congressional approval of the US bailout (Reich 1985: 183–5).

(4) France

Between 1982 and 1985 the French government provided $800 million in capital injections to Renault – over those three years, the firm accumulated FF25 million in losses and FF60 million in debts (*L'Express* 25 July 1986). After a government policy review in 1984, continued public support to the industry was linked to major reductions in employment and investments in modernization. Renault embarked on a programme of restructuring which involved job cuts amounting to about one third of the workforce, despite militant union opposition. It also sold off to Chrysler in 1987 its troubled American subsidiary, AMC. As a consequence of these changes, over the last three years losses have been reduced from about FF12 billion to about FF5 billion (estimated) in 1986 (*Economist* 11 October 1986) and the firm is expected to break even in 1987.

(e) Steel

The steel crisis of the mid-1970s gave rise to extensive use of subsidies, in addition to trade protection and, in the European Community, temporary cartelization.

(1) France

The nationalization of France's ailing steel giants Usinor and Sacilor in 1983 was the culmination of a long-standing tradition of government intervention in and subsidization of the industry. As Priouet remarks, 'this very special industry linked by its origins with the aristocracy, privileged and protected in its activities, was never fully subjected to the stern laws of competition' (Priouret 1963). The general rate of industry-specific subsidization in the post-war period (until the massive interventions following the crisis of 1974–5) has been estimated as between 25 and 30 per cent of production costs (Goldberg 1986; Hayward 1986). Subsidies included bounties on coking coal for the domestic industry and special, high prices in government contracts, in return for guarantees from the industry to sustain certain employment levels, as well as grants for research and development (Levy 1986). The French Government augmented subsidization in 1967 with a plan to modernize and expand the industry, assuming 30 per cent of the capital costs of renewal, with loans and grants totalling about Cdn$1.5 billion from 1967 to the early 1970s (Hayward 1986).

The result of the plan was little short of disastrous, because its primary focus was on increased output, and as Goldberg notes, 'the new capacities were ready to be put into production when the crisis came in 1974' (Goldberg 1986: 141). The French government had premised the subsidized expansion on increased demand of 1.9–3 per cent between 1974 and 1979, whereas demand actually declined 17 per cent in that period (Hayward 1986). Since 1978, the French government has changed direction, tying subsidization to a plan to increase productivity while reducing employment and output. Between 1978 and 1985 state aid totalled FF60 billion (Hayward 1986). Even Goldberg, who claims that the 1978 programme did result in 'good progress towards productivity' and that 'some of the steel works today come close to Japanese and

German productivity levels', acknowledges that this was achieved at a high price (Goldberg 1986). However, many of the productivity gains came not from actual modernization but rather from reduction of employment from 160,000 in 1975 to 97,000 in 1981. All predictions are that further massive losses will occur in the industry, which the state will have to bear, and that capacity will continue to be reduced (*Economist* 7 April 1986).

(2) Sweden

Demand for Swedish ordinary (i.e. non-specialty) steel fell 30 per cent between 1974 and 1977, which made 'thoroughgoing structural changes inevitable' (Hook 1982). The government facilitated a merger of the three major steel makers and acquired 75 per cent of the shares of the newly formed conglomerate. Between 1978 and 1981, the government had invested S Kr5,500 million in the industry, with a view to modernization. But government intervention was also tied to shrinking of capacity, and the labour force was reduced by about 20 per cent (Hook 1982).

Pointing to this reduced capacity and also to the fact that by 1983 the company was making a profit, the OECD considers the Swedish programme to be a model of how 'governments can act as a (rather) successful private entrepreneur' (OECD 1987a: 28). However, one Swedish economist claims that subsidies actually retarded creation of new jobs elsewhere. By keeping wage rates artificially high, subsidies made it more costly to hire people away from the industry, and led to less growth in the labour supply elsewhere, keeping up wage rates in general (Carlsson 1983).

The government also intervened to aid the specialty steel sector, which constitutes 70 per cent of Swedish steel production and which in contrast to the ordinary steel industry, is largely privately-owned. In 1978 and 1979 the government provided S Kr1.3 billion 'in the form of loans and guarantees for investments needed for restructuring purposes' (Hook 1982), resulting in an industry 'with more up-to-date equipment and a technology capable of meeting demand for higher quality steel for advanced purposes' (Carlsson 1983). Ballance and Sinclair note, however, that one effect of the government-aided streamlining is that the many small firms in the industry are now increasingly competing with one another for a relatively limited national market share, with a consequent increase in the incidence of bankruptcies – an unintended (although not economically undesirable) consequence of public aid (Ballance and Sinclair 1983: 121).

(3) United Kingdom

It is estimated that between 1975 and 1982 the nationalized British Steel Corporation (BSC) absorbed about £7 billion in public funds (Goldberg

1986: 147). Although significant reductions in employment have been achieved as a condition of continued assistance (60,000 positions cut between 1975-80; Goldberg 1986), little of the massive assistance has been channelled into modernization; while Cockerill and Coke see some modest increase in labour productivity, they note that many mills are still plagued by outmoded and inefficient work practices, and severe difficulties with technological innovation (Cockerill and Cole 1986). The OECD view is, however, more sanguine: it estimates that between 1980 and 1983, labour productivity at British Steel rose by more than 40 per cent, 'partly due to widespread plant closures, but also helped by bringing working practices into line with modern technology' (OECD 1985a: 102). In any case, by late 1986, BSC did appear to be breaking even, although this was partly a consequence of continued paper restructuring of assets and liabilities, and further redundancies (which add social costs of unemployment to the subsidy bill the government has already footed).

(4) The United States

In the US, response to the decline of the American steel industry has come primarily in the form of trade protection, not subsidies. Nevertheless, Magaziner and Reich (1982: 253) note that between 1975 and 1979, about $45 million per year was provided in trade adjustment assistance to workers. Also, as of 1980 there were about $393 million in loans and loan guarantees to the industry outstanding (1982: 253). In addition, the Reagan Administration adopted a conscious policy of not fully enforcing environmental regulations, which results in an estimated subsidy of $10 per ton of output (Goldberg 1986: 176).

It is hard to find a recent study for the US steel industry that does not consider some form of subsidized restructuring to be preferable to continued and increasing trade protection (Hirschorn 1986). A summary of proposals for subsidized renewal is contained in Table 3.5.

The industry itself tends to place trade protection, not subsidization for restructuring, at the top of its list of demands from government (Hirschorn 1986). It also complains about the regulatory burden imposed by pollution control standards, but pollution control-driven expenses constitute a small part of total input costs and their reduction would not substantially enhance the international competitiveness of the industry (Crandall 1984; Adams 1985).

(f) Summary evaluation

Since the early 1960s, there has been a dramatic growth in the use of domestic subsidies among OECD nations, initially attributable – at least in part – to trade liberalization, but in the 1970s primarily due to crises

Table 3.5 Summary of proposals for government-assisted adjustment in the US steel industry

Federal option	Government cost	Administrative burden	Bias against small firms	Promotion of new technology	Applies to steelmaking only
Accelerated depreciation					
Jones-Conable	High	Low	Yes	No	No
Certification of necessity	Moderate	Low	Yes	No	Yes
Investment tax credit					
Increase capacity	Moderate	Low	No	No	Yes
Modernization	Moderate	Low	Yes	No	Yes
Innovation	Moderate	High	No	Yes	Yes
Loan guarantee					
Increase capacity	Slight	Moderate	Yes	Yes	Yes
Modernization	Slight	Moderate	Yes	Yes	Yes
Innovation	Moderate	High	Yes	Yes	Yes
Subsidized interest loan					
Increase capacity	Slight	Moderate	No	No	Yes
Modernization	Slight	Moderate	Yes	No	Yes
Innovation	Slight	High	No	Yes	Yes

Source: Office of Technology Assessment; From Hirschorn 1986

of surplus capacity in declining industries (see Table 3.1, p. 88). In almost all countries, in the sectors we have examined, dramatic declines in employment were experienced in the 1970s and 1980s. These declines have occurred even where government subsidy policy has had as its objective the maintenance of jobs and output (e.g. textiles in the UK). It is impossible to estimate how much faster these changes would have occurred, had subsidies not existed.

What has not happened, despite these declines, is the rapid collapse of major industries – and to some extent, this is what subsidy policies have been intended to prevent. Despite the combined impact of recession and rapidly contracting demand in basic industries, the basic fabric of social democracy has remained intact in the European countries and Japan; despite the heavy indebtedness of many of the firms in the declining industries, the stability of the financial system has not been undermined; and of course massive political violence and social upheaval have been avoided. As Wilkes suggests, the economic role of government in ensuring the stability of the system as a whole is an important one: 'unless government acts to maintain stability, business will cease to invest and unions will become hyper-defensive' (Wilks 1984: 456).

This being said, the respective policies of the various countries to the selected sectors have varied widely in costs and benefits. One factor that differs widely between countries is the rapidity and accuracy with which the nature of industrial decline had been understood. In this respect, the Japanese seem to fare the best. In textiles, shipbuilding, and coal, the Japanese have discerned trends of declining comparative advantage quite quickly – whereas some other countries (France is the best example) only recognized much later that declining demand was not a mere temporary aberration, or that the market forces at play could not be reversed by production subsidies and some modernization.

In the previous chapter, we compared relative adjustment trends in various countries under study with respect to the steel, auto, and textile industries. In the case of coal and shipbuilding, the rapidity and extent of adjustment have also varied considerably from country to country. From 1975 coal production in Japan and West Germany declined at an average annual rate of 1.93 and 1.70 per cent respectively, whereas in France the rate of decline in output was almost twice that figure, and in the UK production actually increased by about 1.03 per cent per year over the same period. In the 1975–83 period, the most dramatic declines in employment were realized by Japan and France (averaging over 3 per cent per year), whereas in the case of Germany and the UK, the rate of decrease was less than 1 per cent per year on average (of course, major employment reductions in the British industry occurred in the 1984–6 period, as detailed above). Productivity increases have been highest between 1975 and 1983 for France and the UK (about 3 per cent per year), but relatively small for Germany and Japan. In the case of Japan, however, this reflects the fact that adjustment occurred much earlier – in the 1955–64 period, average annual productivity increases for Japan were over 16 per cent (Trebilcock 1986).

In the case of shipbuilding, the greatest declines in capacity have been realized in the 1975–85 period by countries that have adopted strategies of exit such as the US, Sweden, Australia and Japan. The case of the US is the most dramatic of all, with output falling from 5.5 million GRT in 1974 to 450,000 GRT in 1985 (OECD 1987b). Japanese output fell from 14.75 million GRT in 1973 to 6.998 million in 1984, and Swedish output declined from 2.29 million GRT to 216,000 over the same period. Even, however, countries which have resisted the exit option nevertheless have had to reduce output substantially. In France, for example, output fell from 1.17 million GRT in 1973 to 196,000 in 1984, not quite as dramatic a reduction as in Sweden, for instance, but nevertheless massive (OECD 1987b). These figures, however, do not tell the full story: in France, employment fell at a much slower rate than output (from 32,500 workers in 1976 to 17,700 in 1985) whereas in Sweden employment declined almost as dramatically as output (from 23,600 workers in 1976 to 3,776 in 1985). This suggests that exit-resisting subsidy strategies are much more successful at maintaining employment than output.

Our study of industrial subsidies confirms the importance of exit subsidies to labour in facilitating efficient adjustment (a phenomenon which we examine in depth in the next chapter). In some instances, governments have learned to use subsidization as a means of 'buying off' the political demand for policies which resist market changes – whereas previously they had used subsidies as an instrument of such resistance. Clear examples of this transformation of subsidy strategy are Swedish steel and shipbuilding policies and the policies of the French and British governments towards their nationalized auto industries. However, in other sectors, market resisting subsidization has persisted; some instances are French, British, and Swedish textiles, and French coal and steel. Notably, these costly market-resisting policies have not been able to prevent significant declines in employment and output in the industries concerned. With the occasional exception (shipbuilding in Sweden and the US: recently, coal in Japan), governments while recognizing the need to adjust have nevertheless avoided adopting strategies of complete exit which accept a permanent, decisive loss of comparative advantage. Instead, they have preferred at enormous cost, to fund modernization and specialization of industries, with the hope of restoring competitivneess by technological innovation and exploitation of market niches. In some instances, such policies, although very costly, have led to renewed competitiveness in world markets (e.g. steel in Sweden). In others (particularly the textile industry) massive gains in productivity (i.e. in the US and Germany), have made industries in some countries competitive, but only within the current framework of trade protection against NIC producers (the MFA).

(g) Subsidies and the normative goals of adjustment policy

The above analysis of the costs and benefits of subsidy instruments has significant implications for the relative capacity of these instruments to vindicate the public values which purport to justify them.

From a utilitarian perspective, stay-oriented production subsidies are the least desirable subsidy instrument as they have, generally speaking, retarded re-allocation of resources to more efficient uses within domestic economies, while at the same time they have only postponed, not prevented, the final costs of large-scale labour-shedding in declining industries. From a social contractarian perspective, these subsidies are problematic as they have, in the case of many of the sectors concerned, benefited relatively advantaged, skilled industrial workers, and not the least advantaged. If anything, this may have impeded job creation elsewhere in the economy, hence leading to higher unemployment, often among relatively uneducated young people.

From a communitarian perspective, production subsidies have served undoubtedly to postpone community disruption from large-scale job losses, but having come later rather than sooner in many instances these disruptions have been all the more traumatic and severe.

Subsidies for rationalization and modernization have in some instances been linked to re-establishment of competitiveness in certain sectors, but much of the gain to productivity has been a direct consequence of labour-shedding – hence, such subsidies have provided rents to firms, while in the end actually encouraging the job losses which, according to all three ethical perspectives, it would be their major virtue to forestall. Although it might be argued that even more jobs would have been lost had the firms in question been allowed to collapse under competitive pressure, this begs the question as to why (as in the case with German textiles) those firms would not have rationalized without subsidies. In part, the answer may be that the expectations of government assistance have provided incentives for firms not to rationalize on their own, with attendant higher social costs from the delay. These perverse effects are not justifiable from any of the three ethical perspectives, and are the product of rent-seeking behaviour by firms.

Exit-oriented subsidies, from a utilitarian perspective, are the most justifiable, as they appear to encourage rapid reallocation of resources in accordance with shifts in comparative advantage. However, it must be observed that since firms hold out for government assistance to do what the market directs them to do without such assistance, even exit-oriented subsidies may retard adjustment.

In the Japanese context, however, such subsidies appear to in fact have played a role in allowing firms themselves to manage worker dislocation costs of exit and have been linked to cartelization aimed at spreading the cost of exit among all the firms in a given sector. Since these efforts reduce the suddenness and severity of disruptions to workers and communities, they would appear to be justified from both a social contractarian distributive justice perspective and a communitarian perspective. Communitarians would particularly welcome exit subsidies which facilitate conversion of resources to other uses within the same community (e.g. Sweden's subsidized conversion of shipyards to auto-parts plants). Such measures do not merely retard disruption to the community, but actually seek to insure its future economic vitality.

In sum, given their actual effects, from all three ethical perspectives, both production and rationalization subsidies have questionable legitimacy, whereas some exit-oriented subsidy instruments display attractive normative properties.

IV. The political determinants of subsidization and the prospects for international discipline of subsidies

The GATT rules on subsidies which emerged from the Tokyo Round of trade negotiations represent the principal, legally binding internationally agreed constraints on subsidization. On the one hand, almost all of the kinds of subsidies which governments use as a response to industrial decline – regional aids, employment maintenance, R&D, exit and restructuring subsidies – are recognized in Article 11 of the GATT Subsidies Code. The article states that the signatories 'do not intend to restrict the right of signatories to use such subsidies to achieve . . . important policy objectives'. On the other hand, the Code provides remedies against the use of subsidies, without regard to their benefit or importance to the subsidizing country.

The remedy provided by Track I of the Code is the imposition, under Article 6 of the GATT, of countervailing duties to counter subsidization of the imported product. This remedy is available only against injury to the importing country's domestic industry – thus, for example, if country A and country B both export a product to country C, and A subsidizes its exports, B would not have a Track I remedy against A, even though the subsidization injured B's trade with C.

Track II, by contrast, provides a procedure for reference of a dispute between trading partners concerning subsidization to a GATT committee, which may order 'appropriate measures' as a remedy. Unlike Track I, Track II applies to purely domestic subsidies as well, and also to the injury of trade with a third country (the situation between A, B, and

C described above). Use of Track II is rare, and it is questionable whether Track II action ever resulted in a substantive limitation on a subsidy policy. While the GATT rules themselves provide no clue as to how to balance the legitimacy of domestic subsidization to achieve important policy goals against the negative impact on other countries' trade, Track I allows a unilateral determination that a subsidy is countervailable, and of course unilateral remedy. Only export subsidies are explicitly prohibited by the GATT Subsidies Code.

The main effect of GATT subsidies rules has been to encourage trade retaliation against subsidies which the injured states themselves find illegitimate. This retaliation has been exercised largely by the US, where domestic trade laws provided for countervailing duties (CVDs) against subsidized imports long before the existence of the GATT Code. Between 1980 and 1984, the US initiated 123 CVD actions, as compared to 8 by Canada, 6 by the European Community, and 1 by Japan (Hufbauer and Erb 1984: 16). There is little evidence that use of CVD's has provided any deterrent against subsidization. What it has done is to fuel the growing political market for protection in the US. As Horlick, Quick and Vermulst remark, 'the Subsidies Code enhances reactions against all kinds of assistance to industries, reactions which can be used as important barriers, particularly in times of high dollar rates, economic recession or high trade deficits' (Horlick, Quick and Vermulst 1986: 1).

The argument that CVDs correct or neutralize the distortion of trade caused by subsidies is highly questionable. For one thing, it is very unclear which domestic subsidies cause a distortion. As Barcelo argues, subsidies which correct market distortions or address externalities are treated no differently under the CVD rules than any others (Barcelo 1977). Secondly, subsidization often occurs due to national values and preferences for certain kinds of government intervention; it is unclear why these values and preferences should not simply be considered as another aspect of comparative advantage or disadvantage. Most importantly, responding to a domestic subsidy by a tariff is very likely to reduce net economic welfare. Consider the following example evoked by Barcelo:

> even if we start with an assumption that the wage subsidy is inefficient within Utopia, it does not follow that the United States would improve its own efficiency (expand its consumption possibilities) by countervailing against subsidized Utopian shoes. An inefficient subsidy in Utopia could of course have negative consequences for the United States. The misallocation of resources to shoe production in Utopia would generate higher costs and higher prices for some other Utopian product,, for example, widgets. If the United States is an importer of Utopian widgets, it will be hurt by the higher widget prices. But is

a countervailing duty the proper remedy for such harm? If the new American duty does not induce Utopia to abandon its wage subsidy, American consumers and intermediate producers will have the worst of both worlds: higher prices for Utopian widgets and higher prices for Utopian shoes.

(Barcelo 1980: 278).

An examination of the use of CVDs under US trade law discloses that even though the process used is adjudicative and supposedly impartial, decisions tend to reflect ideological bias much more than any well-defined economic logic. For example, many tax concessions are exempted from the definition of countervailable subsidies, because the approach is to consider them to actually reduce rather than increase government intervention. Yet in terms of economic theory it makes no difference whether government reduces the costs of an industry or firm by a benefit or relief from a burden. This logic has to some extent become apparent to the present US Administration, whose tax reform proposals recognize firm and industry-specific tax relief as wasteful subsidies, and seek their elimination in favour of lower overall rates of taxation (Howse et al. 1990). Yet at the same time, the Administration has taken up regulatory relief, i.e. from pollution control standards, as a response to declining industries without considering it as a production subsidy.

Nor, despite its major effects on employment and output in manufacturing, is defence spending deemed to contain an element of subsidization, but as Markusen argues, 'Military spending operates as a disguised sectoral policy in two important ways. First, it acts as an intermediate-run stimulant, filtered predominantly through the manufacturing portion of the economy. Second, it serves as a long-term planning strategy, both by encouraging innovation in certain product lines and by bolstering the balance of payments by a distinctive specialization in arms trade' (Markusen 1985: 73).

The recent softwood lumber case is indicative of a trend in US trade policy to consider as subsidization the setting of resource rents at rates below those which would maximize short term profit for the government owner. However, as a Committee of the American Bar Association has pointed out, this not only assumes that the appropriate behaviour of government with respect to resource management is that of a private profit-maximizing company, but that also 'only one market strategy is available to a private company – that of maximizing short term profits' (American Bar Association 1986: 299).

In the British Steel case, US steel producers sought CVDs on British steel imports, claiming that both equity injections by the British government and labour adjustment assistance provided to help the industry reduce employment and capacity, were injurious subsidies. The American

International Trade Court held that 'to the extent in any year that the government realized a rate of return on its equity investment in the British Steel Corporation which was less than the average rate of return on equity investment for the country as a whole its equity infusion is considered to confer a subsidy' (605 F Supp. 286 (1985) at 291). This of course assumes that a private, purely market-driven investor would never put money into company that did not realize every year at least the average rate of return – an economically irrational caricature of market economies where many investments are made with the expectation that after perhaps several years of losses a compensating rate of return will be realized.

In recent literature on subsidies in international trade, it has become fashionable to talk of the need to develop a three-way taxonomy of subsidies: black (red), grey (yellow) and white (green), identifying subsidies that are unqualifiedly bad (black), those that may or may not be bad, but are in any event legitimately contentious (grey), and those that are wholly benign (white). However, these taxonomies are, in many respects, problematic.

Conventional understanding has it that pure export subsidies (cases where a government subsidizes goods for export but not for domestic consumption) are the most objectionable (trade-distorting) forms of subsidies and provide the strongest case for both international and domestic sanctions (countervail). This understanding is reflected in Track I of the Tokyo Round GATT Subsidies Code.

While it may be true that such subsidies represent a foolish misallocation of resources by the subsidizing state (in effect giving away its goods to foreigners below cost), and may distort the efficient global allocation of resources (e.g. by squeezing out more efficient third country producers from the importing country's market), why the importing country, in terms of its own economic welfare, should have the slightest reason for objection has remained as large an economic (but not necessarily political) mystery as why importing countries should object to dumped (low-priced) imports. In the case of subsidized imports, the importing country should instead express its gratitude to the subsidizing country, noting only its regret that the subsidies are not larger and timeless. This is subject to the narrow exception of predatory subsidization, which if it exists, should be dealt with, along with predatory dumping, under domestic anti-trust laws relating to predation. In addition, to the extent that export subsidies undermine pre-existing tariffs bound by agreement, the appropriate response would seem to be a complaint of nullification or impairment of an obligation or benefit under Article XXIII of the GATT.

White subsidies are seen as wholly benign and as not justifying either international or unilateral sanctions. Conventionally, generally available subsidies, because they do not disproportionately influence the price of particular categories of goods, are not seen as trade-distorting with respect to either imports or exports. Hence, general social, educational and infrastructure expenditures would widely be viewed as 'white' subsidies. This view reflects in part a rather static conception of comparative advantage – clearly many developed economies owe a significant part of their international comparative advantage to social investments in health, education, law and order, basic research, and physical infrastructure. Most modern international trade theorists accept that comparative advantage is a dynamic concept and is not wholly exogenously determined. In many cases of generally available subsidies, public goods characteristics may justify the subsidies on efficiency grounds. Some selective subsidies may also be able to find support on similar grounds: for example, subsidies to R&D in certain industries to offset positive externalities, subsidies for pollution abatement in certain industries to respond to negative externalities. However, generally available subsidies may be presumptively more benign than selective subsidies, because they are less likely to be the product of special interest group rent-seeking.

It may also be the case that generally available subsidies are reflected more fully in exchange rate adjustments than selective or targeted subsidies, but in an international environment where exchange rates are determined increasingly by international capital flows rather than goods flows, it is not clear how robust this assumption is, or when one can be confident that generally available subsidies have induced appropriate exchange rate adjustments but more selective subsidies have not.

In any event, setting aside the exchange rate issue, it is clear that even though generally available subsidies may well substantially shape international comparative advantage, it would be inconceivable that any domestic government would accept bilateral or multilateral constraints on its sovereign capacity to pursue such basic policies of the modern democratic state or accept that such policies should be countervailable. This concern is reflected in the highly ambivalent language of Track II of the Tokyo Round GATT Subsidies Code. This view also necessarily implies that we no longer have any easy touchstone for what subsidies should or should not be objectionable: 'black' subsidies seem wholly unobjectionable, on economic welfare grounds, to importing countries; 'white' subsidies should properly be unobjectionable, on political sovereignty grounds, sometimes on public goods grounds, and to the extent that they make our exports to foreign markets cheaper, then also in terms of the net economic welfare effects on the importing country (as in the case of subsidized exports).

Grey subsidies appear to fall into two principal sub-categories. The first category, selective domestic subsidies with export spill-overs, subsidizes selective domestic producers, and hence reduces the prices faced by consumers of their products in both domestic and export markets (i.e. the subsidies are not confined to goods sold and consumed in foreign markets).

113

In such cases, the analysis, on economic grounds, is the same as for 'black' subsidies. Net economic welfare in the foreign market is increased by the subsidies and hence there is no conceivable domestic economic justification for unilateral countervailing duty actions. To the extent that a third country's exports are being squeezed by the subsidies, then it should, as in the case of 'black' subsidies, have a right of complaint to a GATT Panel, which may result in a basis for a demand for compensation, or a right of retaliation (but, obviously, not countervail, since the subsidized products are not entering the third country's markets).

With respect to the second category, selective domestic subsidies having the intent or effect of squeezing out imports, the conceptual problem is how to distinguish such subsidies from 'white' subsidies, given that all of them are likely to shape comparative advantage in some degree or another. In this case, countervail is, by its nature, not available – the subsidized goods are being consumed domestically in preference to foreign imports as a result of the subsidies. However, assuming we can solve the conceptual question, some sanctions may be necessary in such cases. Domestic subsidies can be designed to replicate the effect of a tariff, and to the extent that a country has agreed to lower or eliminate its tariffs on given products, the introduction of such subsidies may be a nullification or impairment of a benefit conferred or obligation undertaken by prior agreement. Presumably, Article XXIII of the GATT can be invoked to make such determinations, and, in appropriate cases, direct compensation or authorize retaliation.

In Chapter 6, these concerns are addressed at greater length as we present detailed proposals for reform of the GATT approach to subsidies and countervailing duties, advocating the creation of an institutional framework for negotiated, reciprocal reductions in trade-injurious subsidies.

Chapter four

Labour market adjustment policies

I. Introduction: economic change and employment

Economic change proceeds through both the destruction and creation of jobs. Although the net effect of economic adjustment is to increase aggregate national welfare, it is also clear that change creates losers. In the past two decades economic change has been a discontinuous process in which employment in growth sectors has not necessarily compensated for job losses in the contracting ones. The creation of new jobs has not always kept pace with the decline of jobs. This is especially a problem when the displacement process derives from rapid external shocks. New jobs may also require different skills or may occur in different locations from the old ones. Beyond these imbalances in the process of change, labour adjustment problems have been aggravated by the regional concentration of many declining industries, as well as by the poor overall economic performance that has troubled many OECD countries. Positive adjustment involves efforts to encourage the shift of labour to activities in line with their comparative advantage and relative prices reflecting international competitive developments (OECD 1983a: 9). The focus of this chapter is on the ways in which political decision makers in industrialized countries have used labour market policies in dealing with the pressures of economic change. We will describe the major types of labour market policy instruments and evaluate them against economic, ethical and political perspectives. Then we will profile and compare the principal labour market adjustment strategies followed in Australia, the UK, Canada, France, Japan, Sweden, the US and West Germany. In the final section we will attempt to identify those labour market policies which allow governments to cushion the impacts of change while promoting adjustment and growth.

Pressures for change come from various sources including trade liberalization, technological developments, shifts in demand and alterations in the international patterns of competition. For the most part there are continuous labour adjustments as businesses go through a life cycle.

115

Workforce displacements at any one time may seem large but they are often offset by the number of new jobs in expanding firms. However, throughout the 1970s and into the 1980s, in the midst of the overall increase in unemployment, massive labour shedding has taken place in many hard-hit industries. For example, between 1972 and 1980, 400,000 jobs in the steel industry were lost in the OECD nations. This represented some 20 per cent of employment in the steel industry (OECD 1982a). From 1973 to 1981, Germany, France and the UK lost about one-third of their 1973 textile labour force, while in the US the labour shrinkage in textiles for the same period was almost one-fifth (Shepherd 1983: 31). In Japan between 1973 and 1980, employment in the world's largest ship-building industry dropped from 274,000 to 157,000 (McKersie and Sengenberger 1982). During the severe slump in the auto industry from 1978 to 1980 in the US, an estimated 217,000 permanent jobs were lost. Table 4.1 shows the magnitude of the curtailment of production and employment in several sectors.

Adjustment occurs when workers who lose their jobs because of a firm's decline move to other firms that are expanding. To the extent that new jobs are not immediately available, or are not seen to be available, potential losers have often sought to resist economic change and to shield themselves from the costs of change. Major employment dislocations that inflict economic and social damage upon workers, firms and communities have made labour adjustment a crucial political issue. The losers from change have looked to government to cushion them from the negative consequences of the market economy or they have resisted the change itself.

(a) Costs of adjustment

Adjustment and attendant economic growth are not without cost. It is the uneven distribution as well as the magnitude of adjustment costs that generate demands to retard market processes. Private adjustment costs are the difference between the worker's situation before the lay-off and income after job separation. These costs include not only temporary and permanent income losses but also asset losses and the psychological impact of job loss (Hufbauer and Rosen 1986: 31).

Studies of displaced workers have provided some estimates of adjustment costs of laying off workers in industries under severe competitive pressures. Table 4.2 compares the findings of recent Canadian research on the adjustment costs for the average worker. Each of these studies have found that the costs are greater for older workers. They also point to the importance of macro-economic conditions for determining the duration of unemployment and hence adjustment costs (Canada, Labour Force Tracking 1979; Glenday *et al.* 1982). Although

Table 4.1 Changes in production and employment in selected industries and countries: two-year rate change between 1980 and 1982

		Country					
Industry	*Indicator*	*US*	*Japan*	*Sweden*	*W Germany*	*France*	*UK*
Textiles	Production	− 9.7	− 2.7	− 6.4	− 9.7	− 8.0	−12.5
	Employment	−13.2	− 3.5	−20.5	−16.1	− 9.5	−19.5
Iron and steel	Production	−33.3	− 9.6	− 4.2	−14.8	−16.4	+ 6.0
	Employment	−26.1	− 3.6	−12.8	− 9.2	− 9.2	−28.4
Shipbuilding and repairing	Production	− 8.3	+ 5.1	+ 2.1	+ 5.1	n.a.	+13.0
	Employment	− 8.2	− 2.0	−14.7	+ 2.0	+ 4.2	− 8.0
Motor vehicles	Production	− 7.4	− 2.3	n.a.	+ 4.1	−10.7	− 4.6
	Employment	− 9.6	+ 7.2	− 2.0	− 2.5	− 9.6	−26.4

Source: R.A. Jeness *Positive Adjustment in Manpower and Social Policies* (1984).
n.a. = not available

Table 4.2 The private and social costs of adjustment

Study	Site	Sectors	Private income losses per worker	Social or economic costs
Jenkins *et al.* 1978	Ontario and Quebec (1971)	Textiles	$1,294 – $4,895[+] (over 3 yr period)	$4,839 –$5,387[+] (over 5 yr period)
Canadian Lab. Force Tracking Study 1979	Nova Scotia, New Brunswick, Ontario, Quebec, Montreal (1977)	Textiles and Clothing	$2,100* (3 yr period)	$15,440* (3 yr period)
		Electronics	$4,800* (3 yr period)	$19,170* (3 yr period)
Alam 1985	Ontario	Footwear	$1,623[•] (gain over 5 yr period)	$1,749[•] (gain over 5 yr period)
	Quebec (1983)		$3,416.81[•] (gain over 5 yr period)	$699[•] (gain over 5 yr period)

Notes:
+ 1971 dollars.
* 1977 dollars.
• 1981 dollars.

the economic gains associated with deferring lay-offs may in some cases appear to be substantial, these gains must be weighed against the costs to consumers and taxpayers of postponing lay-offs by means of tariffs, quotas, and subsidies. The enormous costs per job saved of these measures have been described in Chapters 2 and 3.

Glenday, Jenkins and Evans (1982) give an example of the calculus in heavily protected industries such as textiles and clothing:

> The economic benefits of delaying the layoff of an average vulnerable job in the Sherbrooke region, is at most 36 per cent of a worker's present wage. With 1978 yearly wages estimated at about $11,200, the benefits of maintaining this job over 5 years equals approximately $20,000 in present value terms. The economic cost of protecting such a job in the clothing sector for 5 years by way of trade restrictions amounts to approximately $30,400 in present value terms. Protecting employment by imposing trade restrictions therefore means a net loss to the economy of some $10,400 per job.
>
> (Glenday, Jenkins and Evans 1982: 6)

Pearson and Salembier (1983) summarize the North American research on labour adjustment costs. Findings from these studies are an important starting point for analysing government intervention in labour markets:

- Adjustment costs differ considerably by industry.
- Higher adjustment costs are borne by older, more skilled, and higher-wage workers.
- The general level of economic activity is important in determining the duration of unemployment and the subsequence wage, both of which in turn strongly influence adjustment costs.
- The majority of US workers receiving Trade Adjustment Assistance (TAA) benefits experienced temporary unemployment and were recalled to their old jobs.
- There was a major difference in adjustment costs to workers who returned to their initial jobs as compared to those who did not.
- Workers who were not recalled suffered large real earnings losses that were not offset by TAA and UI benefits (Pearson and Salembier 1983: 46–47)

(b) Three perspectives on policy

The dilemma for governments in industrialized nations is how to encourage (or at least not hinder) the continual resource reallocation process that is crucial to economic growth while reconciling the dictates of economic efficiency with other widely held values including redistributive justice, job stability and community preservation. Political reality gives greater focus to the problem as those adversely affected may seek to resist changes and to veto socially beneficial policies. In other words, for government policy makers the problem is how to balance the need for economic efficiency with some sharing of the burdens and costs of change.

From an economic perspective, the objective is the relatively simple notion of allocative efficiency, which calls for the unfettered movement of resources to higher valued uses. Within this framework, market failures provide the basic rationale for government intervention. Market failures derived from the inability of the labour market to fully internalize the costs and benefits of adjustment impede displaced workers from moving on to jobs in growing sectors. The most significant failures within the labour market include: (i) *imperfect and asymmetric information* about future changes in patterns of comparative advantage and subsequent employment opportunities which makes it difficult for employees to devise their own adjustment and/or diversification strategies; (ii) *externalities in the accumulation of human capital* which may mean that employers underinvest in worker training because the benefits of that training can be appropriated by other employers. Workers themselves may be unable to afford the direct opportunity costs of training. Moreover, employers have an incentive to provide specific training which is less transferable to another employment setting. From the point of view of societal adjustment, this is the least desirable form of human capital (Wonnacott and Hill 1987: 25), and (iii) *congestion* in the labour market may mean that if there are mass lay-offs each worker's search efforts increase the search costs of other workers; these costs are external to workers and employers in the declining firm. In making a decision whether to relocate in such situations, a worker will value the move less than its value to society (Gunderson 1985; Saunders 1984; Richardson 1982; Trebilcock *et al.* 1985).

Distributional effects rather than adverse allocative efficiency consequences are at the heart of the utilitarian and Kantian social contractarian ethical rationales for intervention in the labour market. The utilitarian paradigm in general suggests directions similar to neo-classical economics. However, utilitarians evaluating claims for compensation will consider private as well as social costs. Besides these costs, utilitarian policy makers may wish to take account of individual disutilities arising from demoralization due to uncertainty and disaffection within the political system (Trebilcock 1985a: 18).

A Kantian social contractarian perspective emphasizes a more clearly redistributive order. The social contract framework, like the utilitarian, dictates compensation for private losses due to change but in the social contract case, the compensatory principle is directed specifically toward the least well-off members of society. Thus within the Rawlsian (1971) framework, all displaced workers are not necessarily to be aided. Compensatory adjustment policy is to be directed toward those in society who are least advantaged.

The third of the mainstream ethical paradigms, communitarianism, derives from individual ties to particular communities rather than distributive claims. The ethical claims generated by communitarianism focus on stability and the preservation of significant attachments to the extended family, community and region.

The political perspective must include both allocative efficiency and distributional concerns. No decision-maker has the objective of decreasing national welfare; therefore, the efficient functioning of the market for human capital must be a primary consideration (Blais 1986a). However, it is also through the political system that industrialized societies typically address equity concerns and operationalize ethical objectives. Political feasibility entails more than just efficiency and equity. The logic of the political system may make some distributional concerns more important than others and some demands more salient than others to policy makers (Trebilcock *et al.* 1985). Job losses are immediate and highly visible. The costs are concentrated. The diffused long term benefits of new jobs or even the long-term costs of opportunities that will never emerge due to earlier failures to adjust, are less conducive to political mobilization. Such benefits may be incapable of offsetting the concerns of those who are immediately threatened and who will try to block change. In contrast to the politics of trade policy in which it is possible for the aggregate or consumer interest to be effectively bolstered by mobilized, organized anti-protectionist interests that stand to lose from trade protection measures (Destler and Odell 1987), there is much less likelihood of mobilizing effective constituencies or groups congruent with the consumer interest in efficient labour market adjustment. Pressures to assist losers from change and possibly to retard adjustment may also derive from the range of moral values within society. Demands to reconcile desires for economic growth with society's moral concerns make labour market issues a critical problem for the political economy.

In summary, the issue of labour adjustment highlights the potential conflicts among policy objectives. It raises questions regarding the basic efficiency goal of promoting growth through the reallocation of resources. As Gunderson (1985) points out, perfectly functioning markets can generate efficiency but not necessarily equity. The political system must however deal with both allocative efficiency and distributional consequences. Moreover, regardless of fairness considerations, a free market approach to problems of decline is seldom politically feasible. Losers from change can and do turn to the political system for assistance (Chandler 1985). Recognizing the multiple and often competing objectives of labour market adjustment is an important starting point in analysing the range of policies adopted by the OECD countries. The next section of this chapter reviews the various programmes and policies that have comprised the labour market strategies of industrialized nations. For purposes of this overview we concentrate primarily on labour market programmes which involve public expenditures.

II. The spectrum of labour adjustment policies

In their efforts to cope with declining sectors and increasing rates of unemployment, all OECD nations have turned to some instruments of labour market adjustment. Traditionally, unemployment insurance, employment centres and relief work were the main forms of assistance to labour. In the 1960s, training and mobility subsidies were typically provided to facilitate employment. In the 1970s job maintenance and job creation became important elements in many governments' initial reactions to the economic downturn. At that time the difficulties were perceived to be only temporary or cyclical fall-offs in demand. Often government responses were defensive bridging measures that sought to shield the labour market either through job retention measures or temporary alternative employment for those who had lost their jobs. However, as it gradually became apparent that the performance problems of the early 1970s were not temporary, stop-gap measures of job preservation and public sector employment became less attractive. As the recession continued and the decline seemed deeper and more permanent, problems began to be viewed as possibly structural rather than cyclical. Rising budgetary deficits, restraints on social welfare expenditures and the increasing ineffectiveness of macro-economic stabilization policies further complicated government efforts to cope with the ongoing economic changes. By the 1980s all of the industrialized states have adopted a range of measures to address the employment implications of economic decline.

As in the case of the trade and subsidy instruments described in the two previous chapters, manpower policies encompass a wide spectrum of options. They range from measures that preserve the stay option to programmes that enhance workers' exit option. Job retention measures shield workers from market signals. These measures preserve threatened jobs and are generally justified as temporary expedients in anticipation of a turn around in the economy or in the fortunes of a particular sector or firm. In some cases (Japan and West Germany are two important examples), enhanced exit options (e.g. early retirement) are provided for some workers in order to preserve the jobs of core labour market groups. Compensation schemes may be designed to encourage stay or to facilitate exit. The scope, level and conditionality of income support programmes determine the extent to which they emphasize the re-employment and hence adjustment. Compensation to displaced workers which provides income support but no work incentives or inducements to adjust is a form of passive labour policy which may be viewed as reinforcing the stay option. For example, US experience with Trade Adjustment Assistance (TAA) indicates that funds were used primarily to maintain workers experiencing temporary lay-offs. Some 75 per cent of the workers receiving assistance under the TAA returned to their old jobs (Hufbauer and Rosen 1986; Lawrence and Litan 1985).

Next on the stay-exit policy continuum are measures that are directed toward assisting workers to obtain new employment by enhancing their search for alternative employment. These programmes typically mean providing adjustment services, for example, better job market information, matching unemployed workers to available jobs, and enhancing geographic mobility and occupational training or retraining.

Policies closer to the exit end of the spectrum focus on new employment and job creation in the private and public sectors. For descriptive purposes we have arrayed the variety of government manpower and employment programmes so that the policies range from those preserving workers in their existing jobs to those enhancing the ability of labour to exit and/or obtain new employment. Within each type the modalities may differ from nation to nation or over time within the same country. In some instances the assistance, whether it be to preserve employment or to provide alternatives, is available to all workers. In other cases the assistance is more narrowly targeted.

STAY
    Direct wage subsidies to defer redundancies
    Output subsidies
    In-house training subsidies
    Short-time work
    Employee buy-outs
    Unemployment compensation
    Enhanced compensation
    Information and placement services
    Plant closing laws
    Training assistance
    Mobility assistance
    Early retirement
    Marginal wage subsidies for new private sector jobs
    Public sector employment
EXIT

(a) Maintaining jobs

Policies at the 'stay' end of the spectrum are directed toward preventing economic dislocation by encouraging employment continuity. As part of what Robertson (1986: 278) refers to as a 'guardian' labour market strategy, governments have erected barriers to block some of the effects of competition in labour markets. In nations like West Germany, powerful trade unions have been able to negotiate, on an enterprise basis, safeguards guaranteeing job security (Bosch 1985).

The policy tools depicted on the continuum go beyond establishing procedures facilitating the management of redundancies. The 'stay' policies entail government preservation of employment through some form of direct support programme. These measures to maintain jobs are directed primarily toward cyclical changes in labour demand. Wage and in-house training subsidies to avert redundancies, stockpiling subsidies, as well as short-time subsidies were initial and presumably temporary responses to the widespread economic difficulties in the early 1970s. Subsidized maintenance of employment was introduced as a means for carrying workers over a temporary economic slow down in preference to relying solely on income maintenance. Job preservation measures have entailed several forms of government intervention including: (a) direct wage subsidies; (b) subsidies for output; (c) subsidies for in-house training; (d) short-time work, and (e) facilitating employee buy-outs.

(1) Direct wage subsidies

Government funding to retain workers during declines in the demand for labour has been used in Japan to sustain the permanent employment system during recent periods of relative slow growth and structural adjustment (Rohlen 1979). Under the *Employment Insurance Law* (1975), the Japanese government paid up to two-thirds of the wage bill for excess labour. When this subsidy scheme became incorporated into the Employment Stabilization Service (1977), its emphasis shifted to maintaining employment while a firm is undergoing structural change rather than as an anti-depression tool. Qualifying industries are given a subsidy to defray their payments to temporarily furloughed workers. It is estimated that had even one-quarter of the workers on subsidized furloughs joined the unemployed, Japan's rate of unemployment in the late 1970s would have more than doubled (Rohlen 1979: 247).

In the UK, direct wage subsidies have been used primarily in the textile, clothing and footwear industries to encourage firms to defer redundancies. The Temporary Employment Subsidy (TES) provided a 20 per cent subsidy for up to eighteen months for a worker who would

Labour market adjustment policies

otherwise be laid off. At its height the programme supported some 200,000 workers (OECD 1982a). This direct support of production to prevent redundancies in the UK's textile, clothing and footwear industries was viewed by other European community countries as 'the export of unemployment' and a violation of the Common Market Treaty. Eventually the TES was replaced by short-time measures.

In Sweden temporary employment subsidies were provided for older workers in clothing and textile companies, the pulp and paper industry and for employees of companies that are 'crucial to a local labour market' (Johanneson and Schmidt 1980).

(2) Subsidies for output

Public programmes that promote the build up of inventories during slack periods have also been used temporarily to preserve employment. Sweden has provided the main example of such assistance. The government provides subsidies to local government for purchases from Swedish manufacturers located in areas with high unemployment. As part of efforts to aid the shipbuilding sector, Sweden provided extensive subsidies for firms to build up their inventories during the recessionary environment of the 1970s. The steel industry as well as pulp and paper also received subsidies for inventory build up. Unfortunately the slump in the economy proved to be more than temporary, and without increased demand the stockpiles created a new problem of over-capacity (Ginsburg 1983).

Bailouts of failing firms may also be considered under the rubric of government intervention to preserve employment. Although some nations, namely Canada and the UK, have been more likely to use this instrument, virtually all of the nations in our survey have at some time acted to 'save jobs' by propping up a failing firm. It may be feared that the large number of displaced workers from the firm will create congestion externalities for other workers. This may occur where mass lay-offs are involved in communities dominated by the failing firm, where the workers are fairly homogeneous in their skills, where laid off workers are likely to enter the local pool of job seekers, and where the level of unemployment is already high (Trebilcock 1985a: 12).

In most cases the bailouts have been concentrated in declining industries. For example, although Germany has typically rejected requests for bailout aid, it has provided aid to the Krupp conglomerate employing some 110,000 workers in the Ruhr coal and steel district. More recently the German government provided rescue aid to AEG Telefunken, the giant electronics firm that employs 140,000 workers and operates many plants in high unemployment regions (Trebilcock *et al.* 1985: Chap. 9). French governments have seen fit to provide bailouts aid to large

125

firms in such distressed industries as autos, steel, textiles and ship-building. Despite Japan's general pro-adjustment orientation, it too has made limited use of bail-outs in some declining industries (Hills 1983; Ramseyer 1981). Although subsidized employment maintenance within a failing firm may sometimes be less costly to society than firm failure and indeed may be less costly than alternative forms of social relief, the bailout has two significant drawbacks. The circumstances at best justify only temporary subsidies yet there is little to ensure that the assistance does not perpetuate a continuing dependence on government support. Furthermore, while the bailout may provide relief for workers hard hit by economic change, the assistance does nothing to induce worker adjustment through training or mobility (Trebilcock *et al.* 1985).

(3) Subsidies for in-house training of redundant workers

The Swedish *Employment Maintenance and Training Subsidy* (1974) provides funding to keep redundant workers in the firm. The in-plant training subsidy encourages companies to use slack business periods for worker training. During the 1970s some 5 per cent of Sweden's work force spent time in in-plant training programmes (Ginsburg 1983: 134).

Japan has also made extensive use of training subsidies as a way of preserving the employment of redundant workers. Under the 1978 (renewed in 1983) *Law for Temporary Measures for the Unemployed in the Designated Depressed Industries* the Ministry of Labour reimburses firms for most of the retraining expenses incurred when dealing with permanent workers. Also within the context of Japan's internal labour market the Ministry of Labour will reimburse firms for their relocation expenses when they transfer their permanent employees. Indeed, worker transfers proved to be an important vehicle for adjustment when Japan's steel, shipbuilding and other heavy industries were faced with the necessity of cutting labour costs. The larger and more diversified companies were able to transfer their permanent workers to other companies in the 'group'. The flow of workers from the ailing steel and shipbuilding industries to auto makers was the most common pattern (Kikkawa 1983; Ramseyer 1981).

(4) Short-time work

Partial subsidies to compensate workers for lost earnings during abbreviated work hours have been used in several European countries. Short-time work allows employers to keep their experienced work force and avoid the cost of dismissal and rehiring of workers. Workers retain their jobs and the loss of earnings is largely made up by short-time allowances from the government. It is estimated that in Germany the average compensation was about 90 per cent of normal net pay (McKersie and Sengenberger 1983: 54) Adopted in West Germany in 1969, short work time was used heavily in the 1970s to avoid or defer redundancies (*Labour Promotion Act*). By 1975, the number of short-time workers in West Germany equalled the number of unemployed. As of 1982 there were 600,000 short-time workers in West Germany, constituting 2.5 per cent of the employed labour force. Short-time subsidies have also been used extensively in France, Japan and the UK as a way of stabilizing employment.

Introduced in the UK in 1978, short-time working compensation provided 75 per cent wage reimbursements to employees put on short hours in the textile and footwear industries. In 1979 the programme was succeeded by a more comprehensive subsidy scheme. It was designed to preserve jobs that were threatened in the short run but that were thought to be viable in the long run. From April 1979 to October 1984, the UK spent over £800 million on short-time work subsidies. The programme supported almost 120,000 jobs in its first two years (Moon and Richardson 1985: 70).

(5) Employee buy-outs

Another policy option to preserve jobs is to facilitate employee purchases of firms. Worker buy-outs can be encouraged by a number of government strategies including: provision of loan capital, tax incentives and funding of feasibility studies of possible employee buy-outs. Wintner estimates that in the US in the last few years some sixty plants or companies have been bought by employees to avert shutdown (Wintner 1983). In Europe, especially Spain, Italy and France, worker co-operatives are more prevalent than in North America. Sweden has over 100 worker co-operatives, many of which originated with the rescue of failing firms. Several factors that may work in favour of employee bailouts to salvage failing firms include:

(i) Corporate management may misjudge the potential profitability of a firm or branch plant and unjustifiably close it down. Alternatively management may decide on a close-down where the rate of return of the firm or plant is positive but falls below the target threshold set for the firm's operations as a whole. If so, it may be rational for employees (and perhaps other members of the affected community) to buy out the firm or plant, even if the return realized on the investment is lower than would be acceptable to a private investor, given the benefits to the workers and affected community of avoiding the social costs of shutdown which they are better able to internalize into the buy-out calculus and subsequent terms of compensation (Stern, Wood and Hammer 1979).

(ii) Appropriately structured forms of employee control, with meaningful levels of ownership and participation in decision-making, may increase motivation and productivity. Along the same lines, it is argued that employees in a company that they own may be more prepared to accept concessions in wages and fringe benefits and to substitute contingent benefits for fixed remuneration. Where such concessions are required by a private-investor-owned company as a condition of continued operations, information assymetries may make it difficult for workers to determine whether the company is simply 'bluffing' in order to extract concessions or is facing genuine financial difficulties.

There are also a number of factors that may inhibit employee buy-outs of failing firms:

(i) If the firm is failing because the industry in question is declining as a result of loss in long-run competitiveness, it is unlikely, absent continuing public subsidies, that an employee buy-out will render the enterprise successful.

(ii) Where the industry in question is capital, rather than labour intensive, the raising of required capital, especially if substantial technological modernization is needed, may be beyond the resources of the workers, affected community, and available private sources of capital. Again, substantial public subsidies may be required.

(iii) Other difficulties arise in the capitalization of employee-owned companies. With respect to the withdrawal of capital by employees, rules should not be so restrictive as to discourage productive forms of mobility or retirement and replacement by younger workers. However, no restrictions on withdrawal may leave the company exposed to the risk of a run on its capital. In stable firms with a workforce of a given age profile profits can be set aside on a systematic basis to meet reasonably anticipated retirements or departures (Trebilcock *et al.* 1985: 436–8).

(6) Evaluating job maintenance programmes

Typically cast as a bridging measure to maintain jobs during a period of reduced manpower demand, subsidizing the stay option has been justified because in some circumstances the social and private costs of unemployment may be so substantial that government subsidies to prevent lay-offs can be an economically efficient solution. Saunders makes the case that 'if wages are rigid and labour is not highly mobile, allowing an inefficient industry (or firm) to expire may generate more social costs than benefits' (Saunders 1984: 17). Thus it is argued, preserving output and jobs in distressed sectors may be less costly than extended unemployment benefits, forgone tax revenues and additional demands on social services. Subsidizing the stay option has been predicated on a number of extenuating factors. For example, older workers who may have job-specific skills, more accumulated pension or deferred income and seniority rights will have far higher adjustment costs than other displaced workers. Policies that induce firms to maintain redundant workers during periods of weak labour demand have also been justified because they allow enterprise to retain highly trained, skill-specific workers. Temporary subsidies to maintain jobs are posed as a way of dealing with congestion externalities that arguably obtain in depressed regional labour markets with high levels of unemployment. To the extent that stay-oriented programmes are initiated as temporary palliatives and are clearly short-term, these measures can function as a form of advance notification, signalling to workers that their jobs are at risk while providing a period of income support for extended job search. This may be especially important when the workers involved are economically or socially disadvantaged and need special assistance. Temporary job maintenance subsidies can be a vehicle for smoothing the adjustment process if there are clear exit signals to the workers receiving support. Plants in which workers are on job maintenance grants might also receive special adjustment assistance services.

In essence, the time during which the workers receive job subsidies could be used by all parties (government, employers, community businesses and employees) to plan and prepare for the re-employment of those workers in other activities. In this fashion, job maintenance subsidies would ultimately help to make workers more accepting of economic change rather than to support them in opposition to market signals. Potential work force displacements in highly specialized regions or lay-offs involving a significant proportion of a community's workers may cause some congestion in the local labour market. Preservation measures that slow down the job separation process can give the redundant workers the necessary time to find a job while lessening the social costs due to lost output.

Empirically the results of job preservation subsidies have shown few efficiency gains. Direct support to prevent redundancies has been used most widely in the UK and Sweden. In both nations, the subsidies were directed toward industries that were undergoing structural changes (textiles and clothing in the UK; pulp and paper and textiles in Sweden) rather than cyclical downturns. In what began as regional policies for areas with the most severe employment problems, the UK tried to encourage firms to defer redundancies. At the peak of its usage, in 1979, the UK's Temporary Employment Subsidy maintained the jobs of some 200,000 workers. To 'save jobs', Sweden spent some SKr 20 billion between 1976 and 1980. Employment eventually shrunk in all of these sectors and there is no evidence that the delays assisted the workers involved to find subsequent employment (Heikensten 1984).

In the cases of Germany and Japan jobs have been preserved through subsidized short-time work or retaining grants; yet industries like steel and shipbuilding have undergone significant shrinkage. The overall adjustment is realized in part through the operation of a segmented or dualistic labour market. In other words the ability to maintain some workers while also responding to change has been possible because less politically salient workers (women, foreigners, those outside the lifetime employment system) are more easily let go. Adjustment that accompanies job maintenance measures may thus be dependent in part on the existence of an unprotected segment of the labour force (Goldthorpe 1984; Streeck 1984).

The balance sheet on employee buy-outs of failing firms is a mixed one. Whyte has studied worker take-overs as an alternative to plant closure over a ten year period. He found that between 1975 and 1985 in the US in sixty cases, there was a saving of approximately 50,000 positions. In only about four or five instances did the employee-owned firm subsequently go out of business. Worker buy-outs would seem to be a viable strategy in some circumstances. There may be smaller, labour- rather than capital-intensive, enterprises earning, or capable of earning, a modest rate of return where the social costs of closure may render this option the most attractive opportunity available to the workers. In such cases, modest government assistance of the kind described above may be warranted in terms of minimizing social costs (maximizing social welfare), given the absence of less costly alternative forms of employment-maintenance or income-support programmes (Trebilcock *et al.* 1985: 411).

The political rationale for policies to preserve the stay option rests in part on the power of losers to delay socially beneficial changes and to threaten the political futures of those in power. Job preservation is a highly visible response to the demands of losers. It allows policy makers to provide concentrated benefits while diffusing the costs. Ideally it allows broader economic change to continue by buying off political vetoes.

In his analysis of instruments of aid to industry, André Blais (1986A) argues that there is too much emphasis on pressure group activity in explaining adjustment policy. He contends that government decision-makers also respond 'to general demands for good economic performance'. These demands include concerns for growth and stability. Blais stresses the stabilizing role of governments in industrialized societies (Blais 1986A: 149–150). For Blais and others (Krasner 1978; Bloom and Price 1975) who argue that stability is a significant political objective, stay oriented labour policy measures provide a highly visible means of reflecting the importance attached by the polity to stable jobs and community ties.

(b) Income maintenance

The idea of income support for job losers is a fundamental part of the welfare state. Some nations, like Germany, have created an elaborate welfare structure while others like Japan have not (Cameron 1978). Unemployment compensation is a passive form of assistance that provides some level of income maintenance to displace workers. It socializes the risk of unemployment by providing for some economic security in the midst of economic change. Although the primary objective of income maintenance programmes is income support for displaced workers, the system of income support is an important factor in labour market adjustment.

(1) Unemployment compensation

One of the most important national programmes for labour market adjustment has been Unemployment Insurance (UI) which provides income replacement to unemployed workers. As part of the social security net, unemployment insurance provides assistance to workers regardless of the specific cause of dislocation. In providing income protection for displaced workers the unemployment insurance programme also influences the behaviour of employees and firms. Unemployment insurance schemes vary in terms of their funding sources (proportion of revenues from government, business and workers and use of experience rating to determine premiums), their conditionality (the extent to which payments are contingent on worker retraining or mobility, etc.), as well as the level of benefits. Income maintenance payments to displaced workers are available in all of the OECD nations. However, spending on unemployment insurance varies greatly across nations. Total spending on labour market programmes including UI ranges from 0.59 to 3.07 per cent of gross domestic product (see Table 4.3).

Table 4.3 Total labour market expenditures as a percentage of GDP, 1987

France	3.07
Sweden	2.66
UK	2.57
W Germany	2.34
Canada	2.24
Australia	1.53
US	0.83
Japan	0.59

Source: OECD, Employment Outlook, September 1988: 86

Some nations' labour market expenditures are concentrated on getting the employed back to work through 'employment promotion' programmes that facilitate re-entry into the work force. Other labour market expenditures are designed to provide a safety net of income maintenance for displaced workers. Although countries rely on both types of measures, there are important differences in the mix. As shown in Table 4.4

Sweden devotes 30 per cent of its labour market expenditures to income
maintenance, while the US, Japan, Canada, France and Australia devote
over 70 per cent of their labour market expenditures to income
maintenance. (Advisory Council on Adjustment 1989: 45–7).

Table 4.4 Government employment promotion and income maintenance
expenditures as a percentage of total labour market expenditure, 1987

	Employment promotion measures	Income maintenance measures
Sweden	70	30
W Germany	42	58
US	29	71
UK	35	65
Japan	29	71
Canada	25	75
France	24	76
Australia	21	79

Source: Advisory Council on Adjustment *Adjusting to Win* 1989: 46.

Unemployment insurance by itself does not directly induce workers
to adjust. But UI can be used for skill development and re-employment
incentives (Social Planning Council 1989; Ministry of Employment and
Immigration 1989; Advisory Council on Adjustment 1989).

(2) Special income benefits

A two-tiered approach for dealing with income maintenance has emerged
in a number of countries. Beyond the general policy instrument of
unemployment insurance, which is available to displace workers
regardless of the source of their dislocation, additional benefit programmes have been established for some subsets of workers dislocated by
long-term structural change. The US *Trade Expansion Act* (1962) and
its more liberal successor the 1974 *Trade Adjustment Act* provided
benefits to workers certified to have been hurt by imports. From 1962
to 1970 there were no worker adjustment assistance petitions approved
and hence no expenditures under the programme. In the period 1970–4,
82 of 224 petitions by groups of workers were approved. Under the 1974
Trade Act the number of applications, approvals and expenditures
increased dramatically. In 1980 over $2.2 billion in adjustment benefits
were paid to 500,000 workers (Hufbauer and Rosen 1986; Aho and
Bayard 1984). Under TAA, the weekly allowance was 70 per cent of
the worker's average gross wage before lay-off. Benefits were available
for up to fifty-two weeks. TAA claimants received income support some
twenty percentage points higher than those workers who qualified only for

unemployment insurance (UI). The TAA benefits were not contingent on the workers obtaining retraining, relocation or other employment services. The compensation system under TAA provided benefits only while the worker collected unemployment insurance and hence did little to encourage dislocated workers to seek new employment. TAA recipients who changed jobs had an initial spell of unemployment of almost 42 weeks compared to 33 weeks for UI recipients (OECD 1984a: 15–17). In 1981 the programme was revised by the US Congress to shift emphasis away from enriching the level of compensation toward providing labour market services to encourage adjustment. The benefit level was reduced to UI levels and could only be obtained after UI benefits were exhausted. Although the revised programme encouraged trade-displaced workers to pursue retraining (by extending benefits), it did not necessarily result in their obtaining new jobs (Lawrence and Litan 1985: 10).

Special allowances for workers in designated hard-hit industries are also available, for example, in Australia which under the *Structural Adjustment Act* (1974) provides special assistance to workers and firms in which there is a direct relationship between their lay-off and specific government decisions (US 1979: 16). Japan under its 1978 *Law for Temporary Measures for the Unemployed in the Designated Depressed Industries* (renewed in 1983) provides training and relocation benefits to workers in designated depressed industries or designated depressed regions.

In Canada, the second tier of income support is narrowly drawn. The Transitional Assistance Benefits (TAB) Programme (1965–76) provided supplemental income benefits to auto workers laid off as a result of the Canada–US Auto Pact. The Adjustment Assistance Benefits (AAB) Programme (1971–82) provided pre-retirement benefits to displaced workers aged fifty-five and older in the textile, clothing, footwear and tanning industries. The Labour Adjustment Benefits Programme (LAB) established in 1982 continued to provide benefits to older workers who had exhausted their UI benefits. LAB also provided pre-retirement benefits to older workers in designated communities. LAB's pre-retirement benefits for older workers were part of the Industry and Labour Adjustment Programme (ILAP) (1981–3) which provided an array of labour market measures to designated communities. They included enhanced training assistance, enhanced mobility allowance, portable wage subsidies, and direct job creation. The Canadian Industrial Renewal Programme (CIRP) (1981–6) provided labour adjustment measures for displaced workers in the clothing, textile, footwear and tanning industries. Similar to ILAP, CIRP provided short-run assistance in the form of income maintenance as well as improved access to jobs through retraining, relocation and job counselling.

Programme usage for each of these second tier Canadian programmes has been limited. The total number of recipients over the life of the TAB programme (1965–76) was 3,100. The low take-up is for the most part attributable to the fact that the Auto Pact was a success and did not generate mass lay-offs. Under the AAB programme, intended to be an alternative to increased import restrictions in the clothing, textile, footwear and tannery industry, take-up rates were also very low. From 1971 to 1980, only 900 claims for assistance had been approved. In the case of AAB, the limited participation is partly attributable to the strict eligibility requirements of the programme. To qualify for assistance the lay-off had to be certified and the individual worker had to satisfy certain eligibility criteria. A lay-off could be certified if it was determined that it met a minimum size requirement of work force reduction and the cause of the lay-off was a reduction in tariffs or any conditions set by the federal government for special protection. In order for workers in the certified lay-off to be eligible for benefits they had to be fifty-four years of age, to have worked in the industry for at least 1,000 hours in each of the previous fifteen years, have exhausted UI benefits, and be unable to find work.

Under the LAB programme (1982), the eligibility requirements were loosened considerably: if an industry was undergoing non-cyclical adjustment because of either import competition or government-induced contractions the lay-off could be certified. Worker eligibility criteria were also broadened. These changes in lay-off and eligibility criteria broadened the programme's use. In 1981–2 there were 716 claimants in the textile and clothing industries; by 1985–6 the number reached over 5,000.

Under ILAP the range of special benefits for targeted industries and communities increased beyond pre-retirement benefits. These special adjustment programmes were essentially enhanced versions of existing general programmes. In the two years of its existence from 1981 to 1983, the Community Employment Programme (2,354) which promoted job creation and the Industrial Training Programme (1,363) were the most heavily utilized of the labour market assistance programmes available under ILAP (OECD 1984b: 34–5).

(3) Assessing income maintenance measures

From an economic perspective unemployment insurance has the virtue of reducing the costs of job displacement and of facilitating more effective job search. Although these may both be significant in inducing labour adjustment to change, economic analysis also raises some critical concerns regarding the overall impact of unemployment insurance programmes on labour market dynamics and consequent economic adjustment. These concerns focus on the impact of income compensation on the incentive to work, on job search, on worker mobility and on job stability (Cousineau 1985; Courchene 1987). Empirical analyses of Canada's Unemployment Insurance conclude that although UI is an important source of assistance to many Canadians who are victims of unemployment, certain provisions may adversely affect the adjustment mechanism of the labour market. Economic analysis indicates that:

(a)   the UI programme contributes to an increase in the length of unemployment;
(b)   it contributes to an increase in the length of temporary lay-offs;
(c)   it reinforces the concentration of temporary and unstable jobs in high unemployment and low wage regions; and
(d)   it provides too generous a subsidy to Canadians whose labour-force behaviour is characterized by repeated unstable employment (Royal Commission on the Economic Union and Development Prospects for Canada 1985: 610 hereinafter Macdonald Royal Commission).

Economic arguments that UI retards efficient economic adjustments have generated calls for reform to the Canadian UI system. Recent reform proposals have sought to modify the adjustment retarding incentives created by the UI system by raising the eligibility requirements, lowering the level of benefits and eliminating regional differentiations in the level and duration of benefits (Canada 1985; Canada 1986; Courchene 1987).

Although deficiencies in the UI system's ability to facilitate labour market adjustment have been an important focus for reform (Commission of Inquiry on Unemployment Insurance 1986), there is increasing concern that UI systems are too large relative to other labour market programmes (Macdonald Royal Commission 1985: 612). Recent proposals for reform have de-emphasised passive income support measures and have called for more active training and re-employment measures for the unemployed (Ministry of Employment and Immigration 1989; Advisory Committee on Adjustment 1989). Referred to as a 'trampoline' approach, active employment promotion policies are directed toward increasing individual worker's abilities to adapt to changing economic conditions. These measures are in contrast to the 'safety net' approach, which provides short-term income assistance until the worker finds a job. While a crucial element in helping displaced workers, the safety net approach does little to enable workers to benefit from future economic development (Advisory Council on Adjustment 1989: 45–8; Social Planning Council 1989: chap. 3; hereinafter Social Planning Council of Metropolitan Toronto).

The three ethical frameworks also provide perspectives on UI and income compensation more generally. Utilitarianism follows much of the economic perspective on labour adjustment. That is, utilitarians

Table 4.5a Features of programmes to assist displaced workers by selected countries

Country	Extent of programme co-ordination[1]	Extent of target population[2]	Feature Wage subsidies	Relocation assistance
US	Low	Broad	None	Yes
Canada	High	Narrow	Growth firms	Yes
Sweden	High	Broad	Firms which provide training instead of lay-offs	Yes
France	High	Narrow	Employers who hire the difficult to employ	Yes
W Germany	High	Broad	Same as France plus OJT and settling-in allowance	Yes
UK	Medium	Broad	Employers who split a FT job into two PT ones	Yes
Japan	Medium	Narrow	Growth and declining firms ranges from ¼ to ¾ of wages	Yes
Australia	Medium	Narrow	Declining firms	Yes (Special programme)

Table 4.5a (continued)

	Feature		
Country	UI benefits	Income maintenance beyond UI[3]	Training; how provided
US	26–39 wks, amount varies by state: 35–40% of previous wage	Yes. Supplementary Unemployment Benefits (SUB) and/or Trade Adjustment Assistance	Publicly funded in public and private training institutions; OJT in firms.
Canada	Usually 12 months, longer if in training: 50% of previous wage	Workers 55–64 years on permanent layoff with 10 years tenure	Use both public and private institutions
Sweden	300 days if under 55 years of age, 450 days of 55+: 80% of previous wage	Agreements may be negotiated in special circumstances	Public compulsory job vacancy requirement
France	Usually 12 months, 70% of previous wage	Workers in training or designated industries	Gov't financed training agreements between firm and Nat'l Vocat'l Assoc., 1.1% of firms wage bill must be spent on training.
W Germany	312 days at 68% of previous wage; drops to 50% for unlimited time	Workers in designated industries or dismissed unwarrantably	Government incentives to firms to provide training; emphasize occupational mobility training.
UK	312 days at $38/wk if single, $61/wk if married: amount based on need after 1yr.	Lump sum, based on tenure and wage; 30 wks pay maximum or full salary if in training.	Use both public and private institutions: emphasis on training youth.
Japan	Ranges from 300 days if 55+ yrs. and 10 yrs. of tenure to 90 days if under 30 yrs.: and 1 yr. or less of tenure: 60–80% of previous wage.	90 days for workers 40 yrs. + in designated industries	Wage subsidy to firm that conducts training.
Australia	In 1980: $48.50 wk if single, $96.50 wk if married; rec'd while on active job search	No	Training allowances to workers

Table 4.5a (continued)

Features

Country	Tripartite co-ordination	Timing of programme implementation	National advanced notification requirement	Job creation[4]
US	No, but Public Industry Councils under JTPA	Post	No	No
Canada	Yes	Prior	Yes. Industries under Federal jurisdiction and 7 or 12 Provinces: 1 wk to 16 wks.	Government sponsored public or private sector employment
Sweden	Yes	Prior	Yes, notice rises as number affected rises	Temporary public relief work
France	Yes	Post	Yes. 2–14 wks depending upon reason and scale of dismissal	$3,420 from general revenues to unemployed to start own firm.
W Germany	Yes	Post	Yes, 30 days after notifying gov't	Government funded jobs in-the-public-interest for the long term unemployed
UK	Yes	Prior	Yes, rises as number affected rises: up to 90 days	$56/wk from UI plus $1,400 of your own to start new firm.
Japan	Yes	Prior	Yes, 'sufficient' time must be given for workers to comprehend problem	Wage subsidy to firms that hire displaced workers
Australia	Yes	Post	No	Temporary public service and pilot programme to help unemployed to start own ...

Table 4.5a (continued)

	Feature		
Country	Government supported early retirement	Work-time reduction schemes
US	No	No
Canada	Yes	No
Sweden	Yes	No
France	Yes	Yes
W Germany	Yes	Yes
UK	Yes	Yes
Japan	Yes	No
Australia	Yes (Compulsory at age 60)	No

Source: US Government, Secretary of Labour Task Force *Economic Adjustment and Worker Dislocation in a Competitive Society* (1986) Washington D.C.

Notes:

[1] Subjective rank based on an active and visible agency, such as the Canadian Manpower Consultative Service and the German Federal Employment Institute, who has responsibility for overall co-ordination of employment and training policy.

[2] Subjective rank based on whether a country designates specific industries and/or geographical areas for assistance; those that do, received a 'narrow' ranking.

[3] EEC countries also receive money for dislocated workers from EEC funds from levies on steel and coal production.

[4] A number of countries also offer regional development assistance (loans and other incentives) to attract and/or develop jobs in certain localities.

Table 4.5b Distribution of UI benefit in Canada, 1981

	Quintile[a]					Low-income cut-off	
Transfer	First (lowest)	Second	Third	Fourth	Fifth (highest)	Below	Above
Unemployment insurance	11.6	24.6	23.2	21.3	19.3	14.1	85.9
All transfers	29.1	27.4	17.2	14.1	12.2	28.6	71.4

Source: François Vaillancourt Income Distribution and Economic Security in Canada: An Overview' in François Vaillancourt (ed.) *Income Distribution and Economic Security in Canada*, Collected Research Studies of the Royal Commission on the Economic Union and Development Prospects for Canada, No. 1 Toronto: University of Toronto Press 1985), Table 1–20.

Notes:

[a] The sum of UI, Social Assistance, OAS/GIS, CPP/APP, Family Allowance, Child Tax Credit, Veterans Pensions and Workers' Compensation.

while sensitive to the need to help those bearing the burdens of change would also be concerned that whatever the chosen instrument of income compensation, it should maximize social benefits net of costs. If the design of unemployment insurance generates incentives that run counter to an adjustment and these features could be improved, utilitarians would support those changes that increase social welfare and thus average utility.

For social contractarians, the crucial question is whether income compensation programmes are directed toward the least well-off in society. Data from the Canadian case presented in Table 4.5b demonstrates that UI programmes may not be well-targeted toward redistributive goals. The evidence in Table 4.5b shows that over 60 per cent of UI benefits go to the top three income quartiles and that 86 per cent of the benefits go to those *above* Statistics Canada's low-income cutoff (Vaillancourt 1985: 33). Although unemployment insurance is intended primarily to replace employment income, from a social contractarian perspective it is a failing that it does not focus more on those Canadians with lower incomes. In addition both utilitarians and social contractarians would also be critical of the failure of income maintenance programmes to link the size of benefits to the actual costs incurred by displaced workers.

For communitarians, compensating displaced workers may be inadequate for dealing with potentially destructive impacts of change on community stability. Moreover, the more that mobility-enhancing incentives are built into UI and other compensation programmes the less desirable from the point of view of those concerned with the dissolution of existing communities and social structures. Communitarians would directly oppose the neo-classical economic position that seeks to remove regional differentiations in the benefit levels, eligibility criteria and duration of unemployment insurance.

In sum, framework policies for income compensation like UI are arguably neutral policy instruments that may be used to facilitate exit by providing displaced workers with greater opportunities for productive search. They may also encourage the stay option by decreasing workers' incentives to leave regions of high unemployment. Unemployment compensation is a fundamental element in the policies that constitute the welfare state in all industrialized nations. The importance for social and economic stability of socializing the risk of unemployment is recognized by politicians of every political stripe. Although there seems to be a broad consensus on the need for publicly provided unemployment income insurance, using UI as a vehicle to redistribute income across individuals or regions is a more controversial political issue. As various redistributive objectives are built into UI programmes, the less effective they may be as instruments of economic adjustment. UI is typically a complex programme often subject to criticism, but without serious challenge to its existence. It is this legitimacy coupled with a lack of transparency that make it a likely vehicle by which various social objectives can visibly be built into the programme with little public awareness of the real costs and/or effectiveness of using the UI system in these ways.

Table 4.6 Trade adjustment assistance: certification by major industry, cumulative April 1975 to April 1983

Industries	Certifications	
	Number of workers	*%*
Coal	5,436	0.4
Textiles	25,913	1.9
Apparel	156,247	11.3
Footwear	79,477	5.8
Steel	186,455	13.5
Electronics	59,587	4.3
Automobiles	724,143	52.6
Fabricated metal products	30,434	2.2
Other industries	109,702	8.0
Total	1,377,394	100.0

Source: US Department of Labour, Employment and Training Administration, Office of Trade Adjustment Assistance, Washington D.C.

The evaluation of extended benefits to subsets of displaced workers raises a number of questions. Neither economic analysis of market failures nor any of the ethical perspectives suggest a basis for presuming that trade-related adjustment costs differ from the costs engendered by other sources of change. Making a utilitarian or social contractarian case for extended benefits to some workers requires evidence that workers receiving more assistance have either higher costs or are more disadvantaged than other workers. It is not clear that such categorical programmes as the US TAA which helps only trade displaced workers or Canada's Labour Adjustment Benefit (LAB) Programme which focuses on older workers laid off from designated industries can be justified on these grounds.

US studies have found that workers in import-competing industries are more economically disadvantaged than workers in the general category of manufacturing. However, when compared to other displaced workers, TAA beneficiaries are not significantly different in occupational or demographic characteristics (Aho 1985: 233). The equity argument is weakened by the evidence that many trade-displaced workers come from the steel and auto industries in which the average compensation was at least 33 per cent above the manufacturing average (Lawrence 1986). The distribution of TAA recipients across sectors is shown in Table 4.6. There is evidence that Canadian workers in textile, clothing, footwear, and leather industries (the main recipients of job preservation subsidies) are less skilled and generally more disadvantaged than other workers in manufacturing. However, designating the boundaries of communities to receive special assistance and the problem of excluding workers from adjustment assistance because their unemployment is caused by technological and other factors rather than by import competition has raised concerns over the fairness of these special programmes (Robertson and Grey 1986; Aho 1985).

The political rationale for special compensation benefits rests primarily on the power of losers to delay socially beneficial changes and to threaten the political futures of those in power. Extended benefit programmes are a highly visible response to the demands of losers. It allows policymakers to provide concentrated benefits while diffusing the costs. Ideally it allows broader economic change to continue by buying off political vetoes. In both Canada and the US, special compensation for trade-related dislocation appears to be most likely to occur when (i) there are large numbers of workers who might be adversely affected; and (ii) the government is responsible for the change. There is, however, little evidence that such compensation permits the overall process of change to continue while placating vocal losers. In both Canada and the US, targeted income maintenance has not served as a substitute for trade protection (OECD 1984a; Hufbauer and Rosen 1986). For the most part subsidies to preserve jobs or targeted compensation have entailed no significant retraining element. They have constituted a form of compensation or income maintenance without adjustment. Benefits from programmes like the TAA and ILAP have not been used to facilitate job search and re-employment. In the US, some 75 per cent of the workers on TAA went back to their old jobs (OECD 1984a: 21). In Canada, some 65 per cent of the laid off workers in industries receiving assistance under CIRP and ILAP returned to their former employer. This compares with an average of 40 per cent of laid off workers who return to their former employment in all Canadian industries (Robertson and Grey 1986).

(c) Facilitating exit by subsidizing search

The pressure for industrial restructuring in a rapidly changing global environment has led governments to adopt policies that stress labour market flexibility and the acquisition of new skills. In order to reduce the costs individual workers must bear and to shape a labour force that can cope with change, governments have adopted a range of policies to facilitate job search and mobility. Providing adjustment services to encourage workers in their search for new employment combines the resource flexibility necessary for efficiency and adjustment with the cost sharing dictated by equity. Differences among nations do not derive from whether or not they support search activities but rather from differences in the quality and levels of such support. In seeking new jobs unemployed workers need information. They may also require training and/or relocation assistance. Government policies to facilitate workers in their search for new employment are less controversial than those designed to preserve jobs. Subsidizing the search option encourages workers to adapt to change by helping them to enter growth areas of the economy.

(1) Information and placement

Most OECD nations have a central agency with responsibility for collecting and disseminating job information through counselling. Often eligibility for unemployment compensation requires registering with the local or district branch employment agency. Those agencies also attempt to coordinate employment and training policy. Haverman and Saks describe the typical administrative arrangements that have emerged:

> With few exceptions, Western European countries have developed comprehensive and stable institutional structures for addressing employment and training issues. The structure is typically characterized by: (a) a single primary agency established by the national government but often independent of it; (b) an extensive network of local offices emphasizing outreach to employers and employees; (c) participation in policy formulation and implementation by employer groups and trade unions; (d) substantial expenditures on developing a large professional staff of placement, counselling, and training personnel.
>
> (Haverman and Saks 1985: 24)

Adequate labour market information is closely associated with successful training. A key ingredient in the success of any skill training is the identification of skills in high demand enabling candidates to find jobs following completion of their training.

Employment adjustment services which include placement and information services, training and retraining programmes and mobility assistance are the components of the search option. Although the general trend has been to establish more centralized systems for collecting labour market information and building up forecasting capability, the delivery of job seeking assistance (information and placement) seems to work best through tripartite structures that bring the services to the plant level (US Government Labor Task Force on Economic Adjustment 1986 hereinafter Task Force on Adjustment). Virtually all of the surveyed countries have adopted some form of tripartite co-ordination to facilitate the search for alternative employment by displaced workers (Table 4.5a).

The Canadian Industrial Adjustment Service (IAS) is an example of a cost-effective programme that facilitates the operation of the labour market (Task Force on Adjustment 1986). The IAS comes in at an early stage of the lay-off process. The IAS works with both a labour-management committee from the contracting firm and community representatives to assist workers facing lay-off to find new jobs. IAS adjustment committees assist workers in their search activities before and after lay-off (Advisory Council on Adjustment 1989: 39). It is reported that from 1971 to 1981 labour-management committees formed with IAS assistance found jobs (usually within a year) for 66 out of every 100 workers affected by plant closings. Despite their seeming utility as an instrument of adjustment assistance, with the exception of the IAS, job placement services in Canada do not have a strong record of performance. Many job seekers and employers do not seem to view Canada Employment Centres (CEC) as a particularly useful employment service. (Canada, 1981). In 1981 almost two-thirds of those registered with the local CECs received no job referrals and only 18 per cent of job seekers obtained a job with CEC assistance (Magun 1981). Job placement services in Western European countries appear to be more heavily involved in the hiring process. A recent survey of these employment services reports that Western European employment services are involved in from 25 to 60 per cent of new hires (Haverman and Saks 1985: 25).

(2) Plant closing

Plant closing legislation, including mandatory advance notice and severance pay, can ease the hardships of job loss. Advance notification is widely viewed as an essential component of a successful adjustment programme (Task Force on Adjustment 1986: 22–4). Empirical evidence substantiates the positive impact of advance notice periods of 6–12 months on the adjustment process (Folbre, Leighton and Roderick 1984; Weber and Taylor 1987). Advance notice of plant closing can be helpful to the adjustment process because it gives workers more opportunity to prepare for change and to search for new employment as well as allowing unions, business and government to take an early and active role in the process (Advisory Council on Adjustment 1989: 54–55). In addition to aiding the re-employment process, advance notification may ultimately serve to keep plants alive either by providing a signal to workers that the firm is facing genuine difficulties (as opposed to bluffing) and concessions are needed to keep the plant open, or by giving the workers time to consider organization of a buy-out plan. Advance notice requirements are more a part of the labour relations legal framework in Europe than in North America (see Table 4.5c; Gunderson 1985: 138–148).

Severance pay or compensation for termination of employment reflects the loss of human capital built up by workers in their jobs. Compared to advance notification the impact of severance pay on adjustments is more problematic. Mandatory severance pay provisions that are tied to plant closure may create an incentive for firms to begin shedding labour before announcing closure. Even more important, such a regulatory burden may simply drive firms to other jurisdictions and thus intensify the negative impact on the labour force. For workers, severance pay would appear to be a disincentive to finding alternative employment. This may be particularly the case for older workers who may choose an early retirement. There is little empirical evidence that such benefits deter job search for younger workers. Recent experience suggests that firm adjustment programmes beginning well before actual closure help workers find new jobs and are more successful in facilitating re-employment than considerable severance pay benefits with no positive adjustment assistance (Yoder and Staudohar 1985).

(3) Training assistance

Workers with inadequate or inappropriate job skills face several potential problems. They may be uninformed as to which kinds of skills will make them more employable. They may be unable to gain access to a training programme. Redundant workers may not be able to afford the costs of participating in training activities.

Retraining programmes are either institutional and classroom based or industrial and work-place based. In Canada, for example, institutional programmes account for the bulk of public retraining expenditure. In 1983–4, 83.4 per cent of trainees were in institutional programmes (see Table 4.7). In 1979 the Critical Trades Skills Training Programme (CTST) was established to offer extended support for longer training periods for high level skills in short supply. The *National Training Act* (1982) maintained the emphasis on institutional training. Besides general provisions for institutional and employer-based retraining under the *National Training Act*, there are special programmes for workers in communities and industries hard-hit by decline. The Industry and Labour Adjustment Programme (ILAP) (1981) brought together a series of labour adjustment measures including enhanced training support for displaced workers in designated communities or in particular industrial sectors (Canada, Dodge Task Force 1981). Adopted in 1984, the modified ILAP broadens the availability of this support to all displaced workers in designated communities.

Begun in 1985, the *Canada Jobs Strategy* (CJS) reorganized these labour market programmes. It placed more emphasis on on-the-job or

Table 4.7 Canada institutional and industrial training: programme expenditures in summary

	1975–6	1978–9	1980–1
Training expenditures ($000,000)			
Institutional training	455.6	551.4	656.4
Industrial training	48.7	83.7	106.1
Critical trade skills (CTST)	–	–	7.5
Training improvement programme	2.3	2.3	–
Total	506.6	637.3	770.0
Trainees started (number)			
Institutional training	213,184	207,558	223,826
Industrial training	61,389	78,936	79,863
Critical trade skills (CTST)	–	–	4,102
Total	274,573	286,494	307,791

Source: Annual Reports of Employment and Immigration Canada.

industrial training. The major elements of the strategy include: job development, and classroom instruction and on-the-job training. Job development through wage subsidies for hiring and training is by far the major part of the programme. In 1985–6, 96,000 workers participated in the job development programme at a cost of $237 million. The training programmes had approximately 19,000 participants. (Wonnacott and Hill 1987: 100). Recent proposals for labour market programme reform have urged greater private sector input into Canada's training programmes. There is also support for expanding the range of training programmes to include programmes to upgrade skills and reduce skill shortages beyond the CJS emphasis on those workers having only a marginal relationship to the labour market such as the long-term unemployed, social welfare recipients and young people (Advisory Council on Adjustment 1989: 49). The Labour Force Development Strategy unveiled in 1989 is directed both toward ensuring training that is more responsive to labour market needs and toward reallocating UI funds from passive income support to active training and re-employment measures (Ministry of Employment and Immigration 1989).

Australia's largest training programme, Commonwealth Rebate for Apprentice Full-Time Training (CRAFT), spends about $90 million annually on subsidies for full-time training in technical institutions or training centres. In 1981 almost 100,000 workers received CRAFT funding (Morrilus 1984: 235). The Swedish system of training (AMU) is an extremely flexible system that uses Country Labour Market Boards to formulate an annual national plan for training courses. Besides the wide availability of training courses at the Labour Market Training Centres there is extensive use of in-plant training. In 1983, about 44,000 individuals participated in Swedish training programmes. Institutional and industrial training, including in-plant training to avoid lay-offs, accounted for about 25 per cent of the total number of persons participating in labour market programmes. Public training centres in the UK date back as far as 1919. Directed toward correcting the tendency of employers to invest suboptimally in manpower training, the Industrial Training Board system established in 1974 levied a tax on firms in those fields that were not training workers and provided grants to those firms actively engaged in training employees (Lindley 1980). By the late-1970s, there were twenty-seven ITBs in existence covering industries that employed over fifteen million people. The other major public sector training initiative in the UK is the Training Opportunities Scheme (TOPS). With an average of 64,000 course completions per year, TOPS is oriented toward the acquisition of specific skills in demand in the labour market.

Japan and Germany have tended to rely heavily on in-plant training. In Japan, the primary burden of retraining is left to the private sector. Transferring redundant workers to another division, to a subsidiary or an affiliate means that most retraining is internal to large enterprises. At the core of government policy toward labour caught in the process of industrial adjustment is the 1978 *Law for Temporary Measures for the Unemployed in Designated Depressed Industries* (renewed in 1983) which *inter alia* subsidizes retraining of workers. In Germany, the *Labour Promotion Act* (1969) provides for training subsidies to institutional and training institutes. Unemployed workers who refuse to relocate or to participate in a retraining programme may be disqualified from unemployment benefits. A comprehensive vocational training system is at the centre of West Germany's approach to labour market adjustment. In 1985 in West Germany, over 400,000 people participated in vocational training. The proportion of those out of work before starting the training was 65.7 per cent. Workers with jobs are strongly represented among those seeking to improve their skills (Social Europe 1986: 99). A crucial part of the training system is the apprenticeship program. Nearly two-thirds of those who leave high school take vocational training (Munch 1986: 99).

The Mitterrand government in France has developed a policy of 'training leaves' designed to accompany restructuring in French industry. Any company contemplating redundancies may ask the Labour Inspectorate to conclude a retraining agreement which will define the conditions of training and provide state aid for up to 50 per cent of the retraining costs and 30 per cent of wage costs. During training leave employees receive an allowance equivalent to 65 per cent of their former gross pay.

Such agreements have been negotiated within the iron and steel industry and by Citroen and Renault.

In the US the most important federal programme was the *Comprehensive Employment and Training Act* (1973). The central aim of CETA was to provide skills training and other employment related services to jobless low-income persons. It also contained provision for public service employment programmes (PSE) to be triggered by specified unemployment rates. The training elements of CETA were soon overshadowed by the negative perceptions of public service job provision (Johnston 1984).

In 1982, the US Congress replaced the remains of CETA with the *Jobs Training Partnership Act* (JTPA). The new law returned to the original intent of CETA by authorizing training primarily for economically disadvantaged individuals. The JTPA also adds a small programme (the Dislocated Worker Programme) of retraining and other employment assistance for displaced workers who cannot return to their previous occupations regardless of the cause of their displacement. However, the training is quite limited because the only income support to JTPA trainees is UI, which usually lasts only about twenty-six weeks. By providing extended income support for eligible workers enrolled in training programmes, the Trade Adjustment Assistance programme (TAA) has increasingly sought to encourage unemployed workers to upgrade their skills. TAA benefits are available only for institutional retraining.

(4) Mobility

Mobility grants, like training assistance, are in keeping with the notion that adjustment depends on the ability of resources to move to higher valued uses. In some cases like that of the US, mobility assistance is limited to workers in designated trade-impacted industries. In light of the fact that the TAA has proved in large part to be a programme of support for cyclically unemployed workers who return to their previous employer, it is not surprising that the take-up rate for the mobility benefits has been very low. (Less than 1 per cent of TAA funds are spent on relocation assistance.)

In Canada, until 1986 mobility assistance was provided by the Canada Mobility Programme (established in 1967). Financial assistance was provided to unemployed and under-employed workers as well as workers anticipating unemployment who must relocate. In comparison to retraining assistance expenditures ($829.8 million in 1981/82), total spending on mobility assistance ($10.7 million 1981/82) was rather small (Saunders 1984: 57). Use of the enhanced mobility grants available through ILAP was quite limited. Only 118 workers were granted allowances during the life of the programme (OECD 1984b: 35). Mobility assistance is currently financed through the *Canada Jobs Strategy*. For areas experiencing high unemployment or mass lay-offs, enriched mobility assistance is available.

In West Germany, relocation benefits are often part of the 'social plan' negotiated by labour and management in instances of mass lay-offs. France, the UK, Australia and Canada have all instituted some mobility allowance programmes for displaced workers. For the most part these various schemes have had limited results. Japan's mobility programmes reflects the unique character of Japan's labour market. Firms receive subsidies for the internal transfer of permanent workers. The Japanese government will assist firms with the discharge payments (including mobility allowances) to those workers outside the lifetime employment system. Special mobility assistance is available to workers in designated depressed industries and in designated depressed regions.

Of the nations surveyed here, Sweden has paid the most attention to facilitating the mobility of redundant workers. Active manpower policies of the 1960s stressed not only job creation but also focussed on the supply side by encouraging workers to move to where there were jobs. By the late 1960s, opposition to the migration policy increased and regional development took on greater importance. Moving workers to jobs as well as jobs to workers are both now parts of Sweden's policies. If a worker relocates, the government will pay moving and travel expenses and provide an allowance for maintaining two households for up to six months. Mobility expenditures comprise 1 per cent of the National Labour Board (AMS) budget (Ginsburg 1983).

(5) Assessing search policies

Policy measures to assist displaced workers in their search for alternative employment include both the passive route of providing income support while they search, as well as more active measures, including counselling and retraining, that are linked to adjustment. Labour adjustment policies to facilitate exit by subsidizing job information, retraining and relocation are justified by economists because of imperfections in the market for human capital. Three types of market failures are especially relevant:

(a) imperfect information;
(b) externalities in the accumulation of human capital
(c) congestion in labour markets.

Information regarding employment opportunities beyond local job markets and future employment trends upon which retraining should be based is very costly and not easily obtained by individual workers. Private underinvestment in training by employers is tied to the possibility that the benefits of training workers can be appropriated without compensation by others. Employees may also under-invest in training because

149

they cannot finance the costs and are unable to borrow against the security of expected future income. The case for publicly funded mobility assistance rests with the possibility of mass lay-offs in depressed areas creating congestion externalities. Under these conditions when deciding whether to leave a congested labour market workers will only consider their own benefits and costs and not take into account the value of this move to society (Wonnacott and Hill 1987: 28; Trebilcock 1985a: 15). Although there is a strong economic case for governments to facilitate search by subsidizing search activities this is not to say that existing programmes have been able to correct market failures and have effectively encouraged adjustment.

Some evaluations of retraining programmes in Canada have pointed to increases in employability and substantial wage gains resulting from completed training (Saunders 1984; for a more negative evaluation see Davies 1986). Studies of institutional training estimated in 1978-9 a benefit–cost ratio of 2.7 for such training. These results were obtained in spite of the fact that 39 per cent of the individuals in the study were trained in occupations identified as experiencing surpluses (Saunders 1984: 39). Evaluations of Canadian on-the-job training programmes found significant gains in the employability of trainees in all age groups and skill levels. The benefit–cost ratio for previously unemployed trainees was 3.3 and for those previously employed it was 3.6. These results are based on the optimistic assumption that income gains will continue to retirement. A subsequent study (1982) that assumed the net benefits would last only five years after training, estimated a cost–benefit ratio of 2.7 per person in retraining in 1978-9 (Saunders 1984: 40-1).

Leaving aside the gains to the individual (and society) from retraining, assessments point to particular problems encountered using training programmes to facilitate adjustment. Most industrial training is cyclical. During difficult economic times firms cut back thereby reducing training opportunities. It should be noted that the Swedes and to a lesser extent, the Germans, have tried to expand their industrial training during recessions. A second problem' is that often training programmes developed in response to unemployment pressures tend to be unrealistically short for developing the higher skills needed in a changing economy.

Training and retraining programmes directly address the long-term adjustment needs of displaced workers. In West Germany and Japan, continued receipt of unemployment benefits is conditional on participation in retraining. Several countries including Canada and the US, have moved toward emphasizing and enhancing the training opportunities of workers in declining sectors, in contrast to providing them with more income support than other laid off workers. In Canada institutional rather than on the job training receives the bulk of federal training funds.

Several studies have criticised Canada's institutional training efforts because they have been directed at occupations with a surplus of workers. Greater emphasis on subsidizing employer-based training would more closely respond to the labour needs of industry. Reversing the policy emphasis so that on-the-job training schemes dominate institutional training programmes would not only diversify judgements about future employment opportunities but also provide more practical job experience (Trebilcock, 1985a: 342).

Although the redeployment of resources is fundamental to a growing economy, programmes which attempt to encourage worker mobility have been neither effective nor popular. The main problem with Canada's Manpower Mobility Programme (MMP) is quite typical of the difficulties in other nations. Although enhanced mobility may be the MMP's objective, the benefits paid under it have not met the private costs of relocation (Saunders 1984: 32–3). Similarly in the two-year period that it was in operation only three workers received benefits under Australia's *Structural Adjustment Act*. In the case of the UK's Employee Transfer Scheme, evidence indicates that 90 per cent of those assisted would have relocated anyway.

The pressure against relocation programmes has stemmed especially from regional governments. A recurrent theme in Canadian policy making (as well as that of France, the UK and Sweden) is the objection to policies that seek to move workers to jobs. It is argued that government should focus instead on regional development which brings 'jobs to workers'. The political answers have been quite clear. Regional development programmes have attracted far more funding than mobility assistance.

When retraining and relocation subsidies have been attached to more general compensation packages they have not been very successful. In the cases of both the TAA (US) and ILAP (Canada), there has been little usage of the adjustment services provisions. After revisions to the TAA programme in 1981, the proportion of workers receiving benefits under the Act who entered retraining programmes increased from 3.8 per cent on average in 1976–81 to 31.3 per cent during 1982–4. However, the proportion of those actually obtaining jobs in the retrained field fell from 7.6 to 4.1 per cent. Providing workers with an additional twenty-six weeks of benefits if they enter a retraining programme seems to have encouraged workers to retrain for the sake of extending their benefits rather than to obtain new jobs (Lawrence and Litan 1985).

Adjustment services no matter how well designed and executed do not address two important employment problems. First, adjustment services are largely superfluous to cylical unemployment. Temporarily laid off workers do not want, or need placement, retraining, etc. Programmes in which workers have undertaken retraining in order to continue to receive benefits rather than to prepare for a new job are wasteful (Lawrence and Litan 1986). Although it is generally assumed that the displaced workers receiving assistance are permanently separated from their jobs, the problem of distinguishing temporary from permanent displacements inevitably arises in evaluating the effectiveness of adjustment service programmes and compensation schemes (Robertson and Grey 1986; Richardson 1982). An even more difficult problem for the political system arises when adjustment services do not help permanent job losers. Counselling, retraining and mobility assistance are of little value if there are few job vacancies, and unemployment problems go beyond the need for better matching of workers to vacancies.

Ethical perspectives on subsidizing search activities are for the most part positive. For utilitarians such policies present an opportunity of assisting victims of change without slowing down adjustment and diminishing the overall level of social utility. From a social contractarian point of view, search subsidies might be better tailored to the specific needs of the less advantaged. Evidence seems to indicate that mobility and retraining assistance are often inadequate. Social contractarians might also be concerned that some targeted programmes to subsidize the exit option by bearing part of the costs of investing in socially desirable retraining and mobility may result in subsidized workers competing with new entrants and unsubsidized redundant workers. Hence, these programmes may impose costs on other, less advantaged workers in the form of longer durations of job search. Although communitarians would oppose government pressures to induce greater mobility, public subsidies for job placement, counselling and retraining can help to create a more viable economic base in depressed communities. Enhancing these search activities within communities can sometimes provide displaced workers with real alternatives to exiting from the community or region.

Government intervention to provide a range of adjustment services may be justified in terms of compensating for market failures as well as more equitably sharing the burdens of adjustment. However, the political justification can be less compelling. Despite its economic and ethical rationales, the exit option has not always been in the forefront of government-led adjustment. Expenditures for labour market information and training may not produce immediate results. No specific jobs are saved, except perhaps in such cases as Sweden's programme to subsidize in-house retraining for redundant workers. Japan's grants for retraining redundant workers by firms are essentially transfers of costs from workers and firms to the government (Peck *et al.* 1985). These grants are one of the ways that the government helps firms to bear exit costs and maintain Japan's unique lifetime employment system and internal labour market.

To the extent that labour market adjustment mechanisms focus on job preservation and mainly income support for the unemployed, there is little likelihood of muting political pressures to delay or block social change. In those nations such as Japan, West Germany and Sweden that have emphasized adjustment through employment promotion measures there is less political pressure to obstruct economic change. Rather than short term income maintenance, successful employment promotion strategies emphasizing employment services and training are oriented toward developing a skilled workforce that can adapt to rapidly changing economic conditions.

(d) Facilitating exit by creating new jobs

The policy arsenal of most of the OECD nations includes more than policies to facilitate matching workers to existing jobs and/or to compensate them while they search for these jobs. In the prolonged downturn of the 1970s and early 1980s, most governments have gone beyond these tools of labour market adjustment. Through marginal employment subsidies to the private sector, and creation of public sector jobs, some governments have sought to influence the demand for labour by directly expanding employment possibilities.

(1) Private sector job creation

Several governments have facilitated exit by increasing labour market demand through job subsidies to the private sector. Even Sweden, which historically has relied most heavily on expanding the public sector, has increasingly turned to facilitating private sector job creation. The New Recruitment Grants programme begun in Sweden in 1978 provided subsidies to firms making net additions to their work forces. Although Sweden does not generally distinguish among displaced workers in their eligibility for special subsidized employment, some special programmes have been set up, for example, to assist redundant shipbuilding workers. In West Germany the government in 1975 established a job creation fund to subsidize new hirings. French and British authorities have tried to create more private sector employment through worker enterprises. Under these schemes, unemployed workers use their unemployment insurance benefits to start their own firms.

Japan uses subsidies to the private sector to generate employment for targeted workers. The Ministry of Labour provides 10 per cent of the annual salary of newly hired workers formerly unemployed in a designated depressed industry or designated depressed area. In the UK, the Adult Employment Subsidy, a spinoff of the Small Firm Employment Subsidy which funded the creation of new jobs, was applied to adults who were unemployed for at least one year in the assisted areas of Merseyside, Tyneside and Leeds. (The scheme ended after one year and about 1,500 placements.)

(2) Public sector job creation

One of the ways in which governments have sought to cope with the uneven distribution of the costs of change has been to establish new jobs for displaced workers. Transitional jobs created by government temporarily to augment labour market demand have been tried in several countries. However, often such jobs are temporary and do little to provide workers with skills for future employment. In Sweden direct job creation is a long established instrument of labour market policy. Relief jobs in Sweden are not targeted to any special group. Sweden has used public sector jobs on a large scale to provide short-term employment. Local governments formulate development plans in advance of any decline in employment so that when employment difficulties affect a particular area these projects can be started without delay. The local level of government receives from the national government 75 per cent of the labour costs of each project. In 1978 there were 95,000 people unemployed and the number of relief jobs equalled almost 46,000 (Ginsburg 1983: 131). By 1983, the number of workers involved in relief work and other related forms of labour market measures accounted for 3.7 per cent of the labour force. This compares with an unemployment rate of 3.5 per cent (Herin and Haltunen 1983: 2). Employment creation through relief work continues to be the single largest area of expenditure by the Sweden's National Labour Market Board (AMS), constituting almost one-third of all AMS expenditures (see Figure 4.1).

Australia's Community Employment Programme (CEP) targets relief jobs toward those who have low skills. Introduced in 1983 by the new Labour government, the CEP creates short term public sector jobs lasting 3 to 12 months. The programme suffers from a deficiency common to job creation schemes: providing short duration jobs to unskilled labour with minimal work experience is unlikely to fulfil substantial training and experience objectives (Burgess 1984). The UK's Special Temporary Employment Programme (STEP) was established in 1978 to provide public employment jobs for up to one year. Although begun as a universal programme, it focused increasingly on regions of high unemployment in England's north and in Scotland (Jackson and Hanby 1982). In 1981 STEP was succeeded by the Community Enterprise Programme (CEP). It was intended to create more than twice the number of jobs as STEP with an emphasis on more permanent employment. Unlike STEP in which over five-sixths of the places were provided by local authorities and voluntary organizations, CEP was designed to encourage greater sponsorship by private firms and nationalized industries. The most recent large scale use of public sector jobs to reduce unemployment has been France's increase in the size and employment capacity of the public sector. In the first eighteen months of

Figure 4.1 Sweden: number of individuals benefiting from various labour market policy measures

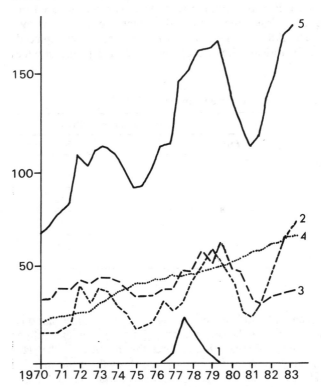

Source: Heikensten 1984: 7

(1) Training to prevent lay-offs
    and dismissals
(2) Relief work
(3) Labour market training

(4) Sheltered work
(5) Total
(Seasonally adjusted quarterly data, first and
third quarter each year, thousand individuals)

the Mitterrand government some 105,000 jobs were created in the public sector.

In Canada, the Community Employment Programme (CEP), 1981, provided temporary employment for displaced workers who had exhausted their unemployment insurance benefits. The CEP was the most heavily used part of ILAP. Between 1981 and 1983 some 2,354 workers took part in this public sector jobs programme (OECD 1984b: 34).

Public sector employment has been far more contentious in the US. In 1979, under CETA some $5.1 billion was spent on transitional public

155

service jobs for the economically disadvantaged and for unemployed persons affected by cyclical economic downturns. In 1978 CETA was amended so that the PSE programme was more narrowly focused on the disadvantaged and less directed toward counter-cyclical unemployment problems. The 1982 *Jobs Training Partnership Act* which replaced CETA, specifically forbade the use of any funds for public service employment.

Table 4.8 Public and private sector employment, 1965–80

Country	Change in employment (%)	
	Private sector	*Public sector*
	(%)	
Australia	+ 15	+31
Canada	+21	+22
France	− 1	+13
W Germany	− 8	+19
Japan	+ 7	+16
Sweden	− 3	+45
UK	− 8	+ 9
USA	+17	+13

Source: Schmidt 1985.

There have been wide differences among the industrialized nations in the degree to which their labour market policies rest on expanding jobs in the public sector. Table 4.8 compares the increases in the size of public sector employment with employment growth in the market sector for several OECD countries. The OECD Secretariat's (1980: 30–2) review of national experiences with public sector job creation programme suggests the following conclusions:

(a) In the 1970s the number of jobs created amounted to 3 to 10 per cent of the total number of unemployed;
(b) they generally lacked a serious training element in terms of preparing workers for permanent employment opportunities;
(c) males dominated enrolments in the programmes;
(d) youth participated to a substantial extent;
(e) the programmes were conceived as a bridge to more permanent employment, but the results were not, in all countries, encouraging;
(f) the jobs created produced useful community services; and
(g) the participants in the programmes were usually satisfied with the experience.

Over the last twenty years, there has been a shift away from general job creation subsidies to a more targeted approach focussing on regional development. Traditionally, regional subsidies have centred on attracting investment capital to depressed areas. To the extent that these subsidies aided rationalization and modernization they did not necessarily add to the employment opportunities in depressed areas. More recently, Sweden, the UK, Canada and Germany among others, have introduced selective regional subsidies for the employment of labour. These subsidies have included such general programmes as the UK's use of Regional Employment Premiums, Germany's Special Labour Market Programmes for Regions with Particular Employment Problems, Sweden's *Act of Parliament on Regional Policy* which established annual employment grants for up to seven years for jobs created in the northern areas and some depressed parts of Sweden's south. Through the *Depressed District Law* Japan extends special assistance to unemployed workers in districts with high unemployment. Its provisions are similar to those for workers in designated distressed industries, i.e. eligible workers may receive twelve months of unemployment insurance benefits; the Ministry of Labour will reimburse firms for most of the retraining and relocation expenses incurred in relation to permanent employees.

Regionally-oriented job creation policies also include more targeted assistance such as the UK's assistance package to preserve shipbuilding on the Clyde and Mersey and Sweden's Swedyard Development Corporation to create new jobs in the shipyards as well as regional aid to generate new job opportunities in the shipbuilding regions. When some 15,000 steel jobs were lost in the late 1970s, the French government provided an industrial adaptation fund ($700 million) to create new jobs in the area of Lorraine. Part of the plan was to induce another large employer, the auto industry, to locate in the area. When the auto industry also came under stress in the late 1970s, this move did not prove feasible.

(e) Assessing job creation strategies

Policies to encourage exit rest on the availability of cash compensation, government-supported adjustment services or the provision of alternative employment opportunities. The efficiency justification for government intervention to increase the number of jobs derives from macro-economic as well as micro-economic considerations. In times of high unemployment and low economic growth, the adjustment costs of displaced workers are very high as alternative jobs are not available. Subsidized adjustment search services are not an effective solution to the extent that unemployment is structural rather than frictional. In these cases the process of economic change may be costly and disruptive involving losses of real resources at least where there are cost effective policies available which would lead to more rapid redeployment of these resources to more highly valued uses. If the economy at large is not generating sufficient jobs, temporary job creation may be an efficient policy response (Harris, Lewis and Purvis 1982; Saunders 1982; Glenday *et al.* 1982).

The benefits from marginal employment subsidies introduced to encourage plants considering expansion to take on, and sometimes train, additional labour are difficult to determine. The gross costs of these subsidies are quite clear; by definition they will be less per job than the 100 per cent subsidy implicit in public sector job creation. However, given rather low estimates of the net jobs actually created by these programmes, the cost of each additional job may be harder to assess. This form of subsidized training and job placement leaves private firms to determine where additional labour will be required rather than having public sector managers try to predict winners. Even with government subsidies, the firm still pays a significant fraction of the new worker's salary and thus has strong incentives to assess correctly its growth prospects as well as to determine the best area in which to train additional workers. Subsidizing these private sector jobs aligns workers' futures and government spending with firms and sectors that expect to expand rather than (as in the case of job preservation subsidies) with firms and sectors that through redundancies have signalled the need to shrink.

The creation of alternative work for those losing their jobs was a frequent governmental reaction to the unemployment levels that developed in the troubled 1970s. Sweden set the lead with up to some 1.1 per cent of the labour force employed in government-created jobs. Employment creation as a way of increasing labour demand differs from job preservation. Programmes to defer redundancies or maintain jobs are more likely to protect structurally weak enterprises and to maintain the attachment of workers to those enterprises. Public sector jobs or incremental employment subsidies to private sector firms are meant to promote additional employment. OECD analysis concludes that a programme of marginal employment subsidies '. . . . would seem to recommend itself as an efficient employment-promoting device on a temporary basis' (OECD 1982a: 83). However, other evaluations are less sanguine. Because there is usually some delay in the policy making process, counter-cyclical job creation programmes are sometimes faulted for not gearing up until after the crisis has passed. Another source of concern about job creation is that the 'new' jobs may simply displace the jobs of other workers rather than be net additions to employment. With respect to public sector jobs, it is also possible that national job creation funds may be used as a substitute for funding for local or regional government jobs with the result that no additional jobs are created. Time lags and substitution problems are two concerns that should be influential in the choice of a job creation strategy. Evidence suggests that there are significant displacement or substitution effects in which employers receive subsidies for hiring workers they would have hired anyway. In the UK, evaluations indicate that 40 per cent of the subsidized jobs were not additions. A study of France's first National Employment Pact also estimates that about 60 per cent of the participants would have been hired without the subsidy (OECD 1982a: 38).

The costs of public sector job creation are not always easy to assess. Not only is it possible to obscure the real cost of expenditures per job, but it is also difficult to measure the product of public sector jobs. The problem of evaluating output relative to the real costs of creating the jobs makes public sector programmes difficult to evaluate as policy options. A public sector job creation programme may be viewed as a 100 per cent employment subsidy, whereas subsidies directed to the private sector are likely to come closer to subsidizing the difference between observed wage rates and real opportunity costs (Haverman and Saks 1985). Unlike the marginal employment subsidy schemes in which individual firms opt to participate, and indeed share the costs, public sector job programmes do not depend on market reactions. In order for these public sector programmes to be more than just 'make work' schemes, government managers are placed in the dubious position of trying to use the jobs to equip workers with those skills and training that will be in future demand.

Although public sector job creation programmes bear some similarities to private sector employment subsidies, there are some important efficiency-related differences. Private sector subsidies are incentive-based, involving cost-benefit analysis by individual firms. Temporary public sector job programmes are primarily seen as supplements to job creation in the private sector. Often their main objective is to provide training and experience for subsequent employment elsewhere. They can provide a transitional stage for those not adequately equipped for permanent employment. Temporary public programmes can also enable some displaced workers to retain their skills and improve their chances of re-employment.

The few follow-up studies of the subsequent employment histories of those in job creation programmes suggest that 'for many participants a job creation programme provides more of an interruption of unemployment than a step toward integration into regular employment' (Casey and Bruche 1985: 45). The extent to which public sector job creation programmes are targeted on the hard-to-place and disadvantaged groups is an important factor in evaluating the post-programme job results. One recent analysis of public sector employment as a tool of employment generation advanced this mixed review:

Evaluations of public sector job creation programs are limited, especially the extent to which the temporary period of employment actually resulted in workers adusting to changing market conditions more efficiently. Generally, there was no evidence that temporary public employment reduced joblessness in the long run. The available evidence suggests that public sector job creation programmes may serve as an effective bridge between jobs provided alternative employment opportunities become available. However, there was very little flow from these jobs to ones in the private sector. In some cases they have caused an extended dependence on public employment in that workers remain in these jobs longer than was anticipated when the program was established. (Task Force on Adjustment 1986: 23)

Ethical perspectives on job creation programmes focus on issues similar to those raised regarding 'stay' or 'search' policies: labour adjustment programmes are generally to be encouraged as a way of sharing the burdens of transition with the losers from economic change. The grounds for targeting workers from specified industries is that they are more economically disadvantaged than workers as a whole. Subsidized job creation may also be justified because there appears to be a societal preference for workers to obtain income through employment (even if this means lower aggregate wealth) rather than through unemployment insurance or welfare (Blais 1986a). That being said, if the jobs do not lead to the integration of displaced workers into the mainstream of the economy or if they maintain a dependence on public benefits in depressed communities, then job creation may not be a preferred instrument to serve these ethical objectives.

From the perspective of political efficacy, job creation programmes are not particularly successful. Although they allow policy makers to respond visibly to the problem of unemployment, the programmes are very expensive. Moreover, job creation programmes are unlikely to fulfil their crucial political function: to neutralize group demands for protection or to buy-off vetoes. Obtaining a short-term job in the public sector or a temporary subsidized position in the private sector is less attractive than keeping one's job through more enduring policies or than receiving compensation while searching for another position. Private sector job creation programmes with low marginal impact have proved to be a very costly means of reducing the burden of unemployment on some job losers. Public sector programmes do not solve – nor are they meant to solve – the long-term adjustment problems of permanently displaced workers.

III. Country profiles

Each of the industrialized nations has adopted its own approach to the problem of unemployment and adjustment. Although attempts to characterize these approaches can over-emphasize differences among nations, synopses of government policies do illustrate significant variations in the ways various nations have sought to develop effective mechanisms to redistribute the costs of change in socially and politically acceptable ways while ensuring some continuing adjustment to market forces.

Given that a strong economy lowers the costs of adjustment because it is easier for workers to find alternative employment, another difficulty in comparing national experiences with labour market policies is that the adoption of particular policy instruments and their subsequent effects may very much depend on each country's particular institutional and social context. For example, Japan's system of lifetime employment constitutes a distinctive context in which Japan's firm-oriented job preservation subsidies have not retarded the adjustment process, although in settings without a segmented labour force, the outcomes might be very different (Peck *et al.* 1985; Lawrence 1986). Recognizing these limitations, this section reviews comparative experience with labour market policies with reference to considerations of efficiency, equity and political feasibility. Table 4.5a compares the many features of the policies adopted by the eight nations in our review. Table 4.9 provides an overview of the expenditures on selected manpower policies.

(a) Sweden

The Swedish approach is characterized by strategies to increase demand for labour and to enhance supply by reducing labour market rigidities through training, counselling and placement services. Measures directed toward reducing the effects of lay-offs include relief work (public service jobs), wage subsidies and in-plant training. Annual expenditures on these policies equal almost 3 per cent of the GNP. Notably, Sweden's expenditures on income maintenance has been, relative to other OECD nations, quite small. The Swedish training system focusses on three diverse needs: training for the unemployed through courses at the AMUs (Labour Market Training Centres), training via vocational courses in the regular school system and subsidized internal training through firms (Cavallius 1988). Sweden's labour market policies have created what has been described as a sheltered secondary labour sector (Johannesson and Schmidt 1980). By 1982 a total of 160,000 individuals were involved in various labour market programmes. This amounted to almost 4 per cent of the labour force at a time when unemployment was a little more than 2 per cent (Heikensten 1984: 7) (See Figure 4.1). The Swedish tripartite approach to labour market adjustment attempts to facilitate structural changes while reducing the burden of change on individual workers.

Table 4.9 Spending on selected manpower adjustment policies in selected countries in the period 1960–77

		As a percentage of gross domestic product				As a percentage of public expenditure	Unemployment rate
		Measures to improve labour placement	Training	Job creation and job maintenance	Total	Total	
Canada	1968	0.06	0.26	0.03	0.35	1.05	4.8
	1969	0.07	0.30	0.00	0.37	1.09	4.6
	1977	0.19	0.30	0.23	0.73	1.82	8.1
W Germany	1968	0.13	0.04	0.15	0.32	0.87	1.2
	1969	0.13	0.06	0.16	0.35	0.98	0.7
	1976	0.16	0.19	0.61	1.00[a]	2.24[a]	4.1
Japan	1969	0.15	0.02	0.08	0.25	1.64	1.1
	1970	0.18	0.02	0.07	0.27	1.75	1.1
	1976	0.19	0.04	0.07	0.30	1.63	2.0
Sweden	1961	0.07	0.09	0.36	0.51	1.65	1.5
	1970	0.16	0.28	0.24	0.68	1.59[b]	1.5
	1976	0.28	0.72	1.10	2.16[b]	3.99[b]	1.6
UK	1968	0.04	0.03	0.00	0.07	0.18	3.3
	1970	0.06	0.04	0.00	0.09	0.23	3.1
	1976	0.09	0.34	0.38	0.82[c]	1.77[c]	5.5
USA	1969	0.05	0.09	0.05	0.19	0.62	3.5
	1970	0.06	0.11	0.05	0.22	0.66	4.9
	1976	0.04	0.26	0.41	0.71	2.03	7.6
Data available for 1976 only:							
Australia		0.06	0.11	–	0.17	0.50	4.5

Source: OECD 1979

(b) Japan

Japan's approach to labour market adjustment has been to complement market forces. A key element has been policies directed toward reducing manpower in depressed industries by facilitating the exit and retraining of peripheral workers. For the core labour segment, i.e. those workers in the permanent employment system, government support is directed toward reducing the costs to firms of redirecting their permanent employees. Virtually all Japanese programmes for employment preservation and stabilization or exit operate through firms rather than individual workers. In Japan, flexibility and the movement of resources to higher valued uses is often attempted through internal labour markets. Retraining is encouraged either by subsidizing firms or linking retraining to extended income maintenance payments. The relative success with which Japan has dealt with labour adjustment in declining industries must be attributed in part to the overall buoyancy of the economy and low rates of unemployment (Peck *et al* 1985).

(c) West Germany

West German labour market policies have stressed income maintenance and adapting labour supply through retraining, relocation and short-time work. For the most part Germany has eschewed labour market practices which impede change. As in Japan, many of the negative consequences of adjustment have been borne by peripheral parts of the labour force. Germany has relied heavily on early retirement and short-time work schemes to redistribute employment. According to Federal Labour Office (Bundesanstalt für Arbeit) studies, the greatest labour market impact among the various policy measures was associated with reductions in the work week and extensions in holiday entitlements, both instruments of employment policy that are within the collective bargaining system and not a government responsibility (Webber and Nass 1984: 189). German labour market policies have tended to be universal rather than targeted. They have been largely subordinated to the demands of a restrictive budgetary policy. The direct role of the state in maintaining and creating employment has been fairly limited. In 1982 a total of 282,000 persons were involved in short-time work (141,000), vocational training (103,000) and job creation measures (40,000). The number of unemployed was 1.8 million (Social Europe 1983: 82). By contrast, in Sweden, since 1974 the number of individuals in labour market programmes has been equal to or greater than the number of unemployed.

(d) France

France's policies have stressed jobs and full employment rather than compensation. Under Prime Minister Raymond Barre, the priorities were to increase job creating projects and to relocate and redeploy labour. In order to stimulate economic adaptations and to minimize the political costs of unemployment, the French government undertook to fight unemployment using several instruments. Enhanced placement services, training and job preparation were part of the strategy as were early retirement and short-time policies. Raymond Barre's government also tried to increase the flexibility of work contracts which resulted in an increase in temporary employment (Mouriaux and Mouriaux 1984). When the Socialists came to power in 1981 they continued many of Barre's policies: budgets for placement services and training programmes were increased and inducements for older workers to leave the force were enhanced. The Socialists differed from their predecessors in their reliance on public enterprise as a means of creating employment. In its first eighteen months some 105,000 jobs were created in the public sector.

(e) UK and Australia

The British and Australian approaches to labour market policy have focused on protecting existing jobs. Their income maintenance policies provide few incentives for adjustment. The UK's policies have been described as an example of an absence of overall strategy (Richardson and Henning 1984: 309). The UK's textiles, clothing, shipbuilding and steel sectors have been among the least adaptive declining industries, (Shepherd *et al* 1983). Despite large expenditures, the UK's policies have neither diminished demands for protection nor induced resource mobility and adjustment. The policies have emphasized employment maintenance rather than reduction of costs to those displaced. The record in Australia is strikingly similar. In 1981 some $995 million was spent on unemployment compensation, and only $100 million on manpower programmes (job creation, training and relocation assistance) with little evidence of enhanced adjustment or reduced demands for protection (Burgess 1984).

(f) United States

The US stands out as the most market-oriented of the nations in our review. The job of combatting unemployment is left largely to the operation of the private sector. However the 'exceptionalism' which marks its trade policy is also reflected in the special assistance given to some segments of the labour force. The *Trade Expansion Act* of 1962 and the 1974 *Trade Act* both sought to provide adjustment assistance to workers dislocated by import competition. The 1962 Act with its very strict eligibility criteria (to be eligible for assistance it was necessary to demonstrate that imports were a more important factor than all others combined in causing injury and that tariff concessions and injury must have occurred simultaneously), was largely unsuccessful as an instrument of assistance. From 1962 to 1974, only 54,000 workers were certified for assistance involving total expenditures of $85 million (Trebilcock 1985a: 132). Adjustment assistance grew substantially under the 1974 *Trade Act*. The level of benefits increased and the eligibility criteria were greatly relaxed. Betwen 1977 and 1981, 1.2 million workers received benefits. Spending on TAA in 1981 reached $1.5 billion (Lawrence and Litan 1985: 10–11). For the most part assistance under the *Trade Act* turned out to be an instrument of compensation for temporarily laid off workers rather than an instrument to promote adjustment out of declining industries (Hufbauer and Rosen 1986).

(g) *Canada*

Unemployment insurance (UIC) expenditures dominate all other forms of labour market assistance in Canada. In 1988, UIC entailed expenditures of $10.5 billion compared to a $1.7 billion budget for the Canadian Jobs Strategy programmes. Two-thirds of CJS expenditures are devoted to those who face special employment problems (long-term unemployed, youth, women) (Advisory Council on Adjustment 1989: 46–50). Beyond an overall emphasis on compensation and limited traditional adjustment services, Canada's labour adjustment policies have been narrowly directed toward workers in particularly hard-hit sectors and communities. The Industry and Labour Adjustment Programme (ILAP) and Labour Adjustment Benefits (LAB) are recent efforts by Canadian policy makers to direct adjustment assistance to those most severely burdened by economic change. There is, however, little evidence that the programme's boundaries have been effectively targeted on those dislocated by structural change or that the existence of adjustment assistance under these programmes has diminished demands for trade protection (OECD 1984b). Recent proposals have identified Canada's need to shift from its 'safety net' approach to an employment promotion approach which focusses on training and accelerating competitive adjustments (Advisory Council on Adjustment 1989; Ministry of Employment and Immigration 1989).

IV. Labour adjustment, political reality and economic change

Without adjustment, long-run economic growth is impossible. In their efforts to make economic adjustment politically acceptable, OECD nations have adopted myriad labour adjustment programmes. These programmes derive from attempts by politicians to balance the economic objective of promoting market adjustment with non-economic values and political considerations. Our review of labour adjustment policy in this chapter considers the economic, ethical and political implications of efforts by governments to socialize risk and to reduce some of the burdens of change. Demands for government intervention often come from those unwilling to accept the distributive and allocative determinations made by the marketplace. The demands of those who seek to be shielded from change or to be compensated for their losses are strengthened to the degree that others in society regard these as legitimate ethical claims.

In addressing the employment problems generated by declining industries in economies marked by slow growth and high unemployment, political systems sometimes have been faced with what appear to be conflicting pressures for efficiency and equity. At some time during the last two decades each of the industrialized nations has acted to thwart economic change and to protect or save specific jobs in a declining sector (Chandler 1985). However, that being said, it is also clear that in the context of rapid economic change some governments have opted for labour market strategies that facilitate change and positive adjustment (Aho 1985; Freeman 1988; Munch 1986).

The problem for policy makers is how to address society's concerns for those who bear the costs of industrial change within a policy context that encourages flexibility and adaptability within the labour force. In short, moderating the effects of transition on the work force does not necessarily mean policies that resist economic change.

Although the limitation of adverse effects of economic change is a fundamental concern across labour market programmes, the extent to which particular measures stimulate and enhance the ability of workers to meet the challenges of change and reintegrate into the workforce is a distinguishing factor among labour market adjustment programmes. Job maintenance subsidies have a negative adjustment effect. Job maintenance grants which temporarily preserve employment are transparent subsidies that may compare favourably with the much larger costs to consumers/taxpayers of tariffs and other forms of trade protection. Moreover, as opposed to trade measures, there is less leakage of these labour directed benefits to investors. In cases of one-industry towns and situations in which worker mobility is very limited, grants to maintain the jobs of redundant workers may be a reasonable alternative to compensation. However, decisions to maintain a redundant work force in some establishments are likely to be based on political criteria rather than systematic evaluations of the opportunity costs of potentially displaced workers. Temporary wage subsidies to maintain redundant workers would appear to be contrary to market forces in that they maintain worker attachment to a declining industry rather than enhance their potential for exit and future employment in growth sectors. Although job preservation subsidies do provide income support to those who bear a disproportionate share of the costs of economic change, they offer no incentive for recipients to adjust to those changes nor do they assist them in benefiting from the new opportunities presented by economic and technological change.

Support in the form of cash assistance rather than job maintenance has at least a possibility of a more positive adjustment effect. Cousineau (1985: 192) points out that in Canada 'UI benefits are not designed to subsidize job search but to subsidize the unemployed themselves – who can, to a large extent, use the payments as they see fit'. Whether a given compensation programme facilitates or hinders labour market adjustments depends largely on the design of the programme. Those income support schemes that encourage training and mobility have a positive adjustment effect. On the other hand, those that are based on regional differentiation may maintain labour attachment to unpromising employment situations.

Continuing along the labour adjustment spectrum are programmes that facilitate employment search by subsidizing job information and counselling, training and relocation. Policies to promote employment through improved job information, counselling and training have a positive adjustment effect. Displaced workers are encouraged to leave a declining sector and are helped to prepare themselves for alternative employment. Policies that increase the flexibility and adaptability of the workforce need not be confined to recently displaced workers. Government supported training can also be directed toward other adjustment problems including the need to upgrade and update the skills of currently employed workers and to prepare long-term unemployed for entry into the labour market (Social Planning Council 1989: chap. 3).

Comparing employment creation programmes reveals that in the case of public sector job creation, allocative decisions rest with bureaucrats rather than individuals or firms, and although assisted workers are not attached to shrinking sectors as is often the case of job maintenance, neither are they linked to growth prospects. For the most part public sector job programmes do not position workers to participate in or benefit from the process of economic change and therefore cannot be said to have a positive adjustment effect.

Among the measures to increase labour demand, marginal employment subsidies lessen the burden of adjustment on job losers while facilitating rather than impeding change. Public sector job programmes may direct public expenditures toward losers but there is little reason for such programmes to be the policy of choice. An even less attractive alternative are job preservation subsidies which tie income support to workers remaining in a declining sector. Proposals directed to all unemployed workers are preferable on both equity and efficiency grounds to those targeted to trade displaced and/or sector specific workers. Moreover, Canadian experience indicates that special benefits for trade-dislocated workers have not proved to be an effective political 'bribe' to induce acceptance of reduced trade protection.

V. Conclusion

The various labour market policy instruments are clearly imperfect substitutes. They differ significantly in their potential to enhance adjustment and to address the non-economic values at stake. A crude rank ordering of the effects of various labour market programmes reveals that training and other job search services are the best way to help those hurt by change and to meet the challenge of international competition. For the most part, economic efficiency arguments provide little justification for policies to preserve the jobs of redundant workers. Although there may be situations where mobility is very limited and where local labour markets are unable to absorb the unemployed, for the most part the evidence, as reviewed in the trade and subsidies chapters, goes the other way – the costs of job protection are well in excess of the highest estimates of adjustment costs (Glenday, Jenkins and Evans 1982). Moreover, such assistance fails to facilitate the long run redeployment of labour. It provides the wrong signals to workers and in so doing perpetuates some of the same conditions that made it appear necessary in the first place. The primary rationale for job preservation derives from ethical and political desires to cushion the impact of structural change.

The ethical case from a utilitarian perspective would certainly recognize the necessity of government measures to deal with those situations which appear to place an extraordinary adjustment burden on some members of society. However, utilitarians, like economists, would be concerned that such measures do not exacerbate the original problem by removing any incentives for losers to leave and improve their adverse situation. It should be noted that utilitarians and social contractarians would, however, appreciate that unlike the case of business bail outs in which distressed firms receive a subsidy, in a programme of direct assistance to workers there is less leakage of benefits to investors and creditors. However, social contractarians who favour measures to moderate the burden of change on the least advantaged in society will not necessarily favour policies that compensate for the costs of change in this way. First of all, such assistance raises the question of horizontal equity. Are all those who are most disadvantaged going to be helped by these measures? More significantly, stay-oriented assistance perpetuates the disadvantageous position by maintaining poor workers in industries with dim future prospects. Such policies, it may be argued, act to maintain an underclass of workers who are discouraged from pursuing the long-term benefits of change.

From a communitarian perspective, policies that allow workers to retain their communal ties are favoured. However, this value is not necessarily synonymous with maintaining all existing jobs in a community. Younger workers with less entrenched community ties may place a higher value on assistance that facilitates employment in higher paid or more challenging jobs outside the community that offer greater prospects of personal development. Older workers may be receptive to generous early retirement arrangements that allow them to remain in the community but avoid more costly job preservation policies. Other workers may be able to be assisted to find alternative employment with other firms or other industries within the same community. In yet other cases, it may be feasible for governments to foster or encourage the location of self-sustaining economic activities in the community. Moreover, the single-minded pursuit of a policy of maintaining all existing jobs in a community is likely to be counter-productive even in communitarian terms. In terms of the economic health and social vitality of a community, it is likely, in many cases, to be a recipe for stagnation, decline and sclerosis – in other words a community that holds very few virtues for its inhabitants. In sum, although all three ethical paradigms favour moderating the effects of transition, labour market policies that simply maintain workers in distressed industries cannot be justified within those frameworks.

Adequately funded worker training and search services are the best strategy for reducing adjustment costs. Training, retraining, mobility and counselling benefits need to be delivered as soon as joblessness occurs. The programmes should be available to all workers displaced by economic change of any kind, and directed toward both the income maintenance and job search needs of displaced workers. Although there is little merit in focusing labour assistance on particular causes of displacement or on specific sectors of the economy, it is necessary to recognize there are different adjustment problems within the workforce. While oriented toward the common goal of preparing the workforce to meet the continuing challenges of economic and technological change, effective training and search programmes need to respond to the distinctive adjustment problems of diverse segments of society including older workers facing dismissal, skilled workers facing obsolescence, newly displaced workers, and the long-term unemployed. At a minimum this means going beyond policies that seek to tide workers over through a spell of unemployment. What is required is a multi-pronged training system that recognizes that dynamic change is a crucial ingredient of economic growth.

Chapter five

The politics of adjustment

I. Introduction

In the preceding three chapters we have explored in detail the costs and benefits of, respectively, trade restrictions, industrial subsidies and labour policies. One general lesson that stands out is that trade restrictions – particularly in the forms typical of the New Protectionism – are the most costly and least well targeted instruments with which governments can address legitimate normative concerns that arise from trade-induced dislocations. Understanding why governments have, nevertheless, adopted trade restrictions as instruments of choice is a necessary precondition to proposing reform of substantive policies. It would be futile to make reform proposals that simply assume away the policy making processes that have generated current policies. Thus, before proceeding to the reform agenda we must first identify the dysfunctions or biases in current policy making processes, measured against the economic and ethical perspectives outlined in Chapter 1.

In this chapter we consider several different approaches to the policy processes which have generated the New Protectionism. We begin with the 'public choice' approach to politics, according to which economically irrational policy choices are explicable as inevitable responses to rent-seeking behaviour by concentrated interests. This approach, if persuasive, would indeed provide a clear explanation of the preference for trade restrictions – precisely the characteristic that makes them least justifiable against our normative framework, i.e. that they confer rents on producer interests, makes them most politically attractive. The 'public choice' view, however, leaves little room for a reform agenda, as it is unclear why concentrated interests that purportedly now predominate the policy process would permit reforms that diminish their influence. The second approach that we consider focuses upon institutions as explanatory of policy outcomes. In this view even with a given pre-determined configuration of interests and exogenous factors, different institutional arrangements will generate quite different policy outcomes. Since the institutionalist perspective tends to understand institutional structures as entrenched in a fixed political culture, it too threatens to paralyse reforms.

In place of the determinism of both pure public choice theory and pure institutionalism we advocate a political perspective sensitive to the dynamics that can be generated by rent-seeking behaviour, but which also recognizes a fluid interaction between interests, ideas and institutions. Such an approach leaves considerable latitude for reform proposals that address institutional biases, or lacunae in existing institutional arrangements, as significant causes of normatively unjustifiable policy outcomes.

II. The public choice approach

Over the last two decades or so, economists have developed an increasing interest in the positive analysis of politics. The basic economic model of politics that has been developed – commonly referred to as the theory of 'public choice' – models the political process as an implicit market with demanders (voters or interest groups) of government policies exchanging political support in terms of votes, information/propaganda, campaign contributions or other material forms of asssistance for desired policies. Government (politicians and their agents, bureaucrats and regulators) will supply policies that maximize the governing party's prospects of re-election (or in the case of opposition parties, election). This view of the political process contrasts with that conventionally assumed hitherto by economists which viewed governments as attempting to maximize some social welfare function by correcting for various forms of market failure (monopoly, public goods, externalities, etc.) (Trebilcock *et al.* 1982: chap. 2). Implicit in the public choice approach is the view that neither the effect nor intent of most government policies is to advance the common good, but rather to construct minimum winning coalitions, often through redistributional policies, even though the impact of such policies will often, perhaps mostly, be to reduce aggregate social welfare.

Robert Baldwin has identified five different models in the literature for explaining inter-industry differences in both levels of, and changes in, trade protection (Baldwin 1985: chapter 1). These are:

(1) Common interest or pressure group model: The ability of an industry to organize for the purpose of raising funds for lobbying activities.
(2) Adding machine model: the voting strength of an industry.
(3) Status quo model: The historical levels of an industry's protection and the ability of the industry to adjust to increased import competition due either to proposed decreases in protection or to changes in basic economic conditions.

(4) Social change model: The income and skill levels of workers in the industry, the nature of the international competition faced by the industry, and its importance in terms of promoting such social changes as an improved national defense capability and better environmental conditions.

(5) Foreign policy model: The bargaining ability, political importance, and income levels of the countries from which competing imports are supplied.

Baldwin (1985: 31) notes:

> Both the common interest group and adding machine models are based on a view of the political decision-making process that considers the state largely as an intermediary responding to the short-run economic interests of various pressure groups. In contrast, the other three models rest on a view of the political process that considers private citizens and government officials as either taking a long-run view of their self-interest or being concerned about the economic welfare of other groups and the state.

With respect to the two variants of the public choice model, Downs (1957) and subsequently Olson (1965) argue that narrow producer interests are likely to dominate over thinly-spread consumer interests. This is largely a function of the differential mobilization and hence lobbying costs faced by producer and consumer interests. The larger the per capita stakes in an issue, the stronger will be the incentives to overcome information and transaction costs in organizing, and the fewer the affected stake-holders the easier it will be to overcome the free-rider problem that afflicts large interest groups whose individual members have small per capita stakes in the relevant issues. This framework would tend to suggest that highly concentrated industries with few firms, perhaps also highly geographically concentrated, and perhaps also with highly unionized work-forces, are likely to be able to organize most effectively and, therefore, are most likely to be successful in securing favourable policies from government, including trade protection.

Whatever the empirical validity of this model (reviewed later), a major theoretical difficulty with it is that it appears to imply no equilibrium in the political process, at least in the context in which it purports to apply, short of a corner solution entailing infinite protection for the affected industries (a total ban on imports). This is manifestly not what we typically observe, even in concentrated industries, which is sufficient to raise some *prima facie* doubts about the subtlety of the model. As Destler and Odell point out in a recent, important study (Destler and Odell 1987), the weakness in the model is its simplistic assumptions that, on the one hand, domestic producers, who are easily mobilized politically, uniformly favour protectionism and that, on the other, the only or principal cost-bearers are ultimate end-users or lay consumers, who are politically disabled. More specifically, the model first ignores the fact that imports will often be intermediate inputs into another industry, for example, textiles and clothing, steel and automobiles, and the industry purchasing the inputs will normally find it rational to resist cost-increasing policies. Second, the model ignores the fact that export-oriented industries may have reason to fear retaliation by foreign countries to restrictions on their exports in the form of reciprocal trade restrictions, thus creating an incentive for such industries to resist domestically imposed trade restrictions. Third, the model overlooks the fact that importers-distributors and large retail chains that import and sell large quantities of lower priced imports constitute a major producer constituency that will be disadvantaged by trade restrictions. Fourth, while it is true that consumers may face information costs, transaction costs, and strategic impediments to effective group mobilization, as individuals they still possess votes which is a resource that firms, whatever their other political resources, by definition do not possess. The determinants of the political rate of exchange between various political currencies, for example, votes and financial resources, are not well addressed in the special interest group variant of the public choice model of the political process.

Finally, the model fails to disaggregate what may be complex competing interests *within* firms. As Milner argues, domestic firms with strong international ties often face difficult choices as to whether to support or oppose protection. Protectionist measures which may benefit the firm in a sector where it produces domestically, could lead to retaliation by foreign trading partners that could harm the firm's exporting or foreign investment interests (Milner 1988: chap. 2). Milner also points out that large, multinational firms have more ability to pursue their own adjustment policies, by moving assembly or other activities offshore to counter any wage-price advantages maintained by foreign competitors. On the other hand, such firms may demand trade restrictions as a kind of 'stick' with which to threaten foreign trading partners to open up their markets, although the evidence that using trade restrictions in this manner can procure significant market opening is quite ambiguous (Milner and Yoffie 1989). In sum, the behaviour of firms will often be motivated by complex interests that do not necessarily point to a pro-protectionist rent-seeking outcome.

The second variant of the public choice model – the adding machine model attributed to Caves (1976) – predicts that government will adopt policies that represent the views of the majority of those voters who are most concerned about an issue. In a trade context, this means those individuals employed in industries subject to import competition. Governments will favour industries with the largest number of voters, i.e. employees. These industries may or may not be highly concentrated (in contrast to the predictions of the narrow special interest group model) (Baldwin 1985: 13).

Again, as with the latter model, a problem with the adding-machine model is that it does not appear to imply or define a political equilibrium short of infinite protection, at least in those contexts to which it purports to apply. Secondly, in common with the first model, it yields no predictions *per se* as to the *type* of trade restricting instrument that a government will be likely to employ – for example, tariffs, global quotas or VERs.

The issue of choice of governing instrument in a trade context is explicitly addressed by Rowley and Tollison (1986). They first attempt to explain why government might adopt trade policies that a majority of voters would find antithetical to their interests:

(a) Those who lose from specific reductions in tariffs, or other terms of trade protection, are not compensated. Where such losers constitute a decisive voter set, their uncompensated votes will be cast effectively against trade liberalization.

(b) Prospective beneficiaries from trade liberalization have less incentive to inform themselves on the issue, to organize and to support pressure groups, even to vote, than do the losers. The benefits from trade liberalization have strong public good characteristics and are derived in an uncertain future, whereas the associated costs are concentrated, immediate, and highly visible.

(c) Where the beneficiaries of trade protection are geographically concentrated, a geographically-oriented, first-past-the-post vote system may provide them with differential vote representation in the legislature.

(d) Where those who benefit from trade protection evidence differentially intense preferences on the issue, log-rolling or vote trading within representative assemblies may overrule an underlying majority vote, even though it results in an overall net loss of welfare to society (the paradox of log-rolling).

(e) Where trade protection is a source of immediate government revenue (e.g. tariffs), governments may trade off a future generalized loss of political support for current revenue, especially where the latter can be diverted to purchase specific votes among favoured constituencies.

(Rowley and Tollison 1986: 314)

175

The authors also argue that the dead-weight costs of trade restrictions consist not only of consumer welfare losses sustained by consumers priced out of the market by induced price increases (the Marshallian or Harberger triangle in the standard monopoly diagram), but also the prospective transfer of surplus from remaining consumers to producers, which will be largely dissipated in socially wasteful rent-seeking activities (Tullock 1967; Krueger 1976; Posner 1975).

They then proceed to explore the political properties of tariffs, quotas and VERs, and predict a political bias towards the latter two classes of instruments. For example, import quotas guarantee an outer bound on import penetration and if assigned to domestic entitlement holders (e.g. importers) confer scarcity rents on a secondary category of domestic rent-seekers. To the relevant government department they offer a more complex system of administration than tariffs and hence a larger budget. Quotas also render the costs of protection less visible to consumers than tariffs. VERs, like import quotas, confer rents on primary rent-seekers (the protected domestic producers) while also conferring scarcity rents on secondary rent-seekers in the form of enfranchised foreign exporters, which may mitigate the prospects of foreign retaliation. VERs, in part because of their informal nature, impose the least visible form of costs on consumers relative to quotas and tariffs.

However, like the other variants of the public choice framework, that offered by Rowley and Tollison has limited predictive powers as to which industries will be protected and to what extent: even if there is a general domestic political bias towards quantitative restrictions over tariffs, this offers little by way of specific prediction as to which industries will receive which of the three forms of protection, and which none at all, nor does it yield predictions of the level of protection, for example relaxed versus stringent quotas.

The three non-public choice models of the trade policy process noted by Baldwin – the status quo model, the social change model and the foreign policy model – in contrast to the behavioural assumption of short-run economic self-interest adopted by the public choice models, admit of various factors: long-run pursuit of self-interest by economic agents and political actors, autonomous behaviour by public officials who are not simply intermediaries acting on the wishes of the electorate or some part of it, and altruism on the part of public and private actors concerned about the welfare of individuals who may be affected by import competition (or conversely, arguably about the welfare of individuals in foreign countries disadvantaged by denial of access to domestic markets for their goods).

The difficulty with these latter three sets of models as positive frameworks for predicting trade policy decisions is that their behavioural assumptions are so vague as to be largely untestable, and are likely to provide a positive rationalization for almost any conceivable set of trade policies (and thus predict or explain nothing).

A limitation in all five of the above models is that they are essentially static rather than dynamic in their orientation and do not well address changes in the political demand and supply functions for trade protection over time – in our context, the rise of the so-called 'New Protectionism' over the past decade or so.

Some obvious factors that bear on either the scale or the costs of adjustments to changes in trade patterns can be identified (OECD 1985b: chap. 10). The emergence of Japan and the NICs as major industrial powers has increased import penetration in a number of sectors in mature industrialized economies in recent years, increasing the scale of adjustment required relative to rates of downside adjustment experienced in the first two post-war decades. Depressed demand in these sectors as a result of global recession in the early 1970s and 1980s (partly induced by oil price shocks), as well as domestic productivity improvements through technological change that have reduced required labour inputs, have exacerbated the scale of adjustments confronted.

The costs of adjustment have also been exacerbated by slow growth in other sectors of industrialized economies, including export sectors, again in large part a function of the recessionary environment of the early 1970s and early 1980s. The declining efficacy of tools of domestic macroeconomic policy to ensure stable rates of economic growth without inflation, the reduced ability of governments to increase social welfare expenditures in the face of mounting budgetary deficits, highly volatile international exchange rates and increased corporate capital mobility, have all constrained alternative adjustment strategies to trade protection and hence enhanced the political attractiveness of the latter. Reduced flexibility may exist at the level of the firm, through rigid wage policies often resulting from long-term indexed collective agreements or, at the limit, through nationalization (in some countries) of major declining sectors. Reduced flexibility may also exist at the level of the individual, through increasing fixities such as increased levels of home ownership, pension and seniority entitlements, dual wage earner families and higher school leaving age, that reduce geographic mobility (Green 1984). All these factors may have increased the adjustment burden sought to be transferred to trade policies. The decline of the US as the hegemonic world economic power with a substantial economic stake in a liberal global trading regime, and the power and influence to advance this goal, is also often identified as a cause of the rise in protectionism (Keohane 1985).

These factors, and probably others, are clearly pertinent to this trend, but they scarcely add up to a tightly structured dynamic positive theory of the political determinants of trade protection with precise and testable predictive implications.

With this relatively unpromising review of positive models of the trade policy process as back-drop, we now proceed to review briefly the empirical evidence on the political determinants of trade policy.

Empirical evidence on the political determinants of trade protection

The empirical evidence on most postulated political determinants of trade protection is as ambiguous as the positive theories that underlie the postulates.

With respect to industry concentration, Pincus (1975) (US), Helleiner (1977) (Canada), Caves (1976) (Canada), and Ray (1981) (US) (with respect to tariffs), all found that highly concentrated industries received more protection. Anderson and R. Baldwin (1981) (international), J. Baldwin and Gorecki (1985) (Canada), Ray (1981) (US with respect to non-tariff barriers), Finger *et al.* (1982) (US), Cable and Rebelo (1980) (UK) and Lavergne (1983) (US), all found that industry concentration had a negative or insignificant effect on the likelihood of protection.

With respect to geographic concentration, Pincus (1975) (US), Biggs (1980) (Canada) and Cable and Rebelo (1980) (UK), all found that regional concentration had a positive effect on the structure of protection. However, Lavergne (1983) (US), Anderson and Baldwin (1981) (international) and Glismann and Weiss (1980) (West Germany), found regional concentration to have a negative or insignificant effect on the supply of protection.

With respect to industry size, Anderson and Baldwin (1981) (international), R. Baldwin (1985) (US) and Lavergne (1983) (US), found that large industries (in terms of employees) were more likely to receive protection. However, Cable and Rebelo (1980) (UK) found both industry and firm size to be unimportant in explaining trade protection. Baldwin and Gorecki (1985) (Canada) found industry size (in terms of number of employees) to have a negative impact on levels of protection, but that the absolute surplus created by protection is larger for a large industry.

With respect to labour intensity, Anderson and Baldwin (1981) (international), Ray (1981) (US), Riedel (1977) (West Germany), Anderson (1980) (Australia), Mahon and Mytelka (1983) (Canada, France) and Lundberg (1981) (Sweden), found that labour intensity is positively related to the supply of trade protection. Ray (1981) (US), Glissman and Weiss (1980) (West Germany) and Baldwin and Gorecki (1985) (Canada) found that labour intensity had a negative or insignificant effect on the supply of protection.

With respect to wage and skill levels of labour, most studies find that low-wage industries are likely to receive more protection: Baldwin and Gorecki (1985); Anderson (1980); Caves (1976). Studies also find that industries with low labour skill requirements receive higher amounts of protection: Helleiner (1977) (Canada); Herander and Schwartz (1984) (US); Riedel (1977) (W. Germany); Lundberg (1981) (Sweden).

With respect to unionization, Baldwin and Gorecki found that the degree of unionization of an industry's labour force was an unimportant explanatory variable (Baldwin and Gorecki 1985). Both Baldwin and Gorecki and R. Baldwin find that broad-based, not narrowly-based support for trade protection is a more powerful explanation of the level of protection supplied. R. Baldwin argues that models of the trade policy process that postulate that narrow special interest groups acting on their short-run economic self-interest will dominate the process do not fit the evidence as well as models that emphasize long-run self-interest or a concern for the welfare of others. He suggests that 'the lower duty cuts in the Tokyo and Kennedy Rounds to industries characterized by a large proportion of unskilled, low-paid workers, who are generally not well organized for pressure group purposes is an example of such an action' (Baldwin 1985: 178). Baldwin and Gorecki conclude that 'voters do seem willing to consider adversity and adaptability characteristics. Thus, while self-seeking behaviour is an important determinant of the tariff process, altruism would appear to act as a constraint upon the process' (Baldwin and Gorecki 1985: 50).

Destler and Odell (1987) find that in fourteen product-specific trade policy episodes in the US since 1976, importers, exporters and retail chains have often successfully exerted political influence in avoiding or diluting specific trade protection measures, that their influence seems to have increased in recent years in such episodes, but appears to have declined in respect of generic trade protection measures.

One or two observations are in order on these findings. The empirical consensus on the significance of wage and skill levels in industry labour forces and to a lesser extent of industry size (in terms of number of employees) does not address, or readily accommodate, some prominent recent examples of protectionism, in particular quantitative restrictions in the steel and auto industries, where the work-forces protected have often been compensated at wages substantially above the average manufacturing wage. Here, explanations from altruism would need to rely on public perceptions of the fairness of protecting long-standing economic expectations from sudden and substantial diminution (the status quo model), or of maintaining communities, rather than a collectively shared concern for the less well-endowed in society (a Rawlsian 'maximin' value).

Second, even if altruism and status quo values are significant, it is not obvious why this would lead to broad-based support for policies that impose costs on (or 'tax') the cost bearers at levels that are often hugely disproportionate to the gains to the beneficiaries, if other less expensive (more efficient) policies can be deployed which vindicate the same values and interests, with a smaller redistributive impact. This suggests the possibility of information failures in political markets, at least with respect to choice of policy instrument, if not with respect to the case for *some* kind of assistance.

Third, the empirical evidence on the political determinants of trade protection is, in many important respects, so mixed that support can be found for or against almost any positive model of the political process. R. Baldwin concludes 'that an eclectic approach to understanding this behaviour is the most appropriate one currently. Until the various models are differentiated more sharply analytically and better empirical measures for distinguishing them are obtained, it will be difficult to ascertain the relative importance of different motivations of government officials under various conditions' (Baldwin 1985: 180). An 'eclectic approach' is, of course, no model at all in terms yielding testable implications or predictions at the level of positive analysis, and in terms of normative implications, provides very little purchase on those features of the policymaking process which, if modified, are likely to yield superior policy outcomes. Perhaps what can be said is that the evidence does not suggest an iron law of politics that inexorably drives governments, in particular sets of circumstances, to the adoption of particular trade restricting policies.

III. The institutional approach

Institutional analysis attempts to identify the systematic characteristics of the domestic policymaking system that translate political inputs into policy. Under what circumstances will domestic political factors generate policies consistent with a principled reconciliation of diverse normative concerns? What are the characteristics that shape the likelihood of protectionist responses to decline?

From the institutionalist perspective it is a singular failing of Mancur Olson's framework that his portrayal of the determinants of economic growth ignores the role of the state (Krasner 1984; Rogowski 1983). For Olson, variation among governments in policy choices is consigned to a single variable – the length of democratic stability (Mueller 1983). Blais and McCallum's (1986) testing of Olson's thesis finds that the variable 'institutional sclerosis' is negatively related to economic growth. It is, however, never specified what aspects of state structure or governmental functioning are tapped by this variable nor what positive model of the policy process underpins the concept. As it stands, Olson's framework and its several applications treat each political system as a generic, passive register of group activity. Identifying the public sector attributes that seem important in shaping an institutional capacity to supply adjustment policies requires further consideration of the relationship between institutional arrangements and political conflict.

Recent comparative studies in the trade policy making process also emphasize the relationship between centralization and reciprocity. Where trade policy is divided between diverse ministries and public institutions, the gains from reciprocal trade liberalization may receive insufficient attention in the policy process (Nau 1989; Yoshino 1989; Destler 1989). For instance, if agricultural trade policy is the exclusive mandate of the agriculture ministry, the question of whether to increase or reduce protection of agriculture will not directly be linked, say, to the possible concessions in *other* sectors that might be extracted from foreign trading partners in return for liberalizing agriculture (see Golstein 1989).

Corporatist, tripartite arrangements among business, labour and government have been singled out as an institutional basis for supplying the collective good of economic adjustment (Katzenstein 1985). Corporatist policy formation is characterized by extensive bargaining between government and organizations of business and labour and the participation of these associations in the implementation of policy. A key feature for each of the social partners is the centralization of economic and political authority (Banting 1985: 7). All three partners take on an encompassing representative function. The apparent economic success of countries (e.g. Sweden, Germany) relying on corporatist processes has been explained in large part by the inclusive, consensual nature of the corporatist system (Goldthorpe 1984). They are more likely to internalize the costs of policies. The political process is thus marked by a longer term, more broadly conceived perspective on the economy.

It would seem that a high degree of integration of the policy formation responsibilities in public and private sector institutions is conducive to wealth maximizing adjustment policies as opposed to protection (Trebilcock 1985; Chandler 1985). Those characteristics which are typically associated with corporatist systems can also be considered in evaluating the institutional capacity of pluralist systems to supply adjustment policies. In the analysis of institutional capacity, two organizational characteristics have received the most attention: the degree of co-ordination and centralization of bureaucratic responsibility and federal versus unitary structures. In each case the focus is on the impact of the dispersion of responsibility and the interdependence among governmental agencies, and/or levels of government (Atkinson 1986; Zysman 1983; Bakvis and Chandler 1987; Jenkin 1983; Thorburn 1984; Prichard 1983).

(a) Bureaucracy and the state

Co-ordinated and centralized responsibility for adjustment policy are deemed significant in two respects. Zysman argues that strong administrative structures determine a government's capacity to construct economic strategy and to mobilize economic resources to serve it (Zysman: 300–9). For example, the French Inter-ministerial Committee for the Adaption of Industrial Structure (CIASI) included ministers and top-level public officials and bankers. The Committee was able to deal quickly and efficiently with the problems of failing firms (Green 1983a: 176–77). The French CODIS (Inter-ministerial Committee for the Development of Strategic Industries) is another example of a highly centralized structure. The Committee, made up of key economic ministers, was established in 1979. It is chaired by the Prime Minister but has no separate budget. Its purpose is to steer the development of strategic industries and to co-ordinate the various instruments of intervention. Japan's MITI (Ministry of International Trade and Industry), established in 1949, also exemplifies centralization and co-ordination. MITI has wide-ranging responsibilities, but although it has a comprehensive perspective, it is not unconstrained. While it is clear that its impact varies across industries, there is little doubt that MITI is the 'focal point in industrial policy determination, lending to continuity and consistency' (Magaziner and Hout 1981: 33). In the absence of a government's capacity to formulate policies of adjustment it may be more vulnerable to external pressures for protection.

The importance of organizational capacity to promote adjustment need not be predicated always on a highly interventionist view of adjustment. Although some commentators (Zysman 1983; Magaziner and Reich 1982) point to the importance of government in actively promoting structural change, there is also much emphasis on developing the organizational capability to counteract political support for protection. Baldwin (1985) argues that certain institutional changes in the US have reduced the ability of pressure groups to secure protection in particular industries. These changes have entailed not only shifting tariff setting authority from Congress to the President. They also involve constituting the International Trade Commission (ITC) a quasi-judicial agency that plays an important part in determining industry-specific levels of protection. The President and the ITC are much less vulnerable to industry-specific political pressures than Congress (Baldwin 1985: 178). Destler (1986) makes the case for strong administrative capability so that government policy is not simply a function of the balance of outside pressures.

> Their [US trade officials] posture should be one of knowing where they want the trade policy train to go, and one of political capacity to steer it in the direction, together with readiness to plan and execute the journey in ways that maximize the gain and minimize the pain for special interests. Only then will private actors find it in their advantage to climb on board. Only with a balance of strength and

responsiveness can trade leaders cope effectively with the inevitable pressures of an internationalized American economy.

(Destler 1986: 220–1)

When decision-making responsibilities are diffused, concentrated interests are more able to penetrate the policy process and to exploit cleavages among competing agencies and departments. The importance of coherence and co-ordination of responsibility is not that it necessarily leads to more state intervention. Whether adjustment relies on state or market forces will depend on many characteristics of the political system (Gourevitch 1986). Indeed strong executive capability is as important for fending off demands for intervention as it is for mobilizing public action. Ikenberry (1986: 135) argues that 'reimposing the market may be as powerful an expression of state capacity as intervention. The capacity to resist intervention and to maintain market forces is as important a part of public policy as direct intervention'. Centralization of authority appears to be important in promoting policies which produce instruments compatible with broadly based notions of national interests because the diffusion of responsibility for policy making detracts from the clarity of understanding of the costs and benefits to protection. This lack of clarity, which is likely to be accompanied by attenuated accountability, provides greater opportunity for special interests to influence policy and enlist 'clientele' institutions of government.

(b) Federalism

The capacity of federal systems to respond to changing international and domestic economic imperatives raises another question concerning the fragmentation of political authority. Does the disperson of power and greater interdependence between levels of government necessarily spell policy incoherence and vulnerability to special interests? Are federal states less able to produce adjustment-promoting policies?

The problems of economic adjustment have exposed two competing views of federalism. One interpretation stresses the advantages of decentralization, multiple decision-points and access in terms of the capacity to respond to diverse interests, to experiment, to adapt to changing conditions and to avoid the institutional rigidities held to be characteristic of modern bureaucratic unitary states. Breton's model (1986) of competitive federalism best articulates the view of federal divisions as a political resource conducive to flexibility and responsiveness.

Other views of federalism are less sanguine about the positive effects of competition among jurisdictions (Tupper 1986). Proponents of the second view contend that while in an era of prosperity and economic growth a reactive crisis-management style of decision-making may be both popular and reasonably successful, in a period of economic crisis an expanded state capacity for coordinating or directing government activities across several sectors and jurisdictions is a necessity. It is argued that the dispersion of power in a federal system and the necessity of seeking consensual solutions among a large number of policy actors combine to inhibit the prospects for effective economic strategies (Thorburn 1984). This implies that the pattern of industrial policy is more likely to be composed of a series of *ad hoc* actions and uncoordinated initiatives between federal and provincial levels of government, all of which spell a policy pattern lacking in coherence and comprehensiveness. Thus, because federal regimes are decentralized and because bargaining and consultation constitute the essential activity of power-sharing between levels of government, it has been argued that they are unsuited for coping with the challenges of intense international economic competition.

This latter critical view of federalism is premised primarily on what Zysman (1983) calls a 'state-led' notion of adjustment in which government bureaucracy attempts to bring about adjustment by directly influencing the future of particular sectors (Zysman 1983: 91). To the extent that adjustment is viewed in this way, the capacity of the state to promulgate and impose a coherent strategy of state manipulation of the market may well be inhibited by the dispersed decision-making associated with federalism. A related problem from this perspective is that the dispersion of power in federal systems may induce private sector groups to develop fragmented, decentralized organizations which arguably exacerbates the absence of an encompassing public sector perspective on policy making (Coleman 1988). Moreover, if conflicting relations between levels of government come to dominate policy making, less attention can be devoted to improving the relations between labour and business.

If the object is to enhance the capacity for state-led adjustment in a fragmented federal system like Canada's, at least some simple reforms are necessary. Drawing on lessons suggested by the West German experience and by basic elements of game theory (Axelrod 1984) we have suggested elsewhere (Chandler and Trebilcock 1985: 195) that institutional arrangements are more likely to be successful if they:

(a) have a small number of agenda issues; (b) have a small number of players; and (c) consist of repeat players with long-term involvement in the issues. That is the federal-provincial structures that hold out promise for more coherent development of economic policy in a federal-provincial framework might (a) focus on reaching accords on, for example, certain classes of interprovincial barriers to trade; (b) involve senior appointees of government with some permanence of tenure and with professional or technocratic expertise in the subject area, who would temper transitory considerations of political expediency with greater continuity in decision making, and (c) meet regularly and privately.

If a more neutral model of adjustment is considered, one which leaves open the question of whether the state or market should be the primary allocator of the costs and benefits of change, then the question of the impact of federalism can focus on the differences in the capacity of government to withstand the rent-seeking demands of narrow interest groups. Put more positively, the focus will be on the ability of the political process to produce instrument choices in keeping with societal interests and important public values. If viewed from the perspective of whether the political process allows public appreciation of the relative costs and benefits of different policy instruments, then the qualities of federal systems can be quite attractive. As Prichard (1983) points out, overlapping and concurrent jurisdictions may permit 'more precise registration of citizens' demands from governments. Overlap in other words, increases opportunities for signalling. . . . Overlap gives individuals more opportunities to remedy, moderate or avoid harmful consequences resulting from the policy preferences of others' (Prichard 1983: 45). Prichard also points out that overlap may contribute to public information and understanding of policy issues:

> Issues under consideration appear to receive more exposure than might be the case if they were being handled within one jurisdiction. Public information may be improved by the focusing of resources by both the media and the governments involved. Government participants have sufficient resources and self-interest to make investment in analysis and information worthwhile. Finally, delays which are often attributed to the complexity of intergovernmental co-ordination may also increase opportunities for citizen involvement in decision-making.
> (Prichard 1983: 43)

In sum, federalism may present some institutional impediments to reflection of anti-protection interests in the policy process. However, federalism does not automatically mean the triumph of pro-protection interests. Indeed, federal systems may be able to tailor and adopt policies to produce outputs more reflective of the ethical pluralism that characterizes liberal democracies.

IV. Public choice, institutionalism and the possibilities for reform

Both the public choice and institutionalist views of politics, in their purest form, suggest very limited possibilities for reform of trade policies. From a public choice perspective, the preference for more over less costly instruments to achieve given goals is explicable by the purportedly inevitable capture of government by rent-seekers. Precisely the most normatively unjustifiable feature of these more costly instruments – that they confer benefits on firms – make them the most attractive to governments, which want simultaneously to win votes from worker *and* from business interests.

From an institutionalist perspective, those features of the policy process which lead to adoption of either superior or inferior (judged against legitimate normative criteria) policy responses to trade pressures tend to be presented as part of the background political order – as part of national political culture. Reform proposals in the trade policy area which entail, say, North American or European societies adopting institutional arrangements typical of Japanese political culture seem highly unlikely to succeed. Similarly, for the US or Canada to adopt the corporatist arangements of Sweden or West Germany (however superior those country's adjustment policies might be) would involve upturning the very bedrock of our political life. One salutary feature of institutionalism is to remind us that other countries' approaches to specific problems cannot simply be imported into our own, since those approaches are intertwined with deeply rooted general social, political, and ethical approaches at variance from our own (see Glendon 1987: introduction). Yet taken to extremes, institutionalism risks paralysing the spirit of reform just as much as public choice theory (Goulet 1989). If we cannot improve trade and adjustment policies without overturning arrangements which are an essential element of our own political culture, then the possibilities for reform seem quite distant.

V. The idea of non-incremental reform: re-evaluating the margins for change

In the 1970s and 1980s, significant political trends in areas other than trade and adjustment policy have provided a powerful challenge to the deterministic strands of both public choice theory and institutionalism. Specifically, the adoption of privatization, deregulation, and tax reform by a large number of countries evokes the very real possibility of achieving non-incremental policy reform without radical changes in the basic structure of society (Howse, Prichard and Trebilcock 1990).

These policy shifts challenge public choice fatalism, in that in a very real sense they represent a victory of more dispersed interests or new coalitions of interests (including consumers) over entrenched, concentrated interests that were assumed by the 'capture' theory of regulation to be gaining an ever tighter vicehold over public policy (see especially Olson 1982). The reforms also challenge the historical/cultural determinism of the institutionalist approach, in that a wide variety of nations

- with very different political cultures and traditions - appear to have adopted similar reform measures. And, by and large, these reform measures have been implemented without abandoning the distinctive features of background institutional arrangements.

In explaining deregulation, privatization, and tax reform, two of us have elsewhere developed a multi-factor approach to non-incremental policy reform, which eschews a deterministic view of politics (Howse, Prichard and Trebilcock 1990). This approach emphasized synergies between conceptual analysis, interest group politics, exogenous (e.g. technological) changes, and broader social and ideological trends. Understanding the margins for significant reform of trade and adjustment policy requires understanding these factors and the interaction between them.

(a) Synergies between ideas, institutions and interest groups

Although the most unadulterated versions of public choice and institutionalist theory tend to deprecate the role of rational analysis and discourse in determining policy outcomes, the most sophisticated articulations of these points of view do allow some scope for the influence of ideas. For instance, Buchanan's version of public choice theory (in contrast to that of the Chicago School) admits and indeed relies upon the appeal of 'constitutional' economic rights. According to Buchanan, at certain junctures society can achieve the collective will to reform the background institutional arrangements that allow politics to be captured by rent-seekers (Brennan and Buchanan 1985).

The cultural determinism of the institutionalist approach is qualified by the recognition of some institutionalist thinkers that inasmuch as institutions reflect biases and concepts that predominated in the *past*, they may be open to change in that those biases and concepts may no longer, once carefully scrutinized, command wide acceptance (Smith 1988). As Goldstein (1988: 180) remarks, 'state structures . . . reflect the biases of decisionmakers present at their creation. Critical in decisions of protection is the evaluation by the state of the legitimacy of claims brought forth by social actors'.

Accepting that ideas have an influence on politics does not mean that this influence is autonomous from interest group demands. The relationship between ideas and interest group politics can be quite complex. Reich points to one aspect of this complexity in observing that the way in which a given policy issue is conceptualized usually results in 'the implicit selection of certain groups to participate' from among many potential losers and gainers (Reich 1988). A concrete example is to be found in the deregulation movement - emphasizing the consumer welfare impacts of traditional regulatory strategies, economists and legal academics

187

legitimized the claim of consumer interests to an important stake in the regulatory process (Eads 1975). By contrast, a focus on allocative efficiency (the traditional basis of the economists' theoretical critique of rate-setting regulation) had achieved a minimal impact on policy, for allocative efficiency is a pure public good in which no salient interest group has a particularly significant stake.

In the trade and adjustment policy area, the way the issues have been traditionally *conceptualized* presents at least as plausible an explanation for why pro-protection interests have prevailed over anti-protection interests, as does the public choice view. As discussed earlier in this chapter, the public choice hypothesis that concentrated interests prevail over more dispersed ones is of limited explanatory power, given that concentrated, anti-protection interests exist as well. The existence of a mercantilist bias in the trade policy process, on the other hand, might well go far toward explaining why anti-protection interests, whether concentrated *or* dispersed, tend to be marginalized by the existing trade and adjustment policy institutions.

The mercantilist bias perceives the essential costs of protectionist measures as costs imposed on *foreign* trading partners and the benefits as accruing to the domestic national interest. The bias is reflected in the rules and procedures of 'administered protection' in most industrialized countries. Such rules rarely provide explicitly for consideration of the cost to consumers of imposing anti-dumping or countervailing duties, since such duties are viewed as responses to the 'unfair' trading practices of a foreign producer, not as a redistribution of wealth from domestic consumers to domestic producers (Finger *et al.* 1982: Howse 1988). Even where the rules do permit consideration of the consumer interest, standing and disclosure requirements, and other aspects of procedure, in practice marginalize the consumer perspective and reinforce the image of anti-dumping and countervailing duty proceedings as an adversarial dispute between a foreign producer (who wants to export his product) and a domestic producer (who wants to protect his market and who claims the foreigner is acting unfairly) (Rugman 1987; Howse 1988).

The founders of GATT understood the neo-classical case for the domestic welfare gains even from unilateral trade liberalization, both in terms of the consumer gains and the overall efficiency gains through a more optimal allocation of resources (Dam 1970). Reciprocity at a sophisticated level can be understood as a means of insuring that other states which benefit from a policy shift which is in one's own interest nevertheless pay something for the benefit.

Yet in the public imagination, reciprocity continues to be seen through mercantilist lenses – the national interest is identified with domestic producers, and the domestic redistributive effects of policies (above all from consumers to producers) remain largely removed from public consciousness.

In sum, rent-seeking behaviour by producer interests may well be an essential ingredient in explaining why more rather than less costly policies have been adopted to achieve legitimate public goals. But a major reason why this behaviour has had such an impact on instrument choice is that the institutional framework for trade policy has marginalized the interests of those who ultimately, so to speak, pay the rents (consumers). These features of the institutional framework are amenable to reform inasmuch as they are the product not simply of government responses to rent seeking behaviour, or of inevitable historical forces, but of biases and concepts that can be publically contested.

(b) Synergies between exogenous changes, interest groups and institutions

It is not only ideas that determine the way in which interest groups are able to influence policy reform, but exogenous changes as well, which rearrange coalitions of interests, or which make traditional rent-seeking demands less salient. Here, again, we draw on the experience of regulatory reform in the 1970s and 1980s. For example, as two of us have argued elsewhere, 'in the case of telecommunications and financial services deregulation, new technologies created new interest groups – potential entrants to the market – which stood to benefit from the dismantling of regulated monopolies' (Howse, Prichard and Trebilcock 1990: 32). To what extent are there synergies between exogenous forces and interest group configurations which could be exploited by reformers in the trade policy area?

It is possible to identify several such potential synergies.

First of all, the increasing globalization of firms' interests makes protectionism a much more problematic policy instrument – where bargains are to be struck that advance firms' interests abroad, they may well be willing to accept some loss of rents from protection of their domestic production in order to gain or secure access to foreign markets. Secondly, to an increasing extent, comparative advantage is portable. Lipsey, Schiberni and Lindsay argue: 'The competitiveness of the multinational firm depends on the firm's characteristics rather than on those of its home country. It may rest on the possession of patents or other technological assets based on the firm's R&D. It may rest on the ability to manage or control certain types of production or distribution operations. It may originate in access to raw materials on favorable terms or in access to home-country markets. All these factors have in common that they can be exploited wherever the firm operates. That is they are mobile geographically within the firm but relatively immobile between firms' (Lipsey, Schimberni and Lindsay 1988: 492).

A plausible response to trade restrictions is for a foreign manufacturer to set up shop in the protecting country, where comparative advantage is based on knowledge of technical processes or managerial excellence rather than wage differentials, or other fixed factors of production. To what extent, under these circumstances, will workers identify their concerns with job security with protecting domestic firms? On one view, the outcome will simply be substitution of demands for trade restrictions with demands for foreign investment controls. But equally plausibly, if foreign firms are able to guarantee good, secure jobs, the pro-protection coalition of workers and firms in trade-threatened sectors may well become unstable. And in addition to the fact that trade restrictions can be circumvented by mobility of comparative advantage, workers will also have to reckon with the realization that often when protectionist policies are aiding a domestic firm, the jobs they are protecting are not in the domestic economy but jobs which the firm itself has already moved offshore, to exploit wage cost differentials (Reich 1989).

In sum, the ethical concerns posed by trade-induced adjustment costs to workers could become increasingly detached both conceptually and politically from the rent-seeking interests of firms. The focus may increasingly have to be placed where, as we have argued, from an ethical perspective it should be placed – on the adjustment costs to workers, who are immobile in important senses in which other factors of production are not. And because a *nation* wishes to retain or gain comparative advantage, it must focus on the quality of its domestic workforce, the only ingredient of comparative advantage that, in the long-term, will resist globalization.

Since the institutional framework through which policy is made reflects the conditions which prevailed at its inception, rather than these emerging trends, institutional reform may well be a necessary condition of harnessing the synergies in question. One cannot rely upon exogenous forces to bring reform in and of themselves. Conversely reform depends upon the capacity of the reformers to identify and exploit such forces.

(c) Synergies between general social and ideological trends, trade policy institutions and interest groups

We have emphasized that reforming the trade policy process is possible without actually requiring the radical alteration of background institutional arrangements (e.g. the role of the bureaucracy in government or division of powers in a federalist state). This is not to say, however, that important general tendencies which affect these background institutional arrangements cannot themselves lead to synergies supportive of reform. The last two decades have witnessed an increasing expansion of the range of dispersed interests, such as environmental and consumer groups, thought to have a legitimate claim to participation in the regulatory process. The recent introduction of access to information legislation in many jurisdictions reflects the importance attached to values of openness and transparency in government.

Trade policy reformers can appeal to these same values in proposing institutional changes which allow fuller representation of anti-protection interests in the policy process. The regulatory reform movement in North America has been closely linked with expansion of public interest group participation in the regulatory and judicial process (Derthick and Quirk 1985).

The point of opening up the policy process is not, it should be emphasized, that consumer interests ought to trump other interests. Rather, it is to ensure a principled, democratic outcome, where in making instrument choices to serve legitimate public goals policymakers take into account the relative costs to consumers of different policy mixes. Here again, the example of regulatory reform is relevant – the significant public values which underlay traditional regulation have not been abandoned, but rather the presence of consumer interests in the policy process has facilitated the adoption of better targeted policies which promise to vindicate these values at less cost to consumer welfare. Consumer interests can counteract the arguments of rent-seekers in the regulatory process that public values *necessarily* entail adopting policies that provide rents to firms (see, for instance, Cooper 1987). And rent-seeking, concentrated interests would have a hard time arguing explicitly against values of openness and participation which legitimate empowerment of the consumer interest. Finally, once the legitimacy of consumer participation is recognized a logical implication is that the substantive criteria employed in the policy process should reflect the importance of what consumers and other domestic industrial users of imports have at stake.

VI. Conclusion

Ideas can give new salience and can influence previously disenfranchised or marginalized interest groups. Democratic process concerns for participation and transparency can be harnessed to introduce procedural reforms that can counteract the tendency for the trade policy process to be captured by selective interest groups. Some exogenous factors – such as the increasing global mobility of comparative advantage also suggest margins for reform. The political art of the reformer is to exploit such synergies, which constitute the windows of opportunity for change. An inordinate focus on any single factor, by contrast, is likely to result in an under- or overestimation of the margins for change. But again, the failure of single-factor explanations of politics to generate empirically verifiable theories of any real robustness give intellectual weight to a decision to focus on multiple factors and the synergies between them. In this vein, we proceed in the following chapter to elaborate a reform agenda which emphasizes specific institutional changes that permit the full range of values at stake in the trade policy process to be appropriately weighed without consumer or other pro-liberalization domestic interests being marginalized.

Chapter six

The reform agenda

I. The nature of the crisis

Given the economic inefficiency of protectionist policies, and the proven welfare gains to trading nations from post-war trade liberalization (Katzenstein 1985), the rise of the New Protectionism would seem an ominous, if not regressive trend in contemporary history. Such reversals of liberalization have occurred before (e.g. the 1930s), with grave consequences for global economic welfare (Milner 1988). Yet despite the increased use of quantitative restrictions, subsidies and contingent protection in the 1970s and 1980s, the total amount of world trade has actually continued to increase at a modest rate and shows no sign of declining (IMF 1988; Milner 1988; Gilpin 1987). Indeed, given the pressures to protect jobs under the recessionary conditions of the mid and late 1970s, the extent to which the liberal trading order has remained intact may be remarkable, when compared with the consequences of similar pressures at earlier historical junctures (Milner 1988).

Moreover, the choice of policies which do not maximize economic efficiency does not suggest, in itself, any bias or irrationality in the political process. Demands for intervention often stem from non-economic values and interests which have a legitimate place in the policy calculus. From each of the three ethical perspectives outlined in Chapter 1 of this study (utilitarianism, social contractarianism and communitarianism) there is an argument for government intervention to address trade-induced employment dislocations. The argument rests on the consequences of such dislocations for workers, their families and their communities. While a total disregard of the consequences of policies for economic efficiency would clearly constitute a form of folly, it is entirely understandable that voters will make some sacrifice of efficiency in order, for example, to preserve community stability or enhance social justice.

The findings of this study suggest that where the dysfunction in the policy process lies is in the choice of instruments often employed to vindicate the non-economic ethical goals of protection. Utilitarian, social contractarian and communitarian ethical theories are all compatible with 'net benefit maximization' (Reich 1988): since there are scarce resources available with which to achieve legitimate public ends, the particular benefit sought by a given policy should be achieved at the least economic cost, and with fewest harmful side-effects to other legitimate policy goals. Assuming net benefit maximization, the preference for quantitative trade restrictions which is typical of the New Protectionism, is irrational from any of the three ethical perspectives. These restrictions typically cost consumers an amount per job saved far in excess of the full wage in the industry. A 100 per cent labour subsidy would be a less costly means of assisting workers, and would still vindicate communitarian values by preserving employment opportunities within a given community. Utilitarians and social contractarians would likely be satisfied with even less costly policies than an employment maintenance subsidy – compensation to workers for the costs of searching, retraining and relocating for new employment would be an optimal response.

From a social contractarian perspective, one must reckon also with the fact that many of the protectionist policies reviewed in this study are not addressed to the least advantaged – job preservation in industries such as steel and autos, where wages are high and workers are represented by powerful unions, seems contrary to Rawls' difference principle, since many of the taxpayers and consumers who end up paying the bill for such policies are less economically advantaged than those benefited. Of course, the least advantaged do not necessarily buy much steel or many autos, but the price of these goods affects the costs of many other goods and services, and the results are felt throughout the consumer economy. In the case of textiles, clothing and footwear, low-income domestic consumers are directly disadvantaged by restrictions on lower priced foreign imports.

From all three ethical perspectives, a preference for trade restrictions that confer windfall benefits (rents) on the shareholder/owners of firms, would seem redistributively perverse. There is no ethical case that firms should be compensated for the costs of adjustment. From a utilitarian point of view, the rent-seeking behaviour induced by the availability of such benefits represents a waste of scarce resources (e.g. costs of lobbying politicians, hiring lawyers to demand administered protection, etc.). In addition, in the case of VERs and some quotas, the scarcity rents conferred on foreign producers represent a pure loss to aggregate domestic welfare. From a Rawlsian contractarian perspective, transfers of wealth from taxpayers and consumers at large to shareholder/owners, who almost by definition constitute a privileged sub-group in the polity, is redistributively regressive. From a communitarian perspective it is undesirable that the rents in question often will not be used to preserve employment in the community but rather will be channelled into overseas investment or into modernization which increases capital/intensity of production, and hence leads to further shedding of labour.

Finally, stay-oriented policies – whether trade restrictions or indusrial subsidies – have often failed to achieve their goal of preventing massive and sudden exit of labour from declining industries. Indeed, inasmuch as they have functioned to artificially postpone change, such policies may, if anything, actually exacerbate the severity of the disruptions when they finally occur.

II. The margins of rational choice

We have suggested that certain instrument choices are much more capable than others of reconciling economic efficiency goals and a plurality of the ethical perspectives. From an economic point of view, tariffs in general are less economically pernicious than global quotas, and global quotas are less pernicious than discriminatory quantitative restrictions like VERs. This ranking is consistent with all three ethical perspectives: the scarcity and/or cartelization rents which characterize quotas and VERs represent an unjustified transfer of wealth from domestic consumers to domestic and foreign producers.

With respect to industrial subsidies, an economic perspective would suggest that subsidies which provide incentives/compensation to firms to exit from declining industries are the least undesirable instrument. Utilitarians and social contractarians would question, however, the ethical justification for compensating firms for the negative effects of economic change. Communitarians might prefer the economically much more pernicious instrument of production subsidies, as they guarantee maintenance of employment in a particular community or region. From all three ethical perspectives, subsidies for modernization would be acceptable if in fact they led to preservation of jobs in a revitalized, newly competitive industry. However, the evidence presented in Chapter 3 above suggests that where industrial policy has focused on modernization or rationalization, the productivity gains have primarily been realized through shedding of labour by substituting capital. Since from all three ethical perspectives the dislocation effects of change on workers, their families and communities are of paramount importance, there is reason for concern that modernization subsidies may not in fact retard, or may even accelerate such dislocation effects. A form of subsidy consistent with all three ethical perspectives would be an incentive to non-declining firms within a given community or region to retrain and employ displaced workers. Assuming new permanent jobs were thus created, this kind of subsidy would be preferable from an economic perspective to production subsidies to the declining industry, as it would be broadly consistent with the exit option.

With respect to labour market adjustment, the economically optimal instrument would be adequately funded adjustment services, encompassing training, retraining, mobility and counselling benefits, as well as income support during the job search process. Such assistance would also be consistent with both the utilitarian and social contractarian ethical perspectives, which view compensation to workers for the real costs of change as the principal goal of industrial policy. From the communitarian perspective, however, adjustment assistance which emphasizes mobility of labour between communities and regions will be counter-indicated. However, adjustment assistance policies which focus on successful relocation of workers *within* a given region or community will be consistent with communitarian goals. From an economic perspective, public sector job creation and income support tied to continued employment of workers in the declining industry are clearly inferior to adjustment assistance. While communitarians in particular may have an inclination to favour these policies because they keep workers employed within a given community, such policies do not address the long-term economic viability of the community and they threaten to create permanent dependence on public assistance. Communitarians must be concerned not only about the preservation of community life, but about its future quality.

This ranking of instruments from the economic and diverse ethical perspectives considered in this study suggests that some instrument choices are inferior from all perspectives (i.e. discriminatory quantitative restrictions such as VERs). However, the relative desirability of many of the other instruments considered varies depending upon the perspective adopted. Policy makers must take up the challenge of finding a mix of instruments which more adequately reconcile economic efficiency and a plurality of ethical goals in the particular circumstances of the case.

For instance, in a small community in Québec where a textile plant employs a large, middle-aged, mainly unskilled workforce, and where few alternative job opportunities exist within the same locality, trade restrictions or job maintenance subsidies may be the only means of vindicating communitarian goals. In other situations, where a declining firm has a diverse workforce of young, middle-aged and older employees, and where some employment alternatives exist within the community, the margins are wider for a creative instrument mix. The younger workers might be offered adjustment assistance to relocate elsewhere or retraining for other jobs within the same community; some, after all, will probably prefer enhanced personal opportunity over community ties. The middle-aged workers might be given jobs elsewhere in the community through an employment creation subsidy, and older workers could be offered an early retirement package, partly subsidized by government.

The existence of these under-utilized margins for more rational choice in domestic policies challenges the frequent characterization of the New Protectionism as a failure or dysfunction in the international liberal trading order, with *national* self-interest triumphing over global welfare and international legal norms (e.g. see Trade Policy Research Centre 1984). Nor can the New Protectionism be characterized as a conscious social choice for justice over economic efficiency, since the policy outcomes chosen are often sub-optimal from *both* economic, *and* legitimate non-economic ethical perspectives. This evokes a dysfunction in the domestic political process, which produces instrument choices incompatible with any widely-held normative concept of the national interest.

The appropriate starting point for reform would therefore be analysis and correction of those aspects of the domestic policy process that produce measures which have relatively high domestic costs and relatively modest, illusory, or redistributively regressive benefits, and which lead to a preference for more over less costly instruments to achieve given objectives.

III. The sources of domestic political dysfunctions

In explaining how the domestic policy process frequently yields trade policies which are indefensible on any of the legitimate normative criteria which might be invoked to justify protection, we believe five factors loom large.

(1) Information asymmetries exist which prevent voters at large from judging the actual costs and benefits of trade and adjustment policies against their purported goals.

(2) The institutional structure of administered protection is such that key anti-protection interests are either excluded from participation, or marginalized.

(3) The substantive mandate and criteria for formal trade policy regimes do not reflect the full range of values at stake in trade policy, but rather give unjustifiable weight to some values, and too little to others.

(4) Some trade policy instruments (VERs and OMAs negotiated between governments at the executive level) are not subject to *any* legally mandated participatory process in which policies can be evaluated against (sometimes conflicting) public goals.

(5) Trade and adjustment policy in many countries is fragmented beween various agencies, each of which has a narrow mandate that excludes a comprehensive weighing of the full range of policy instruments available to vindicate the public values at issue.

Understanding each of these characteristics of the existing policy process is a necessary precondition for the recommendation of specific institutional reforms. We therefore discuss each in more detail, drawing freely upon the current legal and institutional arrangements for trade and adjustment policy formation in Canada, the US and the European Community.

(a) Information asymmetries

Where more costly measures are chosen over less costly alternatives which could equally or better serve the same values, this may be because voters at large are not adequately supplied with the information necessary to assess whether in fact the specific policies mandated are likely to achieve their stated objectives, much less whether there might be less costly, more efficient alternatives. Indeed, the specifics may be left to future administrative determination, and at that level rent-seeking behaviour and not the original ethical or economic objectives may determine their actual shape and impact.

While in the case of trade restrictions, there are doubtless some concentrated anti-protection interests which are well informed in the product-specific debates which most directly concern them (Destler and Odell 1987; Milner 1988), outcomes in many trade policy debates will affect such concentrated interests less directly, leaving the anti-protection argument to be carried by more dispersed interests (e.g. consumers) who face the free rider, collective action problems identified by public choice theory (Downs 1957; Olson 1982). In the trade policy area, the information problem is particularly acute for an additional reason: because of a still widespread mercantilist bias that what is at stake is a conflict between domestic and foreign national interests, adversely affected domestic interests may not even be aware that they are adversely affected, in the absence of high-profile, publicly provided information on the costs of protection. Equally significant is good information about the actual, as opposed to anticipated, benefits of policies.

A major conclusion of our empirical work is that industrial policies have rarely achieved their own goals; significantly, very little publicly-supplied information exists to allow concerned voters to make a reasoned judgement about the actual fit or lack of fit between means and ends in current policies.

(b) Participation asymmetries

Participation of a full range of interest groups (including public interest organizations) in the administrative process has been increasingly considered as essential to ensure that agencies are not 'captured' by special concentrated interests. Enhanced possibilities for participation have been credited with significantly advancing the cause of regulatory reform in the US (Derthick and Quirk 1984). Trucking and airline deregulation are both cases where participation went hand in hand with an increasing role for consumer welfare considerations in the design of regulatory instruments (see Cooper 1987; Howse, Prichard and Trebilcock 1989).

There are formal, conceptual and related institutional barriers evident in the trade policy processes of many industrial countries that inhibit full participation of all affected interests in proceedings which determine administered protection.

The most evident example of formal/legal barriers is to be found in the anti-dumping and countervailing duty laws of the European Community. The right to participate in hearings on the application of these laws is limited by Article (74) of the EC Dumping and Subsidies Regulation to 'the complainant and the importers and exporters known to be concerned, as well as the representatives of the exporting country'. While some anti-protection interests are granted a right to be heard (i.e. importers), consumer interest groups are excluded, as are producer-users of imported goods who themselves are not importers. While the Regulation does permit other 'interested parties' to make written representations, these parties do not have a right to any information concerning the case of the complainant or of the European Commission, which renders even the more attenuated form of participation exemplified in written briefs largely impossible.

With respect to judicial review of countervail and anti-dumping decisions, even importers may not have standing, if they are not explicitly named in the measures being appealed against (*Alusuisse Italia Spa* v. *EEC Council* 1982 E. Comm. Ct J. Rpts 3463; *Allied Corp*, v. *EC Commission (No. 1)* 44 Common Mkt L.R. 57, 611 1985).

In the case of Canadian and American countervailing duty and anti-dumping laws, there are few formal constraints on participation of consumer and other anti-protection interests as *intervenors*. But the general structure of administered protection, which characterizes the foreign producer (who wants to export its product) and the domestic producer (who wants to protect its market) as the *parties* to the dispute, still does not treat equally the domestic losers, the latter being entertained merely as intervenors.

Public interest and dispersed interest groups face the difficulty of raising adequate funds to intervene effectively. Given the inherent tendency (due to the bias of the adversarial party-based approach to regulation) to give priority to arguments of *parties* over those of intervenors, the capacity of intervenors to make sophisticated arguments, bolstered by state of the art economic research, become especially important. In some cases (particularly in the US) a government department or agency with a consumer interest mandate may intervene, in recognition of the cost barriers that consumer organizations face in doing so (see Crawford 1986). In Canada, however, the Federal Department of Consumer and Corporate Affairs rarely intervenes in countervail and anti-dumping proceedings on behalf of the consumer interest, the recent Hyundai anti-dumping case being an exception that shows the potential effectiveness of such intervention to highlight the negative consumer welfare effects of imposing administered protection (see Kronby 1988).

A further, related participatory asymmetry inheres in the fact that under Canadian, American and European Community trade laws, investigation and research into the harm to domestic producer interests of supposedly 'unfair' foreign trade practices is conducted at public expense, whereas no public agency is legally mandated to inquire into the consumer welfare effects of the proposed remedies. In effect, pro-protection interests are provided with a free public good (Palmeter 1985).

(c) Exclusionary mandates and criteria of trade policy regimes

Broadened participation is of limited significance where the values represented by anti-protection interests are simply excluded from agency deliberation by technical legal criteria, or statutory limits to the agency's mandate.

In US trade law, for example, the legal requirements for imposition of anti-dumping or countervailing duties are a finding of dumping or subsidy by the Department of Commerce, and of material injury by the International Trade Commission (10 USC Subsection 1671). As Finger notes, the law, which is completely consistent with the GATT, allows no such investigation of gains to users of imports – either to other producers who use the imported good as an input or to consumers of a finished good (Finger 1982: 370).

While both Canadian and European trade laws do permit consideration of the consumer interest, the relevant provisions and the manner of their implementation have not led to consumer welfare concerns playing a major role in regulatory outcomes. Articles 11 and 12 of the European Community Regulation on Dumping and Subsidization by Non-Community States provide that after a determination of dumping or subsidy, and of injury, the Commission must go on to inquire whether 'the interests of the Community call for intervention' (Reg. No. 2176/84). However, there is no statutory or administrative guidance as to how divergent community interests ought to be balanced, which interests count, and for how much. In a few cases, of which the best known is *Wrought Titanium from Japan*, the Commission did decide that the costs of protection to domestic industrial users of imports outweighed the benefits to protected domestic producers. Apparently, EC trade officials view the Community Interest provision with distaste – they assume that it will be extremely rare that harm to consumers will be anything but trivial in comparison to that done to the domestic industry by the dumping or subsidy (Bourgeois 1985). Indeed, perverse definitions of the consumer interest have occasionally been invoked – in the *Kraft Line Paper Board* case, for instance, the consumer interest was held to be entirely consistent with that of the injured producer, because it was not in the interest of the consumer to become 'dependent' on a non-EC source of supply! (Council Reg. 551/83).

In Canada, a 'public interest' provision in the *Special Import Measures Act* (SIMA) allows consumer interests to be considered in anti-dumping and countervail proceedings. Where the Canadian International Trade Tribunal considers that the imposition of a duty, although otherwise mandated by law, 'would not or might not be in the public interest', the Tribunal may recommend to the Minister of Finance that the duty, or part of it, not be imposed. As Rugman and Porteous note, '(while) originally heralded as an important victory for downstream users and consumers, the public interest provision has languished in an environment of indifference since the enactment of SIMA. In the four years this provision has been in existence only three public interest hearings have been commenced from a pool of twenty-nine findings of material injury and consequent assessments of anti-dumping and/or countervailing duties' (Rugman and Porteous 1988: 28). Only in one case has the tribunal actually recommended that a duty should be foregone or reduced (Rugman and Porteous 1988: 29).

There are several reasons why the public interest provision has been largely ineffective. First, as with the European Community 'Community Interest' provision, there are no direct instructions as to the values to be considered, the structure of the inquiry, and the weight to be assigned to divergent values. Second, in the Canadian case consideration of the public interest is not mandatory, and hence there is no obligatory governmental inquiry into consumer welfare losses from protection. Third, even if it determines that not imposing duties would be in the public interest, the Tribunal itself cannot so decide. The best result consumer interests can hope for is that the Tribunal will send a letter to the minister with its recommendation – and at that point the matter presumably becomes one of pure ministerial discretion. The costs of a full-scale intervention by consumer interests, or other anti-protection interests (including the assembling of rigorous empirical evidence on consumer welfare costs) would have to be weighed against the questionable value of even a favourable outcome, namely a recommendation to the minister which has no binding force whatever.

A further, even more basic, problem with the substantive criteria which trade tribunals must apply in Canada, the US and the European Community is how *pro*-protection interests are defined. The injury to which administered protection is a response is injury to the domestic industry. As we have argued at length above, there is no legitimate ethical case for penalizing consumers in order to protect the market share of domestic *firms*. The ethical arguments hinge on the net aggregate social welfare effects of protectionism (utilitarianism), on the distributive justice consequences of lost jobs, and on the effect on communities of job losses. While there have been many trenchant criticisms of the injury tests used by trade tribunals, these generally tend to focus on the technical shortcomings of these tests. A more fundamental problem is that these tests are normatively incoherent: they do not disaggregate the senses in which 'injury' to an industry can be so morally significant as to justify requiring that other domestic interests pay a high price for measures to counter the 'injury'.

(d) Increasing use of trade protection instruments that evade formal justificatory processes

While the recognition given to anti-protection interests in administered protection proceedings is inconsistent, limited, and in practice often ineffective, the use of voluntary export restraints disenfranchises these interests completely. These restrictions are negotiated at the executive level between the governments concerned, and no public inquiry or deliberation is required as a legal precondition of their enactment. Indeed, according to Tumlir (1985: 42), 'for both governments concerned, though more so for that of the importing country, the main attraction of the export restraint is that it effectively abridges the domestic political discussion of the issue.'

In the US, executive enactment of protection without public hearings has been the subject of a legal challenge by a consumer interest group, which relied upon a provision in the *Trade Restrictions Act* (19 USC 1841) requiring hearings of a 'tariff board' before presidential authorization of trade restrictions. The US Appeals Court's rejection of the argument focused upon the 'voluntariness' of the restraints: 'the steel import restraints do not purport to be enforceable either as contracts or government actions with the force of law' (*Consumers Union* v. *Kissinger* 506 F2d 136 (1974) at 143).

This reasoning goes far to explain why, in other trading nations which use VERs, no participatory rights attach to the process by which they are adopted. Since procedural protections are assumed to be primarily aimed at protecting the foreign trading partner (not domestic interests that would be adversely affected by the measures being proposed), they are deemed unnecessary where the foreign partner voluntarily undertakes restraints. Even abstracting from the reality that VERs are usually negotiated under threat of other trade sanctions, there is certainly nothing voluntary about their impact on importing firms and consumers in the importing country or exporters in the exporting country who are left out of the export cartel created by the VERs (see Chapter 2).

(e) Inability of existing formal trade policy regimes
to consider alternative policy instruments

Among the most significant conclusions of our analysis is that less costly substitutes can often serve as effectively or more effectively the public goals to which trade restrictions are purportedly directed. The existing formal trade policy regimes, however, erect significant institutional obstacles to cost-effective instrument choice. Trade tribunals generally have no mandate to consider whether the 'injury' that has been found to the domestic industry can be addressed by alternative policy responses, such as labour adjustment assistance or exit-oriented industrial subsidies. In the case of countervail and anti-dumping actions, this is because the focus is on the supposed 'unfairness' of foreign trade practices – not on who wins and loses domestically from supposedly 'retaliatory' protection. But the rhetoric of 'fair trade' serves to conceal the fact that many industries which seek contingent protection are experiencing serious adjustment problems.

It is thus understandable that more rather than less costly instruments are frequently adopted, given that trade tribunals have little scope to respond to legitimate adjustment concerns of workers or communities except through the unnecessarily costly means of trade restrictions. In the case of safeguard actions, where the pretence of 'unfairness' is not present, this logic is recognized in the US 'escape clause' provisions, which allow the ITC to consider adjustment assistance as an alternative to trade restrictions, or to recommend that restrictions be conditional upon the industry undertaking adjustment programmes (see McGovern 1986: 301).

More generally, in many industrial countries there is a lack of co-ordination in the formulation of adjustment policy. It is difficult to see clearly the relative costs and benefits of substitute instruments when these instruments come under the discrete mandates of often quite diverse agencies and ministries, each of which has its own particular criteria for policy formulation, and its own institutional culture. To be sure, there are occasional recognitions of the possibilities for pareto-superior substitutions (e.g. adoption by several countries of trade adjustment assistance programs for workers subsequent to the Kennedy and Tokyo Round tariff reductions). But trade restrictions and firm-specific subsidies are granted on a case-by-case basis, and the question of whether alternative instruments which would entail significant legislative or structual reforms would be preferable appears abstract, or at least long-term, in

203

contrast to the immediate pressure to remedy a specific problem.

IV. Domestic institutional reform

A series of reforms to existing domestic policy institutions could significantly correct or mitigate these dysfunctions.

(a) Adoption of appropriate evaluative criteria

The mandates of domestic trade tribunals should require explicit balancing of consumer and industrial import-user interests against the utilitarian, distributive justice, and communitarian arguments for protection. This would entail an obligatory inquiry into the consumer welfare effects of the measures being proposed, as well as a specific determination of those costs which workers and communities would have to bear absent protection. Only then would it be possible to engage in a meaningful discourse about the normative justifications for consumers or the community at large bearing these costs.

Ideally, this kind of open normative inquiry would replace the pseudo-economic technical criteria which currently characterize anti-dumping, countervail and subsidy laws. While these criteria in some sense gain their legitimacy from the GATT Tokyo Round Codes, and while they are thought to constrain protectionism, in fact by perpetuating misconceptions about the economic justification for retaliatory tariffs or other trade measures, and concealing the real normative issues at stake, they tend to serve well the interests of firms seeking rents from protection (Sykes 1989).

At the current juncture, however, the rhetoric of 'unfair trade', applied by the US and to a lesser extent by the European Community to its Asian trading partners, seems on the ascendancy. Therefore, such a radical reform in criteria may not be politically feasible. However, *superimposing* a normative inquiry which encompasses all the legitimate values at stake upon a prior conventional analysis of subsidy, dumping and injury, seems possible in Canada and the European Community through strengthening of the 'public interest' and 'Community interest' clauses in their respective trade laws.

In the case of the Canadian law, for instance, explicit normative criteria (consumer welfare, aggregate social welfare, distributive justice, communitarian concerns) might well replace the intractably indeterminate 'public interest' rubric; inquiries into the 'public interest' (thus disaggregated) could be made obligatory; and the Tribunal could be granted the power to itself reduce or abstain from imposition of duties, where not normatively justified. In the European Community, a similar disaggregation of the 'Community Interest' might be undertaken.

In the US, where 'fair trade' rhetoric is most strident, at least a consumer welfare inquiry could be mandated after subsidy or dumping and injury have been found (such an inquiry is in fact mandatory in the case of Article XIX 'escape clause' actions under US trade law (19 USC Section 2252 (c) (4)).

(b) Broader and enhanced participation of all affected constituencies

Consumer groups and domestic industries adversely affected by trade restrictions should have full standing in trade proceedings. They should be able to make their case as fully and effectively as those domestic interests which purport to benefit from protection. This would normally mean the right to oral argument, and to disclosure of the other side's case to the extent that would normally exist given legitimate concerns for commercial confidentiality. Antiprotection interests should be able to benefit from an inquiry at public expense into the consumer welfare effects of trade restrictions (just as pro-protection interests benefit from the research by government officials in dumping and countervail cases). And because the cost of consumer groups participating *routinely* in trade proceedings may be prohibitive (even though consumer interests are always on the table), at least some official presentation of the consumer case should be obligatory. This might be undertaken by the consumer ministry or by competition policy officials.

(c) Coverage of all substitute trade policy instruments

Voluntary export restraints and other negotiated 'managed trade' arrangements should require legislative ratification, and prior to such ratification they should be subject to scrutiny by national trade tribunals. It would perhaps be too much to expect governments to allow their discretion to *negotiate* the deals in question to be fettered by administrative tribunals, but at least a rigorous and public examination of the costs and benefits against legitimate normative criteria would place a significant justificatory burden on the executive. While in the US, the legislative ratification requirement might require a constitutional amendment (because of the constitutionally entrenched separation of powers among the legislative, executive and judicial branches of government), a requirement of public scrutiny would not. Such a requirement is in fact now in place and must be respected before the President can provide 'escape clause' relief. In the European Community as well, legislative ratification would pose difficulties, given the relationship between domestic legislative sovereignty and the supra-national policy-making powers of the Community organs, but scrutiny by the European Commission would be possible.

(d) Ability to recommend alternative policy instruments to trade restrictions; the fit between means and ends

Before trade protection is granted, the applicant should have to prove that such protection is the least costly means available under the circumstances to address ethically significant adjustment costs. It would be open to those opposed to trade restrictions to show that other, less costly measures are available to achieve this end (such as access to government funding for worker retraining, scrapping of capacity, etc.). It would be in the interest of those seeking protection to explore these avenues first, or contemporaneously with applications before trade tribunals – otherwise they would risk not meeting the burden of proof that less costly options were not available. In addition, a proportionality test might also be required: very costly trade protection should not be awarded, where the ethically significant adjustment costs are themselves not great. The fit between means and ends should also be a focus of the tribunal's deliberations. For example, will trade restrictions really save jobs even in the medium term, or will firms merely capture the rents from protection, and substitute technology for workers in rationalizing production? Where it is claimed that restrictions will give the industry breathing room to adjust (thus preserving permanent jobs in a given community), is the firm or industry adjustment plan really viable? Is it based upon realistic macro- and micro-economic assumptions?

Least restrictive means, proportionality, and rational 'fit' tests give structure to normative inquiry, where divergent and potentially contradictory values are at stake. The possibility of such structuring answers the concern of those such as Rugman and Porteous, who fear that once deliberation on the public interest is a routine feature of trade proceedings, ('the task facing the Tribunal and the (government) in selecting from a variety of normative and ethical assumptions would be daunting' (Rugman and Porteous 1988: 30). In Canada, the use of least restrictive means, proportionality, and rational fit tests has become a prominent feature of constitutional rights adjudication, whereby the courts scrutinize government action to determine whether the limits it places on rights are 'reasonable'. In numerous cases, the courts have ruled that less restrictive means are available to vindicate legitimate collective goals or that the fit between ends and means is not sufficiently close to justify limits on rights (see Weinrib 1988; Beatty 1987). In a pluralistic democracy, such tests hold the promise of avoiding zero-sum outcomes to normative conflict, in which some legitimate values and interests come out as complete losers and others complete winners. Such outcomes themselves undermine pluralism, and overshadow possibilities for inventive and principled solutions which give their due to the full range of legitimate public ends in issue.

(e) Capacity to undertake and publicize empirical evaluations of alternative policy choices

An alternative (or possibly complementary) approach to the above reforms of existing policy institutions is to be found in recent literature which advocates the creation of new institutions focused on improving transparency in policy making and policy debate (OECD 1983a); Leutwiler *et al*. 1985). It is advocated that governments be required regularly to publish the costs and benefits of all forms of industrial assistance, whether subsidies, VERs or tariffs. Most of the proposals suggest that the function of estimating these costs and benefits be performed by an agency, which although publicly funded would be independent of existing policy processes and perform a purely informational role (Carmichael 1986; Long *et al*. 1987; Corbet 1986). A few commentators recommend the expansion of the mandate of existing agencies or tribunals in the trade regulation field to incorporate this function (Destler 1986; Economic Council of Canada 1988). Moreover, a particularly novel aspect of the proposals is that they generally would involve states binding themselves internationally, through the GATT, to provide domestic transparency (see especially, Carmichael 1986 and Long *et al*. 1987).

The model cited in most instances for a domestic transparency agency is the Australian Industries Assistance Commission (IAC). Established in 1974 as an initiative of the Australian federal government, the IAC is not subordinate to any government agency or department, but operates pursuant to independent statutory authority (the *IAC Act*). The most distinctive feature of its mandate is that the federal government is required to refer any proposed industrial assistance measures, except those of a temporary nature, for investigation before such measures are adopted into law (OECD 1983a: 43). Assistance is defined extremely broadly as any act 'that would in any way directly or indirectly, assist a person to carry on a business or activity or confer a pecuniary benefit on, or result in a pecuniary benefit accruing to, a person in respect of the carrying on of a business or activity' (quoted in OECD 1983a: 41). References require a public investigation by the IAC, including oral hearings, at which the various interests at stake, including consumers, are represented. No obligation exists whatever for the government to accept the IAC's recommendations. The IAC may initiate its own investigations, and is required to review existing programmes on a periodic basis. In addition, the IAC must report annually the 'amounts of protection afforded all industries, the economic performance of those industries and the effects of industry assistance on the economy' (quoted in Rattigan 1986: 159).

The objectives to be used by the IAC in evaluating requests for assistance are also spelt out in a general way in the enabling legislation. Theses include: making the allocation of productive resources in the community more efficient; facilitating 'adjustment to changes in the economic environment by industries and persons affected by those changes'; and recognizing the interests of consumers and consuming industries (Rattigan 1986: 187).

In a number of respects a domestic transparency agency would address the main dysfunctions in the policy process identified in this study. First of all, by publicizing the costs to consumers of various protection instruments, the agency would be an important means of combatting the conceptual bias which leads voters at large to assume that it is the foreign trading partner which bears the main costs of protection. Even sophisticated voters may well be surprised – as indeed we were – to discover just how expensive trade protection really is, in terms of costs to consumers per job saved.

Second, a domestic transparency agency would at least reduce some of the information costs which, as noted above, confront dispersed groups and limit their political efficacy. And, moreover, with respect to subsidies, there will be few concerted interest groups opposed to subsidization. Since subsidization (unlike trade restrictions) does not increase domestic prices above world prices, domestic producers who use imports will be largely indifferent to domestic subsidy policies.

Third, the fragmentation of the policy process – with different government agencies having responsibility for different policy instruments – makes overall coherence in the choice of instruments highly problematic. We have seen a persistent preference for more costly (quantitative trade restrictions) over less costly (labour or industrial subsidies) instruments to achieve the same goals. This may to a significant extent be due to the rent-seeking behaviour of producers, who capture – at consumers' expense – higher rents from the more costly instruments. When a public comparison of the relative costs of all instruments is available, governments may be less willing to respond positively to such rent-seeking behaviour.

Fourth, on-going scrutiny of the actual costs and benefits of policies once they begin to be implemented, and the comparison of those costs and benefits with the initial objectives of the policies, can counterbalance extravagant claims by proponents of intervention – whether claims about job maintenance or the benefits of subsidized rationalization – with a more sober estimate of the future returns from public assistance. Broad public support for many policies may be driven by unrealistic expectations about the capacity of government to resist, reverse, or retard market forces. These expectations are encouraged by the understandable tendency of bureaucrats and politicians – either out of instinctive professional bias or calculated self-interest – to make inflated claims for their own powers. One of the most prominent trends which emerges from our empirical analysis is the tendency for adjustment policies to fall short of their purported objectives, particularly when these involve resisting, minimizing, or making more gradual, employment dislocation.

Finally, the prospect of independent public scrutiny should discourage governments from proposing pure 'porkbarrel' assistance measures that would be profoundly embarrassing to the politicians once publicly disclosed. And ongoing surveillance of the full range of assistance measures would doubtless identify duplication and waste which even a government beholden to pro-protectionist interest might be desirous of eliminating.

Most of the proposals for internationally mandated domestic transparency measures emphasize the purely informational role of the proposed model agency (e.g. Long *et al* 1987: 36). However, as the example of the Australian IAC indicates, an 'informational' function may in fact have folded into it several distinctive roles.

For example, the agency's deliberations on the costs and benefits of protection may involve extensive public consultations and hearings, directly empowering not only concentrated anti-protection but also more dispersed anti-protection interest groups (such as consumer groups) to participate in the scrutiny of existing and proposed assistance measures. This participatory aspect to the agency's role, perhaps even more so than the reporting function itself, may lead to heightened awareness of the full range of interests at stake in adjustment policy debates, and contribute significantly to erosion of the mercentilist conceptual bias. Destler and Odell note that 'up to the present, a major constraint on politial participation on the anti-protection side, in product-specific episodes, has been that many companies, unions, cities and others who have a special interest in that particular trade decision have not been fully informed of their own interests in time to make a difference' (Destler and Odell 1987: 131). A transparency agency might be required to notify the full range of special interests affected by the proposed measures, and invite and in appropriate cases, subsidize the costs of their participation (Engelhart and Trebilcock 1981).

In addition, there is a thin dividing line between providing information and providing policy advice. Should the transparency agency, in presenting costs and benefits, make policy recommendations on which measures, if any, ought to be adopted by governments? The Australian IAC is explicitly assigned this role, strongly reinforced by legal constraints which prevent the government from acting before the IAC has completed its evaluation.

In fact, the very way in which costs and benefits are calculated or presented may represent a concealed, or even overt policy choice. Most of the proposals for a domestic transparency agency focus on economic efficiency as the basic measure of costs and benefits, excluding from the calculus the social costs and benefits recognized by the utilitarian, liberal contractarian and communitarian ethical perspectives (see e.g. Long *et al*. 1987: 69).

In the case of the IAC, the exclusion of such claims, and a narrow focus on economic efficiency, has led to a significant erosion of the public credibility of the agency, with pro-protection forces able to claim that its recommendations stemmed from a bias which disregarded or depreciated legitimate and widely held values, such as community stability (Howse 1988; Glezer 1982).

Once a transparency agency is recognized to possess its own distinctive bias, then the general 'constitutional' principles of openness and participation cease to provide a convincing justification for its function. Rather than generating the most comprehensive estimate of the impact of adjustment policies and facilitating voice for the widest range of normative claims, the agency become itself merely another player in the game and loses its 'constitutional' character.

Moreover, political support for less costly adjustment policies requires in practice that these policies be able to vindicate the variety of legitimate ethical concerns which underlie the justification for intervention. Exclusion of such concerns from the function of the transparency agency would substantially weaken its capacity to ameliorate the most dramatic policy making dysfunction identified by this study – the disproportion between the normative justifications for adjustment policies and the actual redistributive effects that many such policies actually have.

Indeed, one of the major benefits of such an agency would be its capacity to require those interests demanding trade protection measures or other forms of intervention to justify such measures through normative claims (i.e. distributive justice or communitarian values) that enjoy broad legitimacy in our democracies and that in each case can claim a measure of internal coherency that mercantilist claims for protectionism wholly lack.

An additional issue is whether a domestic transparency agency should be restricted to reactive assessments of the costs and benefits of existing or proposed trade restrictive measures or as well be able to canvass the merits of a broader array of adjustment policies. In our view, however, it would be precisely the capacity of the agency to present and publicize such alternatives (e.g. subsidies in lieu of VER) that would facilitate adoption of what economists (often scathingly) refer to as second best policies – i.e. those which vindicate non-economic values and interests at lower efficiency costs than the policies most preferred by rent-seekers.

In any case, an advisory role for the transparency agency, would – if the advice reflected not only economic but other legitimate perspectives on adjustment – have the advantage of essentially requiring a formal response by the government, and of publicizing in some instances alternative policy approaches, around which anti-protection forces (instead of merely decrying the logic of intervention) might plausibly rally broad public support.

V. From domestic to international reform: reconceiving the relationship between domestic interests and international co-operation

It has become commonplace to view the New Protectionism as symptomatic of a crisis in the multilateral trading system (see, for instance, Trade Policy Research Centre 1984). The system is seen as a means of constraining by rules domestic self-interest, for the sake of global welfare (Jackson 1983). In the simplest sense, our focus on the domestic determinants of protection shows the limits of this view – protectionist policies generate a combination of domestic winners and losers, both within the protecting and the exporting state. Indeed, conceiving the multilateral system as a world order where domestic interests are transcended by law actually encourages the conceptual bias behind many of the structural dysfunctions of domestic institutions, namely that the domestic interest is the producer (pro-protection) interest.

Both realists (e.g. Krasner 1976) and traditional liberal internationalists (Jackson 1983) judge the multilateral system by its capacity to constrain domestic self-interest in the service of an ideal of world order. The realists view the tensions in the system in the 1970s and 1980s as proof that (in the absence of a Hobbesian sovereign) relations between states remain, in essence, anarchic, with very limited possibilities for sustained co-operation (Grieco 1988). They attribute the apparent early success of the GATT to the existence of American hegemony, and the fact that liberalization was, during the period in question, in the domestic interest of the hegemon (Krasner 1976; Gilpin 1987). On a realist view, it would be folly to attempt to return to multilateralism. The best one can hope for are bilateral or regional deals or alliances, none very stable, and the inducement of some restraint by the threat of retaliation, at least where trading partners are of equal strength. And as between the weak and the strong, there is (as Thucydides' Athenian General puts it) 'no justice'.

The traditional liberal internationalists by contrast hope to reinvigorate the multilateral system, stressing the importance of a global vision, of farsighted statesmanship that places global welfare and common interest over immediate domestic self-interest. On this view, what has weakened the GATT has been erosion of respect for rules and principles that constrain self-interest (Bhagwati 1987). On this view, it was a belief in the global rule of law, and a firmness of vision that made the multilateral economic system successful in the first place.

In recent years, however, a third view of multilateral institutions has come to prominence, which interprets differently the relationship between domestic self-interest and global welfare (Keohane 1985; Ikenberry 1986; Lipson 1984). On this view, often referred to as the new liberal internationalism (Grieco 1988), multilateralism is a framework for the negotiation and maintenance of mutually advantageous bargains among states. Co-operation will occur or not occur depending upon whether the players have adequate information about the existence of possibilities for pareto-superior bargains, and whether means exist to deter cheating and to insure that the balance of the bargain is maintained. This view is liberal in the sense that it presumes that in many situations, once the transaction costs are appropriately managed, co-operation will ensue. But it is also realist, in that no *transcendence* of self-interest is presumed or required, and hence the persistence of incentives to cheat and renege on obligations is openly admitted. Hence, of central importance in the development of this new liberal institutionalist vision has been Axelrod's interpretation of the Prisoner's Dilemma, a paradigmatic game where players move – operating always within self-interested rationality – from non-cooperation to a relatively stable state of co-operation punctuated with intermittent episodes of cheating (Axelrod 1984).

In our view, the new liberal institutionalist approach is the most fitting as an explanation of the multilateral trading system and its limits. First of all, in emphasizing that co-operation is not an all or nothing proposition, the new liberal institutionalism allows the possibility for incremental reforms in institutions, precisely targeted at further reducing transaction costs. The traditional liberal internationalists, by contrast, depend to a large extent on exhortations to a return to the rule of law, and in as much as they advocate specific reforms, these are aimed simply at closing the gaps in an existing system of rules. Realists, on the other hand, have great difficulty explaining why the multilateral system has not unravelled almost completely – why for example, any liberalization could have occurred during the Tokyo Round (when the strains which have produced the New Protectionism were at least as great, if not greater than today, as the world was facing the full impact of the second oil shock). As Milner has pointed out, the realist scenario did in fact occur in the 1930s, but in the 1980s, despite an increase in protection, trade wars have been contained, institutions preserved, and total world trade has continued to increase (Milner 1988).

Moreover, the new liberal institutionalist approach seems much less susceptible to the mercantilist fallacy than either realism or traditional liberal internationalism. What the GATT did was not to create a vision of world order for which domestic self-interest would be justified, but rather to enable new sets of bargains which altered the domestic policy calculus, by expanding the range of domestic interests benefited by liberalization, and securing the greatest gains from domestically self-interested policy shifts.

Consider a two-country, two-product world. Where country A lifts a tariff from product A in return for country B removing a tariff from product B, it is not just country A's consumers who gain, but also country A's producers of product B, who now have access to country B's market. Of course, producers of product A in country A, and product B in country B will be losers, but there will be many instances where the losses will be less politically and ethically salient than the gains, or where the losses can be *managed* in such a way that a domestically superior outcome is attained for each country in the bargain (i.e. the tariff can be replaced by a less costly adjustment policy). Of course, arguably, such losses could be so managed in the absence of a bargain with another state (as we suggest above). But the logic of reciprocity is to include in the domestic calculus the additional or incremental gains that accrue from bargained removal of restrictions.

This formulation of the nature of reciprocity significantly qualifies the rationality of unilateral removal of trade restrictions. While our argument for a better domestic policy mix, often substituting adjustment policies for trade restrictions, implies that unilateral liberalization is logical, in a world in which one can get additional benefits from using liberalization as a bargaining chip, moving ahead unilaterally entails the opportunity cost of losing the added benefit of the potential bargain.

This, of course, goes beyond the neo-classical economic and public choice understanding of why reciprocity exists where unilateral policy modification makes sense: according to that understanding, reciprocity merely enlarges the set of domestic interests in favour of liberalization, thereby counteracting the supposedly inevitable domestic bias in favour of concentrated producer interests.

Even if the domestic institutional reforms we advocate were perfectly acceptable, and a domestic consensus were forged on the desirability of changing the policy mix away from protection in favour of labour adjustment policies, domestic welfare might not be served by acting unilaterally. It would make sense, inasmuch as other nations benefit from this shift as well, to try and extract some payment from them in return for undertaking it. It is here that the conceptual confusion between reciprocity and mercantilism lies. Mercantilism evokes the notion that in liberalizing one is giving up something to get something; reciprocity, by contrast, can merely evoke the self-interested rationality of forcing someone else to pay for a benefit which it is in one's interests, even absent the payment, to confer.

Of course, the strategic games played here can be quite complex. If country B knows that the policy shift in question is in country A's own interests, it may resist payment, hoping that even in the absence of payment the benefit will be conferred. On the other hand, if country A knows that its policy shift is something highly desirable to B, it may desist from making the shift (at a cost to itself) until B is prepared to pay. It, is for this reason that, as Axelrod and Keohane note, co-operation may not even occur in 'areas of shared interest' (Axelrod and Keohane 1986).

The multilateral system can fruitfully be understood as a framework which facilitates co-operation where shared interests exist, but where (absent the framework) strategic behaviour as well as information and other transaction costs would obstruct welfare-enhancing bargains. The rules of the system are not constraints on self-interest, but rather on forms of behaviour that threaten to undermine the capacity to make mutually self-interested bargains. Extracting concessions for what is in one's self-interest to do anyway, means promising to the other party, that even if the policy in question ceases to be in one's own interest, one will be bound to follow it. Many bargains may not be concluded: (a) because countries will not want to commit themselves to pursue a currently self-interested policy even if in the future it no longer serves their domestic self-interest (as defined by the relevant normative criteria), except at a price which exceeds the value of the benefit conferred on the other country; and (b) because the other country will not pay much, on the other hand, for an open-ended agreement that permits 'cheating' whenever it is in the first country's self-defined interest to renege on its commitments.

A durable and effective multilateral system will thus make it difficult for countries to unilaterally alter their commitments (thereby ensuring that trading partners get real value for their concessions), while at the same time making *some* unilateral alteration possible (so that a prohibitive price is not demanded for concessions). Hence, as Kravis has noted in his classic study on the GATT safeguards provisions, 'unequivocal commitments, without any avenue of recourse or succour, are rare if not nonexistent in peacetime international treaties and agreements dealing with economic problems' (Kravis 1963). And it is important to note that, in the trade context, when reneging does occur, it is not simply equivalent to defection in Prisoner's Dilemma type games. In the latter case, cheating reflects the constant tension between the realization that co-operation yields the best outcome over a repeated series of plays but that the optimal outcome in each play will be defection while the other player co-operates. In the trade case, as long as co-operative behaviour is in a country's perceived domestic interest *apart* from the alteration in behaviour it induces in the other players, there will be no incentive to cheat. What may happen, however, is that the domestic policy calculus may change, making concessions contrary to perceived domestic self-interest – indeed their cost, in terms of the normative criteria that prevail domestically, may outweigh the benefit that has been bargained for in return. Thus, while in Prisoner's Dilemma games, retaliation is the appropriate strategy to discipline opportunistic defection after a co-operative pattern has been established, and will tend to induce another series of co-operative plays, where domestic interests have actually *changed*, so has the co-operative equilibrium itself, and retaliation against the reneging state will not normally lead to the state in question returning to its previous behaviour.

Clearly, as depicted in our empirical analysis, the economic strains of the 1970s and early 1980s led precisely to a changed understanding of the domestic costs and benefits of liberal policies. This may to a large extent have been due to dysfunctions in the domestic policy process which presented a skewed calculus of costs and benefits against the normative criteria in issue. But in retreating from liberal policies many states have regarded themselves not as cheating, but as responding to irresistible dynamics in the domestic calculus. In some important instances, however, states have not regarded their reneging in this light, but rather as retaliation against the supposed 'cheating' (i.e. the 'unfair trade') of others. This has been the case, even though much the same pressures on domestic policy have in fact motivated the reneging in all of the countries concerned, regardless of whether it be characterized as cheating or as retaliation. The strategic benefit of characterizing one's reneging as retaliation is precisely to avoid subjecting it to the narrow, explicitly bargained for, escape clause provisions.

Because what is at issue is not really 'cheating', the retaliation (for reasons explained above) tends not to lead to the restoration of a co-operative equilibrium. What it does do, however, is to undermine confidence in the capacity of the system to constrain reneging on multilateral bargains sufficiently narrowly to make those bargains worth paying for.

What specific structural or systemic characteristics have led to this situation, and what institutional reforms can help correct those characteristics?

VI. The Tokyo Round approach to adjustment pressures: the relationship between trade and industrial policy misconceived

By the time of the Tokyo Round of GATT negotiations, most of the major industrial countries had already been experiencing severe adjustment pressures. Preferred policy responses to these pressures, as discussed throughout this book, varied considerably from country to country. In general, Europeans preferred subsidies, the US trade protection, the Japanese exit-oriented policies involving a mix of exit subsidy incentives, labour adjustment policies and cartelization. While the preferred American response involved explicit reneging on liberalization commitments, and hence would seem appropriately to have been filtered through Article XIX relief, the instrument choices of other countries had not as such been explicitly the subject of multilateral bargaining and constraint. They thus had almost unlimited room to manoeuvre.

The American response to this asymmetry was to label many of these foreign policies as 'unfair', as cheating on liberalization commitments in the sense that the injury effects of such policies on trading partners were similar to those of explicitly reinstating tariffs which had been removed through multilateral bargains. The economic logic of this view was quite dubious (see Chapter 2). But it did, through increasingly expansive interpretations of subsidy, dumping and injury in US trade law, give the US *its* room manoeuvre.

In the Tokyo Round negotiations, the US sought multilateral legitimacy for its approach to 'fair trade', while major trading partners sought to constrain American reneging under the guise of retaliation for unfairness. The end result, the Subsidies and Anti-Dumping Codes, probably served further to undermine the multilateral system. One approach to supposedly injury-causing industrial policies would have been to negotiate their removal for concessions. Having never explicitly bargained away the use of such instruments, why should the countries that preferred to use them have consented to have their use characterized as unfair, or prohibited without receiving new concessions? The Subsidies Code ended up legitimizing retaliation, without creating any plausible multilateral mechanism for determining trade injury from domestic industrial policies or bargaining for their modification or removal. At the same time, the Contracting Parties failed to reach agreement on a new safeguards regime, i.e. the *explicit* reneging mechanism in the GATT. The overall rebalancing of the system at the Tokyo Round thus gave the Americans their room to manoeuvre, without restricting the room to manoeuvre of other states. Precisely because the industrial policies of its trading partners did not constitute cheating on a pre-established co-operative equilibrium, the US could not have expected retaliation in this instance to lead to changes in those policies. As discussed in Chapter 3 above, the policies were generally undertaken to vindicate domestic normative concerns, and while retaliation would add to their overall cost, it did not (again unlike Prisoner's Dilemma situations) offer a carrot with a stick, i.e. the possibility of a co-operative equilibrium where the same interests (as defined by these normative concerns) could be satisfied at a lower cost than the cost of the present policies, including the cost imposed by retaliation. Indeed, for the complex reasons discussed in Chapter 2, where threats of retaliation produced co-operative behaviour, this was not in the form of changed domestic industrial policies, but of voluntary export restraints, perversely among the most costly means for the *retaliating* state to vindicate its adjustment concerns. But of course, since retaliation was really, in most instances, disguised reneging under adjustment pressures, the fact that it did not modify domestic policies made it no less attractive to states facing adjustment pressures. Indeed, arguably it was thus more attractive, since had the policies been removed, in most cases adjustment pressures would have remained, while the pretext for reneging undisciplined by safeguards strictures would have disappeared.

This is not to argue that some domestic industrial policies and other practices are never injurious to trade. In particular, in declining industries subsidies that serve to maintain excess capacity increase adjustment pressures generally, and hence, the tendency to renege. Altering domestic regulatory structures (e.g. in industries such as financial services and telecommunications) may well be an appropriate subject of multilateral bargaining, and may ease adjustment pressures inasmuch as new export markets are opened for domestic industries. And again, where such policy shifts are in the self-interest of the liberalizing state, the question will be what kinds of bargains can be struck so that other states pay for the benefits they receive. (Of course, at the domestic level, in some instance states will proceed unilaterally, where the costs of holding off in order to strike a bargain outweigh the benefit of the bargain multiplied by the probability of achieving it.)

VII. Underlying institutional/structural impediments to negotiating on industrial policy

(a) Information cost barriers

The success of the Kennedy and Tokyo Rounds of GATT negotiations in substantially reducing tariff barriers by negotiated reciprocity is generally thought to have been greatly facilitated by the practice of 'linear cuts' in tariffs (Winham 1986). Contracting Parties agreed to a given across-the-board reduction in tariffs, which was proportional to the existing tariff rate (so as not to penalize parties who already had relatively low tariffs). A list of exceptions was then tendered by each state, where it was not prepared to reduce tariffs according to the across-the-board formula. Detailed negotiations then ensued with respect to the exceptions.

It is less obvious how a linear formula approach could be applied to subsidies or NTBs. Each subsidy instrument is usually attached to a discrete aspect of government policy, and few nations would likely disrupt policies across-the-board by a fixed percentage reduction. Moreover, unlike tariffs which are *prima facie* trade distorting, with an across the board approach to subsidies there would be the intractable threshold definitional question of which subsidies would be included in bargaining and which would not. The GATT contains no mechanism for evaluating the trade-injurious effects of industrial policies, nor for reducing these injurious effects to a common metric. Without such mechanisms it is very difficult for parties to know whether they are able to achieve a broad balance of concessions through negotiations, and hence the effectiveness of reciprocity in inducing bargains is greatly reduced.

(b) Surveillance/verification

The capacity to achieve co-operation through bargains depends significantly upon the capacity of each side to verify that the other is upholding the bargain (Axelrod 1984). Here tariffs perhaps are among the ideal subjects for bargaining, as it is almost impossible to impose them without the other side noticing. Some possibilities for cheating are reflected in the necessity to accompany such reductions with agreements concerning customs valuation and administration. With respect to subsidies, however, the problems are much more formidable. As developed in detail in Chapter 3 above, the range of instruments available is wide, and some instruments do not even appear as subsidies (e.g. certain tax expenditures). Verifying whether other partners are cheating on a negotiated co-operative equilibrium can be very difficult, requiring ongoing scrutiny of a wide variety of domestic policies within each state. As the OECD has noted (1985b), many such policies are not clearly reported or visible within the countries concerned, let alone to foreign trading partners. Moreover, the durability of an agreement depends also on knowing whether to respond to a given action as *cheating* (hence, undermining the co-operative equilibrium, as well as putting in doubt the value of any bargain with the party in question) or as requiring a fine tuning of the co-operative equilibrium (further negotiations). A state may have any variety of motivations for a domestic policy shift, and automatic characterization of the shift as 'cheating' threatens unnecessarily to undermine trust. It is important, therefore, that parties not only be aware of the complex domestic policy shifts of other parties but also be able to assess the real reasons for these shifts, as well as their likely impacts on trade. Again, the GATT lacks any functional apparatus to perform this ongoing function of surveillance and verification.

VIII. Institutional/structural impediments
to an effective safeguards regime

The increasing use of VERs, quotas, countervailing and anti-dumping duties reflects, we believe, to a significant extent the adjustment pressures on the users, whose domestic policy processes have generated instrument choices more costly to domestic welfare than would be necessary to respond to adjustment pressures in a way which does justice to the legitimate normative concerns which they raise. Yet, from an international (multilateral) perspective, what is of concern is that the instruments chosen have either constituted 'cheating' themselves (VERs, which violate the strictures of the GATT on selectivity and on quantitative restrictions) or involve accusations that others are cheating (countervail and anti-dump).

The GATT itself has a mechanism which is available to allow states to renege within the framework of the GATT, where adjustment pressures are severe. This is the Article XIX (safeguards) provision, which permits temporary reneging under certain conditions (discussed in Chapter 2). The disuse into which Article XIX has largely fallen, reflected in the popularity of reneging through other instruments, may be due to several of its institutional/structural features.

First, Article XIX permits no selectivity whatever, thus requiring the reneging state to impose costs on all sources of imports, even though injury is largely caused by one country's exports. States clearly prefer inherently selective measures which avoid unnecessarily irritating trading partners with a small share of the market (Sampson 1987). Second, Article XIX imposes a compensation requirement on the reneging state, and permits retaliation in the absence of compensation. Under a legal orders view of the GATT, compensation for breach is an appropriate aspect of Article XIX – however, under neo-liberal view (advocated above) a safeguards provision may be understood as a means by which the risk of changed circumstances altering the costs and benefits of the bargain for one party can be shared between the parties. Using domestic legal terminology, the existing safeguards regime takes an efficient breach approach (allowing breach where the partner is fully compensated), whereas the underlying problem is that of impossibility (to what extent the risk of changed circumstances altering the domestic cost of performance should be reallocated between the parties (see Kronman and Posner 1989). A safeguards regime which does not allow some of the costs to be (at least temporarily) shifted or spread, will not adequately serve its purpose.

Third, because in the case of countervailing and anti-dumping duties, the measures in question are regarded as a response to foreign 'cheating', not domestic adjustment pressures, domestic regimes tend to allow imposition of such duties without any consideration of the harm to the exporting state's welfare which may ensue, or of any alternative means to respond to the domestic adjustment pressures which are really motivating in most instances the demand for contingent protection.

IX. Reforms to address institutional/structural dysfunctions

(a) Reforms to promote bargaining on domestic policies

Creating an institutional mechanism capable of surveying and estimating the trade injury effects of the full range of domestic economic policies would significantly reduce the *ex ante* information costs of bargaining over NTBs and especially subsidies. As detailed in Chapter 3 above, techniques (albeit none is clearly uncontroversial) for reducing domestic subsidy policies to a common metric (tariff equivalent) do exist. The creation of an international, GATT-connected, body to undertake the task of surveying and valuing in trade injury terms domestic policies would have several advantages: (1) it would permit comparison of diverse forms of assistance within a sector (for example, US defence contracting vs. European research and development grants in certain high tech industries); (2) it would also allow bargaining between sectors, which was highly important in the Kennedy and Tokyo Round tariff negotiations in breaking deadlocks on specific issues (Winham 1986); and (3) ultimately, it would perhaps permit the integration to some extent of tariff with NTB negotiations, with subsidy reductions being bargained against tariff reductions.

While such a mechanism might at first seem intrusive into domestic policy making, it should be noted that Article XVI of the GATT already requires that the Contracting Parties be notified in writing of 'any subsidy, including any form of income or price support' which will have either a direct or indirect effect on exports or imports of the subsidizing country. These requirements have rarely been complied with (Dam 1970), but it must be recognized that without any plausible institutional capacity to analyse the data, little pressure has been exerted on parties to comply. Furthermore, in an area with considerable domestic political sensitivity (that of government procurement) it appears that the GATT, with respect to the Code on Government Procurement, has been able to create a workable institutional framework to examine and evaluate trade impacts of diverse domestic policies (see Stern and Hoekman 1987).

Because in some instances the key concern of states about the trade impact of subsidies focuses on the balance of governmentally conferred advantages within a sector, the 'tariff-equivalent' approach just described may still need to be supplemented by negotiations within particular sectors, aimed at creating a negotiated balance between the aids that different countries provide. Sectoral negotiations may be a particularly useful technique where differing policy styles among the parties lead to disagreement at the definitional level as to what constitutes a subsidy. An existing example is the Code on Civil Aircraft negotiated during the Tokyo Round. As Winham (1986: 240) notes, 'the aircraft code essentially represented a trade-off between the US desire to regulate the use by other nations of non-tariff measures in the aircraft trade and other countries' wish to eliminate tariffs in the US market'. While the Europeans were concerned with US 'hidden' subsidies, through padded defence contracts to civil aviation manufacturers which permitted them in effect to 'cross-subsidize' production of civil aircraft, the Americans pointed to export credits provided to purchasers on favourable terms by the Europeans. Agreement on neither of these instruments was reached, but there were other trade-offs that did succeed, and Stern and Hoekman (1987: 65) suggest that 'experience with the Code suggests that it has facilitated trade in civil aircraft and, since it is nondiscriminatory, has been beneficial to other GATT members whether or not they are signatories'. While disagreements exist still between the Americans and Europeans on the operation of the Code, and on NTBs that are not clearly disciplined by it, these have been contained within an institutional framework which has increased trade within the sector, rather than resulting in costly retaliatory measures in response to purported 'cheating'. Here also, an institutional information-gathering/surveillance mechanism can aid the sector-specific institutional framework within the GATT, providing impartial data which may further assist in containing a dispute within the framework, and focusing it on technical issues rather than accusations of 'unfair' practices.

(b) Surveillance/verification

An institutional mechanism which gathers data on an on-going basis about the full range of trade and industrial policies, and measures their trade injury effects against a common metric, can also be used to address the surveillance and verification problems which may impede bargains on NTBs. While many proposals exist for a multilateral GATT-related agency playing such a role (e.g. see Leutwiler *et al.* 1985; Blackhurst 1986), it is important to define the role precisely. One view would be that the institution in question should actually perform an adjudicative role, determining whether in fact the domestic policies in question violate GATT rules, perhaps within the context of a requirement that policies which could be considering as reneging on existing bargains be submitted in advance for scrutiny. Another would be that the institution would simply provide sophisticated information about the trade impacts of given policy shifts, leaving the parties to evaluate whether in fact cheating or reneging has occurred, or whether perhaps new bargains are needed. Differences would be worked out in through the institutional frameworks established by specific agreements (e.g. government procurement, aircraft), through existing dispute resolution mechanisms, or even in some cases through *ad hoc* negotiations.

An adjudicative approach (which would have the institution passing direct judgement on domestic policies) has already created consternation in the Uruguay Round on the part of some Contracting Parties, who see this role as highly intrusive of domestic sovereignty (*News of the Uruguay Round* 27 May 1987). This has been further exacerbated by the fact that the proposal for a surveillance mechanism which is on the table (designed by the Australians on the IAC model) appears to entail the mechanism actually passing judgement on the domestic wisdom of the policies (*News of the Uruguay Round* 27 May 1987).

At the Montreal meeting of GATT Ministers, agreement in principle for a trade policy review mechanism was reached at the expense of abandoning an adjudicative approach. This is reflected in the wording of the Montreal communique: 'The review mechanism will enable the regular collective appreciation and evaluation by the CONTRACTING PARTIES of the full range of individual Contracting Parties' trade policies and practices and their impact on the functioning of the multilateral trading system. It is not intended to serve as a basis for the enforcement of specific GATT obligations or for dispute settlement procedures, or to impose new policy commitments on Contracting Parties' (GATT Secretariat 1988: 35).

While on a 'legal orders' view of the multilateral trading system this might be considered a highly undesirable compromise, on our neo-liberal view, it is entirely appropriate. Bargains can effectively be self-enforcing, and co-operation can be preserved, where appropriate surveillance and verification mechanisms exist, often in the absence of an independent adjudicator/enforcer. These mechanisms should allow rapid detection of violations, and allow the actors to distinguish violations from areas of interpretive disagreement, or lacunae in the agreement itself that require new bargains to be struck. Here, the analogy to arms control agreements (which can be highly stable forms of co-operation where appropriate surveillance and verification measures exist) is most salient. Such agreements virtually never have enforcement/adjudication mechanisms, but do typically possess a framework for resolving interpretative disputes, and an agreed approach to collection and evaluation of data relevant to assessment of compliance (Axelrod 1985; Schelling 1963; Axelrod and Keohane 1986).

It is worth exploring in somewhat greater detail the importance of distinguishing instances of defection/cheating from other kinds of behaviour that alter in some way a bargain, or appear to. Rapid retaliation may be an appropriate means of responding to defection, within a Prisoner's Dilemma framework. This is the case where the other party is in fact consciously defecting: retaliation followed by co-operation indicates that defection will be punished but a return to co-operation is clearly desired. However, where the other side does not consciously cheat, and retaliation is adopted because cheating is *assumed* to occur, it appears to the side retaliated against that retaliation is in fact defection by the side that believes itself to be retaliating. Thus understood, the 'retaliation' may be taken as a signal of abandonment of the co-operative equilibrium rather than a wish to return to it. Note that what is important here in preserving co-operation is not the absence of behaviour that may change the value of the bargain but the interpretation of that behaviour. This distinction also underlies our approach to safeguards reform.

(c) A safeguard based approach for contingent prohibition

The possibility of achieving a separation of subsidies and dumping issues from the case for 'reneging' under adjustment pressures depends significantly upon the capacity to fashion a safeguard regime that embodies some of the attractive features (for protecting states) of unilateral measures, including countervail, antidumping and VERs.

Among the most attractive features of these instruments is their selectivity – they are applied in a discriminatory fashion against individual country(ies) understood to be the source of the threat rather than against all suppliers. This, of course, limits compensation that has to be paid and the political fallout which would ensue from 'sideswiping' of minor suppliers.

Can a measure of selectivity be introduced into safeguards provisions of the GATT without largely undermining the principle of unconditional MFN, entrenched in Article 1? Some, such as Bhagwati, think that it cannot (Bhagwati 1988). In one sense the trade-off would be (especially with respect to VERs) to accept a dilution of principle for the benefits which might occur through subjecting discriminatory protection to multilateral discipline and surveillance (Richardson 1987).

Yet the realism/idealism dilemma ill fits our understanding of the GATT as a framework for bargaining, rather than a self-contained normative order. The question, then becomes, what *function* does MFN serve in the GATT? One function is to expand, through a kind of multiplier effect, the benefits from free trade, by generalizing each concession. Indeed, arguably without such an effect, developing countries – which often have little to bargain with – would have gained little access to export markets crucial to their economic growth. Another function of non-discrimination in facilitating bargains is evoked by Axelrod and

Keohane: when several actors negotiate separately and sequentially over issues that are substantially interdependent, subsequent bargains may call previous agreements into question by altering the value of concessions that have been made (Axelrod and Keohane 1986). A role that ensures that all players have the benefit of all future bargains counters concerns about how these bargains will alter value for previous concessions, and hence makes states less reluctant to make the concessions.

Would either of these positive functions of MFN be undermined by introducing a measure of selectivity into the safeguards regime, which is concerned *not* with directly facilitating new bargains but with constraining reneging from previous ones? In our view, only the second function is potentially at issue – if other states fear that they will each be treated differently by a reneging state, they will likely withhold some concessions from the multilateral bargaining process, in order to bargain them bilaterally for preferential treatment by a reneging state.

However by interpreting 'non-discrimination' as equality of treatment in the safeguards regime, one could introduce a means of selectivity without undermining the functions of MFN. In imposing a burden on the exporting state, the reneging state should do so in proportion to the degree of injury that each exporting state is causing by the exports in question. On this approach, no 'special deals' need be feared, while at the same time an exporting state that has made only a *de minimis* contribution to the injury might be exempted from safeguard actions. In sum, states could not buy exemptions through bilateral concessions, but would be entitled to receive them on an 'equality of treatment' principle. Equality may well mean treating like alike, and unlikes differently, rather than treating all the same (Aristotle 1976).

Hence incorporating 'equality of treatment' and *de minimis* exemptions into the safeguards regime does not threaten to undermine the key functions of MFN in the GATT. An example of an appropriate *de minimis* test is to be found in Article 1102 of the Canada–US Free Trade Agreement, which exempts from safeguards action imports that are not 'substantial' or are not 'contributing' importantly to the 'serious injury' of the 'importing party'. Imports in the range of 5–10 per cent of total imports are deemed normally to meet this test.

(1) Defining the object of the injury

It is a reflection of an enduring mercantilist legacy to be concerned about import-induced injury to domestic produces *per se*, when both theory and the empirical evidence overwhelmingly suggest that the costs to domestic consumers of trade restrictions, even safeguard restrictions, far exceed any producer benefits. No non-economic values can possibly justify protecting the owners of capital in affected industries by imposing disproportionate losses on consumers. However, not only less well-endowed and immobile workers, but dependent communities may also be able to make normatively defensible claims that are not vulnerable to a utilitarian social welfare calculus. Thus, a new safeguards regime should require proof not of serious injury to domestic producers of like products to the imports in question but, rather, serious injury to less-endowed and immobile workers or long-established and dependent communities.

(2) Compensation/retaliation

A new safeguard regime should not require compensation to the exporting state – the very logic of permitting states to renege is to allow some spreading of the risk that changed circumstances may alter dramatically the immediate costs and benefits of a previous bargain. But, the degree of risk that exporting states are subject to should be constrained by a 'minimal impairment' principle. Under this principle, reneging would only be permitted where other means were not available to address adjustment concerns which were less detrimental to exporting states' welfare. These measures would include labour markets policies, exit oriented subsidies and other means to address the adjustment pressures driving the normative claims for protection.

Making safeguard action conditional upon adoption of a specific set of adjustment policies by the reneging state would be highly intrusive of domestic policy sovereignty (Trebilcock 1989). Thus, states might be left to choose the mix of instruments they deem most appropriate, but the revenues from protectionist safeguard measures should be requested to be allocated to the funding of adjustment policies (see Bhagwati 1988).

(3) Forms of safeguards

In order to render the costs, both domestically and internationally, as transparent as possible, the only possible forms of safeguard actions should be tariffs or auctioned quotas. Other forms of quantitative restrictions should be prohibited. It is noteworthy that under the bilateral track for emergency actions under the Canada–US Free Trade Agreement (Article 1101), only tariffs may be invoked; auctioned quotas might also be permitted under a GATT safeguard regime because the transparency qualities are similar. In both cases, an additional virtue is their revenue-raising potential (unlike, e.g. VERs, which simply confer scarcity rents on foreign producers). These revenues will provide new sources to domestic governments out of which to finance generous adjustment programmes for affected workers or communities, if required.

(4) Degressivity and time limitations

Again, the bilateral emergency track under the FTA offers some useful guidance. Emergency actions are limited to three years and no renewals are permitted. Perhaps in some domestic sectors most severely impacted by off-shore imports, five years might seem a more realistic time limit.

Alternatively, the function of monitoring adherence to safeguards strictures might be confided to the international surveillance and verification mechanism described previously. Its institutional capacity to deal with the substitution effects of trade and domestic adjustment policies and technical capacity to evaluate injury to exports would seem to make it well placed to monitor the 'minimum impairment' and 'positive adjustment' requirements of a new safeguards regime.

In the Tokyo Round negotiations, however, a key impediment to agreement on safeguards reform was precisely the immovable opposition of the European Community to multilateral enforcement of safeguards strictures. On the other hand, many developing countries had been prepared to accept a degree of selectivity in the regime as long as multilateral enforcement procedures were available (Winham 1986: 240–7)

It may be possible, however, to envisage a multilateral institutional surveillance and verification role that does not involve a quasi-judicial *ex ante* scrutiny of safeguard action. Ongoing *ex post* surveillance would provide significant benefits in reinforcing bargains and disciplining reneging, even in the absence of a legal orders type of enforcement mechanism. Here once again we make an analogy to arms control agreements and their verification provisions and emphasize the importance of facilitating *identification* of co-operators and defectors (Axelrod and Keohane 1986: 24). Since 'governments with good reputations can more easily make agreements than governments with bad ones' (p. 24) clear identification as a defector is an important self-activating sanction, whether or not the identification comes through a judicial process.

X. Conclusion

The above reforms map out an institutional framework that can structure co-operative, positive-sum responses to the present impasse. The use of protection premised upon the supposed 'cheating' of others has led to a retaliatory spiral that threatens co-operation. The precise point at which the spiral will end probably depends at least as much on the evolution of domestic understanding of self-interest as on the existence of appropriate international institutional arrangements for co-operation. Our study has focused on clarifying the normative claims at issue in the domestic policy arena and how well different sets of policies respond (or, more frequently, how badly) to the substance of these claims. Identifying conceptual and institutional failures allows us to map a direction for reform, although without any determinative certainty that it will occur. Much depends on political will. But without ideas and institutions, the political will to reform has little to nourish it. It is in the clarification of concepts and norms, and the redesign of institutions that lawyers and scholars of political economy can make a vital contribution. Wisdom is a necessary, but not sufficient condition of prophetic statemanship, whether domestic or international (Weber 1963).

Bibliography

Abonyi, A. and Atkinson, M. (1983) 'Technological innovation and industrial policy', in M. Atkinson and M. Chandler (eds) *The Politics of Canadian Public Policy*, Toronto: University of Toronto Press.

Adams, F.G. (1985) 'Industrial policy impacts on the US steel industry: a simulation study', in F.G. Adams (ed.) *Industrial Policies for Growth and Competitiveness: Vol. II: Empirical Studies*, Toronto: D.C. Heath/Lexington Books.

Adams, F.G. and Klein, L. (eds) (1983) *Industrial Policies for Growth and Competitiveness*, Toronto: D.C. Heath/Lexington Books.

Adams, R.J. (1982) 'The federal government and tripartism', *Industrial Relations* 37: 606–16.

Adlercreutz, A. (1985) 'Sweden', in R. Blanpain (ed.) *International Encyclopedia for Labour Law and Industrial Relations* 9: Kluwer Publishers.

Advisory Council on Adjustment (1989) *Adjusting to Win*, Ottawa: Supply and Services.

Aggarwal, V.K. and Haggard, S. (1983) 'The politics of protection in the US textile and apparel industries'. in J. Zysman and L. Tyson (eds) *American Industry in International Competition*, Ithaca: Cornell University Press.

Ahmad, J. (1988) 'Trade-related, sector-specific industrial adjustment policies in Canada: an analysis of the textile, clothing and footwear industries'. (background study) Ottawa: Economic Council of Canada.

Aho, C.M. (1985) 'US labor market adjustment policies in a changing world economy', in C. Stirling and J. Yochelsm (eds) *Under Pressure: US Industry and the Challenges of Structural Adjustment*, Boulder, Colorado: Westview Press.

Aho, C.M. and Bayard, T.O. (1984) 'Costs and benefits of trade adjustment assistance', in R.E. Baldwin and A.O. Krueger (eds) *The Structure and Evolution of Recent US Trade Policy*, Chicago: University of Chicago Press.

Akerlof, G.A. (1970) 'The market for "Lemons": quality, uncertainty and the market mechanism', in *The Quarterly Journal of Economics* 84: 488–500.

Aldcroft, D. (1982) 'Britain's economic decline 1870–1980', in G. Roderick and M. Stephens (eds) *The British Malaise*, Basingstoke: Falmer Press.

Allen, G.C. (1979) 'Government intervention in the economy of Japan', in P. Maunder (ed.) *Government Intervention in the Developed Economy*, Beckenham: Croom Helm.

—— (1980) *Japan's Economic Policy*, London: Macmillan Press.

—— (1981a) 'Industrial policy and innovation in Japan', in C. Carter (ed.) *Industrial Policy and Innovation*, London: Heinenmann.

—— (1981b) *The Japanese Economy*, London: Weidenfeld & Nicolson.

Allen, K. (1979) *Balanced National Growth*, Toronto: D.C. Heath/ Lexington Books.

Alt, J. (1979) *The Politics of Economic Decline*, New York: Columbia University Press.

Alt, J. and Chrystal A. (1983) *Political Economics*, Berkeley, CA: University of California Press.

American Bar Association (Committee on International Trade Law) (1986) 'The natural resource subsidy debate: a critique of proposed legislative action', *The International Lawyer* 21.

Anawaty, W.A. (1979) 'The US legal response to steel dumping', *Canada–United States Law Journal* 2: 60–70.

Anderson, D. (1986) 'Marketing arrangements for Western Canadian coking coal', *Canadian Public Policy* 12, 3: 473–83.

Anderson, J. and Gunderson, M. (1982) *Union-Management Relations in Canada*, Toronto: Addison-Wesley.

Anderson, K. (1980) 'The political market for government assistance to Australian manufacturing industries', *Economic Record* 56 (June): 132–43.

Anderson, K. and Baldwin, R.E. (1981) *The Political Market for Protection in Industrial Countries: Empirical Evidence*, World Staff Working Paper, 492, Washington DC.

Andras, R.K. (1979) 'The federal government's response to the task force on the Canadian shipbuilding industry', *Seaports and the Shipping World* 35–8, 70.

Anton, T.J. (1980) *Administered Politics*, Boston: Martinus Nijhoff Publishing.

ANZ Bank (1983) *Australia in Figures*, Melbourne: ANZ Bank.

Ardagh, J. (1982) *France in the 80's*, London: Martin Secker & Warburg.

Aristotle, *The Ethics*, trans. J.A.K. Thomson, 1976. Harmondsworth: Penguin.

Armstrong, J. (1973) *The European Administrative Elite*, Princeton, NJ: Princeton University Press.

Ashford, D. (1981) *Policy and Politics in Britain: The Limits of Consensus*, Oxford: Basil Blackwell.

Atkinson, M. (1986) 'The bureaucracy and industrial policy' in Vol. 44, Studies for Royal Commission on the Economic Union and Development Prospects for Canada, Toronto: University of Toronto Press.

Atkinson, M. and Chandler, M. (eds) (1983) *The Politics of Canadian Public Policy*, Toronto: University of Toronto Press.

Atkinson, M. and Coleman, W. (1983) 'Corporatism and Industrial Policy', paper presented to European Group for Organizational Studies, Florence.

Aucoin, P. and Bakvis, H. (1983) 'Organizational differentiation and integration: the case of regional economic development policy in Canada', paper presented to the Canadian Political Science Association, Vancouver, June.

Axelrod, R. (1984) *The Evolution of Co-operation*, New York: Basic Books.

Axelrod, R. and Keohane, R. (1985) 'Achieving cooperation under anarchy', in K. Oye (ed.) *Cooperation Under Anarchy*, Princeton, NJ: Princeton University Press.

Bacon, R. and Eltis, W. (1978) *Britain's Economic Problem: Too Few Producers*, 2nd edn, London: Macmillan Press.

Bain, G.W. and Price, R. (1980) *Profiles of Union Growth: A Comparative Portrait of Eight Countries*, Oxford: Basil Blackwell.

Bakvis, H. and Chandler, W. (eds) (1987) *Federalism and the Role of the State*, Toronto: University of Toronto Press.

Balassa, B. (1985) 'French industrial policy under the Socialist government', *American Economic Review* 75.

—— (1986) 'Selective vs general economic policy in postwar France', in F.G. Adams and C. Stoffaes (eds) *French Industrial Policy*, Washington DC: The Brookings Institution.

Balassa, B. and Michalopoulos C. (1987) 'The extent and cost of protection in developed–developing country trade', in D. Salvatore (ed.) *The New Protectionist Threat to World Welfare*, New York: North-Holland, Elsevier Science.

Balassa, C. and Balassa, B. (1984) 'Industrial protection in the developed countries', *The World Economy* 7: 179–96.

Baldwin, C. *et al.* (1983) 'Budgetary time bombs controlling government loan guarantees', *Canadian Public Policy* (September) 9: 338–46.

Baldwin, J. (1982) 'Trade policy in developing countries', in R.W. Jones and P. Kener (eds) *Handbook of International Economics* 1, Amsterdam: North Holland.

Baldwin, J.R. and Gorecki, P.K. (1985) 'The determinants of the Canadian tarif structure before and after the Kennedy round'. Discussion Paper no. 280. Ottawa: Economic Council of Canada.

Baldwin, R. (1985) *The Political Economy of US Import Policy*, Cambridge, MIT Press.

Ballance, R. and Sinclair, S. (1983) *Collapse and Survival: Industrial Strategies in a Changing World*, London: Allen & Unwin.

Banks, G. and Tumlir, J. (1986) *Economic Policy and the Adjustment Problem*, London: Trade Policy Research Centre.

Banting, K. (1982) *The Welfare State and Canadian Federalism*, Montreal: McGill-Queen's University Press.

—— (1986) 'The State and economic interests: an introduction' in *Vol. 32, Studies for Royal Commission on the Economic Union and Development Prospects for Canada*, Toronto: University of Toronto Press.

Barcelo, J.J. III (1971–2) 'Antidumping as barrier to trade', *Cornell Law Journal* 57: 491.

Barcelo, J. (1977) 'Free trade and efficiency implications of subsidies and countervailing duties', *Law and Policy in International Business* 9: 779.

—— (1980a) 'Subsidies, countervailing duties and anti-dumping after the Tokyo round', *Cornell International Law Journal* 13: 257.

—— (1980b) 'The two track subsidies code – countervailing duties and trade retaliation', in J. Quinn and P. Slayton (eds) *Non-Tariff Barriers after the Tokyo Round*, Montreal: Institute for Research on Public Policy.

—— (1984) 'An 'injury-only' regime for imports and actionable subsidies', in D. Wallace (Jr.) (ed.) *Interface Three: Legal Treatment of Domestic Subsidies*, Washington DC: International Law Institute.

Bartel, H. and Wragge, P. (1981) 'A conceptual framework for government bailouts', paper for Department of Consumer and Corporate Affairs, Government of Canada, Ottawa.

Beatty, D. (1987) *Putting the Charter to Work: Designing a Constitutional Labour Code*, Montreal: McGill-Queen's University Press.

Bebchuk, L. (1988) 'A new approach to corporate reorganizations', *Harvard Law Review* 101, 4: 775.

Becker, G.S. (1983) 'A theory of competition among pressure groups for political influence, *Quarterly Journal of Economics* XCVIII: 371–400.

Beer, S. (1982) *Britain Against Itself: The Contradictions of Collectivism*, New York: Norton.

Beigie, C. and Stewart, J. (1985) 'Canada's industrial challenges and business–government relations: toward effective collaboration', in V.V. Murray (ed.) *Theories of Business–Government Relations*, Toronto: Trans-Canada Press.

Bendick, M., Jr. (1981) 'National industrial policy and economically distressed communities', *Policy Studies Journal* 10: 220–35.

Berger, S.D. (ed.) (1981) *Organizing Interests in Western Europe*, New York: Cambridge University Press.

Bergsten, C.F. (1975) 'On the non-equivalence of import quotas and voluntary export restraints', in F. Bergsten (ed.) *Toward a New World Trade Policy*, Lexington, Massachussetts: D.C. Heath & Co.

Bergsten, C.F., Elliot, K.A., Schott, J., and Takacs, W.E. (1987) *Auction Quotas and United States Trade Policy*, Washington: Institute for International Economics.

Berndt, E.R. and Fuss, M.A. (1986) 'Productivity measurement with adjustments for variations in capacity utilization and other forms of temporary equilibrium'. Working Paper no. 8602. Toronto: Department of Economics, and Institute for Policy Analysis, University of Toronto.

Berstein, J.I. (1985) 'Research and development, patents, and grant and tax policies in Canada', in *Technological Change in Canadian Industry*, in Vol. 3, Studies for Royal Commission on the Economic Union and Development Prospects for Canada, Toronto: University of Toronto Press.

Berstein, J. and McFetridge, D. (1986) 'The consequences and determinants of research and development and their implications for public policy', in Vol. The Royal Commission on the Economic Union and Development Prospects for Canada, Toronto: University of Toronto Press.

Bhagwati, J. (1987) 'Economic costs of trade restrictions', in *World Bank 1987*.

—— (1988) *Protectionism*, Cambridge, Massachussetts: MIT Press.

Biggs, M.A. (1980) *The Challenge: Adjust or Protect?*, Ottawa: The North-South Institute.

Bird, R. (1984) 'Few jobs in high tech', *Policy Options* 5: 23–7.

Birnbaum, P. (1981) 'State, centre and bureaucracy', *Government and Opposition* 16: 58–73.

Black, A.P. (1986) 'Industrial policy in West Germany: policy in search of a goal', in G. Hall (ed.) *European Industrial Policy* Beckenham: Croom Helm.

Blackaby, F. (1978) *British Economic Policy 1960–1974*, New York: Columbia University Press.

—— (ed.) (1979) *Deindustrialization*, London: Heinemann.

Blackhurst, R. (1986) 'The economic effects of different types of trade measures and their impact on consumers', in OECD, *International Trade and the Consumer*, Paris.

Blais, A. (1986a) *The Political Sociology of Industrial Policy* Vol. 45, Research Studies prepared for Royal Commission on Economic Union and Development Prospects in Canada, Toronto: University of Toronto Press.

—— (1986b) 'Industrial policy in advanced capitalist democracies', Vol. 44, Research Studies prepared for the Royal Commission on the Economic Union and Development Prospects for Canada, Toronto: University of Toronto Press.

Blais A. and Foucher, P. (1981) 'La politique industrielle dans les économies capitalistes avancées', *Canadian Journal of Political Science* 14: 3–35.

Blais, A., Foucher, P., and Young, R. (1986) 'La dynamique de l'aide financière directe du government fédéral à l'industrie manufacturière au Canada', *Canadian Journal of Political Science* 19, 1: 29–52.

Blais, A. and McCallum, J. (1986) 'Government, special interests and economic growth', in D. Laidler (ed.) *Responses to Economic Change*, Toronto: University of Toronto Press.

Blank, S. (1978) 'Britain: the politics of foreign economic policy', in P. Katzenstein (ed.) *Between Power and Plenty*, Madison: University of Wisconsin Press.

Bliss, M. (1982) *The Evolution of Industrial Policies in Canada*, Ottawa: Economic Council of Canada.

—— (1985) 'Forcing the pace: a reappraisal of business–government relations in Canadian history', in *Theories of Business–Government Relations*, Toronto: Trans-Canada Press.

Bloom, H. and Price, H.D. (1975) 'Voter response to short-run economic conditions: the asymmetric effect of prosperity and recession', *American Political Science Review* LXIX, 4 (December): 1240–54.

232

Bluestone, B. and Harrison, B. (1982) *The Deindustrialization of America*, New York: Basic Books.

Bluett, A.N. (1939) *Report on Economic and Commercial Conditions in Sweden*, London: Department of Overseas Trade.

Blythe, C. (1979) 'The interaction between collective bargaining and government policies in selected member countries', OECD, *Collective Bargaining and Government Policies*: 59–95.

Bobe, B. (1983) *Public Assistance to Industries and Trade Policy in France*, Washington, DC: World Bank Staff Working Paper

Boltho, A. (ed.) (1982) *The European Economy: Growth and Crisis*, Oxford University Press.

Borcherding, T.E. (1983) 'Towards a positive theory of public sector supply arrangements', in J.R.S. Prichard (ed.) *Crown Corporations in Canada*, Toronto: Butterworths.

Borg, G. and Vedin, B.-A. (1982) 'Knowledge – the basis for industrial success', in B. Ryden and V. Bergstron (eds) *Sweden: Choices for Economic and Social Policy in the 1980's*, London: Allen & Unwin.

Bornstein S. (1984) 'States and union: from postwar settlement to contemporary stalemate', in S. Bornstein, D. Held and J. Krieger (eds) *The State in Capitalist Europe*, London: Allen & Unwin.

Borooah, Vani and van der Ploeg, F. (1983) *Political Aspects of the Economy*, London: Cambridge University Press.

Bosch, G. (1985) 'West Germany', in Cross (ed.) *Managing Workforce Reduction*, Beckenham: Croom Helm.

Bourgeois, J.H.J. (1985) 'EC anti-dumping enforcement – selected second generation issues', *Annual Proceedings of the Fordham Corporate Law Institute* (1985), Chap. 27.

Bower, R. (1983) *The Two Faces of Management*, New York: Houghton Mifflin.

Bowles, S. and Eatwell, J. (1983) 'Between two worlds: interest groups, class structure and capitalist growth', in D. Mueller (ed.) *The Political Economy of Growth*.

Bowles, S. and Gintis, H. (1982) 'The crisis of liberal democratic capitalism: the case of the United States', *Politics and Society* 11, 1: 51–93.

Boyer, E. (1983) 'How Japan manages declining industries', *Fortune*, January 10: 58–63.

Bratt, H.A. (1974) 'Assisting the economic recovery of import-injured firms', *Law and Policy International Business* 6: 1–36.

Brennan, G. and Buchanan, J. (1985) *The Reason of Rules*, Cambridge: Cambridge University Press.

Breton, A. (1974) *A Conceptual Basis for an Industrial Policy*, Ottawa: Economic Council of Canada.

—— (1985) 'Supplementary statement', in Macdonald Commission, *Report* 3: 486–526. The Royal Commission on the Economic Union and Developed Prospects for Canada.

Brierley, W. (1987) *Trade Unions and the Economic Crisis of the 1980s*, Aldershot: Gower Publishing.

Bibliography

Brittain, S. (1978) 'How British is the British sickness', *Journal of Law and Economics* 21: 245–68.

Brodin, A. and Blades, D. (1986) 'The OECD compatible trade and production data base, 1970–1983' (Department of Economics and Statistics Working Paper no. 31) Paris: OECD.

Brown, C.J.F. (1980) 'Industrial policy and economic planning in Japan and France', *National Institute Economic Review* 93: 59–75.

Brown, D. and Eastman, J. (1981) *The Limits of Consultation*, Ottawa: Science Council of Canada.

Brown, L. and Shue, H. (eds) (1981) *Boundaries: National Autonomy and its Limits*, Ottawa: Rowman & Littlefield.

Browning, P. (1977) 'Protectionism: a game everyone wants to play', *Far East Economic Review* 90: 46–7.

Buchanan, J. (1975) *The Limits of Liberty*, Chicago: University of Chicago Press.

Bulbeck, C. (1983) 'State and capital in tariff policy', in B. Mead (ed.) *State and Economy in Australia*, Melbourne: Oxford University Press.

Bureau of Industry Economics (1981) *Australian Industrial Development – Some Aspects of Structural Change*, Research Report 2, Canberra: Australian Government.

—— (1981) *The Structure of Australian Industry – Past Developments and Future Trends*, Research Report 18, Canberra: Australian Government.

—— (1983a) *Structural Adjustment in the Australian Footwear Industry*, Research Report 13, Canberra: Australian Government.

—— (1983b) *Structural Adjustment in the Australian Whitegoods Industry*, Research Report 12, Canberra: Australian Government.

Burgess, J. (1984) 'An evaluation of the community employment program', *Australian Quarterly* 56: 239–48.

Burstedt, A. *et al.* (1972) *Social Goals in National Planning*, Bkforlaget Prisma: Stockholm.

Burton, J. (1979) *The Job Support Machine: A Critique of the Subsidy Morass*, London: Centre for Policy Studies.

Cable, V. and Rebelo, I. (1980) *Britain's Pattern of Specialization in Manufactured Goods with Developing Countries and Trade Protection* Washington, DC: World Bank Staff Working Paper no. 425.

Cable, V. and Weale, M. (1983) 'Economic costs of sectoral protection in Britain', in *The World Economy* 6, 4: 421–38.

Calabresi, G. (1985) *Ideals, Beliefs, Attitudes and the Law*, New York: Syracuse University Press.

Calame, A. (1980) 'Impacts and costs of wage subsidy programmes', *Experiences in Great Britain, Sweden, and the USA*, Discussion paper 11M 80–1a, Wissenschaftszentrum, Berlin.

Cameron, D.R. (1978) 'The expansion of the public economy: a comparative analysis', *American Political Science Review* 72: 1243–61.

—— (1984) 'Social democracy, corporatism, labour quiescence and the representation of economic interest in advanced capitalist societies', in J.H. Goldthorpe (ed.) *Order and Conflict in Contemporary Capitalism*, New York: Oxford University Press.

Campbell, R.M. (1984) 'From the post-war period to the 1970's: a comparative investigation of political economic policy processes and institutions', paper presented to the Canadian Political Science Association, Guelph, June.

Canadian Import Tribunal (1985) 'Report respecting the Canadian footwear industry', Ottawa: Supply and Services.

Canadian Shipbuilding and Ship Repairing Association (CSSRA) (1985) 'Report', in *Seaports and Shipping World*, June 1985.

Cape Breton Development Corporation (1985) *Annual Report*.

—— (1986) *Annual Report*.

Caplan, B. (1985) 'Sweden's winds of change', in *The Banker* 135, 709: 53–60.

Careless, A. (1977) *Initiative and Response*, Montreal: McGill-Queen's University Press.

Carlsson, B. (1983) 'Industrial subsidies in Sweden: macro-economic effects and an international comparison', *Journal of Industrial Economics* 32: 1–23.

Carmichael, W.B. (1986) 'National interest and international trade negotiations', in *World Economy* 9, 4: 341–58.

Carter, C. (ed.) (1981) *Industrial Policy and Innovation*, London: Heinemann.

Casey, B. and Bruche, A. (1985) 'Active labour market policy: an international overview', *Industrial Relations* 24, (Winter): 37–61.

Cass, R. (1989) 'Economics in the administration of US international trade law', working paper, International Business and Trade Law Programme, University of Toronto, 31 May 1989.

Cassing, J., McKeown, J. and Ochs, J. (1986) 'The political economy of the tariff cycle', *American Political Science Review* 80, 843–62.

Castles, F.G. (1975) 'Swedish social democracy', *Political Quarterly* 46: 171–85.

Cavallius, L. (1988) 'AMS: the Swedish labour market board', in G. Olsen (ed.) *Industrial Change and Labour Adjustment in Sweden and Canada*, Toronto: Garamond Press.

Caves, R.E. (1976) 'Economic models of political choice: Canada's tariff structure', *Canadian Journal of Economics* 9.

Caves, R. and Krause L. (eds) (1980) *Britain's Economic Performance*, Washington, DC: Brookings Institution.

Chaison, G. (1982) 'Unions: growth, structures and internal dynamics', in J. Anderson and M. Gunderson (eds) *Union-Management Relations in Canada*, Toronto: Addison-Wellesley.

Chandler, A. and Daems, H. (eds) (1980) *Managerial Hierarchies*, Cambridge, Massachussetts: Harvard University Press.

Chandler, M. (1982) 'State enterprise and partisanship in provincial politics', *Canadian Journal of Political Science* 15: 711–40.

—— (1985) 'The state and industrial decline', in *Industrial Policy*, Vol. 44, Research Studies prepared for Royal Commission on Economic Union and Development Prospects in Canada, Toronto: University of Toronto Press.

Bibliography

Chandler, M. and Trebilcock, M. (1985) 'Comparative survey of industrial policies in selected OECD countries', in *Economics of Industrial Policy and Strategy*, Vol. 5, Research Studies prepared for the Royal Commission on the Economic Union and Development Prospects for Canada, Toronto: University of Toronto Press.

Chandler, W. and Siaroff, A. (1984) 'Post-materialist politics in Germany and the rise of the Greens', paper presented to Canadian Political Science Association Meetings, Guelph.

Charette, M.F. *et al.* (1986) 'The evolution of the Canadian industrial structure: an international perspective', Ottawa: The Royal Commission on the Economic Union and Development Prospects for Canada.

Christelow, D. (1979–80) 'National policies toward foreign direct investment', *Federal Reserve Bank of New York Quarterly Review* 4: 4.

Cline, W.R. (ed.) (1983) *Trade Policy in the 1980's*, Washington, DC: Institute for International Economics.

—— (1984) *Exports of Manufactures from Developing Countries*, Washington, DC: Brookings Institution.

—— (1984) *Footwear Imports and the Consumer*, Washington: Volume Footwear Retailers of America.

Coates, D. (1979) *Labour in Power*, London: Longman.

—— (1982) 'Britain in the 1970s: economic crises and the resurgence of radicalism', in A. Cox (ed.) *Politics, Policy and the European Recession*, London: Macmillan.

Coates, D. and Hillard, J. (eds) (1986) *The Economic Decline of Modern Britain*, London: Wheatsheaf Books.

Cockerill, A. (1980) 'Steel', in P.S. Johnson (ed.) *The Structure of British Industry*, London: Granada.

Cockerill, A. and Cole, S. (1986) 'British steel', in W.H. Goldberg (ed.) *Ailing Steel: The Transoceanic Quarrel*, Berlin: WZB Publications.

Cohen, C.D. (ed.) (1982) *Agenda for Britain 1: Micro Policy*, Oxford: Phillip Allan.

Cohen S. (1982) 'Informed bewilderment: French economic strategy and the crisis', in S. Cohen and P. Gourevitch (eds) *France in the Troubled World Economy*, London: Butterworth.

Cohen S. *et al.* (1982) 'Rehabbing the labyrinth: the financial system and industrial policy in France', in S. Cohen and P. Gourevitch (eds), *France in the Troubled World Economy*, London: Butterworth.

Coleman, W. (1986) 'Canadian business and the state in Vol. 32, Studies for Royal Commission on the Economic Union and Development Prospects for Canada, Toronto: University of Toronto Press.

—— (1988) *Business and Politics: A Study of Collective Action*, Montreal: McGill-Queens.

Commission of Inquiry on Unemployment Insurance (1986) *Report*, Ottawa: Supply and Services.

Conlon, R.M. (1982) 'Trade practices control in Australia', in T.G. Parry (ed.), *Australian Industry Policy*, Melbourne: Longman, Cheshire.

Conybeare, J.A. (1983) 'Tariff protection in developed and developing countries: a cross-sectional and longitudinal analysis', in *International*

Organization 37, 3: 441–67.

Coombes, D. (1982) *Representative Government and Economic Power*, London: Heinemann.

Cooper, R. (1987) 'Why liberalization meets resistance', in *World Bank*.

Coopers & Lybrand Consulting Group (1986) *The Five Years Since the Introduction of the Voluntary Export Restraints (Quotas) on the Import of Japanese Cars into Canada*, Willowdale, Ontario: Canadian Association of Japanese Automobile Dealers.

Corbet, H.D. (1985) 'Public scrutiny of the costs and benefits of public assistance to industries: an international perspective', *Australian Outlook*, November.

Corbet, H. (1986) 'Public scrutiny of protection: trade policy and the investigative branch of government', in OECD, *International Trade and the Consumer*, Paris.

Corden, W.M. and Fels, G. (1976) *Public Assistance to Industry*, Boulder, Col.: Westview Press.

Cordes, J.J., Goldfarb, R.S. and Barth, J.R. (1983) 'Compensating when the government harms', in R.J. Zeckhauser and D. Leebaert (eds), *What Role for Government*. Durham, North Carolina: Duke University Press.

Corrigan, R. (1983) 'Choosing winners and losers: business, labour and political leaders are searching for a US industrial policy', *National Journal* 15: 416–43.

Cottrell, E. (1981) *The Giant With Feet of Clay, The British Steel Industry 1945–81*, London: Centre for Policy Studies.

Courchene, T. (1980) 'Towards a protected society: the politicization of economic life', *Canadian Journal of Economics*: 556–77.

—— (1981) 'A market perspective on regional disparities', *Canadian Public Policy*, Vol. 7.

—— (1983) 'Analytical perspectives on the Canadian economic union', in M.J. Trebilcock *et al.* (eds) *Federalism and the Canadian Economic Union*, Toronto: Ontario Economic Council.

—— (1987) *Social Policy in the 1990's: Agenda for Reform*, Toronto: C.D. Howe Institute.

Cousineau, J.M. (1985) 'Unemployment insurance and labour market adjustments', in *Income Distribution and Economic Security in Canada*, vol. 1, Research Studies for Royal Commission on Economic Union and Development Prospects, Toronto: University of Toronto Press.

Cox, A. (1981) 'Corporatism as reductionism: the analytic limits of the corporatist thesis', *Government and Opposition* 16: 78–95.

—— (ed.) (1982) *Politics, Policy and the European Recession*, London: Macmillan.

Crafts, N.F.R. and McCloskey D.C. (1979) 'Did Victorian Britain fall?', *Economic History Review*, 2nd series 32: 533–7.

Crandall, R.W. (1984) 'Import quotas and the automobile industry: the costs of protectionism', *Brookings Review* 2, 4: 8–16.

Crawford, C.T. (1986) 'Trade policy and the consumer: the consumer advocacy role of the federal trade commission in trade proceedings', in OECD.

Cross, M. (ed.) (1985) *Managing Workforce Reduction* Beckenham: Croom Helm.

Crouch, C. (1983) 'New thinking on pluralism', in *The Political Quarterly* 54, 4, October–December: 363–74.

Curt, H. and Olsson, P. (1986) 'A welcome to our foreign colleagues', *Skandinaviska Enskilda Banken Q.R.*: 14.

Curzon-Price, V. (1981) *Industrial Policies in the European Community*, London: Macmillan.

Dahmen, E. (1970) *Entrepreneurial Activity and the Development of Swedish Industry, 1919–1939*, trans. by Alex Leijonhufvud, Richard D. Irwin, Inc., U.S.A.

Dahrendorf, R. (ed.) (1982) *Europe's Economy in Crisis*, London: Weidenfeld and Nicolson.

Davenport, M. (1983) 'Industrial policy in the United Kingdom', in F.G. Adams and L.K. Klein (eds) *Industrial Policies for Growth and Competitiveness: An Economic Perspective*, Toronto: Lexington Books.

Davenport, P. *et al.* (1982), *Industrial Policy in Ontario and Quebec*, Toronto: Ontario Economic Council.

Davidson, F.G. and Stewardson, B.R. (1974) *Economics and Australian Industry*, Victoria, Australia: Longman.

Davies, J. (1986) 'Training and skill development' in Vol. 18, Studies for Royal Commission on the Economic Union and Development Prospects for Canada, Toronto: University of Toronto Press.

Dauphin, R. (1978) *The Impact of Free Trade in Canada*, Ottawa: Economic Council of Canada.

Dean, J.W. (1983) 'Polyarchy and economic growth', in D. Mueller (ed.) *The Political Economy of Growth*, 217–30.

DeCarmoy, G. (1978) 'Subsidy policies in Britain, France and West Germany: an overview', in S.J. Warnecke (ed.) *International Trade and Industrial Policies*, London: Macmillan.

de la Torre, J. (1981) 'Decline and adjustment: public intervention strategies in the European clothing industries', European Institute of Business Administration.

Dell, E. (1973) *Political Responsibility and Industry*, London: Allen and Unwin.

Denison, E. (1979) *Accounting for Slower Economic Growth: The US in the 1970s*, Washington, DC: Brookings Institution.

Denny, M., and Fuss, M. (1981) 'Intertemporal changes in the levels of regional labour productivity in Canadian Manufacturing'. Working Paper no. 8131 Toronto: Institute for Policy Analysis, University of Toronto.

Denton, G. (1976) 'Financial assistance to British industry', in W.M. Corden and G. Fels (eds) *Public Assistance to Industry*, London: Macmillan.

Denton, G. et al., (1975) *Trade Effects of Public Subsidies to Private*

Enterprise, London: Macmillan.

Denzau, A. (1988) 'The Japanese automobile cartel', *Regulation* 1 11–16.

Department of Consumer and Corporate Affairs, Ottawa (1986) *Annual Report*.

Department of Finance (1984) *Economic Review*, Ottawa: Minister of Supply and Services, Canada.

Department of Industry, Trade and Commerce (1979), *A Report on the Labour Force Tracking Project/Cost of Labour Adjustment Study*, Ottawa: Government of Canada.

Derthick, M. and Quirk, P. (1985) *The Politics of Deregulation*, Washington: The Brookings Institution.

De Silva, K. (1988) 'An economic analysis of the shipbuilding industry assistance program'. (Background study.) Ottawa: Economic Council of Canada.

Destler, I.M. (1980) *Making Foreign Economic Policy*, Washington, DC: Brookings Institution.

—— (1986) *American Trade Politics: System Under Stress*, Institute for International Economics, Washington, DC.

—— (1989) 'United States', in H. Nau, 1989.

Destler, I.M. and Odell, J. (1987) *Anti-Protection: Changing Forces in United States Trade Politics*, Washington, DC: Institute for International Economics.

de Vos, D. (1982) *Governments and Micro-electronics: The European Experience*, Ottawa: Science Council of Canada.

Diebold, W. Jr. (1980) *Industrial Policy as an International Issue* McGraw Hill: New York.

Doern, G.B. and Phidd, R.W. (1983) *Canadian Public Policy*, Toronto: Methuen.

Doern, G.B. and Toner, G. (1985) *The Politics of Energy*, Toronto: Methuen.

Dohlman, E. (1984) 'Evolution of Swedish textile trade policy', *European Free Trade Bulletin*, no. 1. 25, January/March, pp. 13–16.

Dolan, M.B. (1983) 'European Restructuring and Import Policies for a Textile Industry in Crisis', *International Organization*, Oxford: Martin Robertson.

Done, K. (1985) 'Restructuring Swedish banking', in *The Banker* 135, 718: 37–40.

Donges, J.B. (1980) 'Industrial policies in West Germany's not so market-oriented economy', *The World Economy* 3: 185–204.

Dore, R., (1986) *Flexible Rigidities*, London: Athone Press.

Dore, R.P. with Taira, K. (1986) *Structural Adjustment in Japan, 1970–82*, Geneva: International Labour Office.

Downs, A. (1957) *An Economic Theory of Democracy*, New York: Harper.

Dunlop, B.D.M. and Trebilcock, M. (1987) *Canadian Competition Policy*, Toronto: Canada Law Book, Co.

Dunlop, J.T. and Galenson, W. (ed) (1978) *Labour in the Twentieth Century*, New York: Academic Press.

Dunn, J. (1972) 'Railroad policies in Europe and the United States', *Public*

Policy 25: 205–40.

Dunnett, P.J.S. (1980) *The Decline of the British Motor Industry: The Effects of Government Policy, 1945-1975*, Beckenham: Croom Helm.

Dyer, D., Salter, M., and Webber, A. (1987) *Changing Alliances: The Harvard Business School Project on the Auto Industry and the American Economy*, Boston: Harvard Business School Press.

Dyson, K. (1977) *Party, State and Bureaucracy in Western Germany*, Beverly Hills: Sage.

—— (1979) 'The ambiguous politics of Western Germany', *European Journal of Political Research* 7: 375–96.

—— (1980) *The State Tradition in Western Europe*, Oxford: Martin Robertson.

—— (1981) 'The politics of economic management in West Germany', in W. Paterson and G. Smith (eds) *The West German Model*, London: Frank Cass.

—— (1982a) 'The politics of economic recession in Western Germany', in A. Cox (ed.) *Politics, Policy and the European Recession*, 32–64.

—— (1982b) 'West Germany: the search for a rationalist consensus', in J. Richardson (ed.) *Policy Styles in Western Europe*, London: Allen and Unwin.

—— (1983) 'The cultural, ideological and structural context', in K. Dyson and S. Wilks (eds) *The Industrial Crisis: A Comparative Study of the State and Industry*, Martin Robertson.

Dyson, K. and S. Wilks (eds) (1983) *The Industrial Crisis: A Comparative Study of the State and Industry*, Oxford: Martin Robertson.

Eads, G. (1985) 'Economists vs. regulators', in J.C. Miller (ed.) *Perspectives on Federal Transportation Policy*, Washington, DC: American Enterprise Institute.

Economic Council of Canada (1975a) *Looking Outward: A New Trade Minister of Strategy for Canada*, Ottawa: Minister of Supply and Services Canada.

—— (1975b) *Beyond the Frontiers*, Ottawa: Minister of Supply and Services Canada.

—— (1982) *Intervention and Efficiency*, Ottawa: Minister of Supply and Services Canada.

—— (1983) *The Bottom Line: Technology, Trade and Income Growth*, Ottawa: Minister of Supply Services Canada.

—— (1987a) *Innovation and Jobs in Canada*, Ottawa: Supply and Services.

—— (1987b) *Trade Policy for Vulnerable Sectors*.

—— (1988) *Managing Adjustment*, Ottawa: Economic Council of Canada.

The Economist, 7 April 1986.

The Economist, 2 August 1986.

The Economist, 11 October 1986.

The Economist, 1 November 1986.

The Economist, 23 April 1988.

The Economist, 'The world's richest people', 13 April 1974, pp. 5–6 of survey.

The Economist, 'Can technology revise Sweden's Economy?', 24 November 1979, p. 109.

The Economist, 'Sweden survey', no. 15, 1980, pp. 1–26, special insert.
The Economist, 'All change here', 15 November 1980, p. 3 of survey.
The Economist, 'Business brief', 4 April 1981, pp. 78–9.
The Economist, 'Swedish industry's thin upper crust', 4 April 1981, pp. 78–80.
The Economist, 'Sweden sinks one', 13 February 1982, p. 63.
The Economist, 'West Germany: survey', 4 February 1984, pp. 1–30 of survey.
Edel, M. (1979) 'A note on collective action, Marxism, and the prisoner's dilemma', *Journal of Economic Issues* XIII, 3 (Sept): 751–61.
Edelman, M. (1965) *The Symbolic Uses of Politics*, Urbana: University of Illinois Press.
Edmunds, M. (1983) 'Market ideology and corporate power: the United States', in K. Dyson and S. Wilks (eds.) *The Industrial Crisis: A Comparative Study of the State and Industry*, Oxford: Martin Robertson.
Elder, N. (1970) 'Continuity and innovation in Sweden in the 1970s' in A. Cox (ed.) *Politics, Policy and the European Recession*, London: Macmillan.
Emminger, O. (1982) 'West Germany – Europe's driving force?' in R. Dahrendorf (ed.), *Europe's Economy in Crisis*, London: Weidenfeld and Nicolson.
Englehardt, K. and Trebilcock, M. (1981) 'Public participation in the regulatory process: the issue of funding', working paper, Ottawa: Economic Council of Canada.
Esping-Anderson, G. (1980), *Social Class, Social Democracy and State Policy*, Copenhagen: New Social Science Monographs.
Esping-Anderson, G. and Friedland, R. (1981) 'Class coalitions in the making of West European economies', in G. Esping-Andersen and R. Friedland (eds) *Political Power and Social Theory*, Greenwich, Connecticut: Jai Press.
Esser, J. *et al.* (1982) 'Steel crisis and steel policy: a comparison of state intervention in Europe', *Inter-economies* 17, 279–85.
Esser, J. and Fach, W. with K. Dyson (1983) 'Social market and modernization policy: West Germany', in K. Dyson and S. Wilks (eds) *Industrial Crisis: A Comparative Study of the State and Industry*, Oxford: Martin Robertson.
Estrin, S. and Holmes, P. (1983a) 'French planning and industrial policy', *Journal of Public Policy* 3: 131–48.
—— (1983b) *French Planning in Theory and Practice*, London: Allen and Unwin.
Etzioni, A. (1983) 'The mitization of America?', *The Public Interest* 70–73: 44–51.
L'Express, 25 July 1986.
Faramond, G. de *et al* (1982) 'Sweden seen from the outside', in B. Reyden and V. Bergstrom (eds) *Sweden: Choices for Economic and Social Policy in the 1980s*, London: George Allen and Unwin.
Far East Economics Review, 4 March 1974.
Faucher, P. *et al* (1984) 'L'aide financier directe des gouvernements du

Quebec et de l'Ontario l'industrie manufacturier 1960–1980', *Journal of Canadian Studies* 18: 54–78.

Feenstra, R.C. (1984) 'Voluntary export restraint in US autos, 1980–81: quality, employment, and welfare effects', in R.E. Baldwin and A.O. Krueger (eds) *The Structure and Evolution of Recent US Trade Policy*, National Bureau of Economic Research Conference Report, Chicago: University of Chicago Press.

Finger, J.M. (1982) 'Incorporating the gains from trade into policy', *The World Economy*, December.

Finger, J.M. and Olechowski, A. (1987) *The Uruguay Round: A Handbook for the Negotiations*, Washington, DC: World Bank.

Finger, J.M. *et al* (1982) 'The political economy of administered protection', *American Economic Review* 72, 452.

Flam, P., Perssom, P. and Svensson, J. (1983) 'Optimal subsidies to declining industries: efficiency and equity considerations', 22, *Journal of Public Economics* 3: 327–45.

Flanagan, R., Soskice, D. and Ulman, L. (1983) *Unionism, Economic Stabilization and Incomes Policies: The European Experience*, Washington: Brookings Institution.

Fleming, M.C. (1980) 'Industrial policy', in W.P.J. Maunder (ed.) *The British Economy in the 1970's*, London: Heinemann.

Folbre J., Leighton, A. and Roderick, B. (1984) 'Plant closings and their regulation in Maine, 1971–1982', *Industrial and Labour Relations Review*, 37: 185.

Foster, P. (1984) *Other People's Money: The Banks, the Government and Dome*, Toronto: Collins.

Frank, I. (1981) *Trade Policy for the Developing Countries in the 1980s*. Staff working paper no. 478. Washington, DC: World Bank.

Franko, L.G. (1979) 'Industrial policies in Western Europe: solution or problem', *The World Economy* 2: 3–50.

Freeman, B. and Mendelowitz, A. (1982) 'Programme in search of a policy: the Chrysler loan guarantee', *Journal of Policy Analysis* I: 4–18.

Freeman, C. (1988) 'Japan: a new national system of innovation?', in G. Dosi, *et al.* (eds) *Technical Change and Economic Theory*, London: Pinter Publishers.

French, R. (1980) *How Ottawa Decides*, Ottawa: Canadian Institute for Economic Policy.

Gamble, A. (1981) *Britain in Decline: Economic Policy, Political Strategy and the British State*, London: Macmillan Press.

Gannicott, K.G. (1982) 'Research and development incentives', in T.G. Parry (ed.) *Australian Industry Policy*, Melbourne: Longman, Cheshire.

GATT Secretariat (1987) News of the Uruguay Round. Various dates. Lausanne: GATT Information and Media Relations Division.

—— (1988) 'Montreal Meeting of the Trade Negotiation Committee, 19 December, NUR 023. Lausanne: GATT, Information and Media Relations Division.

General Agreement on Tariffs and Trade (1979) *Code on Subsidies and Countervailing Duties* [27 BISD 31]. The Contracting Parties to the General Agreement on Tariffs and Trade, Geneva, Mar. 1981.

George, R. (1983) *Targeting High Growth Industry*, Montreal: The Institute for Research on Public Policy.

Gerlach, K., Peters, W. and Sengenberger, W. (eds) (1984) *Public Policies to Combat Unemployment in a Period of Economic Stagnation*, New York: Campus Verlag.

Gerschenkron, A. (1962) *Economic Backwardness in Historical Perspective*, Cambridge, Massachusetts: Harvard University Press.

Gilpin, R. (1987) *The Political Economy of International Economic Relations*. Princeton, N.J.: Princeton University Press.

Ginsburg, H. (1983) *Full Employment and Public Policy: The United States and Sweden*, Lexington, Massachusetts.: Lexington Books.

Glenday, G. and Jenkins, G. (1981) *Labour Adjustment: An Overview of Problems and Policies, Labour Market Development Task Force*, Technical study no. 11, Ottawa: Minister of Supply and Services, Canada.

Glenday, G., Jenkins, G. and Evans, M. (1982) 'Worker adjustment policies: an alternative to protectionism', in North-South Institute, *Canada in a Developing World Economy: Trade or Protection* Ottawa: North-South Institute.

Glendon, M. (1987) *Abortion and Divorce in Western Law*, Cambridge, Massachusetts: Harvard University Press.

Glezer, L. (1982) *Tariff Politics: Australian Policy-Making 1960–1980*, Carlton, Victoria: Melbourne University Press.

Glissman, H.H. and Weiss, F.D. (1980) 'On the political economy of protection in West Germany', World Bank staff working paper no. 427, Washington, DC.

Globe and Mail, 4 May 1985.

Globe and Mail, 14 May 1985.

Globe and Mail, 14 March 1987.

Goldberg, W.H. (1986) *Ailing Steel: The Transoceanic Quarrel* Berlin: WZB Publications.

Golden, D.G., and Poterba, J. (1980) 'The price of popularity: the political business cycle re-examined', *American Journal of Political Science* 24, 4 (Nov.): 696–714.

Goldman, G. (1974) *The German Political System*, New York: Random House.

Goldstein, J. (1988) 'Ideas institutions and American trade policy', vol. 42 (1) *International Organizations* 179.

—— (1989) 'The impact of ideas on trade policy', vol. 43 (1) *International Organization* 31.

Goldthorpe, J.M. (1974) 'Industrial relations in Great Britain: a critique of reformism', *Politics and Society* 4, 4: 419–52.

Goldthorpe, J.H. (ed.) (1984) *Order and Conflict in Contemporary Capitalism*, New York: Oxford University Press.

Gollner, A. (1986) 'The effects of business-government relations on industrial policy' in Vol. 44, Studies for Royal Commission on the Economic Union and Development Prospects for Canada, Toronto: University of Toronto Press.

Goulet, D. (1989) 'Reflections on the new institutionalism', unpublished manuscript, Department of Political Science, University of Toronto.

Gourevitch, P. (1977) 'International trade, domestic coalitions and liberty: comparative responses to the crises of 1873–1896', *Journal of Inter-Disciplinary History* (Autumn): 281–313.

—— (1982) 'Making choices in France: industrial structure and the politics of economic policy', in S. Cohen and P. Gourevitch (eds) *France in the Troubled World Economy*, London: Butterworth.

—— (1984) 'Breaking with orthodoxy: the politics of economic policy responses to the Depression of the 1930's', *International Organization* 38, 1, winter: 95–129.

—— (1986) *Politics in Hard Times*, Ithaca: Cornell University Press.

Gourevitch, P., Martin, A., Ross, G., Bornstein, S., Markovits, A., and Allen, C. (1984) *Unions and Economic Change*, London: Allen and Unwin.

Government of Quebec (1979) *Challenges for Quebec: A Statement on Economic Policy* White Paper, Quebec.

Gray, V. and Lowry, D. (1988) 'Interest group politics and economic growth in the US' *American Political Science Review* 82, 1 March: 109–31.

Grant, G. (1967) *Lament for a Nation*, Toronto: Anansi.

Grant, R.M. (1983) 'Appraising selective financial assistance to industry: a review of institutions and methodologies in the United Kingdom, Sweden and West Germany', in *International Public Policy* 3, 4: 369–96.

Grant, W. (1982) *The Political Economy of Industrial Policy*, London: Butterworths.

—— (1983) 'The political economy of industrial policy', in R.J.B. Jones (ed.) *Perspectives on Political Economy* London: Frances Pinter.

Grant, W. and Wilks, S. (1983) 'British industrial policy: structural change, policy inertia, *Journal of Public Policy* 3: 13–28.

Green, C. (1984) *Industrial Policy: The Fixities Hypotheses*, Toronto: Ontario Economic Council.

Green, D. (1981a) *Managing Industrial Change*, London: Her Majesty's Stationery Office.

—— (1981b) 'Promoting the industries of the future: the search for an industrial strategy in Britain and France', *Journal of Public Policy*, 1: 333–51.

—— (1983a) 'Strategic management and the state: France', in K. Dyson and S. Wilks (eds) *Industrial Crisis: A Comparative Study of the State and Industry*, Oxford: Martin Robertson.

—— (1983b) 'Giscardisme – industrial policy', in V. Wright (ed.) *Giscard, Giscardians and Giscardism*.

—— (1984) 'Industrial policy and policy-making, 1974–82', in V. Wright (ed.) *Continuity and Change in France*.

Greenaway, D. (1986) 'Estimating the welfare effects of voluntary export restraints and tariffs: an application to nonleather footwear in the UK' *Applied Economics* 18, 10, October: 1065–83.

Grieco, J. (1988) 'Anarchy and the limits of cooperation: a realist critique of the newest liberal institutionalism', vol. 42 (3) *International Organization* 485.

Gunderson, M. (1985) 'Alternative mechanisms for dealing with permanent layoffs, dismissals and plant closings', in *Adapting to Change: Labour Market Adjustment in Canada*, Vol. 18, Research Studies prepared for Royal Commission in Economic Union and Development Prospects in Canada, Toronto: University of Toronto Press.

Gunter, H. (1975) 'Trade unions and industrial policies in Western Europe', in S.J. Warnecke and E.N. Suleiman (eds) *Industrial Policies in Western Europe*, New York: Praeger.

Guzzardi, W. (1983) 'How to foil protectionism', *Fortune* 21 March: 76–82, 85.

Hager, W. (1981) 'Industrial policy, trade policy and European social democracy', in J. Pinder (ed.) *National Industrial Strategies and the World Economy* Totowa, N.J.: Allanheld, Osmun; London: Croom Helm, 1982.

Hall, P.A. (1982) 'Economic planning and the state', *Political Power and Social Theory* 3, 175–213.

—— (1984) 'Patterns of economic policy among the European states', in S. Bornstein, D. Held and J. Kreiger (eds) *The State in Capitalist Europe*, London: Allen & Unwin.

Hall, P. (1986) *Governing the Economy*, New York: Oxford University Press.

Hallvarsson, M. (1981a) *Swedish Industry*, Vimmerley, Sweden: VTT-Grafiska.

—— (1981b) *Swedish Industry Faces the 80s*, trans. V. Kayfetz, VIT-Grafiska, Sweden.

Hamilton, C. (1980) 'Effects of non-tariff barriers to trade on prices, employment and imports: the case of the Swedish textile and clothing industry', Washington DC: World Bank staff working paper.

—— (1983) 'Public subsidies to industry: the case of Sweden and its shipbuilding industry, Washington, DC: World Bank staff working paper.

—— (1984) 'Swedish trade restrictions on textiles and clothing', in *Skandinaviska Enskilda Bankens Quarterly Review*, no. 3.

—— (1984) 'Voluntary export restraints on Asia: tariff equivalents, rents and trade barrier formation', Seminar paper no. 276. Stockholm: University of Stockholm, Institute for International Economic Studies, April.

—— (1985) *An Assessment of Voluntary Restraints on Hong Kong Exports to Europe and the USA* Stockholm: University of Stockholm Institute for International Economic Studies.

Hardin, H. (1974) *A Nation Unaware*, Vancouver: J.J. Douglas.

Harkanson, L. and Danielsson, L. 'Structural adjustment in a stagnating economy: regional manufacturing subsidies in Sweden, 1975–1980' in *Regional Studies* 19: 329–42.

Harris, R. with Cox, D. (1984) *Trade, Industrial Policy and Canadian Manufacturing*, Toronto: Ontario Economic Council.

Bibliography

Harris, R., Lewis, F.D. and Purvis, D.D. (1982) 'Market adjustment and government policy', paper presented at 2nd John Duetsch Roundtable on Economic Policy, Kingston: Queen's University.

Harris, R.G. (1985) *Trade, Industrial Policy and International Competition*, in Vol. 13, Studies for Royal Commission on the Economic Union and Development Prospects for Canada, Toronto: University of Toronto Press.

Harrison, R.J. (1980) *Pluralism and Corporatism: The Political Evolution of Modern Democracies*, London: Allen and Unwin.

Hartle, D. (1979) *Public Policy, Decision-Making and Regulation*, Montreal: Institute for Research on Public Policy.

—— (1980) 'The need for adjustment and the search for security: the barriers to change', in Ontario Economic Council, *Developments Abroad and the Domestic Economy*, Toronto: Ontario Economic Council.

Hartley, K. (1977) *Problems of Economic Policy*, London: Allen and Unwin.

Hartmann, U. (1985) 'Experiences in restructuring the textile industry in West Germany and some other industrialized countries' in *World Textiles: Investment, Innovation, Invention*, London: The Textile Institute London: World Conference, 1985.

Haverman, R. and Saks D. (1985) 'Transatlantic lessons for employment and training policy', *Industrial Relations* 24, 1 Winter: 20–36.

Hayward, J. (1972) 'State intervention in France: the changing style of government-industry relations', *Political Studies* 20: 287–98.

—— (1976) 'Institutional inertia and political impetus in France and Britain', *European Journal of Political Research* 4: 341–59, London: Allen and Unwin.

—— (ed.) (1980) *Trade Unions and Politics in Western Europe*, London: Frank Cass.

—— (1982) 'France: strategic management of impending collective impoverishment', in A. Cox (ed.) *Politics, Policy and the European Recession*.

—— (1986) *The State and the Market Economy*, Praeger: New York.

Hayward, J. and Berki, R. (eds) (1979) *State and Society in Contemporary Europe*, Oxford: Martin Robertson.

Hayward, J. and Watson, M. (eds) (1975) *Planning, Politics and Public Policy*, Cambridge: Cambridge University Press.

Hazeldine, T. (1981) 'The costs of protecting jobs in 100 Canadian manufacturing industries'. Technical study no. 16. Ottawa: Task Force on Labour Market Development, July.

Hazeldine, T. and Wigington, I. (1985) *Protection in the Canadian Automobile Market: Costs, Benefits and Implications for Industrial Structure and Adjustment*, Ottawa: Federal Dept of Consumer and Corporate Affairs.

Hazeldine, T., *et al.* (1985) 'The post-1973 productivity slowdown in Canadian manufacturing'. (Working paper series) Toronto: Ontario Economic Council.

Heclo, H. and Madsen, H. (1987) *Policy and Politics in Sweden*,

Philadelphia: Temple University Press.

Heikensten, L. (1984) *Studies in Structural Change and Labour Market Adjustment*, Stockholm: Stockholm School of Economics, Economic Research Institute.

Helleiner, G.K. (1977) 'The political economy of Canada's tariff structure: an alternative model', *Canadian Journal of Economics* 40: 318.

Henning, R. (1984) 'Industrial policy or employment policy? Sweden's response to unemployment', in J.J. Richardson and R. Henning (eds) *Unemployment and Policy Responses in Western Democracies*, Los Angeles, California: Sage.

Herander, M.G. and Schwartz, J.B. (1984) 'An empirical test of the impact of the threat of US trade policy: the case of antidumping duties', *Southern Economics Journal* 51: 59.

Herin, J. and Haltunen, H. (1983) 'Economic developments and politicalism in Finland and Sweden', in *European Free Trade Bulletin* 3, 26, (July/October): 1–14.

Hibbs, D.A. and Fassbender, H. (ed) (1981) *Contemporary Political Economy*, Amsterdam: North-Holland Press.

Hickok, S. (1985) 'The consumer cost of US trade restraints', *Federal Reserve Bank of New York: Quarterly Review* 10, 2 (summer): 1–12.

Hieminz, U. and Rabenau, K.V. (1976) 'Effective protection of German industry', in W.M. Cordon and G. Fels (eds) *Public Assistance to Industry*, London: Trade Policy Research Centre and Macmillan Press.

Hills, J. (1981) 'Government relations with industry: Japan and Britain – a review of two political arguments', *Polity* 14 15–24.

—— (1983) 'The industrial policy of Japan', *Journal of Public Policy* 3: 63–80.

Hindly, B. (ed.) (1983) *State Investment Companies in Western Europe*, London: Macmillan Press.

Hirsch, F. (1978) 'The ideological underlay of inflation', in F. Hirsch and J. Goldthorpe (eds) *The Political Economy of Inflation*, Cambridge: Harvard University Press.

Hirsch, F. and Goldthorpe, J. (1979) *The Political Economy of Inflation*, Cambridge: Harvard University Press.

Hirsch, J. (1980) 'Developments in the political system of West Germany', in R. Scase (ed.) *The State in Western Europe*, Croom Helm: Beckenham.

Hirsch, M. (1982) 'Regulation of mergers in Germany', *Business Lawyer* 37: 559–90.

Hirschorn, J. (1986) 'Restructuring of the US steel industry requires new policies', in Goldberg (ed.) *Ailing Steel: The Transoceanic Quarrel*, Berlin: WZB Publications.

Hobsbawm, E. (1982) 'The state of the Left in Western Europe', *Marxism Today* 26: 10.

Hogan, W.T. (1983) *World Steel in the 1980s*, Lexington, Massachussets: Lexington Books.

Hogwood, B. (1979) *Government and Shipbuilding: The Politics of Industrial Change*, England; Saxon House Westmead.

Hook, E. (1978) 'Cyclical and structural problems in the Swedish steel industry', *Skandinaviska Enskilda Banken Q.R.* 3–4: 67.

Hook, E. (1982) 'The restructuring of the Swedish steel industry', in *European Free Trade Bulletin* 3, 23: 11, 12.

Horlick, G., Quick, R. and Vermulst, E. (1986) 'Government actions against domestic subsidies, an analysis of the international rules and an introduction to United States practice', *Legal Issues of European Integration* 1: 1.

Howard, L. and Stanbury, W.T. (1984) 'Measuring Leviathan: the size, scope and growth of governments in Canada', in G. Lermer (ed.) *Probing Leviathan*, Vancouver: The Fraser Institute.

Howse, R. (1988) 'Participation, transparency, and the domestic determinants of trade liberalization', unpublished manuscript.

Howse, R., Prichard, J.R.S. and Trebilcock, M.J. (1990) 'Smaller or smarter government?', *University of Toronto Law Journal.*

Hufbauer, G. and Erb, J. (1984) *Subsidies in international trade*, Washington DC: Institute for International Economics.

Hufbauer, G.C. and Schott, J. (1985) *Trading for Growth*, Washington, DC: Institute for International Economics.

Hufbauer, G.C., Beliner, D.T., Elliot, K.A. (1986) *Trade Protection in the United States: 31 Case Studies*, Washington DC: Institute for International Economics.

Hufbauer, G.C. and Rosen, H.F. (1986) *Trade Policy for Troubled Industries*, Washington, DC: Institute for International Economics.

Hunker, J.A. (1984) *Structural Change in the US Automobile Industry*, Massachusetts: Lexington Books.

Ikenberry, J. (1986a) 'The state and strategies of international adjustment', *World Politics* 39, 1: 53–77.

—— (1986b) 'The irony of state strength: comparative responses to the oil shocks of the 1970s', *International Organization* 40 (winter): 105–37.

IMF (1988) *Issues and Developments in International Trade Policy.* Occasional paper no. 63. Washington, DC: International Monetary Fund.

Industries Assistance Commission of Australia (1980) *Annual Report, 1978–79*, Canberra.

International Labour Organization (1982) *Workforce Reductions in Undertakings*, Geneva: ILO.

—— (1983) *Yearbook of Labour Statistics*, Geneva: ILO.

Jackson, J. (1983) 'Gatt machinery and the Tokyo Round agreements in W. Cline (ed.) *Trade Policy in the 1980s.*

Jackson, M. and Hanby, V. (1982) *British Work Creation Programmes*, Aldershot: Gower.

Jackson, T.H. (1986) *The Logic and Limits of Bankruptcy Law*, Cambridge, Massachusetts: Harvard University Press.

Jacobs, J. (1984) *Cities and the Wealth of Nations*, New York and Toronto: Random House.

Jacquemin, A. (ed.) (1984) *European Industry: Public Policy and Corporate Strategy*, Oxford: Clarendon Press.

James, P. (1984) *The Future of Coal*, London: Macmillan.

Jenkin, M. (1984) *The Challenge of Diversity In Canadian Federation* Ottawa: Science Council of Canada.

Jenkins, G. (1980) *Costs and Consequences of The New Protectionism: The Case of Canada's Textile Sector*, Ottawa: North-South Institute.

Jenness, R. (1984) *Positive Adjustment in Manpower and Social Policies*, Paris: OECD.

Johannesson, J. and Schmidt, G. (1980) 'The development of labour market policy in Sweden and in Germany: competing or convergent models to combat unemployment', *European Journal of Political Research* 8: 387–406.

Johnson, C. (1982) *MITI: The Ministry of International Trade and Industry*, Berkeley: University of California Press.

Johnson, H. (1965) 'Optimal trade intervention in the presence of domestic distortions, in H. Johnson et al. (eds.), *Trade, Growth, and the Balance of Payments*,

Johnston, J. (1984) 'An overview of US federal employment and training programmes' in J. Richardson and R. Henning (eds) *Unemployment Policy Responses of Western Democracies*, Beverly Hills, California: Sage.

Jones, M.A. (1983) *The Australian Welfare State: Growth, Crisis and Change*, Sydney: George Allen and Unwin.

Kalantzopoulos, O.K. (n.d.) *The Cost of Voluntary Export Restraints for Selected Industries in the US and the EC*, Washington, DC: World Bank.

Kanthrow, A. (1983) 'The political realities of industrial policy', *Harvard Business Review* vol 61: 76–87.

Kaplow, L. (1986) 'An economic analysis of legal transitions', *Harvard Law Review* 99: 509.

Katzenstein, P.J. (ed.) (1978) *Between Power and Plenty*, Madison: University of Wisconsin Press.

—— (1984) *Corporatism and Change: Australia, Switzerland, and the Politics of Industry*, Ithaca, New York: Cornell University Press.

—— (1985) *Small States in World Markets*, Ithaca: Cornell University Press.

Kavanagh, D. (1985) 'Whatever happened to consensus politics, *Political Studies* 33, 4 (December): 529–46.

Keohane, R.O. (1978) 'Economics, inflation, and the role of the state: political implications of the McCracken report', in *World Politics* 31: 108–28.

—— (1984) 'The world political economy and the crisis of embedded liberalism', in J. Goldthorpe (ed.) *Order and Conflict in Contemporary Capitalism*, Oxford: Clarendon Press.

—— (1985) *After Hegemony*, New York: Princeton University Press.

Kesselman, M. and Krieger, J. (ed.) (1982) *European Politics in Transition*, Lexington, Massachussets: D.C. Heath.

Kiewiet, D.R. (1983) *Macroeconomies and Micropolitics*, Chicago: University of Chicago Press.

Kikkawa, M. (1983) 'Shipbuilding, motor cars and semiconductors: the diminishing role of industrial policy in Japan', in G. Shepherd *et al* (eds.) *Europe's Industries: Public and Private Strategies for Change*, London: Frances Pinter.

King, A. (1973) 'Ideas, institutions and the policies of government: a comparative analysis', *British Journal of Political Science* 3,: 291–313; 409–23.

—— (1986) 'What Thatcher has done to beer', paper presented to American Political Science Association meeting, Washington, DC.

Kirby, M. (1984) 'Restructuring the Atlantic Fishery: a case study in business-government relations', paper presented at Dalhousie University, Halifax, Nova Scotia.

Korpi, W. (1980) 'Social policy strategies and distributional conflict in capitalist democracies', *West European Politics* 3, (October): 296–316.

—— (1982) 'The historical compromise and its dissolution', in B. Ryden and V. Bergstron (eds) *Sweden: Choices for Economic and Social Policy in the 1980s*, London: George Allen and Unwin.

Krasner, S. (1976), 'State power and the structure of international trade', *World Politics* 28: 317.

—— (1978) 'US commercial and monetary policy: unravelling the paradox of external strength and internal weakness', in P. Katzenstein (ed.) *Between Power and Plenty*, Madison: University of Wisconsin Press.

—— (ed.) (1983) *International Regimes*, Ithaca: Cornell University Press.

—— (1984) 'Approaches to the State: alternative conceptions and historical dynamics', *Comparative Politics* 16: 223–46.

Kravis, I. (1963) *Domestic Interests and International Obligation: Safeguards in International Trade Organization*, Philadelphia: University of Pennsylvania Press.

Krauss, M. (1978) *The New Protectionism*, New York: Viking.

Kreile, M. (1978) 'West Germany: the dynamics of expansion', in P. Katzenstein (ed.) *Between Power and Plenty*, Madison: University of Wisconsin Press.

Kronby, M. (1988–9) 'Kicking the tires: assessing the Hyundai Antidumping decision from a consumer welfare perspective', working paper, International Business and Trade Law Programme, University of Toronto Law School.

Kronman, A.J. and Posner, R.A. (1979) *The Economics of Contract Law*, Boston: Little Brown and Co.

Krueger, A.O. (1976) 'The political economy of the rent seeking society', *American Economic Review* 6: 291.

—— (1980) 'Impact of foreign trade on employment in United States industry', in J. Block and B. Hindley (eds) *Current Issues in Commercial Policy and Diplomacy*, London: Macmillan.

Krugman, P.R. (1984) 'Targeted industrial policies: theory and evidence', Boston: Massachussets Institute of Technology, mimeo.

—— (ed.) (1986) *Strategic Trade Policy and the New International Economics*, Cambridge: MIT Press.

Kurth, J.R. (1979) 'The political consequences of the product cycle: industrial history and political outcomes', *International Organization* 33, 1 (winter): 1–34.

Kuster, G. (1974) 'Germany', in R. Vernon (ed.) *Big Business and the State*, Cambridge, Massachussets Harvard University Press.

Kuttner, R. (1984) *The Economic Illusion: False Choices Between Prosperity and Social Justice*, Boston: Houghton Mifflin Company.

Labour Canada (1985) *Labour Adjustment Benefits Policy Review*, Ottawa: Department of Supply and Services.

Lange, P., Ross, G. and Vannicelli, M. (1982) *Unions, Crisis and Change*, London: Allen and Unwin.

Lange, P. and Garrett, G. (1985) 'The organizational and political determinants of economic performance 1974–1980', *Journal of Politics* 47, 3,: 792–827.

Larkey, P.D. Stolp, C. and Winer, M. (1981) 'Theorizing about the growth of government: a research assessment', in *Journal of Public Policy* 1: 157–220.

Lauber, V. (1986) 'The political economy of industrial policy in Western Europe', in S. Shull and J. Cohen (eds) *Economics and Politics of Industrial Policy*, New York: Praeger.

Lavergne, R.P. (1983) *The Political Economy of US Tariffs*, New York: Academic Press.

Lawrence, R.Z. (1983) 'Is trade deindustrializing America? A medium term perspective', Brookings Papers on Economic Activity no. 1, Washington, DC: Brookings Institution.

—— (1984a) 'The myth of US deindustrialization', in Petri *et al.* (eds) *National Industrial Policy*, Boulder, Colorado: Westview.

—— (1984b) *Changes in US Industrial Structure*, Washington DC: Brookings Institution.

—— (1985) *Can America Compete?*, Washington, DC: Brookings Institution.

—— (1986) 'Myths and realities in America's need for an industrial policy' in S. Shull and J. Cohen (eds) *Economics and Politics of Industrial Policy*, New York: Praeger.

—— (1987) 'A depressed view of policies for depressed industries', paper delivered at Conference on US -Canadian Trade and Investment Relations with Japan, University of Michigan, mimeo.

Lawrence R.Z. and Litan, R. (1985) 'Living with the trade deficit adjustment strategies to preserve free trade', *Brookings Review* 4, 1 (Fall): 3–13.

—— (1986) *Saving Free Trade*, Washington, DC, Brookings Institution.

Lazarus, S. and Litan, R. (1984) 'The Democrats coming civil war over industrial policy', *Atlantic Monthly*, September: 92–8.

LeCraw, D.J. (1984) 'Industrial policies in the United States: A survey', paper presented at the University of Western Ontario, June.

Lee, D. (1988) 'Politics, ideology, and the power of public choice', *Virginia Law Review* 74, 2: 191.

Leibhafsky, H.H. (1977) *American Government and Business*, New York: John Wiley.

Lembruch, G. (1979) 'Consociational democracy, class conflict and the new corporatism', in P. Schmitter and G. Lembruch, *Trends Towards Corporatist Intermediation,*

Leslie, P. (1987) *Federal State, National Economy,* Toronto, University of Toronto Press.

Leutwiler *et al.* (1985) *Trade Policies for a Better Future: Proposals for Action,* Geneva: GATT Secretariat.

Levy, R. (1986) 'Industrial policy and the steel industry', in F.G. Adams and C. Stoffaes (eds) *French Industrial Policy,* Washington DC: The Brookings Institution.

Lindbeck, A. (1975) *Swedish Economic Policy,* R. and R. Clark.

—— (1984) 'International and domestic preconditions for economic stability', *Skandinaviska Enskilda Banken Q.R.* 2: 34.

Lindberg, L. (1975) *Stress and Contradiction in Modern Capitalism,* Lexington Massachussets: D.C. Heath.

Lindblom, C.E. (1977) *Politics and Markets,* New York: Basic Books.

Lindley, R.M. (1980) 'Economic policy in transition' in R.M. Lindley (ed.) *Economic Change and Employment Policy,* London: Macmillan.

Lindmark, K. (1985) 'Free trade for whom?', *European Free Trade Bulletin* 26, 2: 9–11.

Lipsey, R.G. and Smith, M.G. (1985) *Taking the Initiative: Canada's Trade Options in a Turbulent World* Toronto: C.D. Howe Institute.

Lipson, C. (1984) 'International cooperation in economic and security affairs', *World Politics* 37: 1.

Litvak, I.A. (1981) 'Government intervention and corporate government relations', *Business Quarterly* 46: 47–54.

—— (1982) 'National trade associations: Business-government intermediaries', *Business Quarterly* (Autumn): 34–42.

Loveday, P. (1982) *Promoting Industry: Recent Australian Political Experience,* St. Lucia, Queensland: University of Queensland Press.

Long, O., et al. (1987) *Domestic Transparency in the Uruguay Round,* London: Trade Policy Research Centre.

Lowi, T. (1970) 'Decision-making vs policy-making: four systems of policy, politics, and choice', *Public Administration Review* 30.

—— (1979) *The End of Liberalism: Ideology, Policy and the Crisis of Public Authority,* 2nd edn, New York: Norton.

Lucas, N. (1985) *Western European Energy Polices,* Oxford: Clarendon.

Lundberg, L. (1981) *Patterns of Barriers to Trade in Sweden: A Study in the Theory of Protection,* Washington, DC: World Bank Staff Working Paper, no. 494.

Lundmark, K. (1983) 'Welfare state and employment policy: Sweden', in K. Dyson, and S. Wilks (eds) *Industrial Crisis: A Comparative Study of the State and Industry,* Oxford: Martin Robertson.

Lynn, L. (1983) 'Japanese technology: successes and strategies', *Current History* 82: 366–70.

Lyon, J. (1983) *Dome: The Rise and Fall of the House that Jack Built,* Toronto Macmillan.

Macdonald Commission (1985): see Royal Commission on the Economic

Union and Development Prospects for Canada.

MacNeil, M. (1982) 'Plant closings and workers' rights', *Ottawa Law Review* 14.

Magaziner, I.C. and Hout, T. (1981) *Japanese Industrial Policy*, Berkeley: University of California Press.

Magaziner, I.C. and Reich, R.B. (1982) *Minding America's Business*, New York: Harcourt Brace Jovanovitch.

Magun, S.D. (1981) *The Impact of the Canadian Placement Service on the Labour Market*, Ottawa: Employment and Immigration Canada.

Mahon, R. (1984) *The Politics of Industrial Restructuring: Canadian Textiles*, Toronto: University of Toronto Press.

Mahon, R. and Mytelka, L.K. (1983) 'Industry, the state and the new protectionism: textiles in Canada and France', *International Organization* 37 (autumn): 551–81.

March, J. and Olsen, J.P. (1984) 'The new institutionalism: organizational factors in political life', *American Political Science Review* 78 (September) 3: 734–49.

Markovic, M. (1982) *Democratic Socialism*, London: St. Martins Press.

Markovits, A. (ed.) (1982) *The Political Economy of West Germany: Modell Deutschland*, New York: Praeger.

Markusen, A. (1985) 'Defense spending as industrial policy', in S. Zukin (ed.) *Industrial Policy*, New York: Praeger.

Markusen, J.R. and Melvin, J.R. (1984) *The Theory of International Trade and Its Canadian Applications*, Toronto: Butterworth.

Martin, A. (1986) 'The politics of employment and welfare: national policies and international interdependence' in Vol. 32, Studies for Royal Commission on the Economic Union and Development Prospects for Canada, Toronto: University of Toronto Press.

Martin, P.L. (1983) *Labour Displacement and Public Policy*, Lexington, Massachusetts: D.C. Heath.

Martin, R.M. (1983) 'Pluralism and the new corporatism', *Political Studies* xxi, 1: 86–102.

Maslove, A. (1983) 'Loans and loan guarantees: business as usual versus the politics of risk', in G.B. Doern (ed.) (1983) *How Ottawa Spends Your Tax Dollars*, Toronto: James Lorimer.

Matthews, R.A. (ed.) (1982) *Federal Policies in Two Federal Countries: Canada and Australia*, Canberra: Centre for Research on Federal Financial Relations, The Australian National University.

Matthews, T. (1980) 'Australian pressure groups', in M. Mayer and M. Nelson (eds) *Australian Politics* 5, Melbourne: Longman, Cheshire.

Maunder, W.J.P. (ed.) (1979) *Government Intervention in the Developed Economy*, Beckenham: Croom Helm.

—— (ed.) (1980) *The British Economy in the 1970's*, London: Heinemann.

Maxwell, J. and Pestieau, C. (1980) *Economic Realities of Contemporary Confederation*, Montreal: C.D. Howe Research Institute.

Mayer, G.E. (1983) 'Past and projected labor productivity trends and their potential impact on the structure of the world automobile industry of 1990', *Volkswirtschaftliche Forschung und Entwicklung*, Band 7,

Munich: Florentz.

Mayer, M. and Nelson, M. (eds) (1980) *Australian Politics*, Melbourne: Longman, Cheshire.

McArthur, J.B. and Scott, B.R. (1969) *Industrial Planning in France*, Cambridge, Massachusetts: Harvard University Press.

McBride, S. (1983) 'Public policy as a determinant of interest group behaviour', *Canadian Journal of Political Science* 16: 501–17.

McCallum, J. and Blais, A. (1985) 'Government special interest groups and economic growth', in *Responses to Economic Change*, Vol. 27, Research Studies prepared for the Royal Commission on the Economic Union and Development Prospects for Canada, Toronto: University of Toronto Press.

McCorquodale, S. (1983) 'The management of a common property resource and fisheries policy in Atlantic Canada', in M. Atkinson and M. Chandler (eds) *The Politics of Canadian Public Policy*, Toronto: University of Toronto Press.

McFetridge, D. and Warda, J. (1983) 'Canadian R & D incentives: their adequacy and impact', *Canadian Tax Paper* 70, Toronto: Canadian Tax Foundation.

McGovern, E. (1986) *International Trade Regulation*, Exeter: Globefield Press.

McKay, D. (1983) 'The political economy of economic policy', in R.J.B. Jones (ed.), *Perspectives on Political Economy*, London: Frances Pinter.

—— (1983) 'Industrial policy and non-policy in the United States', *Journal of Public Policy* 3: 29–48.

McKay, D. and Grant, W. (1983) 'Industrial policies in OECD countries: an overview', *Journal of Public Policy* 3: 1–12.

McKersie, R. and Sengenberger, W. (1983) *Job Losses in Major Industries*, Paris: OECD.

McKinnon, W.A. (1982) 'Structural change in Australia', in R.L. Matthews (ed) *Federal Policies in Two Federal Countries: Canada and Australia*, Canberra: Australian National University, Centre for Research on Federal Financial Relations.

McQueen, H. (1982) *Gone Tomorrow: Australia in the 80's*, Melbourne: Angus and Robertson.

Mead, B. (ed.) (1983) *State and Economy in Australia*, Melbourne: Oxford University Press.

Medley, R. (ed.) (1982) *The Politics of Inflation: A Comparative Analysis*, New York: Pergamon.

Messerlin, P. and Saunders, C. (1983) 'Steel: too much investment too late', in Shepherd *et al.*, *Europe's Industries: Public and Private Strategies for Change*, London: Frances Pinter.

Metcalfe, L. and Quillan, W. (1979) 'Corporatism or industrial democracy?', *Political Studies* 27, 266–82.

Michalet, C.A. (1974) 'France', in R. Vernon, *Big Business and the State*, Cambridge, Massachussets: Harvard University Press.

Michelman, F. (1967) 'Property, utility, and fairness', *Harvard Law Review* 80: 1165.

Middlemas, K. (1979) *Politics in Industrial Society*, London: Andre Deutch.

Migue, J.L. (1979) *Nationalistic Policies in Canada: An Economic Approach*, Montreal: C.D. Howe Research Institute.

Miller, R. and Isbester, F. (eds) (1977) *Canadian Labour in Transition*, Scarborough,: Ontario Prentice-Hall.

Milner, H. (1987) 'Resisting the protectionist temptation: industry and the making of trade policy in France and the US During the 1970s', *International Organization* 41, 4, (Autumn): 639–66.

—— (1988) 'Trading places; industries for free trade', *World Politics* XL, 3 (April): 350–76.

Milner, H. and Yoffie, D. (1989) 'Between free trade and protectionism: strategic trade policy and a theory of corporate demands', *International Organization*: 43(2).

Ministry of Economic Affairs (1981) *The 1980 Medium Term Survey of the Swedish Economy*, Stockholm: Sweden.

Ministry of Employment and Immigration (1989) *Success in the Works: A Labour Force Development Strategy for Canada*, Ottawa: Supply and Services.

Ministry of Industry, Trade and Commerce (1979) *Doing Business in Canada: Federal Incentives to Industry*, Ottawa.

Mintz, I. (1973) *US Import Quotas: Costs and Consequences*. Domestic Affairs Study 10. Washington, DC: American Enterprise Institute for Public Policy Research.

Molot, M.A. (1977) 'The domestic determinants of Canadian foreign economic policy: beavers build dams', paper delivered at American Political Science Association Meetings, Washington, DC.

Monroe, K. (ed.) (1983) *Political Process and Economic Change*, New York: Agathan Press.

Moon, J. (1984) 'The responses of British governments to unemployment' in J. Richardson and R. Henning (eds) *Unemployment Policy Responses of Western Democracy*, Beverly Hills, California: Sage.

Moon, J. and Richardson, J.J. (1985) *Unemployment in the UK*, Aldershot: Gower.

Moore, M. (1988) 'What sort of ideas become public ideas' in R. Reich (ed.) *The Power of Public Ideas*, Cambridge, Massachusetts: Ballinger.

Morici, P. and Megna, L.L. (1983) *US Economic Policies Affecting Industrial Trade: A Quantitative Assessment*. NPA Report no. 200: CIR report no. 13, Washington, DC: National Planning Association, Committee on Changing International Realities.

Morici, P., Smith, A. and Lea, S. (1982) *Canadian Industrial Policy*, New York: National Planning Association.

Morkre, M.E. (1984) *Import Quotas on Textile: The Welfare Effects of the United States Restrictions on Hong Kong*. Bureau of Economics Staff Report to the FTC, Washington, DC: US Federal Trade Commission.

Morkre, M.E., and Tarr, D.G. (1980) *Effects of Restrictions on US Imports: Five Case Studies and Theory*. Bureau of Economics Staff

Report to the FTC, Washington, DC: US Federal Trade Commission.

Morton, D. (1982) 'The history of Canadian labour', in J. Anderson and M. Gunderson, *Union-Management Relations in Canada*.

Mottershead, P. (1978) 'Industrial policy', in F. Blackaby (ed.) *British Economic Policy, 1960–74*.

—— (1983) 'Shipbuilding: adjustment-led intervention or intervention led-adjustment', in Shepherd, G., Duchene, F. and Saunders, C. (eds) *Europe's Industries: Public and Private Strategies for Change*, London: Frances Pinter.

Mouriaux, M.F., and Mouriaux R. (1984) 'Unemployment policy in France, 1976–82' in J. Richardson and R. Henning (eds) *Unemployment Policy Responses of Western Democracies*, Beverly Hills, California: Sage.

Mueller, D.C. (ed.) (1983) *The Political Economy of Growth*, New Haven: Yale University Press.

Muller, R. (1980) *Revitalizing America: Politics for Prospects*, New York: Touchstone.

Munch, J. (1986) *Vocational Training in the Federal Republic of Germany*, 2nd ed Berlin: European Centre for the Development of Vocational Training.

Munger, M.C. (1983) 'The costs of protectionism: estimates of the hidden tax of trade restraint'. Working paper no. 80. Washington University, Centre for the Study of American Business, July.

Murray, V.V. and McMillan, C.J. (1984) 'Business-government relations in Canada: a conceptual map', *Canadian Public Administration* 27,: 591–609.

Mytelka, L.K. (1982) 'The French textile industry: crisis and adjustment', in *The Emerging International Economic Order*, H.K. Jacobson and D. Sidjanski (eds) Berverley Hills, California: Sage.

—— (1986) 'The State and foreign capital in the advanced industrial countries', Ottawa: The Royal Commission on the Economic Union and Development Prospects for Canada.

Nau, H. (ed.) (1989) *Domestic Politics and the Uruguay Round*, Ithaca New York: Cornell University Press.

Neale, A.D. and Goyden, D.G. (1980) *The Antitrust Laws of the USA*, Cambridge, Massachusetts: Cambridge University Press.

Neufeld, E. (1982) 'Industrial policy in Canada in the 1980s', *Western Economic Review* 1: 14–33.

Norgren, M. and C. (1971) *Industrial Sweden*, Victor Pettersons, Bokindusti AB.

Norrie, K. (1984) 'Energy, Canadian federalism and the West', *Publius* 14: 79–91.

North, D. (1981) *Structure and Change in Economic History*, New York: Norton.

Oberg, S. and Oscarsson, G. (1979) 'Regional policy and interregional migration-matching jobs and individuals on local labour markets', in *Regional Studies* 13,: 1–14.

OECD (1973a) *Area Redevelopment and Regional Development Policy in*

France, Paris: OECD.
—— (1973b) *Industrial Policy of Australia*, Paris: OECD.
—— (1976a) *Measures of Assistance to Shipbuilding*, Paris: OECD.
—— (1976b) *Economic Surveys: Canada*, Paris: OECD.
—— (1976c) *Regional Problems and Policies*, Paris: OECD.
—— (1978) *Selected Industrial Policy Instruments: Objectives and Scope*, Paris: OECD.
—— (1979a) *The Case for Positive Adjustment Policies: A Compendium of OECD Documents*, Paris: OECD.
—— (1979b) *Concentration and Competition Policy*, Paris: OECD.
—— (1979c) *Collective Bargaining and Government Policies*, Paris: OECD.
—— (1979d) *Economic Surveys: Canada* Paris: OECD.
—— (1979e) *Perspective Review of Industrial Policy Development and of the Situation in Industry: Japan*, Paris: OECD.
—— (1980) *Direct Job Creation in the Public Sector*, Paris: OECD.
—— (1981a) Special Group of the Economic Policy Committee on Positive Adjustment Policies, 'Positive adjustment policies in Australia: annex 1', Paris: OECD.
—— (1981b) Directorate for Science, Technology and Industry, Working Party no. 6 of the Industry Committee, 'Regional policy developments in the Federal Republic of Germany', Paris: OECD.
—— (1982a) *The Challenges of Unemployment*, Paris: OECD.
—— (1982b) *Labour Force Statistics 1969–80*, Paris: OECD.
—— (1982c) Directorate for Science, Technology and Industry, 'Survey of recent developments in regional problems and policies', Paris: OECD.
—— (1983a) *Positive Adjustment Policies, Managing Structural Change*, Paris: OECD.
—— (1983b) *Investment Incentive and Disincentives*, Paris: OECD.
—— (1983c) *Textile and Clothing Industries: Structural Problems and Policies in OECD Countries* Paris: OECD.
—— (1983d) Directorate for Science, Technology and Industry, Working party no. 6 of the Industry Committee, 'Survey of recent developments in regional problems and policies', Paris: OECD.
—— (1984a) *Textile Industry in OECD Countries in 1982*, Paris: OECD.
—— (1984b) *The Effectiveness of Trade-Related Worker Adjustment Policies in Canada and the US* Paris: OECD.
—— (1984c) *High Unemployment: A Challenge for Income Support Policies*, Paris: OECD.
—— (1984d) *Economic Surveys: Australia*, Paris: OECD.
—— (1984e) *Economic Surveys: Canada*, Paris: OECD.
—— (1984f) *Historical Statistics 1960–1982*, Paris: OECD.
—— (1984g) *Economic Surveys: Sweden*, Paris: OECD.
—— (1985a) *The Iron and Steel Industry in 1983*, Paris: OECD.
—— (1985b) *Costs and Benefits of Protection*, Paris: OECD.
—— (1986a) *Productivity in Industry: Prospects and Policies*, Paris: OECD.
—— (1986b) *International Trade and the Consumer*, Paris: OECD.
—— (1987a) 'Structural adjustment in industry: study of the steel industry'

Paris: OECD.
—— (1987b) 'Structural adjustment in industry: study of the shipbuilding
industry', Paris: OECD.
—— (1987c) 'Structural adjustment in industry: study of the textile
industry', Paris: OECD.
Office of the Auditor General (1983) *Report of the Auditor General, 1982*,
Ottawa: Office of the Auditor General.
Ohlin, G. (1978) 'Subsidies and other industrial aids',in S.J. Warnecke
(ed.) *International Trade and Industrial Policies*, London: Macmillan.
Olson, M. (1965) *The Logic of Collective Action*, New York: Schoken.
—— (1982) *The Rise and Decline of Nations*, New Haven: Yale University
Press.
—— (1985) 'Beyond the measuring rod of money: the unification of
economics and the other social sciences', Law and Economics Workshop
University of Toronto Faculty of Law, 20 November 1985.
Ontario Economic Council (1980) *Developments Abroad and the Domestic
Economy*, Toronto
Ontario Ministry of Consumer and Commercial Relations (1984–85) *Final
Report of the Commission of Inquiry into Wage Protection in Insolvency
Situations*, Ontario: Ontario Ministry of Labour.
Ouchi, W. (1984) *The M-Form Society*, New York: Addison-Wesley.
Oulton, N. (1976) 'Effective protection of British industry', in W.M.
Cordon and Gerherd Fels (eds) *Public Assistance to Industry*, London:
Trade Policy Research Centre and Macmillan Press.
Owen-Smith, E. (1979) 'Government intervention in the economy of the
Federal Republic of Germany', in W.J.P. Maunder (ed.) *Government
Intervention in the Developed Economy*, Beckenham: Croom Helm.
Palmeter, N.D. (1985) 'Torquemada and the Tariff Act: the inquisitor rides
again', *International Law*, 20: 641.
Panitch, L (1979) 'Corporatism in Canada', *Studies in Political Economy* 1
(spring): 43–92.
Parkin, F. (1971) *Class Inequality and Political Order*, London: Granada
Publishing.
Parry, T.G. (ed.) (1982) *Australian Industry Policy*, Melbourne: Longman
Cheshire.
Paterson, W.E. and Smith, G.(eds) (1981) *The West German Model*,
London: Frank Cass.
Patrick, H. (ed.) (1976) *Japanese Industrialization and Its Social
Consequences*, Berkeley: University of California Press.
Patrick, H. and Rosovsky, H. (eds) (1976) 'Japan's economic performance: and
overview' in *Asia's New Giant*, Washington, DC: Brookings Institution.
Peacock, A. *et al.* (1980) *Structural Economic Policies in West Germany
and the UK*, London: Anglo-German Foundation for the Study of
Industrial Society.
Pearson, C. (1983) *Emergency Protection in the Footwear Industry*, Thames
Essay no. 36, London: Trade Policy Research Centre.
Pearson, C. and Salembier, C. (1983) *Trade Employment and Adjustment*,
Montreal: Institute for Research on Public Policy.

Peck, M., Levin, P. and Goto, A. (1985) 'Picking losers: public policy toward declining industries in Japan', mimeo.

Peltzman, S. (1976) 'Toward a more general theory of regulation', *Journal of Law and Economics* 211–48.

Pempel, T.J. (1978) 'Japanese foreign economic policy: the domestic bases for international behaviour', in P. Katzenstein (ed.) *Between Power and Plenty*, Madison: University of Wisconsin Press.

—— (1982) *Policy and Politics in Japan* Philadelphia: Temple University Press.

Pestieau, C. (1978) *The Quebec Textile Industry in Canada*, Montreal: C.D. Howe Institute.

Peters, G. (1986) 'Politics of industrial policy in the United States', in S. Shull and J. Cohen (eds) *Economics and Politics of Industrial Policy*, New York: Praeger.

Petersmann, U. (1986) 'Trade policy as a constitutional problem: on the domestic policy functions of international trade rules', *Aussenwirtschaft*, September: 405–39.

Phidd, R. and Doern, G.B. (1978) *The Politics and Management of Canadian Economic Policy*, Toronto: Macmillan.

Pickering, J.F. *et al.* (1982) 'Industrial performance and policy', in C.D. Cohen (ed.) *Agenda for Britain: Micro Policy*, Oxford: Philip Allan.

Picot, W.G. (1986) *Canada's Industries: Changes in Jobs over Three Decades*, Statistics Canada.

Pincus, Jonathan J. (1975) 'Pressure groups and the pattern of tariffs', *Journal of Political Economy* 83: 757.

Pollard, S. (1982) *The Wasting of the British Economy*, Beckenham: Croom Helm.

—— (1983) *The Development of the British Economy*, 3rd edn, Australia: Edward Arnold.

Porteous, S. and Rugman, A. (1989) 'Canadian unfair trade laws and corporate strategy', *Review of International Business Law* 3, 2.

Posner, R.A. (1975) 'The social costs of monopoly and regulation', *Journal of Political Economy* 83: 807.

Prest, A.R. and Coppock, D.J. (1976) *The UK Economy: A Manual of Applied Economics*, 6th edn, London: Weidenfeld and Nicolson.

Presthus, R. (1973) *Elite Accommodation in Canadian Politics*, Toronto: Macmillan.

Price-Waterhouse Inc. (1986) *An Evaluation Study of the Sector Firms Program and the Industrial Development Program for the Canadian Industrial Renewal Board*, Ottawa: Price Waterhouse.

Prichard, J.R.S. (ed.) (1983) *Crown Corporations in Canada*, Toronto: Butterworth.

Priouret, R. (1963) *Origines du Patronat Francais*, Paris: Grasset.

Pross, A.P. (1984) 'The Fishery: Ali versus Frazier', in B. Jamieson (ed.) *Governing Nova Scotia Policies, Priorites and the 1984–85 Budget*, Halifax, Nova Scotia: School of Public Administration, Dalhousie University.

Protheroe, D.R. (1980) *Imports and Politics: Trade Decision Making in*

Canada 1969–1970, Montreal: Institute for Research on Public Policy.

Pryor, F.L. (1972) 'An international comparison of concentration ratios', *Review of Economics and Statistics* 54, 130–40.

Przeworski, A. and Wallerstein, M. (1982) 'The structure of class conflict in democratic capitalist societies', *American Political Science Review* 76, 2 (June); 215–38.

Quinn, J. (1985) 'Corporate reorganization and strategic behaviour: an economic analysis of Canadian insolvency law and recent proposals for reform', *Osgoode Hall Law Journal* 21: 1–36.

Quinn, J. and Trebilcock, M. (1982) 'Compensation, transition costs, and regulatory change', *University of Toronto Law Journal* 32: 117.

Ramseyer, J.M. (1981) 'Letting obsolete firms die: trade adjustment assistance in the United States and Japan', *Harvard International Law Journal* 22: 595–619.

Rattigan, A. (1986) *Industry Assistance, the Inside Story*, Melbourne: Melbourne University Press.

Rawls, J. (1971) *A Theory of Justice*, Cambridge, Massachussets: Harvard University Press.

Ray, E.J. (1981) 'The determinants of tariff and non-tariff trade restrictions in the US', *Journal of Political Economy* 81: 105.

Reich, R. (1982a) 'Making industrial policy', *Foreign Affairs* 60: 852–81.

—— (1982b) 'Why the US needs an industrial policy', *Harvard Business Review* 60: 74–81.

—— (1983a) 'An industrial policy of the right', *Public Interest*: 3–17.

—— (1983b) *The Next American Frontier*, New York: Times Books.

—— (1983c) 'Why democracy makes economic sense', *The New Republic* 19 December: 25–32.

—— (1985) *New Deals: The Chrysler Revival and the American System*, New York: Times Books.

—— (ed.) (1988) *The Power of Public Ideas*, Cambridge, Massachussets: Ballinger.

Report to the Congress, (1979) General Accounting Office, US 'Considerations of adjustment assistance under the 1974 Trade Act: a summary of techniques used in other countries', 1, 2.

Resa, G. (1980) 'Government and industry in the Federal Republic of Germany', *International and Comparative Law* 29: 87–111.

Reyden, B. and Berstrom, V. (1982) 'Sweden in the 1980s: how gloomy are the prospects?', in B. Reyden and V. Bergstrom (eds) *Sweden: Choices for Economic and Social Policy in the 1980s*, George Allen and Unwin.

Reynaud, J. (1980) 'Industrial relations and political systems: some reflections in the crises in industrial relations in Western Europe', *British Journal of Industrial Relations*: 1–13.

Rhys, D.G. (1980) 'Motor vehicles', in P.S. Johnson (ed.) *The Structure of British Industry*, London: Granada.

Rich, D. (1987) *The Industrial Geography of Australia*, Beckenham: Croom Helm.

Richardson, J. (1980) *Understanding International Economics*, Boston: Little Brown.

—— (ed.) (1982) *Policy Styles in Western Europe*, London: Allen and Unwin.

—— (1982) 'Trade adjustment assistance under the US Trade Act of 1974: an analytical examination and worker survey' in J. Bhagwati (ed.) *Import Competition and Response*, Chicago: University of Chicago Press.

—— (1987) 'Safeguard issues in the Uruguay Round and beyond', mimeo.

Richardson, J. and Henning, R. (eds) (1984) *Unemployment Policy Responses of Western Democracies*, Beverly Hills, California: Sage.

Richardson, J. and Jordan, A. (1979) *Governing Under Pressure: The Policy Process in a Post-Industrial Democracy*, London: Macmillan Press.

Ridell, W.C. (1986) 'Adapting to labour market adjustment in Canada: an overview' in Vol. 18, Studies for Royal Commission on the Economic Union and Development Prospects for Canada, Toronto: University of Toronto Press.

Riedel, J. (1977) 'Tariff concessions in the Kennedy Round and the structure of protection in West Germany' *International Economics* 7: 133.

Ritchie, G. (1983) 'Government aid to industry: a public sector perspective', *Canadian Public Administration* 26: 36–46.

Rivers, R. and Greenwald, J. (1979) 'The negotiation of a code on subsidies and countervailing measures: bridging fundamental policy differences', *Law and Policy of International Business* 11: 1447.

Robertson, D.B. (1986) 'Mrs Thatcher's employment prescription: an active neo-liberal labour market policy', *Journal of Public Policy* 6, 3: 275–96.

Robertson, J. (1983) 'Inflation, unemployment and government collapse: a Poisson application', *Comparative Political Studies* 15: 425–44.

Robertson, M. and Grey, A. (1986) 'Trade related worker adjustment policies: the Canadian experience', in J. Whalley (ed.) *Domestic Policies and the International Economic Environment*, Toronto: University of Toronto Press.

Rogowski, R. (1983) 'Structure, growth and power: three rationalist accounts', *International Organization* 37, 4: 713–38.

Rohatyn, F. (1983) *The Twenty First Century*, New York: Random House.

Rohlen, T. (1979) 'Permanent employment faces recession, slow growth and an ageing work force', *Journal of Japanese Studies*: 235–72.

Rosenblatt, S.M. (1977) 'Trade adjustment assistance: crossroads or dead end?', *Law and Policy in International Business*: 1065–100.

Rotstein, A. (ed.) (1972) *An Industrial Strategy for Canada*, Toronto: New Press.

Round, D.K. (1982) 'Concentration in Australian markets', in T.G. Parry (ed.) *Australian Industry Policy*, Melbourne: Longman, Cheshire.

Rowley, C.K. and Tollison, R.D. (1986) 'Rent seeking and trade protection', *Aussenwirtschaft* 41: 303.

Royal Commission on the Economic Union and Development Prospects for Canada (Macdonald Commission) (1985) *Report* 3 vols, Ottawa: Supply and Services.

Ruggie, J.G. (1983) *The Antimonies of Interdependence*, New York, Columbia University Press.

Rugman, A. (1986) 'US protectionism and Canadian trade policy', *Journal of World Trade Law*: 63.

—— (1987) *Administered Protection in America*, Beckenham: Croom Helm.

Rugman, A. and Porteous, S. (1989) 'Canadian and US unfair trade laws: a comparison of their legal and administrative structure', *Canadian Business Law Journal*, December.

Salamon, L.M. and Siegfried, J.J. (1977) 'Economic power and political influence', *American Political Science Review* 71: 1026–43.

Sampson, G. (1987) 'Safeguards', in J.M. Finger and A. Olechowski (eds) *The Uruguay Round: A Handbook for Negotiation*

Samuels, R. (1987) *The Business of the Japanese State*, Ithaca: Cornell University Press.

Samuelson, P. and Scott, A. (1980) *Economics*, Toronto: McGraw-Hill.

Sandel, M. (1982) *Liberalism and the Limits of Justice*, Cambridge: Cambridge University Press.

Saunders, C. (ed.) (1981) *The Political Economy of Old and New Industrial Countries*, London: Butterworth.

Saunders, R. (1984) *Aid to Declining Industries*, Toronto: Ontario Economic Council.

Sawer, G. (1980) 'The constitution and its politics' in M. Mayer and M. Nelson (eds) *Australian Politics 5*, Melbourne: Longman, Cheshire.

Saxonhouse, G. (1979) 'Industrial restructuring', *Journal of Japanese Studies* 5: 273–320.

Scase, R. (1980) *The State in Western Europe*, New York: St. Martin's Press.

Scharf, F. (1984) 'Economic and institutional constraints on full employment strategies: Sweden, Austria and West Germany 1973–82' in J.H. Goldthorpe (ed.) *Order and Conflict in Contemporary Capitalism*.

Scherer, F.M. (1980) *Industrial Market Structure and Economic Performance*, 2nd edn, Boston: Houghton Mifflin.

Schmid, G. (1979) 'The impact of selective employment policy: the case of a wage cost subsidy scheme in Germany 1974–5', *Journal of Industrial Economics* XXIII (June): 339–55.

Schmidt, I. (1983) 'Differential approaches and problems in dealing with control of market power', *Antitrust Bulletin* 28: 417–60.

Schmidt, M. (1982) 'The role of parties in shaping macroeconomic policy', in F. Castles (ed.) *The Imapct of Parties*, Beverly Hills: Sage.

—— (1985) 'The politics of labour market policy', paper presented at World Congress of International Political Science, Paris.

Schmiegelow, M. (1985) 'Cutting across doctrines: positive adjustment in Japan', *International Organization* 39, 2, (spring): 261–96.

Schmitter, P. (1981) 'Interest intermediation and regime governability in contemporary Western Europe and North America', in S. Berger (ed.) *Organizing Interests in Western Europe*, New York: Cambridge University Press.

Schmitter, P. and Lembruch, G. (eds) (1979) *Trends Toward Corporatist Intermediation*, London: Sage Publications.

Schnitzer, M. (1970) *The Economy of Sweden*, New York: Praeger.

Schultz, R. (1980) *Federalism, Bureaucracy and Public Policy: The Politics of Highway Transportation Regulation*, Montreal: McGill-Queen's University Press.

Schumpeter, J. (1975) *Capitalism, Socialism and Democracy*, Cambridge, Massachussets: Harvard University Press.

Schwartz, G. (1980) *Being Number One: Rebuilding the US Economy*, Lexington, Massachusetts: Lexington Books.

Schwartz, W.F. and Harper, E.W. (1970–71) 'The regulation of subsidies affecting international trade', *Michigan Law Review* 70: 831.

Science Council of Canada (1979) *Forging the Links: A Technology Policy for Canada*, Report no. 29, Ottawa: Ottawa Minister of Supply and Services.

—— (1979) *The Politics of Industrial Strategy: A Seminar*, Ottawa: Minister of Supply and Services.

Science Statistics Centre (1983) *R & D Expenditures in Canada 1963–1983*, Ottawa: Statistics Canada.

Scott, B.R. (1982) 'Can industry survive the welfare state?', *Harvard Business Review* 60: 70–84.

—— (1984a) 'American competitiveness: concepts, performance, and implications', mimeo, Cambridge, Massachussetts: Harvard Business School.

—— (1984b) 'National strategies: key to international competition', mimeo, Cambridge, Massachussets: Harvard Business School.

Seers, D., Schaffer, B. and Kiljuner, M. (eds) (1979) *Underdeveloped Europe*, Hassocks: Harvester.

Sengenberger, W. (1984) 'West German employment policy restoring worker competition', *Industrial Relations* 23, 3 (Fall): 323–43.

Seyfarth, S. *et al.* (1969) *Labor Relations and the Law in West Germany and the United States*, Ann Arbor: Bureau of Business Research.

Shalev, M. (1980) 'Industrial relations theory and the comparative study of industrial relations and industrial conflict', *British Journal of Industrial Relations* 18, 1, (March): 26–43.

—— (1983) 'The social democratic model and beyond: two generations of comparative research on the welfare state', *Comparative Social Research*, 6: 315–51.

Shepherd, G. (1983) 'Textiles: new ways of surviving in an old industry', in G. Shepherd, F. Duchene and C. Saunders (eds) *Europe's Industries and Private Strategies for Change*, London: Frances Pinter.

Shepherd, G. and Duchene, F. (1983) 'Industrial change and intervention in Western Europe', in G. Shepherd, F. Duchene and C. Saunders (eds) *Europe's Industries: Public and Private Strategies for Change*, London: Frances Pinter.

Shue, H. (1980) *Basic Rights: Subsistence, Affluence, and US Foreign Policy* Princeton, New Jersey Princeton University Press.

Shull, S. and Cohen, J. (eds) (1986) *Economics and Politics of Industrial Policy*, New York: Praeger.

Simeon, R. (1976) 'Studying public policy', *Canadian Journal of Political Science* 9, 4: 548–80.

—— (1979) 'Criteria for choice: a survey of the issues', Toronto: Working

Paper, Law and Economics Programme, Faculty of Law, University of Toronto.

—— (1980) 'Intergovernmental relations and the challenges to Canadian federalism', *Canadian Public Administration* 23: 14–32.

Singer, P. (1979) *Practical Ethics*, Cambridge: Cambridge University Press.

Skidelsky, R. (1979) 'The collapse of the Keynesian consensus', in C. Crouch (ed.) *State and Economy in Contemporary Capitalism*, Beckenham: Croom Helm.

Skocpol, T. (1985) 'Bringing the State back in: strategies of analysis in current research', in P.B. Evans, (eds) *Bringing the State Back In*, Cambridge: Cambridge University Press.

Smith, G. (1976) 'The politics of centrality in West Germany', *Government and Opposition* 11, 4.

Smith, R. (1988) 'Political Jurisprudence, the 'New Institutionalism' and the Future of Public Law', *American Political Science Review* 82, 1

Social Europe, Commission of the European Communities, Directorate-General for Employment, Social Affairs and Education 1983.

Social Planning Council of Metropolitan Toronto (1989) *Target on Training: Meeting Workers' Needs in a Changing Economy*, Toronto.

Soltwedel, R. (1987) 'Labour market barriers to employment – the case of West Germany', *Fraser Forum*, Vancouver: Fraser Institute.

Staiger, R.W., Deardorff, A.V. and Stern, R.W. (1987) 'Employment effects of Japanese and American protectionism', in D. Salvatore (ed.), *The New Protectionist Threat to World Welfare*, New York: North-Holland, Elsevier Science.

Stanbury, W.T. (1985) 'Government as leviathan: implications for business-government relations', in V.V. Murray (ed.), *Theories of Business-Government Relations*, Toronto: Trans-Canada Press.

Stanbury, W.T. and Lermer, G. (1984) 'Regulation and the redistribution of income and wealth', *Canadian Public Administration* 26, 3 (Fall): 378–401.

Statistics Canada (1984) *Federal Government Finance*

—— (1985a) *Canada Year Book 1985*,

—— (1985b) *Women in Canada: A Statistical Report*,

—— (1987) *Canadian Statistical Review*,

—— (1987) 'Capacity utilization rates in Canadian manufacturing' (second quarter 1987: Nov) (cat. 31–003) Ottawa: Supply and Services.

—— (1988) *Canada Year Book, 1988*.

Stephens, J.D. (1979) *The Transition from Capitalism to Socialism*, London: Macmillan.

—— (1981) 'Impasse and breakthrough in Sweden', *Dissent* 28: 308–18.

Stern, R. and Hoekman, B. 'The codes approach', in J.M. Finger and A. Olechowski (eds) *The Uruguay Round: A Handbook for Negotiation*,

Stern, R., Wood, H. and Hammer, T. (1979) *Employee Ownership in Plant Shutdowns*, Kalamazoo, Michigan: W.E. Upjohn Institute for Employment Research.

Stigler, G. (1971) 'The theory of economic regulation', *Bell Journal of Economics and Management Science* 2, 1 (spring): 3–21.

Stockwin, J.A.A. (1975) *Japan: Divided Politics in a Growth Economy*, London: Weidenfeld and Nicolson.

Stoffaes, C. (1978) *La Grande Menace Industrielle*, Paris: Colmann-Levys.

Strange, S. (1979) 'The management of surplus capacity: or how does theory stand up to protectionism 1920s style?', *International Organization* 33: 303–34.

—— (1985) 'Protectionism and world politics', *International Organization* 39, 2: 233–59.

Strath, B. (1986) 'Redundancy and solidarity: tripartite politics and the contraction of the West European shipbuilding industry', *Cambridge Journal of Economics* 10: 147–63.

Streeck, W. (1983) 'Between pluralism and corporatism: German business association and the State', *Journal of Public Policy* 3: 265–84.

—— (1984) 'Neo-corporatist industrial relations and the economic crisis in West Germany', in J.H. Goldthorpe (ed.) *Order and Conflict in Contemporary Capitalism*

Stubbs, P.C. (1982) 'Government policy and technology', in T.G. Parry (ed.) *Australian Industry Policy*, Melbourne: Longman, Cheshire.

Studies of Foreign Competition Policy and Practice (1976) vol. 2, Ottawa: Minister of Supply and Services Canada.

Study Group on Structural Adjustment (1979) Canberra: Australian Government.

Suleiman, E. (1975) 'Industrial policy formation in France', in S.J. Warnecke and E. Suleiman (eds) *Industrial Policies in Western Europe*, New York: Praeger.

Sundelius, R. (1984) 'Interdependence, internationalization and foreign policy decentralization in Sweden', in *Cooperation and Conflict* 19, 2.

Sundqvist, E. (1985) *The Costs and Benefits of Protection*, Paris: OECD.

Suzuki, Y. (1980) *Money and Banking in Japan*, New Haven: Yale University Press.

Svenska Handelsbanken (1984) *1984 Annual Report*.

Swann, D. (1983) *Competition and Industrial Policy in the European Community*, London: Methuen.

Sykes, A. (1989) 'Countervailing duty law: an economic perspective', *Columbia Law Review* 89: 199.

Szenberg, M., Lombardi, J.W., and Lee, E.Y. (1977) *Welfare Effects of Trade Restrictions: A Case Study of the US Footwear Industry*, New York: Academic Press.

Tarr, D.G. and Morkre, M.B. (1984) *Aggregate Costs to the United States of Tariffs and Quotas on Imports: General Tariff Cuts and Removal of Quotas on Automobiles, Steel, Sugar, and Textiles*. Bureau of Economics Staff Report to the FTC. Washington, DC: US Federal Trade Commission, December.

—— (1987) 'Aggregate costs to the United States of tariffs and tariffs and quotas on imports', in D. Salvatore (ed.) *The New Protectionist Threat to World Welfare*, New York: North-Holland, Elsevier Science.

Task Force on Labour Market Development (1981) *Labour Market Development in the 1980s* (Dodge Report), Canada: Ministry of Employment and Immigration.

Taylor, J.B. (1982) 'The Swedish investment funds system as a stabilization policy rule'. Brookings Papers on Economic Activity. Washington, DC: Brookings Institution.

Taylor, V. and Yerbury, D. (1985) 'Australia' in Cross (ed.) *Managing Workforce Reduction*,

Thorburn, H.G. (1984) *Planning and the Economy*, Toronto: Canadian Institute for Economic Policy.

Thunholm, L.-E. (1978) 'The crisis in the Swedish shipyards', *Skandinaviska Enskilda Banken Q.R.* 3–4: 64.

Thurow, L. (1980) *The Zero-Sum Society*, New York: Basic Books.

—— (1983) *Dangerous Currents: The State of Economics*, New York: Random House.

Todd, D. (1985) *The World Shipbuilding Indusry*, Beckenham: Croom Helm.

Tomasson, R.F. (1970) *Sweden*, New York: Random House.

Trade Policy Research Centre (1984) *Has the Cavalry Arrived? Report on Trade Liberalization and Economy Recovery*, London: TPRC.

Trebilcock, M. (1985a) *The Political Economy of Economic Adjustment*, Vol. 8, Research Study prepared for Royal Commission on Economic Union and Development Prospects in Canada, Toronto: University of Toronto Press.

—— (1985b) 'The politics of positive sum', in T.J. Courchene, D.W. Conklin and G.C.A. Cook (eds) *Ottawa and the Provinces: The Distribution of Money and Power*, Toronto: Ontario Economic Council.

—— (1988) 'The case for free trade', *Canadian Business Law Journal* 14: 387.

—— (1989) 'Reforming trade remedy laws'. Working paper. Toronto: International Business and Trade Law Programme, University of Toronto Law School.

Trebilcock, M.J. and Quinn, J. (1979) 'The Canadian Antidumping Act', *Canada - US Law Journal* 101.

Trebilcock, M.J. and Quinn, J. (1982) 'Compensation, transition costs and regulatory change', *University of Toronto Law Journal* 32: 117–75.

Trebilcock *et al.* (1983a) 'Provincially induced barriers to trade in Canada'', in M.J. Trebilcock *et al.* (eds) *Federalism and the Canadian Economic Union*, Toronto: Ontario Economic Council and University of Toronto Press.

Trebilcock, M.J. *et al.* (1983b) *Federalism and the Canadian Economic Union*, Toronto: Ontario Economic Council, Institute for Economic Policy.

Trebilcock, M.J., Prichard, J.R.S., Hartle, D., and Dewees, D. (1982) *The Choice of Governing Instrument*. Study prepared for the Economic Council of Canada. Ottawa: Minister of Supply and Services Canada.

Trebilcock, M.J., Chandler, M., Gunderson, M., Halpern, P., and Quinn, J. (1985) *The Political Economy of Business Bailouts*, Toronto: University of Toronto Press.

Tresize, P. with Y. Suzuki (1976) 'Politics, government and economic growth in Japan', in H. Patrick and H. Rosovsky (eds) *Asia's New Giant*, Washington, DC: Brookings Institution.

Tsoukalis, L. and da Silva Ferreira, A. (1980) 'Management of industrial surplus capacity in the European Community', *International Organization* 34.

Tsoukalis, L. and Strauss, R. (1985) 'Crisis and adjustment in European steel: beyond laisser-faire', *Journal of Common Market Studies.*

Tullock, G. (1967) 'The welfare costs of tariffs, monopolies & theft', *Western Economic Review* 5: 224.

Tumlir, J. (1985a) *Protectionism*, Washington: AEI.

—— (1985b) 'The need for a multilateral trading system', *World Economy*,

Tupper, A. (1981) *Public money in the private sector*, Kingston: Institute for Intergovernmental Relations.

—— (1986) 'Federalism and the politics of industrial policy', in Vol. 44, Studies for the Royal Commission on the Economic Union and Development Prospects for Canada, Toronto: University of Toronto Press.

United Nations Centre on Transnational Corporations (1983) *Salient Features and Trends in Foreign Direct Investment*, New York: United Nations.

United Nations Department of International Economic and Social Affairs (1982) *Yearbook of Industrial Statistics*, 1980 ed., vol. 1, New York: United Nations.

United Nations Economic Commission for Europe (1986) 'Alternative measures of productivity growth in the manufacturing sectors of the market economies' Ch. 2.10 in United Nations, *Economic Survey of Europe in 1985-1986*, New York: United Nations.

United Nations Statistical Office (1981) *Yearbook of National Accounts Statistics, 1981*, New York: United Nations.

US General Accounting Office (1979) *Considerations for Adjustment Assistance Under the 1974 Trade Act: A Summary of Techniques Used in Other Countries* 1 and 2, Washington, DC: US Government Printing Office.

US Government Labor Task Force on Economic Adjustment and Worker Dislocation (1986) *Economic Adjustment and Worker Dislocation in a Competitive Society*, Washington, DC.

US International Trade Commission (1982) *Economic Effects of Export Restraints*. USITC Publication no. 1256. Washington, DC June.

—— (1985a) *Analysis of the International Competitiveness of the US Commercial Shipbuilding and Repair Industries*. Washington, DC: US GPO.

—— (1985b) *A Review of Recent Developments in the US Automobile Industry, Including an Assessment of the Japanese Voluntary Restraint Agreements*. USITC Publication no. 1648. Washington, DC, February.

Urban, P. (1984) 'Recent approaches to industrial policy in Australia', in F.G. Adams and L.R. Klein (eds) *Industrial Policies for Growth and Competitiveness: An Economic Perspective*, Toronto: Lexington Books.

Usher, D. (1983) 'The benefits and costs of firm-specific investment grants: a study of five federal programmes. Discussion paper no. 511. Queen's University, Institute for Economic Research, Kingston, Ontario.

Vaillancourt, F. (1985) 'Income distribution and economic security in Canada: an overview' in F. Vaillancourt (ed.) *Income Security and Economic Security*, Toronto: University of Toronto Press.

Vernon, R. (1974) *Big Business and the State*, Cambridge, Massachusetts: Harvard University Press.

Vogel, D. (1978) 'Why businessmen distrust their State: the political consequences of American corporate executives', *British Journal of Political Science* 8: 45–78.

Vogel, E. (1979) *Japan As Number One: Lessons for America*, Cambridge, Massachusetts: Harvard University Press.

Volkman, L. (1983) *The Political Economy of France: From Pompidou to Mitterrand*, New York: Praeger.

Von Beyme, K. (1978a) 'The politics of limited pluralism? The case of West Germany', *Government and Opposition* 13, 3.

—— (1978b) 'The changing relationships between trade unions and the Social Democratic Party in West Germany', *Government and Opposition* 13, 4,: 399–415.

—— (1983) 'Neo-corporatism: a new nut in an old shell', *International Political Science Review* 412: 173–96.

Von Beyme, K. and Ionscu, G. (1977) 'The politics of employment in Germany and Great Britain', *Government and Opposition* 12: 88–107.

Von Otter, C. (1980) 'Swedish welfare capitalism', in R. Scase (ed.) *The State in Western Europe*.

Wagenhals, G. (1983) 'Industrial policy in the Federal Republic of Germany: a survey', in F.G. Adams and L.R. Klein (eds) *Industrial Policies for Growth and Competitiveness*.

Waingelin, J. (1981) 'The restructuring of the Swedish steel industry', *EFTA Bulletin* 22: 12–15.

Ward, M. (1985) 'Purchasing power parities and real expenditures in the OECD', Paris: OECD.

Warhurst, J. (1982) *Jobs or Dogma? The Industries Assistance Commission and Australian Politics*, St. Lucia, Queensland: University of Queensland Press.

—— (1986) 'Industrial assistance issues', in B. Head (ed.) *The Politics of Development in Australia*, London: Allen and Unwin.

Warnecke, S.J. (ed.) (1978) *International Trade and Industrial Policies: Government Intervention in An Open World Economy*, London: Macmillan Press.

Warnecke, S.J. and Suleiman, E. (1975) *Industrial Policies in Western Europe*, New York: Praeger.

Warren, J.H. (1978) 'Canada's role in the GATT negotiations', *Canadian Business Review* 36–41.

Watson, W. (1983) *A Primer on the Economics of Industrial Policy*, Toronto: Ontario Economic Council.

Weber, A. and Taylor, D. (1987) 'Problems of advance notice', in D. Staudohar and H.E. Brown (eds) *Deindustrialization and Plant Closure*, Lexington, Massachussetts: Lexington Books.

Weber, M. (1958) 'Politics as a vocation', in *From Max Weber*, trans. and

ed. H.H. Gerth and C.W. Mills, New York: Oxford University Press.
Webber, D. and Nass, G. (1984) 'Employment policy in West Germany' in
  J. Richardson and L. Henning (eds) *Unemployment: Policy Responses of
  Western Democracies*.
Weeks, A. and Mazany, L. (1983) *The Future of the Atlantic Fisheries*,
  Montreal: Institute for Research on Public Policy.
Weidenbaum, M.L. and Munger, M.C. (1983) 'Protectionism at any
  price?', *Regulation* 6: 14–18.
Weinrib, L. (1988) 'The Supreme Court of Canada and Section One of the
  Charter', *Supreme Court Law Review* 10: 469.
West, E. and Winer, S. (1980) 'The individual, political tension and
  Canada's quest for a new constitution', *Canadian Public Policy* 6: 3–15.
Westerstahl, J. (1982) 'What will happen to democracy in the 1980s?', in
  B. Ryden and V. Bergstrom (eds) *Sweden: Choices for Economic and
  Social Policy in the 1980s*, London: George Allen and Unwin.
Whalley, J. (1985) *Canadian Trade Policies and the World Economy*, Vol.
  9, Studies for the Royal Commission on the Economic Union and
  Development Prospects for Canada, Toronto: University of Toronto
  Press.
—— (1984) Review of Harris, *Canadian Journal of Economics* 17: 386.
Whyte, W.F. (1985) 'Employee ownership: lessons learned', in
  *Proceedings of the Thirty-Seventh Annual Meeting of the Industrial
  Research Association*, Madison, Wisconsin.
Wildavsky, A. (1975) *Budgeting: A Comparative Theory of Budgetary
  Process*, Boston: Little Brown.
Wilks, S. (1983) 'Liberal state and party competition: Britain', in K. Dyson
  and S. Wilks (eds) *The Industrial Crisis: A Comparative Study of the
  State and Industry*, Oxford: Martin Robertson.
—— (1984) 'The practice and the theory of industrial adaptation in Britain
  and West Germany', *Government and Opposition*, 19: 451–70.
Williams, D. (1986) 'Canadian adjustment policy–beyond CIRB', paper
  delivered at North South Institute Research Workshop, 18 March 1986.
  Ottawa: North South Research Institute, Mimeo.
Williams, G. (1981) *Not for Export*, Toronto: McClelland and Stewart.
Wilson, F.L. (1982) 'Alternative models of interest intermediation: the case
  of France', *British Journal of Political Science* 12: 173–200.
—— (1983) 'French interest group politics: pluralist or neo-corporatist',
  American Political Science Review 77: 895–910.
Wilson, G. (1979) 'Incidence of subsidies to the nationalized fuel industries
  in Britain', *Scottish Journal of Political Economy* 26, 3: 261–73.
Winham, G. (1986) *International Trade and the Tokyo Round Negotiations*.
  Princeton: Princeton University Press.
Wintner, L. (1983) Employee Buy-Outs: An Alternative to Plant Closings,
  US Conference Board Research Bulletin no. 104 (New York).
Wolf, M. (1983) 'Managed trade in practice: implications of the textile
  arrangements', in W.R. Cline (ed.) *Trade Policy in the 1980's*,
  Washington DC: Institute for International Economics.
Wolfe, D. (1983) 'Backing winners? Constraints on industrial strategy in

the New International Division of Labour', paper presented to Association of Political Economy, Montreal.

Wolff, A.W. (1983) 'The need for new GATT rules to govern safeguard actions', in W.R. Cline (ed.) *Trade Policy in the 1980's*, Washington, DC: Institute for International Economics.

Wolinetz, S. (1986) 'The Role of trade unions in industrial policies, 1945 to 1984', in Vol. 44, Studies for Royal Commission on the Economic Union and Development Prospects for Canada.

Wonnacott, R. with R. Hill (1987) *Canadian and US Adjustment Policies in a Bilateral Trade Agreement*, Toronto: C.D. Howe.

Woodside, K. (1979) 'Tax incentives versus subsidies: political considerations in government choice', *Canadian Public Policy* 5 (Spring): 248–56.

World Bank (1987) *The Uruguay Round: A Handbook on the Multilateral Trade Negotiations*, Washington, DC: IBRD.

Wright, V. (ed.) (1983) *Giscard, Giscardians and Giscardism*, London: Allen and Unwin.

—— (ed.) (1984) *Continuity and Change in France*, London: Allen and Unwin.

Yamazawa, K. (1983) 'Renewal of the textile industry in developed countries and world textile trade', *Hitotsubashi Journal of Economics* (June): 28–39.

Yemin, E. (ed.) (1982) *Workforce Reductions in Undertakings*, Geneva: ILO.

Yoder, D. and Staudohar, P.D. (1985) 'Management and public policy in plant closure', *Sloan Management Review* 26: 45.

Yoffie, D. (1983) 'Adjustment in the footwear industry: the Consequences of orderly marketing arrangements', in J. Zysman and L. Tyson (eds) *American Industry in International Competition*, Ithaca: Cornell University Press.

Yoshini, B. (1989) 'Japan', in H. Nau (ed.) *Domestic Politics and the Uruguay Round*.

Young, S. (1974) *Intervention in the Mixed Economy*, Beckenham: Croom-Helm.

Yudelman, D. (1985) *The Ambiguous Legacy of Federal Mineral Policy*, Kingston: Centre for Resource Studies, Queen's University.

Yuill, D. and Allen, K. (eds) (1982) *European Regional Incentives*, Glasgow: Centre for the Study of Public Policy.

Zysman, J. (1978) 'The French State in the international economy', in P. Katzenstein (ed.), *Between Power and Plenty*, Madison: University of Wisconsin Press.

—— (1983) *Governments, Markets and Growth*, Ithaca: Cornell University Press.

Zysman, J. and Cohen, S. (1983) 'Double or nothing: open trade and competitive industry', *Foreign Affairs* 61: 1113–39.

Zysman, J. and Pontosson, J. (1980) 'Industrial adjustment and the politics of business-state relations', prepared for British Social Science Research Council.

Zysman, J. and Tyson, L. (eds) (1983) *American Industry in International Competition*, Ithaca: Cornell University Press.

Index